REVERSE DISCRIMINATION IN THE EUROPEAN UNION

Discriminatierecht in theorie en praktijk / Discrimination law in theory and practice

Editors
Stefan Sottiaux en Jogchum Vrielink

REVERSE DISCRIMINATION IN THE EUROPEAN UNION

A Recurring Balancing Act

Valérie Verbist

intersentia
Cambridge – Antwerp – Portland

Intersentia Ltd
Sheraton House | Castle Park
Cambridge | CB3 0AX | United Kingdom
Tel.: +44 1223 370 170 | Fax: +44 1223 370 169
Email: mail@intersentia.co.uk
www.intersentia.com | www.intersentia.co.uk

Distribution for the UK and Ireland:
NBN International
Airport Business Centre, 10 Thornbury Road
Plymouth, PL6 7 PP
United Kingdom
Tel.: +44 1752 202 301 | Fax: +44 1752 202 331
Email: orders@nbninternational.com

Distribution for Europe and all other countries:
Intersentia Publishing nv
Groenstraat 31
2640 Mortsel
Belgium
Tel.: +32 3 680 15 50 | Fax: +32 3 658 71 21
Email: mail@intersentia.be

Distribution for the USA and Canada:
International Specialized Book Services
920 NE 58th Ave. Suite 300
Portland, OR 97213
USA
Tel.: +1 800 944 6190 (toll free) | Fax: +1 503 280 8832
Email: info@isbs.com

ISBN 978-1-78068-458-1
D/2017/7849/7
NUR 823

GPRC
Guaranteed
Peer Reviewed
Content

British Library Cataloguing in Publication Data. A catalogue record for this book is available from the British Library.

ACKNOWLEDGEMENTS

This book arises out of my PhD thesis written at the KU Leuven. It would not have been possible without the support of many people. First, I would like to thank my PhD supervisor and co-supervisors, Professor Dr Marie-Claire Foblets, Professor Dr Piet Van Nuffel and Professor Dr Geert De Baere, for their suggestions, debate and discussion. I am also very grateful to Emeritus Professor René Foqué and my colleagues at the KU Leuven for their support and intellectual stimulation. Moreover, I owe gratitude to FWO for granting me a scholarship which made it possible to carry out research. I would also like to thank Pascale Van Houtte, publisher at Intersentia, for her invaluable cooperation in steering this book to publication. Finally, I would like to express my heartfelt thanks to my friends and family for their ever-present support.

CONTENTS

PART III. REVERSE DISCRIMINATION IN A FEDERAL STATE CONTEXT

TABLE OF CASES OF THE EUROPEAN COURT OF JUSTICE

References are to paragraph numbers.

CHAPTER 1

INTRODUCTION

1. PROBLEM DEFINITION: DISCRIMINATION AND REVERSE DISCRIMINATION

1.1. EQUALITY AND NON-DISCRIMINATION

1. The principle of equality is enshrined in various international instruments and in national constitutions.[1] The classic definition of equality is that of Aristotle, according to which cases that are alike should be treated alike.[2] The principle of equality is complemented by the principle of non-discrimination. Discrimination takes place when two cases that are alike are treated differently without a sufficient justification, or when two different cases are treated as though they are alike without a sufficient justification being given.[3]

2. However, the idea of equality has been criticised for being hollow and incomplete.[4] The particular question that arises is: what are cases that are alike? It is clear that the cases do not have to be identical because 'no two people are alike in every respect'.[5] However, in what respects should they be similar in order for them to be treated alike? In other words, when is 'relevant resemblance' at stake?[6] Westen's definition seems to take this concern into account. He defines equality as being 'the comparative relationship that obtains between two or more distinct persons or things by virtue of their having been jointly measured by a

---

1 Eg Article 14 European Convention on Human Rights (ECHR) determines that: 'The enjoyment of the rights and freedoms set forth in this Convention shall be secured without discrimination on any ground such as sex, race, colour, language, religion, political or other opinion, national or social origin, association with a national minority, property, birth or other status.'

2 Aristotle, Nicomachean Ethics, V.3. 1131a10–b15; Aristotle, Politics, III.9.1280 a8–15, III.12.1282b18–23.

3 De Prins, Vrienlink and Sottiaux, *Handboek discriminatierecht*, Kluwer 2005, p 3.

4 Hart, *The Concept of Law*, 2nd ed, Oxford University Press 1994, p 159 and Westen, 'The Empty Idea of Equality' (1982) 95 *Harvard Law Review* 537, 537–95.

5 Westen, 'The Empty Idea of Equality' (1982) 95 *Harvard Law Review* 537, 544.

6 Hart, *The Concept of Law*, 2nd ed, Oxford University Press 1994, p 160.

relevant standard of comparison and found to be indistinguishable by reference to that standard'.[7]

3. Hart has observed that 'the criteria of relevant resemblances and differences may often vary with the fundamental moral outlook of a given person or society'.[8] That is to say, for instance, that only men had equal access to justice in Ancient Greece; slaves and women were excluded.[9] Another example can be found in the USA's Declaration of Independence which, although it determined that 'all men are created equal', did not include slaves in 1776. As AG Sharpston has summarised, who and which aspects of 'economic, social, political and personal life' are covered by the principle of equality evolves over time in societies.[10] Next, the law reflects this change by prohibiting certain forms of discrimination that have gone 'previously unnoticed or (if noticed) tolerated'.[11]

4. In the context of the European Union (EU), next to a prohibition of discrimination on grounds of nationality, anti-discrimination law was originally confined to equality between men and women in the context of employment. The EEC Treaty of 1957, in particular, already provided that each Member State was to ensure the principle of equal pay for male and female workers for equal work.[12]

5. Since the Amsterdam Treaty of 1999, the EU can take action to combat discrimination on the grounds of sex, racial or ethnic origin, religion or belief, disability, age or sexual orientation.[13] Two important legislative anti-discrimination instruments in particular were adopted on the basis of Article 19 of the Treaty on the Functioning of the European Union (TFEU). Specifically, the Race Directive 2000/43 that prohibits discrimination on the grounds of racial and ethnic origin in different contexts[14] and the Framework Employment Directive 2000/78 that prohibits discrimination in the field of employment on the grounds of religion, belief, disability, age and sexual orientation.[15]

---

7 Westen, *Speaking of Equality*, Princeton University Press 1990, p 39.
8 Hart, *The Concept of Law*, 2nd ed, Oxford University Press 1994, p 163.
9 Opinion AG Sharpston 22 May 2008 in C-427/06, *Bartsch*, para 45.
10 Ibid para 46.
11 Ibid.
12 Then Article 119 TEEC, now Article 157 TFEU.
13 Article 19 TFEU.
14 Council Directive 2000/43/EC of 29 June 2000 implementing the principle of equal treatment between persons irrespective of racial or ethnic origin, in particular Article 3 regarding the scope.
15 Council Directive 2000/78/EC of 27 November 2000 establishing a general framework for equal treatment in employment and occupation.

6. Title III of the Charter of Fundamental Rights, which enjoys the same status as the EU Treaties since the entry into force of the Lisbon Treaty on 1 December 2009, is devoted to equality. Article 21 of the Charter, in particular, prohibits discrimination on any ground. However, only Articles 19 and 157 TFEU grant the EU express legislative competence in relation to the grounds set out in these Articles.[16] Nevertheless, the European Court of Justice (ECJ) has recognised a general principle of equal treatment in EU law, first regarding the equal treatment of men and women, thereafter regarding age and more recently in other areas.[17]

7. Finally, it should be pointed out that Article 18 TFEU determines that 'within the scope of application of the Treaties, and without prejudice to any special provisions contained therein, any discrimination on grounds of nationality shall be prohibited'. The principle of non-discrimination on the grounds of nationality will be discussed in various sections throughout this work.

1.2. REVERSE DISCRIMINATION

1.2.1. The Concept of Reverse Discrimination

1.2.1.1. Unexpected Group is Discriminated Against

8. The word 'reverse' in 'reverse discrimination' indicates that an unexpected group is being discriminated against.[18] It could be expected that a Member State treats its own nationals more favourably than other Member States' nationals. However, this is forbidden in the context of the European Union. Article 18 TFEU, in particular, prohibits discrimination on the grounds of nationality within the scope of the Treaties.

9. By contrast, Union law does not prohibit Member States from treating their own nationals in a purely internal situation less favourably than Union citizens falling within the scope of Union law. If this rather unexpected group

---

16 Craig and de Burca, *EU Law. Text, Cases, and Materials*, 6th ed, Oxford University Press 2015, p 894.

17 See inter alia regarding equal treatment between men and women ECJ case 194/77 *Defrenne III* [1987] ECR 1365, paras 26–27 and ECJ case C-13/94 *P v S* [1996] ECR I-2143, para 19; regarding age discrimination ECJ case C-144/04 *Mangold* [2005] ECR I-9981, para 75 and ECJ case C-427/06 *Bartsch* [2008] ECR I-7245; and regarding parental leave for parents of twins, ECJ case C-149/10 *Chatzi* [2010] ECR I-8489, para 63. See more extensively Craig and de Burca, *EU Law. Text, Cases, and Materials*, 6th ed, Oxford University Press 2015, pp 932–35.

18 See inter alia Davies, *Nationality Discrimination in the European Internal Market*, Kluwer Law International 2003, p 19 and Tryfonidou, *Reverse Discrimination*, Kluwer Law International 2009, p 3.

is treated less favourably, a situation of reverse discrimination arises.[19] Hence, a Member State may treat its own nationals in a purely internal situation more strictly than other Union citizens, understood as being nationals from other Member States and a Member State's own nationals who fall within the scope of Union law. However, as Poiares Maduro observed: 'States do not, in general want to discriminate against their own nationals. Reverse discrimination normally occurs because [Union] law obliges States to treat nationals of other Member States in a way which – by reasons of their own policies and aims – they did not originally intend to treat their own nationals'.[20]

1.2.1.2. The Origins of Reverse Discrimination

10. The issue of reverse discrimination immediately raises the question of why a Member State would treat its own nationals in a purely internal situation more strictly than Union citizens falling within the scope of Union law. It is a common misunderstanding that reverse discrimination occurs because Union law deprives home nationals of certain benefits in some way.[21] In order to clear up this misunderstanding, the following paragraphs will discuss the two main situations in which reverse discrimination typically arises.[22]

11. Often a situation of reverse discrimination will arise after an ECJ judgment holding that Union law precludes a national measure. That is to say, Union law may preclude certain national measures only 'insofar as' they apply to cross-border situations.[23] For instance, in its *Drei Glocken* judgment, the ECJ held that 'it is the extension of the law on pasta products to imported products which is at issue, and … [Union] law does not require the legislature to repeal the law as far as pasta producers established on Italian territory are concerned'.[24] Hence,

---

19 Cornu defines reverse discrimination in the context of the EU as follows: 'Effet paradoxal (pervers?) consistant en ce que le traitement réservé aux ressortissants d'un Etat membre de l'Union européenne est moins favorable que celui dont bénéficient ceux des autres Etats, en application des règles communautaires' (Cornu, *Vocabulaire juridique*, Presses universitaires de France 2011, p 350).

20 Poiares Maduro, 'The Scope of European Remedies: The Case of Purely Internal Situations and Reverse Discrimination' in Kilpatrick, Novitz and Skidmore (eds), *The Future of European Remedies*, Hart Publishing 2000, p 127.

21 Nic Shuibhne, 'Free Movement of Persons and the Wholly Internal Rule: Time to Move on?' (2002) 39 *CMLRev* 771, 763.

22 A third situation in which reverse discrimination may arise will be discussed below. This is where reverse discrimination arises as a result of the implementation of EU minimum harmonisation if the Directive contains a 'market access' clause. See below nn 115–18 and see inter alia Barnard, *The Substantive Law of the EU: The Four Freedoms*, Oxford University Press 2013, pp 663–66 and Tryfonidou, *Reverse Discrimination*, Kluwer Law International 2009, pp 35–36.

23 See inter alia case C-448/98 *Guimont* [2000] ECR I-10663, paras 21, 24–25.

24 See inter alia ECJ case 407/85 *Drei Glocken* [1988] ECR 4233, para 25.

in the wake of the ECJ judgment, the national measure at issue remains valid in purely internal situations and it is this which leads to a situation of reverse discrimination.

12. Nevertheless, reverse discrimination may, in some cases, result from a deliberate choice of the national legislator to (continue to) apply stricter conditions to purely internal situations in order to pursue their own national policy. One such example can be found in the Belgian legislation on family reunification, which will be discussed extensively in Part II of this volume.[25] Here, a deliberate choice was made by the Belgian legislator to introduce stricter conditions for family reunification with Belgian citizens in order to control migration flows. The legislator could not do so for family reunification with Union citizens falling within the scope of Union law since that would have been incompatible with Union law.

These types of reverse discrimination cases are not a deprivation of rights of nationals in purely internal situations. As Nic Shuibhne has argued, Union law should be seen as giving certain rights to Union citizens falling under the scope of Union law 'over and above those available domestically', instead of depriving static home nationals from benefitting from the right at issue.[26]

1.2.1.3. Purely Internal Situations versus Situations with a Connection with Union Law

13. According to the Court of Justice, reverse discrimination is not prohibited by Union law, since purely internal situations fall outside the scope of application of the Treaty provisions on freedom of movement and citizenship.[27] Accordingly, it is crucial to understand which situations are purely internal and which situations have a sufficient connection with Union law. The Court of Justice defines purely internal situations as 'situations which have no factor linking them with any of the situations governed by European Union law and which are confined in all relevant respects within a single Member State'.[28]

14. Traditionally, the connection with Union law was interpreted as comprising actual movement between two or more Member States. However, in light of Union citizenship, the Court of Justice has also accepted a more abstract

---

[25] See below nn 542–84.

[26] Nic Shuibhne, 'Free Movement of Persons and the Wholly Internal Rule: Time to Move on?' (2002) 37 *CMLRev* 771, 763.

[27] See inter alia ECJ 175/78 *Saunders* [1979] ECR I-1129, para 12 and ECJ 35/82 and 36/82 *Morson and Jhanjan* [1982] ECR 3723, para 15.

[28] See inter alia ECJ case C-434/09 *McCarthy* [2011] ECR I-3375, para 45 and ECJ case C-256/11 *Dereci*, para 60.

connection with Union law. The question has arisen as to whether 'having made use of the right of free movement' is still relevant in order to determine the line between the scope of application of Union law and that of national law.

15. It should be noted from the outset that the purely internal situation rule is confined to the context of freedom of movement and Union citizenship. It is not the case that Union law can never apply in a purely internal situation. For instance, Article 157 TFEU provides that 'each Member State shall ensure that the principle of equal pay for male and female workers for equal work or work of equal value is applied'. This imperative also applies to situations in which all the relevant aspects are confined to a single Member State.[29] Moreover, Articles 114 and 115 TFEU make it possible for the EU to adopt harmonised Union rules that replace diverging national rules and can be made applicable to purely internal situations. For instance, Directive 95/46 on data protection[30] is an example of maximum harmonisation that provides equivalent protection in all Member States.[31]

1.2.1.4. Examples of Reverse Discrimination

16. In order to make things clearer, the following will briefly discuss two examples of reverse discrimination, one in the domain of the free movement of goods and one in the domain of the free movement of persons. The illustrations given will be explained not only from the perspective of Union law, but also from the perspective of national law.

17. The first example concerns the Italian legislation on pasta. Article 29 of the law on pasta products[32] provides that only durum wheat is to be used for the industrial manufacture of dry pasta. Mr Zoni, an Italian wholesaler, imported pasta made from common wheat and durum wheat from Germany. He was prosecuted in Italy for contravening Article 29 of the law on pasta products. Mr Zoni claimed, in his defence, that the application of Article 29 of the law on pasta products to imported pasta was incompatible with the free movement of goods and with the prohibition on quantitative restrictions on imports and all measures having equivalent effect in particular.[33]

---

29 See inter alia ECJ case 43/75 *Defrenne* [1976] ECR 455.

30 Directive 95/46/EC of the European Parliament and of the Council of 24 October 1995 on the protection of individuals with regard to the processing of personal data and on the free movement of such data.

31 ECJ case C-101/01 *Lindqvist* [2003] ECR I-12971, paras 95–99. On the purely internal situation doctrine and harmonisation at Union level, see below nn 109–18.

32 Law No 580 of 4 July 1967, *Gazzetta Ufficiale* No 189 of 29 July 1967.

33 Now Article 34 TFEU.

The Court of Justice held in its *Zoni* judgment that the Italian prohibition on the sale of pasta made from a combination of common wheat and durum wheat constituted an obstacle to the importation of pasta that has been lawfully produced in another Member State.[34] The Court held that such an obstacle cannot be justified on the grounds of the protection of public health.[35] Nor can it be justified on the grounds of consumer protection because less restrictive means are available, such as affixing suitable labels.[36] Accordingly, the Court of Justice held that 'the extension to imported products of a prohibition on the sale of pasta made from common wheat or from a mixture of common wheat such as is contained in the Italian law on pasta products' is incompatible with Article 34 TFEU.[37]

Although the prohibition on pasta made from common wheat was disapplied to imported pasta, it continued to apply to pasta produced and sold in Italy. This situation of reverse discrimination was challenged before the Italian Constitutional Court. The Court considered that although reverse discrimination falls outside the scope of application of Union law, it is relevant from the perspective of Italian law and it should be assessed in the light of the Italian principle of equality.[38] The Court ruled that cross-border situations and purely internal situations should be treated equally, unless the difference in treatment could be justified constitutionally. Regarding the industrial manufacture of dry pasta, the Italian Constitutional Court held that the different treatment of purely internal and cross-border situations was incompatible with the principles of equality and non-discrimination.[39] In other words, the Italian Constitutional Court ended the situation of reverse discrimination on the basis of the principle of equality as enshrined in Italian law.

18. The second example concerns the Belgian legislation on family reunification. Specifically, a Belgian adult in a purely internal situation has no right to family reunification with relatives in the ascending line.[40] By contrast, Union citizens falling within the scope of Union law have the right to be united with their dependent direct relatives in the ascending line on the basis of Directive 2004/38.[41] This situation of reverse discrimination has been challenged before the Belgian Constitutional Court.

---

34 ECJ 90/86 *Zoni* [ECR] 1988 4285, para 11.
35 Ibid para 14. 36 Ibid para 16. 37 Ibid para 28.
38 Italian Constitutional Court 30 December 1997, no 443/1997, paras 5–6.
39 Ibid para 6.
40 They are no longer listed in Article 40*ter* of the Belgian Aliens Act of 8 July 2011.
41 Article 2(2) of Directive 2004/38. It should be emphasised that a Belgian citizen who can demonstrate a sufficient connection with Union law can rely on Directive 2004/38.

With the judgments of 26 September 2013, the Belgian Constitutional Court took a position on the compatibility of reverse discrimination with the Articles 10 and 11 of the Constitution, enshrining the principle of equality, for the very first time. In particular, the Belgian Constitutional Court rejected the federal government's argument that purely internal situations and cross-border situations are not comparable because this would render the scrutiny on equality and non-discrimination 'meaningless'.[42] Next, the Court held that the difference in treatment can be justified by the legislation's aim of controlling migration flows.[43] Since the Court considered that the stricter conditions on Belgian citizens in a purely Belgian situation were a relevant and proportionate measure,[44] it held that the legislation did not violate the Articles 10 and 11 of the Belgian Constitution.[45] Hence, the Belgian Constitutional Court, unlike the Italian Constitutional Court, considered the reverse discrimination to be compatible with the principle of equality, as enshrined in national law, and the situation of reverse discrimination has been allowed to continue.

1.2.2. Terminology

19. Although the Court's first cases concerning purely internal situations date back to the late seventies, the term reverse discrimination has only recently emerged in the Court's case law.[46] Previously, the term was used only by legal scholars; since then parties and Advocates General have systematically used it in order to emphasise the paradoxical effect of treating one's own nationals less beneficially than nationals from other Member States.[47]

---

42 Belgian Constitutional Court 26 September 2013, no 121/2013, para B.49 and Belgian Constitutional Court 26 September 2013, no 123/2013, para B.5.3 where the Court used the word '*zinledig*'.

43 Belgian Constitutional Court 26 September 2013, no 121/2013, para B.52.2 and Belgian Constitutional Court 26 September 2013, no 123/2013, para B.6.2.

44 Belgian Constitutional Court 26 September 2013, no 121/2013, paras B.52.2–B.56.2 and Belgian Constitutional Court 26 September 2013, no 123/2013, paras B.6.2 and B.6.7.3.

45 Belgian Constitutional Court 26 September 2013, no 121/2013, para B.57 and Belgian Constitutional Court 26 September 2013, no 123/2013, para B.8.

46 See inter alia ECJ joined cases C-231/06 to C-233/06 *Jonkman* [2007] ECR I-5149, para 25; ECJ case C-104/08 Order *Kurt* [2008] ECR I-97, para 22; ECJ case C-225/09 *Jakubowska* [2010] ECR I-12329, paras 32 and 62; ECJ case C-111/12 *Ordine degli ingegneri di Verona e provincia e.a.*, para 22.

47 See inter alia Davies who defines reverse discrimination as 'a term that tends to be used where an unexpected group is favoured' (Davies, *Nationality Discrimination in the European Internal Market*, Kluwer Law International 2003, p 19).

1.2.2.1. Reverse Discrimination and Positive Action

20. The notion of positive action consists of deliberately creating a legal inequality in order to guarantee the substantive equality of disadvantaged groups.[48] For instance, Article 157(4) TFEU provides that 'with a view to ensuring full equality in practice between men and women in working life, the principle of equal treatment shall not prevent any Member State from maintaining or adopting measures providing for specific advantages in order to make it easier for the underrepresented sex to pursue a vocational activity or to prevent or compensate for disadvantages in professional careers'. Hence, although the difference in treatment is based upon a prohibited ground, that is to say as enshrined in Article 10 TFEU on the basis of sex, the two groups are, in reality, not equal. By treating the traditionally disadvantaged group, woman in working life, for instance, temporarily more favourably than the traditionally favoured group, men, the legislator is aiming for substantive equality.[49]

21. In the Anglo-American tradition, the terms 'reverse discrimination' and 'affirmative action' are very closely linked.[50] Sometimes 'reverse discrimination' and 'affirmative action' are used interchangeably;[51] other authors have a clear preference for the term 'affirmative action'.[52,53]

Conceptually, reverse discrimination and affirmative/positive action can be seen as being two sides of the same coin. Which is which depends on one's point of view. On the one hand, a certain group of persons is treated more favourably, from a Union law perspective; that is to say, those Union citizens falling within the scope of Union law. It could be said that they benefit from affirmative/positive action. On the other hand, a certain group of persons is treated less

---

48 De Prins, Vrielink and Sottiaux, *Handboek discriminatierecht*, Kluwer 2005, p 4.

49 See more in Bamforth, *Discrimination Law: Theory and Context*, Thomson Sweet & Maxwell 2008, Chapters 6 and 7, pp 340–447.

50 According to Iliopoulou and Jauréguiberry, Advocates General and parties were inspired by the Anglo-American tradition when introducing the term reverse discrimination in the context of the European Union (Iliopoulou and Jauréguiberry, 'La première condamnation d'une discrimination à rebours. A propos de l'arrêt du Conseil d'Etat du 6 octobre 2008' [2009] *RFDA* 132, 132).

51 See inter alia Nowak and Rotunda, *Constitutional Law*, 8th ed, West 2010, p 1798. See also Cals, *La discrimination à rebours et le droit communautaire*, Université de Toulouse 2001, p 46.

52 Chang, 'Reverse Racism!: Affirmative Action, the Family and the Dream that is America' [1995–96] *Hastings Const LQ* 1115, 1134. Moreover, sometimes 'positive discrimination' is used to describe 'positive action'. However, since the term discrimination is used to nominate an unjustified difference in treatment, and positive action is justified under certain circumstances, the term 'positive action' seems more appropriate (De Prins, Vrielink and Sottiaux, *Handboek discriminatierecht*, Kluwer 2005, p 4).

53 Bossuyt, *L'interdiction de la discrimination dans le droit international des droits de l'homme*, Bruylant 1976, p 11.

favourably, from the point of view of immobile Union citizens. They suffer from reverse discrimination.

1.2.2.2. Renaming Reverse Discrimination?

22. As explained above, the term discrimination refers to an unjustified difference in treatment. Hence, the term reverse discrimination seems to imply that unjustified differences in treatment are at stake. If we consider every situation of reverse discrimination as a problem to be solved, this terminology is not problematic. However, whether this is the right starting point is open to debate. That is to say, at first glance, reverse discrimination is the result of the combination of national law and Union law as applying to the same territory but with a different scope of application.[54] This point of view seems to imply that not every instance of reverse discrimination is an unjustified difference in treatment necessarily. Hence, the answer to whether or not it is appropriate to rename 'reverse discrimination' depends upon the position taken concerning the question of whether reverse discrimination should be considered to be a problem that requires a solution in each case.[55]

23. Suppose that reverse discrimination is to be renamed, what would the alternative be? A more neutral denomination might be appropriate. One might opt for 'reverse difference in treatment', 'unexpected difference in treatment' or 'more favourable treatment granted by union law vis-a-vis a stricter treatment by national law'.

2. RESEARCH AIM

2.1. RESEARCH QUESTIONS

24. This book examines three main research questions:

1. To what extent does reverse discrimination continue to fall within the scope of law of the Member States and when does it fall within the ambit of Union law?

---

54 See also CANNIZZARO, 'Esercizio di competenze comunitarie e discriminazioni "a rovescio"' (1996) 2 *Il diritto dell'Union Europea* 352: 'La disparità di trattamento deriva allora dall'esistenza di norme comunitarie e norme interne aventi un diverso contenuto materiale in ragione del diverso sistema di finalità al quale rispettivamente si ispirano. Si tratta quindi di un problema di intersezione fra sfere di competenze affidate alle Comunità e sfere di competenze degli Stati membri' and NIC SHUIBHNE, 'Free Movement of Persons and the Wholly Internal Rule: Time to Move on?' (2002) 39 *CMLRev* 771, 738: 'Viewed through this lens, there is no element of blame involved, on the part of either the Community or Member States. But what remains is the material difference in treatment.'

55 This is the third research question to be addressed in this text, see further Chapter 1, section 2.1.

2. On which grounds do the Member States decide whether or not to remedy reverse discrimination?
3. Should reverse discrimination be considered to be a problem that requires a solution in each case? Moreover, if a solution is required, then who should provide this solution: the EU, the Member States, regions or several levels of government in interaction?

2.2. DELINEATING THE SCOPE OF RESEARCH

25. In this work, reverse discrimination is examined within the context of the EU. In particular, reverse discrimination is analysed both from the perspective of Union law and from the perspectives of five Member States (Austria, Belgium, France, Germany and Italy). Moreover, there is a particular focus on reverse discrimination of Union citizens. For instance, regarding family reunification, there is analysis of family reverse discrimination with Union citizens as enshrined in Directive 2004/38 (and Articles 20–21 TFEU) and not family reunification with third country nationals as enshrined in Directives 2003/86 and 2003/109.

26. Although the interpretation of the ECJ's purely internal situation doctrine by the national authorities in the five Member States under analysis is closely related to the issue of reverse discrimination in the EU, it is not discussed here because it is beyond the scope of inquiry of this book.[56] The same applies to the impact the ECJ's judgments have upon the national legislator.[57] Finally, although it has been mentioned in this introductory chapter, the issue of reverse discrimination in the USA will not be examined further, nor will reverse discrimination from the perspective of international law. Whilst Articles 8 and 14 of the European Convention on Human Rights (ECHR) will be mentioned, for instance, they will not be discussed in detail.

---

56 Regarding the interpretation of *Ruiz Zambrano* at national level see inter alia CAMBIEN, 'Recente ontwikkelingen op het vlak van gezinshereniging van Belgen en Unieburgers: a long and winding road?' in *Migratie en migrantenrecht deel 16*, die Keure 2015, p 17; EIJKEN, 'Ruiz Zambrano the aftermath: de impact van artikel 20 VWEU op de Nederlandse rechtspraak' (2012) *NTER* 41–48 and VAN ELSUWEGE and KOCHENOV, 'On the Limits of Judicial Intervention: EU Citizenship and Family Reunification Rights' (2011) 13 *EJML* 433, 455–56.

57 For instance the impact of *Zhu Chen* and *Ruiz Zambrano*. See also BARNARD, *The Substantive Law of the EU: The Four Freedoms*, Oxford University Press 2013, p 526 in particular fn 249; CAMBIEN, 'Citizenship of the Union as a Cornerstone of European Integration', Dissertation, KU Leuven 2011, on implications of *Zhu and Chen*, pp 383–88 and SCHMIDT, 'Judicial Europeanisation: the Case of Zambrano in Ireland' [2014] *West European Politics* 776–81 on the Member States' reactions after *Ruiz Zambrano*.

2.3. ADDED VALUE TO PREVIOUS LITERATURE

27. Previous research on reverse discrimination has mainly examined the issue from the perspective of Union law, from the ECJ's case law in particular. For instance, Tryfonidou has provided a detailed analysis of the ECJ's case law on purely internal situations and reverse discrimination against the background of the post-Maastricht developments; that is to say, the creation of Union citizenship and the formal completion of the internal market.[58] However, in recent years, the ECJ has further refined its purely internal situation doctrine, especially in the aftermath of the *Ruiz Zambrano* judgment. This book will discuss recent developments in the ECJ's case law.

28. Sparse attention has been paid to reverse discrimination from a variety of national perspectives, although scholars have examined examples in their own domestic legal order regarding the five Member States under analysis here. Specifically, the French scholar Cals has discussed some examples in the French legal order[59] while the German scholar Epiney has discussed examples in the light of Articles 3 and 12 of the Basic Law in Germany, enshrining the principle of equality and the freedom to choose a profession.[60] The Italian scholar Spitaleri has described the treatment of reverse discrimination in the Italian legal order in detail.[61]

This work discusses examples of national authorities addressing reverse discrimination in five Member States. Admittedly, Walter has examined the issue of reverse discrimination by comparing four Member States; namely the Netherlands, Germany, Austria and Belgium. However, this work was undertaken only in the field of family reunification.[62] This book will discuss examples in the domain of the free movement of goods and persons, and concerning the latter specifically, both classic economic free movement and family reunification will be examined.

Moreover, special attention will be paid to the specific situation of reverse discrimination arising in a federally structured Member State. In a Member State that has a federal structure, an extra level of governance is added and this makes the issue of reverse discrimination even more complex.

---

58 Tryfonidou, *Reverse Discrimination*, Kluwer Law International 2009.

59 Cals, *La discrimination à rebours et le droit communautaire*, Université de Toulouse 2001.

60 Epiney, *Umgekehrte Diskriminierungen*, Carl Heymans Verlag KC 1995, pp 343–494.

61 Spitaleri, *Le discriminiazioni alla rovescia nel diritto comunitario*, Università di Trieste 2005, pp 159–97.

62 Walter, *Reverse Discrimination and Family Reunification*, Wolf Legal Publishers 2008. See also Hanf, 'Reverse Discrimination' in EU Law: Constitutional Aberration, Constitutional Necessity, or Judicial Choice?' (2011) 18 *MJ* 29. However, this article only briefly notes some illustrations of reverse discrimination in different Member States, without really elaborating on them.

3. METHODOLOGY

29. As Van Hoecke has formulated it: '[D]octrinal legal research ranges between straightforward descriptions …, with some incidental interpretative comments, on the one hand, and innovative theory building (systematisation), on the other. The more "simple" versions of that research are necessary building blocks for the more sophisticated ones.'[63]

30. In Part I, reverse discrimination is examined from the perspective of the European Union. The case law of the Court of Justice is the most important source in this Part. Specifically, the purely internal situation doctrine and the interpretation of a sufficient link with Union law are analysed in the light of both specific Treaty provisions and in terms of general principles of Union law, such as the principles of conferral, subsidiarity and proportionality.

31. Parts II and III examine a variety of national perspectives on reverse discrimination; specifically, there is discussion of cases in Belgium, France, Italy, Germany and Austria. These five Member States were selected for both substantive and pragmatic reasons.

Regarding the first set of reasons, it should be noted first that in those five Member States under analysis, all founding Member States apart from Austria, the issue of reverse discrimination has been explicitly and repeatedly questioned. In particular, France has been selected because, historically, French law exerted considerable influence over Belgian legal tradition and Belgian law is still susceptible to French influence now.[64] Italy is discussed because of its unique position as being against reverse discrimination in general. Finally, Germany and Austria were selected because of their federal state structure, an element which became clear from early on in this research that may add an extra level of complexity to the issue of reverse discrimination.

Concerning the more pragmatic reasons involved, it should be emphasised that the selection of those Member States under analysis is limited to five in order to guarantee the depth and manageability of the research involved.[65] Given the importance of access to sources in the original language in which they

---

63 Van Hoecke, 'Preface' in Van Hoecke (ed), *Methodologies of Legal Research*, Hart 2011, p vi. See also Van Gestel and Micklitz, 'Revitalizing Doctrinal Legal Research in Europe: What About Methodology?', EUI Working Papers Law 2011/05, 26–31.

64 Heirbaut and Storme, 'The Belgian Legal Tradition: from a Long Quest for Legal Independence to a Longing for Dependence?' (2006) 14 *ERPL* 645–83.

65 Kestemont et al, 'Methods for Traditional Legal Research' in Reader, *Methods of Legal Research*, KULeuven – University of Tilburg 2014–15, p 18.

were written, language limitations also obviously explain and limit the choice of those Member States under analysis.[66]

32. Unfortunately, information concerning how Member States interpret and apply Union law is not systematically monitored or reported. No database exists that brings together cases of reverse discrimination dealt with by Member States. However, between 2003 and 2013, under the supervision of the European Commission, the Radboud University Nijmegen's Centre for Migration Law coordinated the European network on free movement of workers within the European Union.[67] In particular, the centre 'kept track of legislation on the free movement of workers and how it is applied; monitored how national courts interpret EU laws [and] raised awareness of the importance of free movement of workers as a fundamental right'.[68] From 2002 to 2013, the network coordinated and published annual reports, Member State by Member State, regarding the application and interpretation of the free movement of workers by the individual Member State. These national reports were an important source for examples of reverse discrimination as discussed from the perspective of Member States.

33. The main research question, regarding a variety of national perspectives on reverse discrimination, is on which grounds the Member States decide whether or not to remedy reverse discrimination. It is not the intention of this book to give an exhaustive overview of every single case of reverse discrimination in the five Member States under analysis. First, this would be virtually impossible because reverse discrimination may arise in the areas of the free movement of goods, services, workers, establishment, capital and Union citizenship and often a situation of reverse discrimination can go unnoticed or will not have been described as such. Secondly, providing an exhaustive overview of every case of reverse discrimination in the five Member States under analysis would not be a particularly thought-provoking exercise because in some cases national authorities seem not to be aware of the issue of reverse discrimination and often do not make their reasoning explicit as to why they remedy or allow reverse discrimination.

Accordingly, the focus is on those cases of reverse discrimination in which the national authorities explain the grounds on the basis of which they decide to remedy, or not to remedy, the situation of reverse discrimination. Moreover, special attention is given to cases of family reunification because this is a topical subject both at Union level and at national level.

---

66 Ibid p 19.

67 This network is no longer active and has been replaced by FreSsco (Free Movement of Workers and Social Security Coordination).

68 <http://ec.europa.eu/social/main.jsp?catId=475&langId=en> accessed 15.06.2016.

34. Legal rulings and decisions are assessed critically in order to encourage the relevant actors, both at the Union level and national levels, 'to improve their reasoning in the future'.[69] In particular, we will examine whether a decisive element can be distinguished at all, and if so which element that is, in order to categorise some situations of reverse discrimination as being unproblematic side effects of the vertical division of competences in the EU and others as problematic situations of reverse discrimination which should be resolved. On this basis, the following section outlines the proposed schema of reasoning for legal practice of assessing reverse discrimination in any particular case.[70]

4. STRUCTURE

4.1. REVERSE DISCRIMINATION FROM A UNION LAW PERSPECTIVE (PART I)

35. Part I analyses the issue of reverse discrimination from a Union perspective. This is a logical starting point given that reverse discrimination arises as a result of the limited scope of application of Union law. More precisely, reverse discrimination is the result of the combination of national law and Union law that apply to the same territory but which have a different scope of application.

36. Chapter 2 in particular examines whether reverse discrimination continues to fall within the scope of application of Member State law or whether it falls within the ambit of Union law. It starts with the ECJ's traditional case law holding that reverse discrimination is not prohibited by Union law. Next, different proposals which seek to address reverse discrimination at the Union level are discussed. The arguments underlying the Court's case law will be balanced against the reasons underlying the proposals given for addressing reverse discrimination at the Union level.

37. Chapter 3 analyses both the applicability and the interpretation of the purely internal situation doctrine. First, it discusses the purely internal situation doctrine's applicability. The general rule is that it applies to the Treaty provisions on free movement and Union citizenship, but the Court refines its case law by not applying the purely internal situation doctrine to domains which are harmonised. Moreover, the Court makes an exception to the purely internal

---

69 Alter, 'Law, Political Science and Legal Studies. A Political Science Perspective' (2002) 3 *EUP* 113, 115.

70 On the prescriptive nature of legal doctrinal research see inter alia Alter, 'Law, Political Science and Legal Studies. A Political Science Perspective' (2002) 3 *EUP* 113, 116 and Vick, 'Interdisciplinarity and the Discipline of Law' (2004) 31 *J Law & Soc* 163, 179.

situation doctrine, in its case law on internal tariff barriers, and an indirect exception via Article 267 TFEU by replying to a question referred for preliminary ruling in which the main proceedings concern a purely internal situation.

Next, the chapter examines the instances in which the ECJ considers a situation to be purely internal or, by contrast, to have a sufficient connection with Union law. The traditional interpretation of a sufficient connection with Union law regarding Treaty provisions on free movement requires both a cross-border element and an economic activity. Only a cross-border element is required regarding the Treaty provisions on Union citizenship. Initially, the cross-border element was interpreted as comprising actual movement between different Member States. However, the Court of Justice has become increasingly generous in accepting a sufficient connection with Union law, both by expanding upon the notion of movement and, at the same time, by reducing the importance of movement.

4.2. REVERSE DISCRIMINATION FROM A VARIETY OF NATIONAL PERSPECTIVES (PART II)

38. The perspective of the Member States is a crucial part of research on reverse discrimination since, according to the ECJ, Union law does not prohibit reverse discrimination and the Member States must individually decide whether to remedy it or not. Therefore, Part II of the book discusses reverse discrimination from five national perspectives. The Member States under analysis are Belgium, France, Italy, Germany and Austria. The focus is on the way in which the national authorities make their assessment of reverse discrimination in order to decide whether they allow reverse discrimination to exist or whether they require the same treatment for purely internal situations.

39. Chapter 4 examines the national authorities' assessment of reverse discrimination in the area of goods whilst Chapter 5 discusses the national assessment of reverse discrimination in the area of persons. In particular, after analysing cases of reverse discrimination in the area of the classic free movement rights of persons, cases of family reunification with Union citizens are discussed.

4.3. REVERSE DISCRIMINATION IN A FEDERAL STATE CONTEXT (PART III)

40. In this book, 'classic cases' of reverse discrimination are distinguished from cases of reverse discrimination in a federal state context.[71] In Parts I and II,

---

71 See also DAUTRICOURT and THOMAS, 'Reverse Discrimination and Free Movement of Persons Under Community Law: All for Ulysses, Nothing for Penelope?' (2009) 34 *ELRev* 454, 443:

the 'classic cases' of reverse discrimination are discussed, that is, those cases in which a Member State treats its own nationals in a purely internal situation more strictly than Union citizens falling within the ambit of Union law. In Part III, the focus is on 'specific cases' of reverse discrimination which concern situations of reverse discrimination in a federally structured Member State. That is to say, it may happen that the reverse discrimination only affects some of the Member State's own nationals, those who do not fall under the jurisdiction of the regional authority granting certain rights to the nationals falling under its jurisdiction in particular.

41. Chapter 6 discusses cases of reverse discrimination in a federal state context from the perspective of Union law. The EU's approach to the federal structure of its Member States in general is described and there is discussion of the ECJ cases which (may) lead to a specific situation of reverse discrimination specifically. Chapter 7 discusses cases of reverse discrimination in a federal state context from the perspective of Belgium and Germany. There is particular examination of the grounds on which the national authorities decide whether or not to remedy or prevent the specific situation of reverse discrimination.

'[A]n important distinction has to be drawn between, on the one hand, the specific category of reverse discrimination resulting from the existence of internal repartition of competences within a Member State and, on the other, reverse discrimination which does not result from the federal organisation of the state but exclusively from the fact that some nationals have not made use of their [Union] free movement rights.'

PART I

REVERSE DISCRIMINATION FROM A UNION PERSPECTIVE

42. Part I examines the issue of reverse discrimination from a Union perspective. It is the Court of Justice's settled case law that reverse discrimination is not prohibited by Union law because the Treaty provisions on free movement and Union citizenship do not apply to purely internal situations. Accordingly, the Member States have to decide individually whether or not to remedy situations of reverse discrimination. The aim of Part I is to answer the first research question: to what extent does reverse discrimination continue to fall within the scope of the law of the Member States and when does it fall within the ambit of Union law?

43. Chapter 2 provides an analysis of the ECJ's case law on reverse discrimination from the very first cases to the most recent ones. The arguments justifying and questioning this case law will be discussed, taking new developments in Union law into account, and the creation of Union citizenship particularly. After balancing all of these elements, the position will be taken that reverse discrimination still falls outside the scope of Union law.[72]

44. The real problem with the ECJ's case law on reverse discrimination seems to lie in its interpretation of what constitutes a purely internal situation. In particular, the unpredictability of whether or not the ECJ will consider a concrete case to be purely internal can be seriously criticised. This assessment's consequences are far-reaching: if a sufficient link with Union law is found, the situation falls under Union law; if no such link is found, by contrast, the situation is purely internal and reverse discrimination may occur. Chapter 3 provides an analysis of the ECJ's interpretation of purely internal situations. Finally, some recommendations on how to make this interpretation more clear and straightforward are given.

---

72 By contrast, see inter alia Tryfonidou, *Reverse Discrimination*, Kluwer Law International 2009.

45. The study of reverse discrimination from a Union perspective should not examine the ECJ's purely internal situation rule as being an isolated doctrine, but should instead involve general principles of EU law and other ECJ doctrines. Accordingly, involved inter alia in this analysis are the principle of conferral, the ECJ's case law on restrictions of free movement, the ECJ's case law on internal tariff barriers and the *Dzodzi* and *Guimont* lines of cases.

46. Although cases regarding the Treaty provisions on the free movement of goods, workers, establishment, services, capital and the right of EU citizens to move and reside on the territory of the EU are all discussed in this Part, the focus is placed on cases regarding the free movement of persons for two reasons. First, the fact that Union law does not prohibit reverse discrimination is currently being criticised principally from the perspective of Union citizenship and fundamental rights. Moreover, the most recent developments of the ECJ's interpretation of a sufficient link with Union law can be situated within the domain of free movement of persons.

47. Finally, the third research question will be addressed: should reverse discrimination be considered as a problem that requires a solution in each case? Moreover, if a solution is required, who should provide this solution: the EU, the Member States, regions or several of these in interaction? In the conclusion to Part I, a determining criterion will be suggested that attempts to distinguish between problematic and unproblematic cases of reverse discrimination. This will be explained from the perspective of Union law and developed further and applied to situations of reverse discrimination presented in Parts II and III.

CHAPTER 2

THE EUROPEAN COURT OF JUSTICE'S APPROACH TO REVERSE DISCRIMINATION

48. In this chapter, the ECJ's position on reverse discrimination is examined. After a brief explanation of the ECJ's case law establishing the purely internal situations rule, there is analysis of the ECJ's case law according to which reverse discrimination does not fall within the scope of Union law and, hence, is not prohibited by Union law. Since this position has not been unanimously approved of, we will also discuss some proposals which aim to address reverse discrimination at the Union level. Finally, the question of whether the underlying rationale of the ECJ's traditional position on reverse discrimination remains valid will be assessed on the basis of the current Treaties.

1. ECJ'S TRADITIONAL APPROACH: REVERSE DISCRIMINATION IS NOT PROHIBITED BY UNION LAW

1.1. THE EARLY CASE LAW ON PURELY INTERNAL SITUATIONS

1.1.1. The Notion of a 'Purely Internal Situation'

49. The Court of Justice used the notion of a 'purely internal situation' for the first time in 1979, in the *Knoors* case. Mr Knoors was a Dutch national residing in Belgium where he had been working as a plumbing contractor. He applied to the Dutch authorities for authorisation to practise the same trade in the Netherlands. However, the Dutch authorities refused his application because he did not possess the necessary qualifications according to the Dutch legislation. They added that Mr Knoors could not be considered a beneficiary of the provisions of Directive 64/427, according to which a Member State has to recognise the actual practice in another Member State as a sufficient proof of the qualifications required. In this context, the question was raised as to whether a national could be considered to be a beneficiary of the Directive towards his own state.

50. The Court of Justice considered that 'although it is true that provisions of the Treaty relating to establishment and the provision of services cannot be applied to situations which are purely internal to a Member State', Article 49 TFEU[73] applies to a Member State's own nationals when they have lawfully resided on the territory of another Member State in which they have obtained a trade qualification which is recognised by Union law, since they are in a similar situation to that of other persons enjoying the rights and liberties guaranteed by the Treaty with respect to their state of origin.[74] The Court concluded that Directive 64/427 may be relied upon by the nationals of all the Member States who objectively enter into one of the situations envisaged by the Directive, even with respect to the State whose nationality they possess.[75]

51. An important aspect of the issue of reverse discrimination can already be seen from this first judgment in which the ECJ used the notion of a purely internal situation. This is that reverse discrimination concerns not only those situations in which Union law urges a Member State to treat nationals of other Member States more favourably, but also the situations in which Union law urges a Member State to treat their own nationals who have enjoyed the rights and liberties guaranteed by the Treaty – or in other words, who have made use of their right of free movement – more favourably than nationals in purely internal situations.

1.1.2. Definition of a 'Purely Internal Situation'

52. A month later in the *Saunders* case, the Court defined the notion of 'purely internal situation'. Mrs Saunders was a British national who had pleaded guilty to a charge of theft. The national court had ordered her to move to Northern Ireland and not to return to England or Wales within the following three years. The national court on appeal posed the question, on the basis that Mrs Saunders was a worker within the meaning of Article 45 TFEU,[76] as to whether the rules of the Treaty on freedom of movement for workers prohibit measures such as those in the main proceedings.

---

[73] Then Article 52 EEC Treaty.

[74] ECJ case 115/78 *Knoors* [1979] ECR I-399, para 24.

[75] Ibid para 28 and more clearly in the summary.

[76] Then Article 48 EEC Treaty.

53. First, the Court of Justice considered that the reply to that question depended upon the determination of the scope of Article 45 TFEU in combination with Article 18 TFEU.[77,78] In this respect, the Court recalled that any discrimination on grounds of nationality is forbidden within the scope of application of the Treaty, under Article 18 TFEU.[79] The Court ruled that, in application of this general principle, Article 45 TFEU intends to abolish national conditions of work and employment according to which a national of another Member State is subjected to more severe treatment than a State's own national facing the same circumstances.[80]

54. Next, the Court considered that 'although the right conferred upon workers by article [45 TFEU] may lead the Member States to amend their legislation, where necessary, even with respect to their own nationals', Article 45 TFEU does not intend to restrict the power of the Member States to impose limits within their own territory on the freedom of movement of all persons subject to their jurisdiction in domestic criminal law.[81] In line with the *Knoors* case, the Court confirmed for the Treaty provisions on the freedoms of movement of workers that they cannot be applied to 'situations which are wholly internal to a Member State, in other words, where there is *no factor connecting them to any of the situations envisaged by [Union] law*'.[82] Accordingly, the Court decided that a situation such as that in the main proceedings, constituted a 'wholly domestic situation which falls outside the scope of the rules contained in the treaty on freedom of movement for workers'.[83]

1.1.3. Justification Put Forward by the ECJ for the Purely Internal Situation Rule

55. Two years later, in the *Morson and Jhanjan* case, the ECJ put forward a two-fold justification for its purely internal situation rule. Mrs Morson and Mrs Jhanjan were nationals of Suriname who applied for permission to reside in the Netherlands together with their daughter and son respectively, both of whom were Dutch nationals and upon whom they were dependant. The daughter and son worked in the Netherlands but had never worked in another Member State. Both Mrs Morson's and Mrs Jhanjan's applications were refused, and they challenged the decision, inter alia, on the basis of the prohibition of discrimination enshrined in Articles 18 and 45 TFEU.

---

77 Then Article 48 EEC Treaty and Article 7 EEC Treaty respectively.

78 ECJ case 175/78 *Saunders* [1979], ECR I-1129, para 7.

79 Ibid para 8.

80 Ibid para 9.

81 Ibid para 10.

82 Ibid para 11, emphasis added.

83 Ibid para 12.

56. The ECJ ruled that Articles 18 and 45 TFEU can only be relied upon when the situation at issue 'comes within the area to which [Union] law applies, which in this case is that concerned with freedom of movement of workers within the [Union]'.[84] According to the Court, this conclusion not only follows on from 'the wording of those articles, but it also accords with their purpose, which is to assist in the abolition of all obstacles to the establishment of a common market in which the nationals of the Member States may move freely within the territory of those states in order to pursue their economic activities'.[85] Correspondingly, the Court confirmed that the Treaty provision on the free movement of workers cannot be applied to cases without a factor linking them with any of the situations governed by Union law.[86] In this respect, the Court ruled that this is definitely the case for 'workers who have never exercised their right to freedom of movement within the [Union]'.[87] The Court concluded, therefore, that Union law does not prohibit a Member State from refusing to grant a residence permit to a third country national who is a relative of a worker employed within the territory of the Member State whose nationality he possesses and who has never made use of his right of free movement within the Union.[88]

57. Hence, the ECJ in its judgment justified the purely internal situations rule on two grounds. First of all, the Court pointed out that this follows from the wording of the Treaty provisions on free movement. For instance, Article 49 TFEU provides that 'restrictions on the freedom of establishment of nationals of a Member State in the territory of *another* Member State shall be prohibited'.[89] Secondly, the Court noted that this corresponds to the Treaty provisions on free movement's principal aim; namely to establish a common market in which the nationals of the Member States may move freely within the territory of those Member States, in order to pursue their economic activities. Accordingly, the ECJ considered the fundamental freedoms as an instrument by which to promote

84 ECJ joined cases 35/82 and 36/82 *Morson and Jhanjan* [1982] ECR 3723, para 15.

85 Ibid.

86 Ibid para 16.

87 Ibid para 17.

88 Ibid para 18.

89 Emphasis added. See also Article 49 TFEU regarding the right of establishment, 'restrictions on the freedom of establishment of nationals of a Member State in the territory of *another* Member State shall be prohibited'; Article 56 TFEU regarding free movement of services 'in respect of nationals of Member States who are established in a Member State other than that of the person for whom the services are intended'; Article 63 TFEU regarding the free movement of capital 'between Member States and between Member States and third countries' and Articles 34 and 35 TFEU regarding quantitative restrictions on import and export 'between Member States'. The only free movement provision which does not explicitly determine that only cross-border situations are envisaged is the freedom of movement for workers since Article 45 TFEU provides that 'the freedom of movement for workers shall be secured within the Union'. However, since the time of the *Saunders* case, the ECJ has applied its purely internal situation doctrine to the freedom of movement for workers. (See also Tryfonidou, *Reverse Discrimination*, Kluwer Law International 2009, p 10.)

the freedom of movement between the Member States.[90] This is why the benefits of the Treaty provisions on the fundamental freedoms were only applied to those individuals who contributed to the common market.[91]

1.2. REVERSE DISCRIMINATION IS NOT PROHIBITED BY UNION LAW

1.2.1. Purely Internal Situations Outside the Scope of Union Law – Reverse Discrimination Not Prohibited by Union Law

58. From its inception, the ECJ made clear that purely internal situations fall outside the scope of the Treaty provisions on free movement. As mentioned above, in the *Saunders* case, the Court ruled that a situation such as that in the main proceedings, constituted a 'wholly domestic situation which falls outside the scope of the rules contained in the treaty on freedom of movement for workers'.[92]

59. In the same vein, the Court ruled that Articles 18 and 45 TFEU can only be relied upon when the situation at issue 'comes within the area to which [Union] law applies, which in this case is that concerned with freedom of movement of workers within the [Union]' in the *Morson and Jhanjan* case.[93] The Court concluded that '[Union] law does not prohibit a Member State from' treating family members of an own national in a purely internal situation more severely regarding their residence permit than family members of Union citizens who fall under the scope of Union law.[94]

60. The ECJ further developed this line of case law over the next few years, inter alia, in the *Hurd* case. Mr Hurd challenged the fact that the UK had granted an exemption from domestic income tax to teachers of a European school, situated on its territory, who are nationals of another Member State, but not to its own nationals. According to Mr Hurd, this constituted a discrimination on the grounds of nationality, contrary to Article 18 TFEU.[95]

The ECJ considered that in order to resolve this question, it was necessary to examine whether the situation falls within the scope of application of the

---

90 Opinion AG Maduro 30 March 2006 in C-524/06, *Heinz Huber*, para 18 and Tryfonidou, *Reverse Discrimination*, Kluwer Law International 2009, p 166.

91 Tryfonidou, *Reverse Discrimination*, Kluwer Law International 2009, p 166.

92 ECJ case 175/78 *Saunders* [1979] ECR I-1129, para 12.

93 ECJ joined cases 35/82 and 36/82 *Morson and Jhanjan* [1982] ECR 3723, para 15.

94 Ibid para 18.

95 Then Article 7 EEC Treaty.

Treaties, in the meaning of Article 18 TFEU in particular.[96] In this respect, the Court ruled on the one hand, that 'it is true that teachers at the European school may be regarded as workers within the meaning of article [45 TFEU],[97] where they are employed in a school situated in another Member State, have made use of their right to free movement within the [Union]'.[98] On the other hand, the Court explicitly considered that this is 'not the case with regard to a teacher who is a national of the Member State in which the European school in question is situated and who has not moved within the [Union] to take up a post with that school'.[99]

Next, the Court referred to the *Saunders* and *Morson and Jhanjan* cases, according to which the principle of non-discrimination, enshrined in the Articles 18 and 45(2) TFEU, cannot be applied to purely internal situations. The ECJ ruled that 'the mere fact that nationals of a Member State are employed by a European school situated on the territory of that State is not sufficient to confer on those persons the benefit of the [Union] rules on the free movement of workers and to limit the power of that Member State to adopt measures in relation to them which are more restrictive than those applied to nationals of other Member States'.[100] Accordingly, the ECJ concluded that 'article [18 TFEU] cannot be relied upon to prohibit a Member State from applying to the teaching staff of a European School situated on its territory tax treatment which is less favourable to its own nationals than to the nationals of other Member States'.[101]

61. A recent confirmation of this position can, for instance, be found in the ECJ's *Ordine degli ingegneri* judgment, which will be discussed in the sections which follow.[102] In particular, after recognising that reverse discrimination may be caused by the Italian legislation involved, the Court explicitly held that 'with respect to a purely internal situation, the principle of equal treatment under European Union law cannot be invoked'.[103]

62. In sum, according to ECJ's established case law, purely internal situations fall outside the scope of Article 18 TFEU. Accordingly, reverse discrimination is not prohibited by the Union's general principle of non-discrimination.[104]

---

96 ECJ case 44/84 *Hurd* [1986] ECR 29, para 54.

97 Then Article 48 EEC Treaty.

98 ECJ case 44/84 *Hurd* [1986] ECR 29, para 54.

99 Ibid. 100 Ibid para 55. 101 Ibid para 56.

102 ECJ case C-111/12 *Ordine degli ingegneri di Verona e provincia e.a.* See below n 148.

103 ECJ case C-111/12 *Ordine degli ingegneri di Verona e provincia e.a.*, para 22.

104 It has been argued that in its *Kenny* judgment (ECJ case 1/78 [1978] ECR 1489, paras 16–21), the ECJ held that reverse discrimination in the domain of social security is prevented by the principle of non-discrimination as enshrined in Article 18 TFEU (see BARNARD, *EC Employment Law*, 3rd ed, Oxford University Press 2006, pp 213–14 and Opinion AG Sharpston 28 June 2007 in C-212/06, *Flemish Care Insurance*, para 148). However, the

1.2.2. Reverse Discrimination Should be Addressed at the National Level

63. In the *Steen* judgment, the ECJ identified another aspect of its approach towards reverse discrimination. The case concerned Mr Steen who began training under a contract of employment with a view to taking up a job at the Deutsche Bundespost (German federal post office) as a civil servant. However, at the end of his training period, Mr Steen asked to be appointed to the post in question under a contract of employment, since his remuneration at that time was higher than the one he would receive as a civil servant. When his application was rejected, Mr Steen brought an action before the employment courts arguing that, insofar as access to posts in the civil service is reserved to German nationals only, they alone were not able to occupy, as contractual employees, a post such as that at issue for an indefinite period and thereby they suffered discrimination within the meaning of Articles 18 and 45 TFEU in relation to nationals of other Member States.

64. The ECJ ruled that relying on Union law with respect to a purely internal situation is precluded.[105] Moreover, the ECJ added that 'it is for the national court, faced with a question of national law, to determine whether there is any discrimination under that law and whether that discrimination must be eliminated and, if so, how'.[106] Accordingly, the Court concluded that '[Union] law does not preclude a national court from examining the compatibility with its constitution of a national rule which, in a situation unconnected with any of the situations contemplated by [Union] law, treats national workers less favourably than nationals from other Member States'.[107]

65. In this judgment, the ECJ stated explicitly for the first time that it is up to the Member States to deal with situations of reverse discrimination. The ECJ has confirmed this in later judgments, as will be seen in the following subsection,[108]

Court did not confirm this in subsequent case law. Moreover, it has been argued that the *Kenny* case did not concern reverse discrimination since it concerned a situation in which people are subjected to different non-harmonised national rules depending upon the country in which they operate. In particular, in that case no discrimination is at stake since the different treatment has to be attributed to two different sources, namely two different Member States (Hanf, '"Reverse Discrimination" in EU Law: Constitutional Aberration, Constitutional Necessity, or Judicial Choice?' (2011) 18 *MJ* 29, 34–35).

105 ECJ case C-132/93 *Steen* [1994] ECR I-2715, para 9. 106 Ibid para 10. 107 Ibid para 11.

108 See inter alia ECJ joined cases C-64/96 and C-65/96 *Uecker and Jacquet* [1997] ECR I-3171, para 23; ECJ case C-253/01 *S.A. Krüger* [2004] ECR I-1191, para 36: 'As is apparent from the case-law of the Court, any discrimination which nationals of a Member State may suffer under the law of that State fall within the scope of that law and must therefore be dealt with within the framework of the internal legal system of that State' and ECJ case C-111/12 *Ordine degli ingegneri di Verona e provincia e.a.*, para 22.

and it is now considered to be settled case law. Whether and how the Member States should address situations of reverse discrimination will be examined in detail in Part II which considers a variety of national perspectives on reverse discrimination.

1.2.3. Confirmation of the ECJ's Traditional Approach on Reverse Discrimination Following the Introduction of Union Citizenship

66. The ECJ's position towards reverse discrimination is not uncontested, as will be discussed in the following section. The case law has been questioned in the light of Union citizenship specifically.[109] However, in its *Uecker and Jacquet* judgment, the ECJ confirmed, at least in principle, its traditional approach on reverse discrimination. The case concerned Ms Uecker and Ms Jacquet, a Norwegian and Russian national respectively. They were married to German nationals who resided and worked in Germany and had never exercised the right to freedom of movement within the Union. Ms Uecker and Ms Jacquet worked as foreign-language assistants in German universities on limited period contracts. They relied on Union law in order to challenge the validity of the limited duration of these contracts of employment. In this context, the national court referred a question for a preliminary ruling to the Court of Justice.

67. First, the ECJ recalled its settled case law according to which the Treaty provisions on freedom of movement and regulations adopted to implement them cannot be applied to cases which have no factor linking them to any of the situations governed by Union law and all elements of which are purely internal to a single Member State.[110] Consequently, the Court ruled that because the German husbands of Ms Uecker and Ms Jacquet had never exercised their right to free movement within the Union, they could not rely upon Union legislation regarding the free movement of workers.[111]

68. Next, the national court asked 'whether the fundamental principles of a Community moving towards European Union still permit a rule of national law which ... is in breach of Article [54 TFEU] to continue to be applied by a

---

109 See below nn 78–80. See inter alia Nic Shuibhne, 'Free Movement of Persons and the Wholly Internal Rule: Time to Move on?' (2002) 39 *CMLRev* 771, 731–71; Spaventa, 'Seeing the Wood Despite the Trees? On the Scope of Union Citizenship and its Constitutional Effects' (2008) 45 *CMLRev* 13, 13–45 and Tryfonidou, 'Reverse Discrimination in Purely Internal Situations: An Incongruity in a Citizens' Europe' (2008) 35 *LIEI* 67, 43–67.

110 ECJ joined cases C-64/96 and C-65/96 *Uecker and Jacquet* [1997] ECR I-3171, para 16.

111 In particular old Article 11 of Regulation No 1612/6. ECJ joined cases C-64/96 and C-65/96 *Uecker and Jacquet* [1997] ECR I-3171, paras 17–19.

Member State against its own nationals and their spouses from non-member countries'.[112] In this respect, the ECJ ruled that 'citizenship of the Union ... is not intended to extend the scope *ratione materiae* of the Treaty also to internal situations which have no link with [Union] law'.[113] The Court considered that 'any discrimination which nationals of a Member State may suffer under the law of that State fall within the scope of that law and must therefore be dealt with within the framework of the internal legal system of that State'.[114] Accordingly, the Court concluded that a third country national who is married to a Union citizen who has never exercised his right to free movement within the Union cannot rely on Directive 2004/38.[115,116]

69. The Court of Justice has confirmed this principled position repeatedly, for instance in the judgments *Garcia Avello* and *Schempp*.[117] However, the impact Union citizenship has had upon the interpretation of the purely internal situation rule is remarkable. This will be discussed in further detail in Chapter 3.

70. As a final remark on the ECJ's settled case law, according to which reverse discrimination is not prohibited by Union law, it is often said that an exception to the general approach is made when reverse discrimination would compromise one of the objectives of Union law. Lenaerts first formulated this in the following way: 'il est fait exception à cette règle lorsque la discrimination à rebours compromet les objectifs de la Communauté'.[118] Afterwards many authors, referring to Lenaerts, confirmed that reverse discrimination has only been prohibited where it would compromise one of the objectives of the Treaties.[119] In particular, Lenaerts refers to the *Knoors* case in order to illustrate this statement. However, that case concerned a so-called 'returning citizen' who exercised his right to free movement and therefore fell under the scope of application of Union law. Accordingly, no exception was at stake since Mr Knoors was not involved in a purely internal situation.[120]

---

112 ECJ joined cases C-64/96 and C-65/96 *Uecker and Jacquet* [1997] ECR I-3171, para 22.

113 Ibid para 23. 114 Ibid.

115 Then Regulation 1612/68.

116 ECJ joined cases C-64/96 and C-65/96 *Uecker and Jacquet* [1997] ECR I-3171, para 24.

117 *Garcia Avello* [2003] ECR I-11613, para 26 and ECJ case C-403/03 *Schempp* [2005] ECR I-6421, para 20.

118 Lenaerts, 'L'égalité de traitement en droit communautaire. Un principe unique aux apparences multiples' (1991) *CDE* 41, 19: 'an exception to this rule is made if the situation of reverse discrimination compromises the goals of the Community' (own translation).

119 See inter alia Spaventa, 'Seeing the Wood Despite the Trees? On the Scope of Union Citizenship and its Constitutional Effects' (2008) 45 *CMLRev* 13.

120 In particular, Mr Knoors was not in purely internal situation because the ECJ considers the fact that a Union citizen has previously exercised his right of free movement is enough to fall under the scope of Union law. See on returning citizens below nn 223–36.

2. PROPOSALS TO ADDRESS REVERSE DISCRIMINATION AT UNION LEVEL

71. As noted above, the ECJ's position on reverse discrimination is not unanimously accepted by legal scholars. We will now go on to look at some proposals which are aimed at addressing reverse discrimination at the Union level, particularly those proposals that seek to reverse the ECJ's traditional approach to reverse discrimination. Although the ECJ has consistently rejected such suggestions, it is worthwhile having a closer look at the arguments which have been put forward in this regard.

72. First, proposals that criticise the ECJ's settled case law on reverse discrimination from the perspective of the common and the internal market are discussed. Next, the proposals that do so more specifically in the context of freedom of movement for persons are examined. The ECJ's approach on reverse discrimination has been decried recently in this area particularly, especially following the creation of Union citizenship and the ECJ's broad interpretation of the related Treaty provisions.

73. As a preliminary remark,[121] it is worth pointing out that those who oppose the purely internal situation rule, arguing that reverse discrimination should be addressed at Union level, seem to presuppose that there is an unjustified discrimination that should be corrected in every event. However, opinions diverge as to whether reverse discrimination should be eliminated by the legislator, through harmonisation, or by the ECJ.

2.1. IN THE LIGHT OF THE COMMON AND INTERNAL MARKET

74. As early as 1986, AG Mischo argued, in the context of free movement of goods, that 'reverse discrimination is clearly impossible in the long run within a true common market, which must of necessity be based on the principle of equal treatment. Such discrimination must be eliminated by means of the harmonisation of legislation'.[122] This remark by AG Mischo in the *Edah* case reveals his belief that reverse discrimination is an unjustified discrimination that should be remedied in every instance. Moreover, the AG made it clear that this should be done at the Union level, in particular by way of harmonisation.

---

[121] And in particular in the light of the third research question of whether reverse discrimination should be considered as a problem that requires a solution in each case.

[122] Opinion AG Mischo in Joined Cases 80 and 159/85, *Edah* [1986] ECR 3375.

75. Following the introduction of the 'internal market', the conviction grew that the ECJ's case law that allowed reverse discrimination should be abandoned.[123] Specifically, D'Oliveira argued that 'it is possible for the European Court to revise its case law in respect of reverse discrimination without having to wait for harmonisation measures bringing nearer the equal treatment of one's own citizens and those of other Member States. The Court should now re-interpret the existing provisions on freedom of movement etc. in the light of the new objective of the [Single European Act] and disallow reverse discrimination in this sector'.[124]

76. D'Oliveira reached this conclusion by beginning with the consideration that the difference between the 'common market' and the 'internal market' is that the latter 'no longer has any internal frontiers'.[125] He argued that this new objective would have an impact upon the interpretation of the principle of non-discrimination and the Union provisions on fundamental freedoms.[126] According to D'Oliveira, it would in particular become increasingly difficult to maintain the distinction between purely internal situations and Union situations.[127] He argued that 'aiming at an internal market, or completing it, while at the same time continuing to attach importance to the crossing of national frontiers is self-contradictory. One cannot remove internal frontiers on the one hand and attribute decisive importance to the existence of those self-same frontiers on the other.'[128] D'Oliveira concluded 'that in the case of contradictory layers of provisions, the Court is free to reconsider its position *vis-à-vis* reverse discrimination'.[129]

77. In sum, the argument made here is that it is illogical to consider the crossing of national borders to be a decisive element while at the same time removing the physical and technical obstacles in order to complete an internal market without internal borders. This view has since been affirmed by several

---

123 See inter alia White, 'A Fresh Look at Reverse Discrimination?' (1993) 18 *ELRev* 527, 532.

124 D'Oliveira, 'Is Reverse Discrimination Still Possible Under the Single European Act?' in *Forty Years On: The Evolution of Postwar Private International Law in Europe: Symposium in Celebration of the 40th Anniversary of the Centre of Foreign Law and Private International Law, University of Amsterdam, on 27 October 1989*, Kluwer 1990, p 86.

125 Ibid 83. However, this is one possible interpretation of the different terms. It might also be that they are basically synonyms (Barnard, *The Substantive Law of the EU: The Four Freedoms*, Oxford University Press 2013, p 12).

126 D'Oliveira, 'Is Reverse Discrimination Still Possible Under the Single European Act?' in *Forty Years On: The Evolution of Postwar Private International Law in Europe: Symposium in Celebration of the 40th Anniversary of the Centre of Foreign Law and Private International Law, University of Amsterdam, on 27 October 1989*, Kluwer 1990, p 84.

127 Ibid. 128 Ibid. 129 Ibid.

authors.[130] Unlike AG Mischo, who argued that reverse discrimination should be removed by way of harmonisation of legislation, D'Oliveira argued that the ECJ is able to reconsider its case law on reverse discrimination on the basis of the aforementioned contradiction. D'Oliveira's proposal seems to be tantamount to requiring the ECJ's abandoning of the requirement of a cross-border element or the exercise of rights of free movement altogether.

2.2. IN THE LIGHT OF FREEDOM OF MOVEMENT FOR PERSONS AND UNION CITIZENSHIP

2.2.1. In the Light of Union Citizenship and EU Fundamental Rights Protection

78. It seems that the arguments put forward, which seek to correct reverse discrimination at the Union level, are even more prevalent in the context of the freedom of movement for persons than they are in the context of other fundamental freedoms.[131] Some authors argue that while reverse discrimination can be accepted in a purely economic context, it is hard to justify it in the light of the creation of Union citizenship.[132] With the introduction of Union citizenship, it became clear that the Union's objectives were no longer exclusively confined to economic aims, but instead included the creation of a sense of identity and solidarity at the EU level.[133]

79. It is certainly true that the change created by the introduction of Union citizenship has brought the legitimacy of the doctrine of purely internal situations into question. So-called 'static' Union citizens may be treated less

---

130 See eg O'Leary, *The Evolving Concept of Community Citizenship. From the Free Movement of Persons to Union Citizenship*, Kluwer Law international 1996, pp 275–76 and Poiares Maduro, 'The Scope of European Remedies: The Case of Purely Internal Situations and Reverse Discrimination' in Kilpatrick, Novitz and Skidmore (eds), *The Future of European Remedies*, Hart Publishing 2000, p 126.

131 Nic Shuibhne, 'Free Movement of Persons and the Wholly Internal Rule: Time to Move on?' (2002) 37 *CMLRev* 771, 764.

132 See inter alia Dautricourt and Thomas, 'Reverse Discrimination and Free Movement of Persons Under Community Law: All for Ulysses, Nothing for Penelope?' (2009) 34 *ELRev* 454, 436; Nic Shuibhne, 'Free Movement of Persons and the Wholly Internal Rule: Time to Move on?' (2002) 39 *CMLRev* 771, 731. See also Tryfonidou, *Reverse Discrimination*, Kluwer Law International 2009, pp 166–71, which will be discussed more in detail below.

133 Dautricourt and Thomas, 'Reverse Discrimination and Free Movement of Persons Under Community Law: All for Ulysses, Nothing for Penelope?' (2009) 34 *ELRev* 454, 436. See also O'Leary, *The Evolving Concept of Community Citizenship. From the Free Movement of Persons to Union Citizenship*, Kluwer Law international 1996, p 277. See also Tryfonidou, *Reverse Discrimination*, Kluwer Law International 2009, pp 166–71, which will be discussed more in detail below.

favourably than 'mobile' Union citizens.[134] Or, in other words, moving or not moving can have far-reaching consequences for Union citizens.[135] For instance, imagine that the German husbands of Ms Uecker and Ms Jacquet[136] had resided and worked in France. Then Ms Uecker and Ms Jacquet might have successfully challenged the validity of the limitation on the duration of their contracts of employment under Union law.[137] In this light, it is not surprising that this case law has been questioned.

80. Nic Shuibhne has argued that although there is a strong argument to leave it up 'to the Member States individually to redress imbalances between national and [Union] standards', this has become less justifiable in the light of EU fundamental rights protection, the Framework and Race Directives and the extending scope of EU citizenship in the ECJ's case law.[138] Therefore, Nic Shuibhne has concluded that 'it does now seem time to move on'.[139] However, she admitted that it is less certain how exactly to proceed.[140] On the one hand, she considers that in the specific context of free movement of persons, there is political merit in assigning responsibility at the national level. On the other hand, in that way, an inconsistency risk exists. Therefore, she prefers to assign this task to the Union. However, she does acknowledge that the next question that arises is whether reverse discrimination should be corrected by the EU legislature or judiciary.[141]

2.2.2. *Reverse Discrimination Incompatible with the Union Principle of Equality*

81. Several Advocates General and academics have argued that Article 18 TFEU, enshrining the principle of non-discrimination on the basis of nationality, should be interpreted as prohibiting reverse discrimination. This was argued as

---

134 See inter alia Opinion AG Sharpston 30 September 2010 in C-34/09, *Ruiz Zambrano*, para 138.

135 Nic Shuibhne, 'Free Movement of Persons and the Wholly Internal Rule: Time to Move on?' (2002) 37 *CMLRev* 771, 748.

136 For a description of the real facts see above nn 66–68.

137 Conversely, if Mr Carpenter had only delivered services within the UK, Mrs Carpenter could not have challenged her deportation under Union law (Nowak, 'Case Note, Case C-34/09, Gerardo Ruiz Zambrano v. Office national de l'emploi (ONEM) & Case C-434/09, Shirley McCarthy v. Secretary of State for the Home Department' (2011) 17 *ColJourEurLaw* 673, 8, fn 50). See more on the *Carpenter* case below n 188.

138 Nic Shuibhne, 'Free Movement of Persons and the Wholly Internal Rule: Time to Move on?' (2002) 37 *CMLRev* 771, 732.

139 Ibid 770.
140 Ibid.
141 Ibid.

early as 1979, specifically in the opinion of AG Warner in the *Saunders* case, discussed above.[142]

82. According to AG Warner, it is doubtful whether the dictum in the *Knoors* case is generally applicable in the areas of the freedom of establishment and freedom of services since it applied only in a very narrow context. In particular, the ECJ had to deal with the argument by the Dutch government that a person should not be allowed to circumvent qualifications required by their home Member State for a particular trade by deliberately going to obtain less strictly managed qualifications in another Member State. In any event, AG Warner is convinced that the *Knoors* dictum cannot be treated as establishing a sweeping principle whereupon no provision of the Treaty, or no provision of it about the free movement of persons, can apply in a case 'wholly internal to a Member State'.[143] He argued that 'the Treaty, in many ways, confers on the citizens of each Member State rights enforceable against the authorities of that State and, secondly, that article [18 TFEU] forbids discrimination by a Member State against its own nationals as much as it forbids discrimination by a Member State against the nationals of other Member States'.[144]

In other words, AG Warner argued that the purely internal situation rule should not be applicable in the context of freedom of movement for persons. According to the Advocate General, the principle of equality and non-discrimination, as enshrined in Union law, prohibits both discrimination on the grounds of nationality (discrimination of nationals from other Member States) and reverse discrimination (discrimination of its own nationals in a purely internal situation).[145]

83. Moreover, several legal authors have argued, over the years, that reverse discrimination should be prohibited by Article 18 TFEU. For instance, O'Leary formulated it in the following way: 'the importance of the principle of equal

---

142 Above nn 52–54.

143 Opinion AG Warner 8 March 1979 in ECJ case 175/78, *Saunders* [1979] ECR 1142.

144 Ibid.

145 Other Advocates General have emphasised the connection between Union citizenship and the Union principle of equality, but rather 'in a specific context or in an embryonic form' (Cambien, 'Citizenship of the Union as a Cornerstone of European Integration', Dissertation, KU Leuven 2011, p 240). In this respect Cambien refers to the Opinions of AG Léger and AG Poiares Maduro. In particular, Opinion AG Léger 14 November 1995 in C-214/94, *Boukhalfa*, para 63: 'Taken to its ultimate conclusion, the concept should lead to citizens of the Union being treated absolutely equally, irrespective of their nationality'; Opinion AG Poiares Maduro 6 May 2004 in C-72/03, *Carbonati Apuani*, para 63 (discussed above) and Opinion AG Poiares Maduro 3 April 2008 in C-524/06, *Huber*, para 18: 'the prohibition of discrimination on the basis of nationality is no longer merely an instrument at the service of freedom of movement; it is at the heart of the concept of European citizenship'.

treatment to the development of Union citizenship further undermines the survival of reverse discrimination. Reverse discrimination is arguably unacceptable if, as they should be, equal treatment and more complete free movement are considered prerequisites of [Union] citizenship. ... The possible effects of Union citizenship and the principle of equal treatment should not be underestimated.'[146]

84. According to Spaventa, who considers Article 18 TFEU to be one of the rights granted to Union citizens, 'so that static Union citizens who find themselves in a comparable situation to migrant citizens would have a right to equal treatment deriving directly from [Union] law ... would be consistent both with the existing case law on article [18 TFEU], and with the demands of a meaningful concept of citizenship'.[147] She emphasised that 'the very idea of citizenship sits uncomfortably with an a priori differentiation between citizens based on the sole ground that a border has been crossed'.[148]

85. Tryfonidou is a prominent advocate of an interpretation of Article 18 TFEU that prohibits reverse discrimination. Tryfonidou firmly insists that reverse discrimination should now be considered to be a difference in treatment that falls within the scope of application of Union law.[149] She argued that reverse discrimination is caused by the realisation of an internal market and the limited scope of application of Union law.[150] In particular, she considered that 'in the context of an organization of purely economic aims, which viewed individuals merely as factors of production, it was not at all surprising that fundamental human rights and, more specifically, the principles of equality and non-discrimination were principally used as vehicles for assisting the completion of the internal market and thus were available to persons only in order to enable them to act in furtherance of the [Union']s goals'.[151] Accordingly, reverse

---

146 O'Leary, *The Evolving Concept of Community Citizenship. From the Free Movement of Persons to Union Citizenship*, Kluwer Law international 1996, pp 276–77.

147 Spaventa, 'Seeing the Wood Despite the Trees? On the Scope of Union Citizenship and its Constitutional Effects' (2008) 45 *CMLRev* 13, 44.

148 Ibid. See also Nic Shuibhne, 'Free Movement of Persons and the Wholly Internal Rule: Time to Move on?' (2002) 37 *CMLRev* 771, 748 who argued that 'the fundamental regulatory shift effected by citizenship strongly challenges the legitimacy of maintaining the wholly internal rule; in particular, it highlights both the deepening consequences of movement and the potentially inferior position of those who stay still'.

149 Tryfonidou, 'Reverse Discrimination in Purely Internal Situations: An Incongruity in a Citizens' Europe' (2008) 35 *LIEI* 67, 54–64; Tryfonidou, *Reverse Discrimination*, Kluwer Law International 2009, p 220.

150 Tryfonidou, 'Reverse Discrimination in Purely Internal Situations: An Incongruity in a Citizens' Europe' (2008) 35 *LIEI* 67, 45–47; Tryfonidou, *Reverse Discrimination*, Kluwer Law International 2009, p 166.

151 Tryfonidou, 'Reverse Discrimination in Purely Internal Situations: An Incongruity in a Citizens' Europe' (2008) 35 *LIEI* 67, 61.

discrimination traditionally fell outside the scope of application of the Union principle of non-discrimination.[152]

However, according to Tryfonidou, at present, the Union's 'all-important aim of ensuring that no discrimination arises as a result of the process of European integration' is incompatible with not prohibiting reverse discrimination at the Union level.[153] Specifically, the creation of Union citizenship and the broad interpretation of the Treaty provision on Union citizenship by the ECJ are, in her opinion, strong catalysts for the extension of the scope of application of human rights as general principles of Union law and, in particular, the Union principle of equality.[154] The fact that reverse discrimination is caused by Union law is, in her opinion, an additional reason to argue that the EU should provide a solution thereto.[155]

86. Tryfonidou argues that reverse discrimination ought to be considered to be a violation of the Union principle of equality. By applying this principle, the Court of Justice will be able to prevent the emergence of reverse discrimination – without inappropriately extending the scope of the internal market provisions as for instance in *Carpenter* and *Jia*.[156] Moreover, Tryfonidou argues that by ruling that the Union principle of equality is directly effective, the Court of Justice will be able to empower the national courts to do the same.[157]

87. Finally, another prominent defender of a wider interpretation of the scope of application of the Treaty provisions on Union citizenship and of Article 18 TFEU is AG Sharpston, in two well-known opinions in particular. First, in her opinion in the *Flemish Care Insurance* case, which will be extensively discussed in Part III,[158] Sharpston argued that the Treaty provisions on Union citizenship potentially challenges at least the sustainability, in its present form, of the purely internal situations doctrine.[159] The Advocate General considered that the group of persons concerned were not only Belgian citizens, but were also citizens of the Union.[160] Article 21 TFEU grants to Union citizens not only a right to move, but also a right to reside anywhere within the territory of the Union.[161]

---

152 Ibid 61–62.

153 Ibid 64.

154 Ibid 62–63; Tryfonidou, *Reverse Discrimination*, Kluwer Law International 2009, pp 166–71.

155 Tryfonidou, 'Reverse Discrimination in Purely Internal Situations: An Incongruity in a Citizens' Europe' (2008) 35 *LIEI* 67, 64.

156 Ibid.

157 Ibid. However, she does not explain further which role the direct effect exactly plays.

158 See below nn 689–91.

159 Opinion AG Sharpston 28 June 2007 in C-212/06, *Flemish Care Insurance*, paras 140 (and 121).

160 Ibid para 142, referring to Article 20 TFEU.

161 Ibid para 143.

AG Sharpston wondered whether Article 21 TFEU 'means "freedom to move and *then* reside" (i.e., freedom to reside derives from/flows from prior exercise of the freedom to move) or whether it means "freedom *both* to move *and* to reside" (so that it is possible to exercise the freedom to reside/go on residing without first exercising the freedom to move between Member States)'.[162]

88. Secondly, in the opinion on the *Ruiz Zambrano* case,[163] AG Sharpston inter alia examined whether Article 18 TFEU could be applied in order to correct situations of reverse discrimination in the context of Union citizenship.[164] She started by pointing out that the creation of Union citizenship entailed important consequences.[165] First, a free-standing right of free movement is conferred on non-economically active individuals.[166] Secondly, following the creation of Union citizenship, 'it became impossible to regard such individuals as mere economic factors of production. Citizens are ... individuals bound to a political community and protected by fundamental rights.'[167] Thirdly, the Advocate General pointed out that citizens are human beings and if their family members are not treated in the same way as Union citizens exercising their rights of free movement then, 'the concept of freedom of movement becomes devoid of any real meaning'.[168] Fourthly, the European Union engaged itself to protect the fundamental rights of citizens exercising their right to the freedom of movement.[169] Finally, she considered that the creation of Union citizenship entails the shared responsibility of the Member States and the EU in dealing with the issues resulting from the exercise of free movement by Union citizens.

89. Next, AG Sharpston criticised the case law of the ECJ which applies the internal market approach with respect to citizenship of the Union.[170] One result of this approach is 'the risk that "static" factors of production will be left in a worse position than their "mobile" counterparts, even though in all other respects their circumstances may be similar or identical. The outcome is reverse discrimination created by the interaction of EU law with national law – a

---

162 Ibid para 144.

163 See below nn 306–09.

164 This is the second proposal in her Opinion in C-34/09, *Ruiz Zambrano*. First, she addressed the question whether young children who possess the nationality of a Member State can invoke rights under Articles 20 and 21 TFEU as citizens of the Union when they have not (yet) moved from their Member State of nationality and whether their parents can obtain a derivative right of residence. Since this concerns the question of whether or not a sufficient link with EU law was present, it will be discussed extensively in Chapter 3. Finally, she enquired into the scope of application of fundamental rights under EU law.

165 Opinion AG Sharpston 30 September 2010 in C-34/09, *Ruiz Zambrano*, paras 125–30.

166 Ibid para 125, referring to ECJ case C-413/99 *Baumbast* 2002 [ECR] I-7091.

167 Opinion AG Sharpston 30 September 2010 in C-34/09, *Ruiz Zambrano*, para 127.

168 Ibid para 128.

169 Ibid para 129.

170 Ibid paras 130 ff.

discrimination that the Court has hitherto left each Member State to solve.'[171] On the basis of the cases *Carpenter*, *Zhu and Chen* and *Metock*, AG Sharpston has demonstrated that the 'traditional, hands-off approach is capable of generating results that are curiously random'.[172] This creates legal uncertainty in delicate areas of both national and Union law.[173]

90. Therefore, the Advocate General suggested that the ECJ should deal openly with the issue of reverse discrimination in cases involving Union citizenship.[174] She confined her proposal to these cases since 'it is in this area that the results of the present case-law are the most clearly damaging; and where a change is perhaps most called for'.[175] AG Sharpston invited the ECJ to interpret Article 18 TFEU as prohibiting reverse discrimination if three cumulative conditions are met.[176] First, the reverse discrimination at issue concerns a 'static' Union citizen whose situation is comparable to that of other Union citizens in the same Member State and who are able to assert rights under Article 21 TFEU.[177] Secondly, the reverse discrimination would entail a violation of a fundamental right, protected under EU law, if it would be considered a violation of a protected right by the Strasbourg court.[178] Thirdly, Article 18 TFEU would only be available where minimally the equivalent protection is not available under national law; hence, it would be a subsidiary remedy.[179] According to AG Sharpston, it is the task of the national court to apply these three criteria and 'to permit EU law to be invoked to prevent reverse discrimination only where those criteria were satisfied'.[180]

3. THE ECJ'S TRADITIONAL APPROACH TOWARDS REVERSE DISCRIMINATION REMAINS VALID

91. As emerges from the proposals discussed in the previous section, two types of objections have been articulated against the ECJ's traditional approach to reverse discrimination. First, it has been argued that it is contradictory to aim at the completion of an area without internal frontiers, while at the same time considering the crossing of national borders to be necessary in order to fall within the scope of Union law. Secondly, it has been argued that the purely internal situation rule is discordant with the status of Union citizenship; in particular, in combination with the Union principle of equality.

However, as will be explained in this section, these arguments are not sufficiently strong to challenge the ECJ's traditional approach on reverse

171 Ibid para 133.
172 Ibid para 135.
173 Ibid para 141.
174 Ibid paras 139 ff.
175 Ibid para 140.
176 Ibid paras 144 ff.
177 Ibid para 146.
178 Ibid para 147.
179 Ibid para 148.
180 Ibid para 149.

discrimination because of the legal and political justifications underlying this approach. Moreover, it is submitted that a general prohibition of reverse discrimination at the Union level is undesirable. Chapter 3 will discuss specific justifications for not considering Union citizenship as such to be a sufficient link with Union law.[181]

3.1. REVERSE DISCRIMINATION AS A SIDE EFFECT OF THE LIMITED SCOPE OF APPLICATION OF UNION LAW

92. The ECJ itself has put forward a two-fold justification for its purely internal situation rule and, correspondingly, to its approach to reverse discrimination in the *Morson and Jhanjan* case. In particular, it held that the purely internal situation rule 'accords with [the] purpose [of the Treaty provisions on non-discrimination on grounds of nationality and freedom of movement], which is to assist in the abolition of all obstacles to the establishment of a common market in which the nationals of the Member States may move freely within the territory of those states in order to pursue their economic activities'.[182] Moreover, the ECJ held that the purely internal situation rule follows from the wording of the Treaty provisions on non-discrimination on the grounds of nationality and freedom of movement.

93. The current Treaty provisions on non-discrimination and free movement explicitly limit their scope of application. Specifically Article 18 TFEU determines that '*within the scope of application of the Treaties*, and without prejudice to any special provisions contained therein, any discrimination on grounds of nationality shall be prohibited'.[183] Moreover, the Treaty provisions on the freedom of movement for goods,[184] for services,[185] for capital[186] and

181 Below nn 167–74.

182 ECJ case 35/82 and 36/82 *Morson and Jhanjan* [1982] ECR 3723, para 15.

183 Emphasis added.

184 Article 28(1) TFEU provides that 'The Union shall comprise a customs union which shall cover all trade in goods and which shall involve the prohibition *between Member States* of customs duties on imports and exports and of all charges having equivalent effect, and the adoption of a common customs tariff in their relations with third countries.' Emphasis added.

185 Article 56 TFEU provides that 'Within the framework of the provisions set out below, restrictions on freedom to provide services within the Union shall be prohibited *in respect of nationals of Member States who are established in a Member State other than that of the person for whom the services are intended.*' Emphasis added.

186 Article 63(1) TFEU provides that 'Within the framework of the provisions set out in this Chapter, all restrictions on the movement of capital *between Member States* and between Member States and third countries shall be prohibited.' Emphasis added.

for establishment[187] explicitly contain the idea that there has to be movement 'between Member States' or that 'another Member State' has to be involved. Only the Treaty provision on freedom of movement for workers does not explicitly mention the necessity of a cross-border element; instead, it merely provides that 'the freedom of movement for workers shall be secured within the Union'.[188] However, since the *Saunders* judgment, it is clear that the purely internal situation doctrine also applies to the freedom of movement for workers.[189]

94. It has been argued that the fundamental rationale underlying the ECJ's traditional case law on reverse discrimination lies in the vertical division of competences between the EU and the Member States, even though this has never been made explicit by the ECJ.[190] The limits of Union competences are governed by the principle of conferral. Article 5(2) TEU determines that the Union has the competences that are conferred upon it by the Member States in the Treaties in order to achieve the goals set out therein. Competences not conferred upon the Union in the Treaties remain with the Member States.[191] Additional references with respect to the Member States' competences have been included since the Lisbon Treaty, in particular in Article 4(1) of the Treaty on the European Union (TEU) and Article 51 EU Charter of Fundamental Rights. Accordingly, it has

---

187 Article 49 TFEU provides that 'Within the framework of the provisions set out below, restrictions on the freedom of establishment of nationals of a Member State *in the territory of another Member State* shall be prohibited.' Emphasis added.

188 Article 45(1) TFEU.

189 ECJ case 175/78 *Saunders* [1979] ECR I-1129.

190 See also CAMBIEN, 'Citizenship of the Union as a Cornerstone of European Integration', Dissertation, KU Leuven 2011, p 273; HANF, '"Reverse Discrimination" in EU Law: Constitutional Aberration, Constitutional Necessity, or Judicial Choice?' (2011) 18 *MJ* 29, 57; NIC SHUIBHNE, 'Free Movement of Persons and the Wholly Internal Rule: Time to Move on?' (2002) 37 *CMLRev* 771, 763–64; RITTER, 'Purely Internal Situations, Reverse Discrimination, Guimont, Dzodzi and Article 234' (2006) 31 *ELRev* 691–92; VAN ELSUWEGE, 'The Phenomenon of Reverse Discrimination: An Anomaly in the European Constitutional Order?' in ROSSI and CASOLARI (eds), *The EU After Lisbon, Amending or Coping with the Existing Treaties*, Springer 2014, p 164 and WIESBROCK, 'Disentangling the "Union Citizenship Puzzle"? The McCarthy Case' (2011) 36(6) *ELRev* 873. By contrast, Poiares Maduro argued that 'reverse discrimination should not be approached as a question of jurisdiction' (POIARES MADURO, 'The Scope of European Remedies: The Case of Purely Internal Situations and Reverse Discrimination' in KILPATRICK, NOVITZ and SKIDMORE (eds), *The Future of European Remedies*, Hart Publishing 2000, p 138).

191 Papadopoulou argued that the notion of purely internal situations has a double function. On the one hand, it delimits the right to freedom of movement from which economic operators benefit in the context of the internal market. On the other hand, the notion is an instrument to delimit the space in which the Member States can act freely without being submitted to control of compatibility with the Union law on freedom of movement. In particular, she argued that 'l'existence d'une situation purement interne, qui conduit à la non-application du droit communautaire de libre circulation, déclenche automatiquement l'application des règles du droit national en excluant le contrôle de leur compatibilité avec le droit communautaire' (PAPADOPOULOU, 'Situations purement internes et droit communautaire: un instrument jurisprudentiel à double fonction ou une arme à double tranchant?' (2002) *CDE* 95, 122).

been argued that reverse discrimination can be seen as a by-product of the division of competences between the EU and the Member States.[192]

95. However, the scope of application of the Treaties and the competences of the EU institutions are not identical issues.[193] Although these two issues are closely connected and partly overlap,[194] it is submitted that it is more precise to consider reverse discrimination as being a possible side effect of the limited scope of application of the Treaty provisions on free movement and citizenship. That is to say, a situation of reverse discrimination is a possible consequence of the fact that different legal spheres – EU law and the law of the individual Member States – are applicable to the same territory; in particular, where Union law grants a more favourable treatment to persons falling within its scope of application than national law does for nationals in a purely internal situation.[195] In other words, reverse discrimination can be seen as a disparity that has 'to be accepted in a system which recognises several levels of government unless

---

192 Ritter, 'Purely Internal Situations, Reverse Discrimination, Guimont, Dzodzi and Article 234' (2006) 31 *ELRev* 702 and Van Elsuwege, 'The Phenomenon of Reverse Discrimination: An Anomaly in the European Constitutional Order?' in Rossi and Casolari (eds), *The EU After Lisbon, Amending or Coping with the Existing Treaties*, Springer 2014, pp 163–64.

193 Dashwood, 'The Limits of European Community Powers' (1996) *ELRev* 113, 114 and Prechal, de Vries and van Eijken, 'The Principle of Attributed Powers and the Scope of EU Law' in Besselink, Pennings and Prechal (eds), *The Eclipse of the Legality Principle in the European Union*, Kluwer 2011, pp 213–47.

194 Prechal, de Vries and van Eijken, 'The Principle of Attributed Powers and the Scope of EU Law' in Besselink, Pennings and Prechal (eds), *The Eclipse of the Legality Principle in the European Union*, Kluwer 2011, p 215.

195 Cannizzaro has argued that 'reverse discrimination, … may well be considered as a consequence of the existence of overlapping spheres of competence in the same matter: of the existence of norms belonging to different legal systems, and having to conform to different objectives and values' (Cannizzaro, 'Producing "Reverse Discrimination" through the Exercise of EC Competences' (1997) 17 *YEL* 29, 29).

Bombois has pointed out that reverse discrimination has traditionally been presented as a confrontation between a situation falling within the scope of application of Union law and a situation that escapes. The author has argued that in reality reverse discrimination is rather about opposing a situation governed exclusively by Union law and a situation autonomously governed by a Member State. This definition leads to many more situations being captured by the concept of reverse discrimination.

Although his argumentation is conceptually solid, it is doubtful whether the situations he brings under the concept of reverse discrimination really add anything to this concept. For instance, Bombois's example about different rules for concession and public procurement touches upon the issue of defining the precise scope of application of regulation. While this is a situation of reverse discrimination for Bombois, this is, arguably, an illustration of the fact that law sometimes regulates domains or cases differently than domains or cases that are related and similar, but nevertheless subjected to other rules and conditions. (Bombois, 'La "discrimination à rebours" et son appréhension par la cour constitutionelle belge' in Cariat and Nowak (eds), *Le droit de l'Union européenne et le juge belge – Het recht van de Europese Unie en de Belgische rechter*, Bruylant 2015, pp 344–54.

no explicit political decision has been taken to eliminate that "inequality"'.[196] Hence, it is submitted that reverse discrimination has to be considered to be a possible side effect of the limited scope of application of Union law, based on the division of competences between the EU and the Member States as governed by the principle of the conferral of powers.

96. Moreover, the question as to whether or not to abandon the purely internal situation rule in order to prevent reverse discrimination at Union level should be considered in the light of the ECJ's case law on restrictions on free movement.[197] This case law has already resulted in an important encroachment upon the Member State's regulatory autonomy: not only in the prohibition of (in)directly discriminatory measures, but also in non-discriminatory restrictions on free movement that have been prohibited.[198] Extending the scope of the five fundamental freedoms to purely internal situations would be an unacceptable interference with the Member States' competences.[199] It would lead to a situation in which all national measures – not only those which constitute non-discriminatory restrictions on trade between the Member States – will be challengeable before the ECJ in the light of the narrow list of public order objectives in Articles 36, 45 and 52 TFEU.[200] In that case, European law would not only govern the access to the market and the trade between the Member States, but also 'the unhindered pursuit of commerce in individual Member States'.[201]

97. In sum, this leads to the conclusion that were the ECJ to change its position on reverse discrimination, by reversing the purely internal situations rule, this would contradict the vertical division of competences as they have been enshrined in the current Treaties, in particular in the principle of conferral and

---

196 Hanf, '"Reverse Discrimination" in EU Law: Constitutional Aberration, Constitutional Necessity, or Judicial Choice?' (2011) 18 *MJ* 29, 58.

197 Verbist, 'De invloed van het Unieburgerschap op zuiver interne situaties' [2011] *RW* 510, 526.

198 Barnard, *The Substantive Law of the EU: The Four Freedoms*, Oxford University Press 2013, p 20 and Dautricourt and Thomas, 'Reverse Discrimination and Free Movement of Persons Under Community Law: All for Ulysses, Nothing for Penelope?' (2009) 34 *ELRev* 454, 449. Regarding (in)directly discriminatory measures and non-discriminatory restrictions in the domain of freedom of movement for persons see Lenaerts and Van Nuffel, *European Union Law*, Sweet & Maxwell, 2011, pp 245–47.

199 Dautricourt and Thomas, 'Reverse Discrimination and Free Movement of Persons Under Community Law: All for Ulysses, Nothing for Penelope?' (2009) 34 *ELRev* 454, 499.

200 Ritter, 'Purely Internal Situations, Reverse Discrimination, Guimont, Dzodzi and Article 234' (2006) 31 *ELRev* 701–02.

201 See Opinion AG Tesauro 27 October 1993 in C-292/92, *Hünermund*, para 1: 1 'Is Article 30 of the Treaty a provision intended to liberalize intra-[Union] trade or is it intended more generally to encourage the unhindered pursuit of commerce in individual Member States?' AG Tesauro defended the first interpretation.

the wording of the Treaty provisions on the freedom of movement. Prohibiting reverse discrimination at the Union level is a far-reaching action that should not be taken by the Union Court. A general prohibition on reverse discrimination at the Union level would only be possible by changing primary law, namely, by a Treaty amendment of the Treaty provisions on freedom of movement and Article 18 TFEU. However, this seems to be not only politically unfeasible in the near future, but, as will be explained in the following subsection, is also arguably both unnecessary and undesirable.

3.2. A GENERAL PROHIBITION ON REVERSE DISCRIMINATION AT THE UNION LEVEL IS UNNECESSARY AND UNDESIRABLE

98. First, the supposition that a general prohibition on reverse discrimination at the Union level would lead to the better protection of Union citizens in all cases can be challenged.[202] In particular, after 70 years of European integration, one single Union market has not yet been completely realised; it is an ongoing process.[203] Instead, we have 28 internal or national markets and one twenty-ninth Union market for those who fall within the scope of Union law.[204] The more favourable conditions for those who fall within the scope of Union law often concern the imposition of fewer requirements in order to benefit from a certain right. However, the stricter conditions for purely internal situations may be seen not only as involving a less favourable treatment for purely internal situations, but also as a means by which to achieve higher standards of quality and protection.

99. Secondly, a general prohibition on reverse discrimination at the Union level would imply that policy decisions actually pass from the national level to the EU.[205] A political justification, in order not to prohibit reverse discrimination

---

202 See inter alia D'Oliveira, 'Is Reverse Discrimination Still Possible Under the Single European Act?' in *Forty Years On: The Evolution of Postwar Private International Law in Europe: Symposium in Celebration of the 40th Anniversary of the Centre of Foreign Law and Private International Law, University of Amsterdam, on 27 October 1989*, Kluwer 1990, p 86.

203 Barnard, *The Substantive Law of the EU: The Four Freedoms*, Oxford University Press 2013, p 12.

204 Ritter, 'Purely Internal Situations, Reverse Discrimination, Guimont, Dzodzi and Article 234' (2006) 31 *ELRev* 709, arguing that the Union market is 'less regulated'.

205 As Nic Shuibhne argued, no longer requiring a cross-border dimension 'would open up a whole swathe of Member State policies and practices to EU scrutiny following decades of express insistence that such issues were not amenable to such scrutiny at all. This would seem all the more curious given the express delimitation of EU and Member State competences recently effected by the Lisbon Treaty' (Nic Shuibhne, 'The Resilience of Market Citizenship' (2010) 47 *CMLRev* 1597, 1615).

at Union level, is a so-called 'virtual representation'.[206] What is meant by that is that since migrants have no access to the political processes of the host Member State generally, Union law protects them by prohibiting discrimination on the grounds of nationality.[207] By contrast, a Member State's own nationals can participate in the national political process and strive to get the rules changed.[208] However, it should be noted that entrusting reverse discrimination to the national political processes also involves risks, such as an 'under-representation of minority interests'.[209] In this respect, the national judicial authorities may play an important role in counteracting this risk.

100. Moreover, national institutions seem better suited to assessing situations of reverse discrimination than EU institutions,[210] given that they are familiar with the national rules, principles and interests which are at stake. It has been argued that the ECJ judges are not in the best position to assess situations of reverse discrimination.[211] This argument can be supported by the fact that the ECJ judges are experts in Union law and that they cannot be experts in the diverse legislative provisions of 28 Member States; instead, they largely depend on the information provided by the national referring court. On the other hand, in some cases, ECJ judges might be in a more adequate position to solve national problems because they are unbiased by a Member State's constitutional structure and the related sensitivities and, therefore, are able to maintain a certain distance. Of course, currently, in cases of internal disagreement on constitutional issues with an EU aspect, the national judicial body is able to refer a question for preliminary ruling to the Court of Justice.[212]

---

206 Barnard, *The Substantive Law of the EU: The Four Freedoms*, Oxford University Press 2013, p 236.

207 Ibid. 208 Ibid.

209 Poiares Maduro, 'The Scope of European Remedies: The Case of Purely Internal Situations and Reverse Discrimination' in Kilpatrick, Novitz and Skidmore (eds), *The Future of European Remedies*, Hart Publishing 2000, p 137.

210 Hanf, '"Reverse Discrimination" in EU Law: Constitutional Aberration, Constitutional Necessity, or Judicial Choice?' (2011) 18 *MJ* 29, 57; Poiares Maduro, 'The Scope of European Remedies: The Case of Purely Internal Situations and Reverse Discrimination' in Kilpatrick, Novitz and Skidmore (eds), *The Future of European Remedies*, Hart Publishing 2000, p 137 and Ritter, 'Purely Internal Situations, Reverse Discrimination, Guimont, Dzodzi and Article 234' (2006) 31 *ELRev* 702.

211 Ritter, 'Purely Internal Situations, Reverse Discrimination, Guimont, Dzodzi and Article 234' (2006) 31 *ELRev* 702: 'The Court of Justice will become the ultimate arbiter of policy choices across the EU. Policy decisions will move away from national authorities and elected parliaments to a "government of the judges"', and 710. Ritter pointed out that past case law demonstrates that the ECJ has no problem in overriding a Member State's policy choices (referring to the following cases: ECJ case C-189/95 *Franzén* [1997] ECR I-5909; ECJ case C-442/02 *Caixa Bank* [2004] ECR 15; ECJ case C-17/00 *De Coster* [2001] ECR I-9445).

212 Cloots, 'Germs of Pluralist Judicial Adjudication: Advocaten Voor de Wereld and Other References from the Belgian Constitutional Court' (2010) 47 *CMLRev* 645, 655, regarding inter alia the *Flemish Care Insurance* case.

101. Finally, it should be emphasised that, at present, remedies for reverse discrimination are available at both the Union and national levels. Correcting reverse discrimination at the Union level is possible by way of the maximum harmonisation of legislation in a specific area.[213] That is to say, in the case of exhaustive harmonisation, the Member States have to treat both cross-border situations and purely internal situations alike; specifically, as they are described in the Union measure.[214] Since no room is left for Member State action, no situation of reverse discrimination can arise.[215] For instance, further harmonisation of national immigration law, on the basis of Article 79 TFEU, could remedy reverse discrimination in the area of family reunification.[216]

102. Concerning possible remedies to reverse discrimination at national level, it should be recalled that reverse discrimination often occurs because Union law obliges Member States to treat nationals from other Member States in a manner other than that provided to their own nationals.[217] As Ritter has argued, 'if the Member States then realise that their restrictive national policies result in reverse discrimination, it must be up to them to decide whether reverse discrimination is a price worth paying or not'.[218] In other words, the individual Member States have to decide, on the basis of their own national values and policies, whether or not they align the national rules applicable to internal situations to the Union rules applicable to cross-border situations.[219] However, this position does not imply that all situations of reverse discrimination should be considered to be acceptable. In this regard, it should be emphasised that the individual Member States are bound to protect the fundamental rights of their own nationals in a purely internal situation. In particular, national authorities are bound by the rules and principles that are protected in their national Constitution. Moreover, the ECHR also provides a 'safety-net' to all Member States.[220] In sum, using

---

213 See also the above discussed Opinion AG Mischo in 80 and 159/85, *Edah* [1986] ECR 3375 and ECJ case 98/86 *Mathot* [1987] ECR 809, paras 9–11. Moreover, see above nn 109–18.

214 Barnard, *The Substantive Law of the EU: The Four Freedoms*, Oxford University Press 2013, pp 658–61.

215 Tryfonidou, *Reverse Discrimination*, Kluwer Law International 2009, p 36.

216 Below n 396.

217 Poiares Maduro, 'The Scope of European Remedies: The Case of Purely Internal Situations and Reverse Discrimination' in Kilpatrick, Novitz and Skidmore (eds), *The Future of European Remedies*, Hart Publishing 2000, p 127.

218 Ritter, 'Purely Internal Situations, Reverse Discrimination, Guimont, Dzodzi and Article 234' (2006) 31 *ELRev* 702.

219 See also Hanf, '"Reverse Discrimination" in EU Law: Constitutional Aberration, Constitutional Necessity, or Judicial Choice?' (2011) 18 *MJ* 29, 57 and Verbist, 'De invloed van het Unieburgerschap op zuiver interne situaties' [2011] *RW* 510, 527.

220 Hanf, '"Reverse Discrimination" in EU Law: Constitutional Aberration, Constitutional Necessity, or Judicial Choice?' (2011) 18 *MJ* 29, 58.

Hanf's words, it can be concluded that 'not all problems and inequalities arising in Europe necessarily relate to Union law and need to be resolved by the ECJ'.[221]

3.3. INTERPRETATION OF THE PURELY INTERNAL SITUATION RULE

103. Finally, it should be pointed out that although the arguments underlying the proposals discussed above to alter the ECJ's approach to reverse discrimination are unconvincing at the level of the principled hands-off approach towards reverse discrimination, they do seem to play a significant role at another level. That is to say, it appears that the concepts of the European Union as an area without internal frontiers and that of Union citizenship have had an impact on the interpretation of the purely internal situation rule. This touches upon the problematic issue of the precise dividing line between the scope of Union law and that of national law. This will be examined in some detail in Chapter 3.

---

221 Ibid. In the same vein, it is argued below nn 206–19 that the ECJ should adopt a more narrow interpretation of restrictions to free movement.

CHAPTER 3

APPLICABILITY AND INTERPRETATION OF THE PURELY INTERNAL SITUATION DOCTRINE

104. In Chapter 2, it was argued that the Court's principled position on reverse discrimination should be approved of on the basis of the current Treaties. Accordingly, situations that do not have a sufficient connection with Union law fall outside of the scope of application of Union law and within the scope of application of national law. However, the sore spot of this case law is the question of what precisely constitutes a situation that falls under Union law. Or, putting it another way, what exactly are purely internal situations? As Van Elsuwege and Kochenov have formulated it: 'the potential for reverse discrimination entirely depends on the dividing line between the scope of EU law and national law. This line is virtually never straightforward'.[222] This is exactly what will be discussed in this chapter; the recent evolutions in the ECJ's interpretation of the purely internal situation doctrine in particular will be examined. The ECJ seems to be increasingly willing to accept that a given issue has a sufficient link with Union law in order to apply the Treaty provisions on free movement and citizenship. The concept of Union citizenship particularly seems to play an important role in this evolution.

105. The major flaw of the Court of Justice's case law, concerning the interpretation of the purely internal situation doctrine is the unpredictability of whether or not a situation will fall within the scope of application of Union law. Accordingly, several Advocates General as well as legal scholars have developed proposals for the ECJ to either widen or to constrain the scope of application of the Union provisions on free movement and citizenship. The common point of departure for these diverse proposals is that the ECJ's case law on purely internal situations should be based upon clear and straightforward guidelines.

---

222 Van Elsuwege and Kochenov, 'On the Limits of Judicial Intervention: EU Citizenship and Family Reunification Rights' (2011) 13 *EJML* 433, 444.

1. APPLICABILITY OF THE PURELY INTERNAL SITUATION DOCTRINE

1.1. THE PURELY INTERNAL SITUATION DOCTRINE IS APPLICABLE TO TREATY PROVISIONS ON FREE MOVEMENT AND CITIZENSHIP

106. We have already been introduced to the ECJ's purely internal situation doctrine in Chapter 2, in which it was noted that the ECJ defined the notion of purely internal situations for the first time in the *Saunders* case.[223] In particular, the ECJ described purely internal situations as being 'situations which are wholly internal to a Member State, in other words, where there is no factor connecting them to any of the situations envisaged by [Union] law'.[224] The present formulation of the ECJ's settled case law goes as follows: 'situations which have no factor linking them with any of the situations governed by European Union law and which are confined in all relevant respects within a single Member State'.[225]

107. The ECJ applies its purely internal situation doctrine to the Treaty provisions governing the free movement of goods,[226] workers,[227] establishment,[228] services[229] and capital[230] as well as to the Treaty provisions governing Union citizenship.[231] Moreover, it should be noted that this doctrine not only applies to Treaty provisions, but also to 'the measures adopted to implement them'.[232]

1.2. REFINEMENTS OF, AND EXCEPTIONS TO, THE PURELY INTERNAL SITUATION DOCTRINE

108. The following section discusses three components of the ECJ's case law which refine and which comprise – directly and indirectly – exceptions to the

223 Above nn 52–54.
224 ECJ case 175/78 *Saunders* [1979] ECR I-1129, para 11.
225 See inter alia ECJ case C-434/09 *McCarthy* [ECR] I-3375, para 45 and ECJ case C-256/11 *Dereci* [2011] ECR I-11315, para 60.
226 See inter alia ECJ case 98/86 *Mathot* [1987] ECR 809, para 9.
227 See inter alia ECJ case 35–36/82 *Morson and Jhanjan* [1982] ECR 3723, para 16.
228 See inter alia ECJ joined cases C-54/88, C-91/88 and C-14/89 *Nino* [1990] ECR I-3537, para 11.
229 See inter alia ECJ case 52/79 *Debauve* [1980] ECR 833, para 9.
230 See inter alia ECJ case C-513/03 *van Hilten-van der Heijden* [2006] ECR I-1957, para 42 and ECJ case C-256/06 *Jäger* [2008] ECR I-123, para 25.
231 See inter alia ECJ joined cases C-64/96 and C-65/96 *Uecker and Jacquet* [1997] ECR I-3171, para 23.
232 See inter alia ECJ case 20/87 *Gauchard* [1987] ECR 4879, para 13; ECJ case C-18/95 *Terhoeve* [1999] ECR I-345, para 26; ECJ case C-434/09 *McCarthy* [ECR] I-3375, para 45 and ECJ case C-256/11 *Dereci* [2011] ECR I-11315, para 60.

Court's settled case law on purely internal situations. First, the ECJ's position will be examined, which is that the purely internal situation rule does not apply if national laws in the domain concerned are harmonised. Secondly, the ECJ's case law on internal tariff barriers will be examined, for which the purely internal situation rule also does not apply. Thirdly, the section will analyse the ECJ's *Dzodzi* line of cases, in which the ECJ responds to a question referred for a preliminary ruling in which the main proceedings concern a purely internal situation.

1.2.1. Harmonisation of National Laws: No Need for the Purely Internal Situation Doctrine

1.2.1.1. No Application of the Purely Internal Situation Doctrine in the Case of Harmonisation of National Laws

109. Although the ECJ firmly upholds the principle that reverse discrimination is not prohibited by Union law, parties continue to question situations of reverse discrimination before the ECJ. This allows the ECJ to refine its position, not its principled position on reverse discrimination as such, but rather the scope of its purely internal situation doctrine. In this context, the Court of Justice has made clear that the purely internal situation doctrine is not applicable to a sector in which the harmonisation of national laws has taken place.

110. This occurred in 1986, for instance, in the *Driancourt v Cognet* case, which concerned the French legislation regarding the fixed price for books.[233] In particular, it was provided that the price is fixed by the publisher for the books which remained in France in the course of being marketed, while the price of books published and printed in France may be freely determined where the books have crossed a border within the Union in the course of being marketed.[234] The question arose as to whether this double system of prices in book trade was prohibited by the Union principle of equal treatment and non-discrimination.

The ECJ ruled that the general principle of non-discrimination does not apply to treatment which works to the detriment of national products, as compared with imported products, 'and which is put into effect by a Member State in a sector which is not subject to [Union] rules in relation to which there has been no harmonisation of national laws'.[235] Accordingly, the Court concluded that neither Article 18 TFEU nor any other provision or principle of the Treaties applies to a difference in treatment which is detrimental to a Member State's own nationals or own products in a purely internal situation.[236]

233 ECJ case 355/85 *Driancourt v Cognet* [1986] ECR 3231.

234 Ibid.

235 Ibid, para 11.

236 Ibid, para 12.

111. At present, this is settled case law. A more recent confirmation can be found in the *Mosconi* order, for instance, which concerned the Italian legislation on classified heritage buildings.[237] In particular, works undertaken on classified heritage buildings were reserved to architects only. That is to say, civil engineers who had qualifications that they received in Italy were excluded. By contrast, people who held a civil engineering qualification which was obtained in another Member State did have access to works on classified heritage buildings on the basis of Directive 85/384.[238]

112. Mr Mosconi claimed that the Italian legislation was incompatible with both Council Directive 85/384/EEC on the mutual recognition of diplomas, certificates and other evidence of formal qualifications in architecture[239] and the Union principle of equal treatment. The Court of Justice emphasised that Directive 85/384 merely aims to guarantee the recognition of those diplomas by other Member States and does not intend to harmonise the access that those diplomas give to the activities involved with architecture within the Member State concerned.[240] Next, the Court considered that the consequence of the Court's case law in the case of a purely internal situation, which was the case in the main proceedings, is that the principle of equality enshrined in Union law cannot be invoked.[241] In this situation, it is up to the national judge to assess whether a discrimination prohibited by national law exists and, where appropriate, to determine how this should be eliminated.[242] Therefore, regarding a purely internal situation of one Member State, neither Directive 85/384, nor the principle of equality precludes a national legislation which recognises, in principle, the equivalence of the qualifications in architecture and civil engineering, but reserves to architects alone the works undertaken on classified heritage buildings.[243]

113. On the other hand, the Court of Justice has confirmed its position *a contrario*, in the *Mathot* judgment of 1987 for instance.[244] The case concerned Belgian legislation on the labelling of butter. The ECJ pointed out that national laws concerning the labelling of butter have been harmonised by Council

---

237 ECJ order in case C-3/02 *Mosconi*, OJ C 118, 30 April 2004, 25–26. See inter alia also Joined cases C-29–35/94 *Aubertin e.a.* [1995] ECR I-301, in particular paras 9–13.

238 Similar legislation exists in France and will be discussed, from the perspective of France, in Part II.

239 Council Directive 85/384/EEC of 10 June 1985 on the mutual recognition of diplomas, certificates and other evidence of formal qualifications in architecture, including measures to facilitate the effective exercise of the right of establishment and freedom to provide services.

240 ECJ order in case C-3/02 *Mosconi*, para 47.

241 Ibid para 53.

242 Ibid.

243 Ibid para 54.

244 ECJ case 98/86 *Mathot* [1987] ECR 809.

Directive 79/112[245] which created obligations without allowing distinctions on the basis of the food's origins.[246] The Court considered that 'national rules which impose those obligations only on domestic products to the exclusion of products imported from other Member States therefore discriminate against certain traders contrary to [Union] law by virtue of the fact that the requirements of the directive are not yet applied to imported products'.[247] The Court of Justice ruled that 'it is for the Commission to ensure that the national authorities put an end to that situation by extending the scope of the national rules to all the products covered by the Directive'.[248]

Hence, a situation of reverse discrimination was present, given that only national traders in a purely Belgian situation were subjected to these obligations. However, since the legislative provisions in this area were harmonised by Council Directive 79/112, Belgium should end the situation of reverse discrimination in order to comply with the obligations arising from Union law.

114. In sum, the Court of Justice only applies its purely internal situation rule if the legislative provisions in this area have not been harmonised. By contrast, if the provisions at issue have been harmonised, the individual Member States have to treat nationals in purely internal situations equally to Union citizens falling within the scope of Union law. However, it should be emphasised that in the cases discussed above the ECJ did not specify which type of harmonisation was concerned. Since this is necessary in order to interpret this case law well, we will now discuss the two main forms of harmonisation found in EU law: maximum harmonisation and minimum harmonisation.

1.2.1.2. Not All Forms of Harmonisation Exclude Application of the Purely Internal Situation Doctrine: Minimum Harmonisation with a Market Access Clause

115. In the case of maximum harmonisation, national rules are replaced by a single European standard.[249] The Member States no longer have any room for independent action, or in other words 'their action is pre-empted'.[250] Since the

245 Council Directive 79/112 of 18 December 1978 on the approximation of the laws of the Member States relating to the labelling, presentation and advertising of foodstuffs for sale to the ultimate consumer.

246 ECJ case 98/86 *Mathot* [1987] ECR 809, para 11.

247 Ibid.

248 Ibid.

249 Barnard, *The Substantive Law of the EU: The Four Freedoms*, Oxford University Press 2013, pp 658–66 and Woods and Watson, *Steiner and Woods EU Law*, 12th ed, Oxford University Press 2014, pp 344–48. See inter alia ECJ case C-150/88 *Provide* [1989] ECR I-3891 and ECJ case 60/86 *Dim-dip lighting* [1988] ECR I-3921.

250 Barnard, *The Substantive Law of the EU: The Four Freedoms*, Oxford University Press 2013, p 658.

Member States must guarantee that their national legal system 'provides exactly what is required' by the harmonising Union measure,[251] it is not possible for situations of reverse discrimination to arise. Accordingly, there is no need to apply the purely internal situation doctrine to an area in which a maximum harmonisation measure has already been adopted.

116. In the case of minimum harmonisation, Union legislation sets minimum requirements and the Member States are allowed to impose stricter requirements.[252] However, minimum harmonisation measures do not always have the same structure. Some minimum harmonisation directives allow Member States to impose stricter requirements on both domestic and imported products. For instance, laws protecting consumers may apply both to the companies established in the Member State imposing stricter requirements and to companies established in another Member State, but that trade in the first Member State.[253]

However, the minimum harmonisation directive may also include a market access clause, particularly in the area of goods.[254] This means that the Member States must provide goods that comply with the minimum standard provided at Union law and are lawfully produced in their Member State of origin access to its market.[255] If a Member State imposes stricter requirements than the Union measure, they only apply to purely internal situations. Accordingly, reverse discrimination may arise. As the Court of Justice has made clear in *Gallaher*, the resulting reverse discrimination is not prohibited by Union law.[256]

117. The *Gallaher* case concerned the implementation by the UK of Directive 89/622.[257] The directive on the labelling of tobacco products provides that certain indications and warnings must appear on cigarette packets and which must cover at least 4 per cent of the surfaces on which they are printed. The British rules implementing this directive provide that these warnings must cover at least 6 per cent of the corresponding surface. However, in order to comply

---

251 Woods and Watson, *Steiner and Woods EU Law*, 12th ed, Oxford University Press 2014, p 344.

252 Barnard, *The Substantive Law of the EU: The Four Freedoms*, Oxford University Press 2013, pp 662–66; Lenaerts and Van Nuffel, *European Union Law*, Sweet & Maxwell 2011, p 296 and Woods and Watson, *Steiner and Woods EU Law*, 12th ed, Oxford University Press 2014, pp 348–51.

253 Barnard, *The Substantive Law of the EU: The Four Freedoms*, Oxford University Press 2013, p 663.

254 Ibid and Tryfonidou, *Reverse Discrimination*, Kluwer Law International 2009, pp 35–37.

255 Woods and Watson, *Steiner and Woods EU Law*, 12th ed, Oxford University Press 2014, p 349 and Tryfonidou, *Reverse Discrimination*, Kluwer Law International 2009, p 35.

256 ECJ case C-11/92 *Gallaher* [1993] ECR I-3545.

257 Now Directive 2001/37.

with the market access clause in that directive,[258] the British rules provided that imported cigarettes from another Member State were to be regarded as complying with the UK regulations if the packets carried a warning in English which complied with the rules of the Member State of origin, covering at least 4 per cent of the surface as imposed by the directive.

Tobacco companies challenged this situation of reverse discrimination and inequality in conditions of competition in the light of Articles 3(3) and 4(4) of Directive 89/662. However, the Court of Justice did not agree with them and held that 'those consequences are attributable to the degree of harmonisation sought by the provisions in question, which lay down minimum requirements'.[259] In other words, the UK was free to demand higher standards, but only with respect to cigarettes produced in the UK.[260]

118. In sum, if the Court of Justice rules that the purely internal situation doctrine is not applicable to a sector in which there has already been a harmonisation of national laws; it should be interpreted as concerning cases of maximum harmonisation and cases of minimum harmonisation without a market access clause. By contrast, if minimum harmonisation with a market clause is at stake, then the purely internal situation doctrine applies and reverse discrimination may arise.

1.2.2. *Internal Tariff Barriers: An Exception to the Purely Internal Situation Rule*

1.2.2.1. An Overview of the ECJ's Case Law on Internal Tariff Barriers

119. It is settled case law of the Court of Justice that a charge proportional to the customs values of goods, levied by a Member State on goods imported from or exported to another Member State by reason of their entry into or their leaving from a region within the first Member State, constitutes a charge which has an effect equivalent to a customs duty on imports and exports. In particular, the Court has emphasised that this conclusion is not altered by the fact that the charge is also levied on goods entering or leaving that region from

---

258 Article 8 Directive 89/622: '(1) Member States may not, for reasons of labelling, prohibit or restrict the sale of products which comply with this Directive. (2) The provisions of this Directive do not affect the right of the Member States to lay down, in compliance with the Treaty, requirements concerning the import, sale and consumption of tobacco products which they deem necessary in order to protect public health, provided such requirements do not imply any changes to labelling as laid down in this Directive.'

259 ECJ case C-11/92 *Gallaher* [1993] ECR I-3545, para 22.

260 The Court of Justice takes the same position as regards exports, see for instance, ECJ case C-1/96 *CWF* [1998] ECR I-1251.

another part of the same Member State.[261] In other words, 'if [a tax] is collected on the occasion of the crossing of a frontier, even an internal frontier, [it] is capable of constituting a charge having equivalent effect to a customs duty. In those circumstances, it makes absolutely no difference whether the tax affects only intra-[Union] trade or internal trade as well'.[262] Or, more briefly, the *Legros*, *Lancry*, *Simitzi* and *Carbonati Apuani* judgments 'have extended the prohibition on tariff barriers to a similar prohibition on regional borders inside a Member State'.[263]

120. Very interesting in this regard is the ECJ's reasoning behind the extension of the prohibition on tariff barriers to purely internal situations. This section goes on to consider the underpinnings of the ECJ's case law, which are of both a practical and a conceptual nature.

121. In its *Lancry* judgment, a case concerning dock dues imposed in the French overseas departments, the ECJ put forward the practical reason behind its case law. In this respect, the ECJ emphasised that the charges at issue were imposed on all goods alike.[264] Therefore, it would be practically impossible 'to distinguish between products of domestic origin and products originating in other Member States'.[265] The Court considered that establishing, in every case, whether or not a particular product originated in another Member State would lead to administrative procedures and further delays which would in themselves constitute obstacles to the free movement of goods.[266]

122. In its *Carbonati Apuani* judgment, the ECJ pinned down its case law in a more conceptual way. The ECJ had to answer the question as to whether or not the Italian legislation establishing a marble tax, levied solely in one municipality of the Member State and imposed upon one class of goods, specifically marble excavated in that municipality's territory, when those goods are transported out of that municipality, constitutes a charge having equivalent effect to a customs duty.

123. First, the Court recalled that the prohibition on customs duties and charges having equivalent effect was justified by the fact that any pecuniary

---

[261] ECJ case C-163/90 *Legros* [1992] ECR I-4625, paras 17–18; ECJ joined cases C-363/93 and C-407/93 to C-411/93 *Lancry* [1994] ECR I-3957, para 32; ECJ joined cases C-485/93 and C-486/93 *Simitzi* [1995] ECR I-2655, paras 20–22 and ECJ case C-72/03 *Carbonati Apuani* [2004] ECR I-8027, para 35.

[262] Opinion AG Poiares Maduro 6 May 2004 in C-72/03, *Carbonati Apuani*, para 3.

[263] Opinion AG Sharpston 28 June 2007 in C-212/06, *Flemish Care Insurance*, para 122.

[264] ECJ joined cases C-363/93 and C-407/93 to C-411/93 *Lancry* [1994] ECR I-3957, para 31.

[265] Ibid. [266] Ibid.

charges imposed upon goods, because they cross a frontier, constituted an obstacle to free movement.[267] The Court then held that 'the very principle of a customs union, as provided for by article [28 TFEU], requires the free movement of goods to be ensured within the union generally, not in trade between Member States alone, but more broadly throughout the territory of the customs union'.[268] The Court specified that the fact that Articles 28 and 30 TFEU only expressly refer to trade between Member States can be explained by the fact that the framers of the Treaty took it for granted that no charges with the features of a customs duty existed within the Member States.[269]

More broadly, the Court went on to consider that Article 26(2) TFEU 'defines the internal market as "an area without internal frontiers in which the free movement of goods, persons, services and capital is ensured", without drawing any distinction between inter-State frontiers and frontiers within a State'.[270] The Court concluded that the reading together of Articles 26 and 28 TFEU implied that the absence of charges between or within a Member State was essential to the realisation of a customs union in which the free movement of goods is ensured.[271]

124. Moreover, the Court of Justice extended its case law in the *Jersey Produce* judgment to non-tariff obstacles to trade in goods.[272] This case concerned the Jersey Potato Export Marketing Scheme Act that established mandatory contributions for the exporting of potatoes from Jersey to the UK.[273] The contested rules provided that the amount of the mandatory contributions may be fixed either with reference to the quantities of potatoes or by reference to the areas used by that party for potato production. By contrast, the rules at issue did not govern the production intended for the consumption on the Jersey market nor the export to other Member States. The rules were questioned in the light of Articles 28, 30 and 35 TFEU.

125. The Court of Justice first examined the situation in the light of Articles 28 and 30 TFEU. In this regard, the states of Jersey argued that since the contested rules governed only the export of potatoes from Jersey to the UK for consumption in that Member State, then only internal trade within the UK was concerned. Therefore, they argued, Articles 28 and 30 TFEU were not applicable.[274]

267 ECJ case C-72/03 *Carbonati Apuani* [2004] ECR I-8027, para 22.
268 Ibid.
269 Ibid.
270 Ibid para 23.
271 Ibid para 24.
272 ECJ case C-293/02 *Jersey Produce* [2005] ECR I-9543.
273 Jersey is the largest island in the archipelago of the Channel Islands. The Channel Islands and the UK must be treated as one Member State (see ECJ case C-293/02 *Jersey Produce* [2005] ECR I-9543, para 54).
274 Ibid para 61.

However, the ECJ referred in this respect to its *Lancry* and *Simitzi* judgments. In those cases it held that a charge proportional to the customs values of goods, levied by reason of their entry into or their leaving a region within a Member State, constituted a charge having an effect equivalent to a customs duty on imports and exports, not only insofar as it was levied on goods entering/leaving that region from other Member States, but also insofar as it is levied on goods entering/leaving that region from another part of that same State.[275]

The Court of Justice first considered that a contribution which is calculated by reference to the quantities of potatoes produced by the party concerned and exported from Jersey to the UK constituted a charge levied on goods exported from one region to another in the same Member State.[276] Next, the Court emphasised that although the contested rules only referred to potatoes from Jersey that are exported to the UK, it was possible that these potatoes were being re-exported to other Member States.[277] Therefore, the ECJ concluded that a contribution calculated by reference to the quantities of potatoes produced and exported to the UK was contrary to Articles 28 and 30 TFEU.[278]

126. Next, the Court of Justice examined the contested rules in the light of Article 35 TFEU, which determines that 'quantitative restrictions on exports, and all measures having equivalent effect, shall be prohibited between Member States'. Regarding the contributions calculated by reference to the areas used for the cultivation of potatoes, the ECJ considered again that although the wording of the contested rules only mentioned potatoes exported to the UK, it was conceivable that those potatoes were being re-exported to other Member States.[279] Accordingly, the ECJ ruled that a contribution such as that at issue in the main proceedings which is calculated by reference to the areas used for the cultivation of potatoes was contrary to Article 35 TFEU.[280] Hence, in the *Jersey Produce* judgment, the Court went further than in the *Lancry*, *Simitzi* and *Carbonati Apuani* cases since it transposed this case law to non-tariff obstacles to trade in goods.[281]

127. Divergent views on this line of cases have been expressed. Both positions will be discussed in the following subsection.

1.2.2.2. Divergent Opinions on the ECJ's Cases on Internal Tariff Barriers

i. Criticisms

128. In his Opinion in *Lancry*, AG Tesauro acknowledged that a paradox exists in 'a single market in which barriers to trade between Portugal and Denmark are

[275] Ibid paras 62–63.
[276] Ibid para 65.
[277] Ibid.
[278] Ibid para 67.
[279] Ibid paras 79–81.
[280] Ibid para 84.
[281] Opinion AG Léger 3 May 2005 in ibid para 142.

prohibited, whilst barriers to trade between Naples and Capri are immaterial'.[282] However, according to the Advocate General, 'neither the Treaty, nor the Court in its decisions can, or could, find a way out of such paradox'.[283] AG Tesauro pointed out that the Treaty provisions on the customs union intended to eliminate obstacles to trade between Member States and not within a Member State.[284]

Ruling differently would call into question the settled case law on wholly internal situations.[285] In particular, AG Tesauro emphasised that it would not only do so regarding the customs union and the free movement of goods, but also regarding the free movement of services and persons.[286] Therefore, the Advocate General did not suggest this alternative to the Court, but instead referred to the *Steen* judgment in which the Court held that the national judge can always assess in the light of its own national law whether the treatment of purely internal situations is discriminatory and whether or not it should be corrected.[287]

129. However, as has been examined in the previous subsection, the Court of Justice did not follow AG Tesauro in that respect. In turn, AG Poiares Maduro challenged the *Legros*, *Lancry* and *Simitzi* judgments in his Opinion in the *Carbonati Apuani* case. Poiares Maduro pointed out the main disadvantages of that case law.[288]

130. First, AG Poiares Maduro held that the foundations of that line of case law are fragile, since Articles 28 and 30 TFEU only refer to the remaining tariff barriers to trade between Member States, not between parts of the territory of a single Member State.[289] He went on to consider that the founding States did not intend to deprive Member States of their competences to govern situations which relate to their territory exclusively.[290]

131. Secondly, AG Poiares Maduro argued that the case law on charges having equivalent effect is inconsistent with the settled case law of the Court according to which the rules on the freedom of movement are not applicable to purely internal situations.[291] The Advocate General reflected that the case law in relation to charges having equivalent effect could have been extended to all matters connected to the provisions on freedom of movement. However, he observed that this is not the route the Court has chosen to take.[292]

---

282 Opinion AG Tesauro 28 June 1994 in C-363/93 and C-407/93 to C-411/93, *Lancry*, para 28.
283 Ibid.
284 Ibid.
285 Ibid.
286 Ibid.
287 Ibid.
288 Opinion AG Poiares Maduro 6 May 2004 in C-72/03, *Carbonati Apuani*, paras 44 ff.
289 Ibid para 45.
290 Ibid para 46.
291 Ibid paras 4 and 47–48.
292 Ibid para 47.

AG Poiares Maduro considered that, at present, 'a seemingly unjustifiable contradiction' exists between the line chosen by the Court in the field of charges having equivalent effect and the line generally taken by the Court in other fields.[293] Although the ECJ has recently been increasingly generous in recognising a sufficient link with Union law, it never called into question the inapplicability of Union law to purely internal situations.[294] According to AG Poiares Maduro, the fact that the Court does not want to start from this principle shows its consciousness of the risk of arbitrarily extending the scope of Union law.[295]

132. As set out above, the Court of Justice did not follow AG Poiares Maduro in the *Apuani Carbonati* case. Subsequently, the Court's case law in the field of charges having equivalent effect was once more questioned, particularly by AG Léger in his Opinion in the *Jersey Produce* case. In that case, AG Léger finds it hard to agree with the interpretation that 'the very principle of a customs union, as provided for in Article [28 TFEU], requires the free movement of goods generally to be ensured not only in trade between States but also, more widely, throughout the territory of the customs union'.[296] Being of the same mind as AG Poiares Maduro, AG Léger argued that the only interpretation which is consistent with the wording of Articles 28 and 30 TFEU and the intentions of the drafters of the Treaty is that the customs union only governs inter-State custom activities.[297]

133. Moreover, according to AG Léger, the additional underpinning in the *Carbonati Apuani* judgment regarding Article 26(2) TFEU cannot compensate for the fragile reasoning followed by the Court in the wake of its *Lancry* judgment regarding the customs union's requirements.[298] The Advocate General emphasised, in this respect, that Article 26(2) TFEU expressly refers to the Treaty provisions in order not to extend the scope of the Treaty rules on the freedom of movement.[299] That is to say, the internal market is defined as 'an area without internal frontiers in which the free movement of goods, persons, services and capital is ensured *in accordance with the provisions of this Treaty*'.[300] Accordingly, AG Léger considered that 'the expression "area without internal frontiers" in Article [26(2) TFEU] means nothing more than an area within which obstacles to trade, between Member States, are prohibited'.[301] Therefore, the Advocate General argued against the transposition of the *Lancry*, *Simitzi* and *Carbonati Apuani* case law to the contested rules in *Jersey Produce* and, hence, to exclude

[293] Ibid para 48. [294] Ibid. [295] Ibid.
[296] Opinion AG Léger 3 May 2005 in C-293/02, *Jersey Produce*, para 122.
[297] Ibid paras 123–25. [298] Ibid para 126. [299] Ibid para 130.
[300] Emphasis added; by contrast, the Court of Justice omitted this part of the definition in its *Carbonati Apuani* judgment (ECJ case C-72/03 *Carbonati Apuani* [2004] ECR I-8027, para 23).
[301] Opinion AG Léger 3 May 2005 in C-293/02, *Jersey Produce*, para 134.

the application of Articles 28 and 30 TFEU to those situations which are purely internal to a Member State.[302]

The Advocate General emphasised that the same conclusion necessarily applies to Article 35 TFEU as well. In particular, he argued against the transposition of the *Lancry*, *Simitzi* and *Carbonati Apuani* case law to the area of non-tariff obstacles to trade in goods, since this would rely on the same fragile arguments as those on the basis of which the ECJ applies Articles 28 and 30 TFEU to purely internal situations.[303] However, as has been examined in the previous subsection, the ECJ also ignored the comments of its Advocate General in the case of *Jersey Produce*. In that case, the ECJ confirmed its case law regarding Articles 28 and 30 TFEU and even extended it as far as Article 35 TFEU.

ii. Proposal to Extend the Case Law on Internal Tariff Barriers

134. Although the Court's case law on internal tariff barriers has been repeatedly criticised, it has also been approved of. In particular, in her Opinion in the *Flemish Care Insurance* case, which will be extensively discussed in Part III,[304] AG Sharpston found in the ECJ's case law on internal tariff barriers, and in particular in the conceptual reasoning behind it, support for her proposal to take the relevant regulatory authority – Member State or regional authority – into account when adjudging alleged restrictions on the freedom of movement within the EU.[305]

135. In this respect, the Advocate General first considered the argument that the Court put forward in its *Lancry* judgment, regarding the practical objections to verifying whether or not products originate in another Member State in each case.[306] AG Sharpston recognised that this practical consideration cannot be transposed to the freedom of movement for persons since the provisions on the freedom of movement for persons do not include a prohibition equivalent to that of tariff barriers in Article 28 TFEU.[307]

136. Next, however, she argued that the conceptual argument, put forward by the Court in *Apuani Carbonati*, could be applied analogously to the freedom of movement for persons.[308] As mentioned previously, the Court considered in that judgment that the very principle of a customs union intends to ensure free movement of goods throughout the territory of the customs union. The ECJ recognised that Articles 28 and 30 TFEU only refer to trade between Member

302 Ibid para 141.
303 Opinion AG Léger 3 May 2005 in C-293/02, *Jersey Produce*, para 142.
304 Below nn 689–91.
305 Opinion AG Sharpston 28 June 2007 in C-212/06, *Flemish Care Insurance*, paras 122–32.
306 Ibid para 124.
307 Ibid para 125.
308 Ibid paras 126–30.

States; however, it also pointed out that the drafters of the Treaty took it for granted that no charges equivalent to a customs duty existed within one Member State. Moreover, the Court held that Article 28 TFEU should be read together with Article 26(2) TFEU which does not draw a distinction between inter-State frontiers and frontiers within one Member State.

AG Sharpston argued that the same reasoning could be applied analogously to freedom of movement for persons, in particular by reading Articles 26(2) and 45 TFEU together.[309] She pointed out that Article 45 TFEU does not explicitly refer only to cross-border situations, but determines that 'freedom of movement for workers shall be secured within the Union'.[310] She considered that, just as with Articles 28 and 30 TFEU, the drafters of the Treaties may well also have assumed for Article 45 TFEU that internal obstacles to the freedom of movement for persons should be abolished.[311]

According to AG Sharpston, the Court of Justice has not yet fully drawn out the consequences of the conceptual justification that it put forward for the abolition of internal tariff barriers.[312] She submitted that an additional argument for doing so could be found in the Treaty provisions on Union citizenship.[313] In this respect, she pointed out that 'the question whether the situation is internal is ... conceptually distinct from the question whether there is a link with [Union] law'.[314] Sharpston argued that internal situations should not automatically be considered as lacking any link with Union law.[315] It seems as though the ECJ has confirmed this with its *Rottmann* and *Ruiz Zambrano* cases, which will be discussed below in section 2 (Purely Internal Situation Versus Sufficient Connection with Union Law).[316]

1.2.3. Guimont *Line of Cases: Indirect Exceptions to the Purely Internal Situation Rule via Article 267 TFEU*

1.2.3.1. *Dzodzi* and *Guimont* Line of Cases

137. The *Dzodzi* line of cases concerns those cases in which the Court of Justice provides a preliminary ruling where, according to the referring judge,

309 Ibid para 129.

310 In this respect, AG Sharpston referred to AG Warner in his Opinion in *Saunders* where he considered that 'the right [enshrined in article 45 TFEU] is *prima facie* one of access to every part of every territory. That is as one would expect, since the free movement of persons has as its object to contribute to the establishment of a common market in which the nationals of all Member States may take part in economic activity anywhere on the territory of the [Union]' (see AG Warner 8 March 1979 in 175/78, *Saunders*, 1143).

311 Opinion AG Sharpston 28 June 2007 in C-212/06, *Flemish Care Insurance*, para 130.

312 Ibid para 132.

313 Ibid para 133.

314 Ibid para 136.

315 Ibid para 136.

316 Below nn 302–09.

the facts of the main proceedings fall outside the scope of Union law, but where provisions of Union law are made applicable by domestic law or by virtue of contractual terms.[317] In *Kleinwort Benson*, the Court of Justice subjected its jurisdiction to the double condition that (1) national law must refer directly and unconditionally to Union law and (2) that the national court must consider itself absolutely and unconditionally bound by Union law.[318] In subsequent cases, however, the Court has been more lenient in also accepting indirect and implicit references to Union law.[319]

138. In the *Dzodzi* line of cases, the Court of Justice justifies its jurisdiction in a two-fold manner. First, the Court considers that nothing, neither in the wording of Article 267 TFEU nor in the aim of the procedure, indicates that it is excluded from the jurisdiction of the Court to answer a request for a preliminary ruling on a Union provision in the case where a Member State's national law refers to the Union provision in order to determine rules applicable to a situation which is purely internal to that Member State.[320] Secondly, the Court points out that 'it is manifestly in the interest of the [Union] legal order that, in order to forestall future differences of interpretation, every [Union] provision should be given a uniform interpretation irrespective of the circumstances in which it is to be applied'.[321]

139. The *Guimont* line of cases concerns those cases in which the Court of Justice provides a preliminary ruling where the facts of the main proceedings are confined to a single Member State and where the rule at issue applies to internal and cross-border situations alike. In particular, the *Guimont* judgment[322] concerned the French legislation reserving the denomination 'emmenthal' for those cheeses 'with a hard, dry rind of a colour between golden yellow and light brown'. Mr Guimont was prosecuted for selling cheese deceptively labelled as 'emmenthal'. He invoked that the French decree should be considered to be a

317 ECJ joined cases C-297/88 and C-197/89 *Dzodzi* [1990] ECR I-3763, paras 29–43, in particular para 36. See also ECJ 166/84 *Thomasdünger* [1985] ECR 3001 which precedes the *Dzodzi* judgment, but which contains less detailed reasoning. See also ECJ case C-88/91 *Federconsorzi* [1992] ECR I-4035 regarding contractual terms which render Union law applicable.

318 ECJ case C-346/93 *Kleinwort Benson* [1995] ECR I-640, paras 16 and 20.

319 See inter alia ECJ case C-28/95 *Leur Bloem* [1997] ECR I-4161, paras 31–33 and ECJ case C-1/99 *Kofisa Italia* [2001] ECR I-207, paras 23–32.

320 ECJ joined cases C-297/88 and C-197/89 *Dzodzi* [1990] ECR I-3763, para 36. See also inter alia ECJ case C-28/95 *Leur Bloem* [1997] ECR I-4161, para 25 and ECJ case C-280/06 *ETI* [2007] ECR I-10893, para 21.

321 ECJ joined cases C-297/88 and C-197/89 *Dzodzi* [1990] ECR I-3763, para 37. See also inter alia ECJ case C-28/95 *Leur Bloem* [1997] ECR I-4161, para 32; ECJ case C-280/06 *ETI* [2007] ECR I-10893, para 21; and ECJ case C-458/06 *Gourmet Classic* [2008] ECR I-4207, para 32.

322 ECJ case C-448/98 *Guimont* [2000] ECR I-10663.

quantitative restriction or a measure having equivalent effect on intra-Union trade and hence violated Article 34 TFEU. However, the French government argued that the facts underlying the preliminary reference related to a purely internal situation to which Article 34 TFEU does not apply.[323]

140. The Court of Justice recognised that a rule such as that at issue in the main proceedings, which applies, according to its wording, without distinction to national and imported products and imposes marketing conditions falls under Article 34 TFEU 'only in so far as it applies to situations that are linked to the importation of goods in intra-[Union] trade'.[324] However, the Court went on to hold that this finding does not lead to the conclusion that there is no need to answer the question referred to the Court for a preliminary ruling in the case at issue – although the facts in the main proceedings were confined to a single Member State.[325]

Next, the Court recalled that it is up to the national courts alone to decide both on the need for a preliminary ruling and on the relevance of the questions asked. The Court considered that a reference for a preliminary ruling is only rejected if 'it is quite obvious that the interpretation of [Union] law sought by that court bears no relation to the actual nature of the case or the subject-matter of the main action'.[326] The Court ruled that this was not obvious in the case at issue and held that 'a reply might be useful to [the national court] if its national law were to require ... that a national producer must be allowed to enjoy the same rights as those which a producer of another Member State would derive from [Union] law in the same situation'.[327] Unsurprisingly, the ECJ subsequently held that the French legislation violated Article 34 TFEU.[328]

141. In other words, the ECJ considers that it has the jurisdiction to answer the referring court in the context of a reference for a preliminary ruling in which all elements in the main proceedings are situated within a single Member State, given that the ECJ's answer may be useful to the referring court; in particular, in the case that the relevant national law would prohibit reverse discrimination.[329] The *Guimont* judgment concerned the area of the free movement of goods,

---

323 Ibid para 18. 324 Ibid para 21.

325 ECJ case C-448/98 *Guimont* [2000] ECR I-10663, para 22.

326 Ibid, referring to ECJ case C-281/98 *Angonese* [2000] ECR I-4139, para 18. The Court of Justice used this formulation for the first time in ECJ case 126/80 *Salonia* [1981] ECR 1563, para 6.

327 ECJ case C-448/98 *Guimont* [2000] ECR I-10663, para 23.

328 Ibid para 35.

329 However, specifically regarding the French legislation at issue in the *Guimont* judgment, the French Court of Cassation held that the stricter treatment of purely internal situations was not a violation of Union law nor of French law. Below nn 424–29.

but the ECJ subsequently extended the 'it might be useful' principle to the free movement of capital,[330] services[331] and establishment.[332]

The ECJ also formulated the basis for its jurisdiction slightly different in subsequent judgments regarding a reference for a preliminary ruling in which the facts of the main proceedings were purely internal, but where the national legislation at issue applied to its own nationals and nationals of other Member States alike. That is to say, the Court emphasised that 'it is far from inconceivable that companies [or nationals] established in Member States other than the Member State concerned have been or are interested in constructing a service station selling fuel'[333] or opening a new pharmacy.[334]

142. It is important to remember that the ECJ's jurisdiction in the *Dzodzi* line of cases is based on a reference in national law to Union law. However, in the *Guimont* line of cases there is no such connection. Accordingly, it may be argued that the ECJ made an indirect exception to the purely internal situation via Article 267 TFEU in the *Guimont* line of cases.[335] This will be explained further in the following subsection.

1.2.3.2. Criticising the Justifications Put Forward in the *Dzodzi* and *Guimont* Line of Cases

143. Each of the three justifications put forward by the ECJ in its *Dzodzi* and *Guimont* line of cases can be criticised. First, the Court's reasoning that Article 267 TFEU does not exclude the ECJ's jurisdiction in the context of a reference for preliminary ruling in which all the elements of the main proceedings are confined to one Member State can be denounced. In particular, AG Mancini argued in his Opinion in *Thomasdünger*[336] that 'in replying to

---

330 See inter alia ECJ joined cases C-515/99, C-519/99 to C-524/99 and C-526/99 to C-540/99 *Reisch* [200] ECR I-02157.

331 See inter alia ECJ case C-6/01 *Anomar* [2003] ECR I-8621 and ECJ case C-380/05 *Centro Europa* [2008] ECR I-349.

332 See inter alia ECJ case C-84/11 *Susisalo*.

333 ECJ case C-384/08 *Attanasio* [2010] ECR I-2055, para 24.

334 ECJ joined cases C-570/07 and C-571/07 *Blanco Pérez* [2010] ECR I-4629, para 40 (and in para 39 the 'may be useful' consideration). See also ECJ case C-159/12 *Venturini*, para 26 and ECJ case C-367/12 *Sokoll-Seebacher*, para 11.

335 In this sense, the present author concurs with Ritter's analysis by making a distinction between the '*Dzodzi* principle' and the '*Guimont* principle' (RITTER, 'Purely Internal Situations, Reverse Discrimination, Guimont, Dzodzi and Article 234' (2006) 31 *ELRev* 690–710). For instance, Lefevre's analysis is slightly different again. Lefevre describes the *Dzodzi* line of cases as a progressive extension of the jurisdiction of the Court of Justice in which he distinguishes five movements. He considers the *Guimont* judgment as being part of the fifth movement. LEFEVRE, 'The Interpretation of Community Law by the Court of Justice in Areas of National Competence' (2004) 29 *ELRev* 501–16).

336 ECJ 166/84 *Thomasdünger* [1985] ECR 3001 is actually the first case in the *Dzodzi* line of cases, see above n 317.

those questions therefore, the Court would in appearance be interpreting the provisions mentioned therein but would in reality be expressing an opinion on the internal rule in which these provisions had been absorbed and by which process they had lost their binding force. That is something which the Court is expressly prohibited from doing by [article 267 TFEU].'[337]

Although it is correct that the Court of Justice cannot rule on the compatibility of national rules with Union law in the context of preliminary rulings,[338] this is not expressly prohibited by Article 267 TFEU. However, it can be inferred from this Article *a contrario* because the ECJ is competent for the interpretation of Union law.

144. Next, the Court's argument that a reply in *Dzodzi*-type cases is necessary for the uniform interpretation of Union law can also be challenged. AG Darmon argued in his Opinion in *Dzodzi* that the Court was not competent to provide the ruling requested of it.[339] In this respect, he recalled the aim of the preliminary ruling mechanism as explained by the Court itself in *Rheinmuehlen*: 'Article [267 TFEU] is essential for the preservation of the [Union] character of the law established by the Treaty and has the object of ensuring that in all circumstances this law is the same in all States of the [Union]'.[340] According to AG Darmon, this 'clearly applies only within the field of application of [Union] law, as it is defined by [Union] law and by [Union] law alone'.[341]

145. Finally, the justification used by the ECJ in the *Guimont* line of cases regarding the discretion of the national judge to decide both on the need for a reference for preliminary ruling and on the relevance of the questions can be criticised. First, the Court's *Guimont* case law seems to be inconsistent with the Court's *Foglia* case law according to which 'the duty assigned to the Court by article [267 TFEU] is not that of delivering advisory opinions on general or hypothetical questions'.[342] That is to say, if the national legislation at issue does not prohibit reverse discrimination, then the question referred for a preliminary ruling could be considered to be 'hypothetical'.[343]

337 Opinion AG Mancini 15 May 1985 in 166/84, *Thomasdünger*, 2.

338 Lenaerts, Arts and Maselis, *Procedural Law of the European Union*, Sweet & Maxwell 2006, pp 232–33 and 237–38.

339 Opinion AG Darmon 3 July 1990 in C-297/88 and C-197/89, *Dzodzi*, 8.

340 Ibid, referring to ECJ case 166/73 *Rheinmuehlen* [1974] ECR 33, para 2.

341 Opinion AG Darmon 3 July 1990 in C-297/88 and C-197/89, *Dzodzi*, 8.

342 ECJ case 244/80 *Foglia II* [1981] ECR 3045, para 18. This is settled case law, see inter alia ECJ case C-343/90 *Lourenço Dias* [1992] ECR I-4673, para 17; ECJ case C-458/06 *Gourmet Classic* [2008] I-4207, paras 25–26; and ECJ joined cases C-94/04 and C-202/04 *Cipolla e.a.* [2006] ECR I-11421, para 25. See also Lefevre, 'The Interpretation of Community Law by the Court of Justice in Areas of National Competence' (2004) 29 *ELRev* 501, 509.

343 See also Ritter, 'Purely Internal Situations, Reverse Discrimination, Guimont, Dzodzi and Article 234' (2006) 31 *ELRev* 694.

Secondly, if national law does not actually prevent reverse discrimination, the referring judge has to disapply the national legislation in cross-border situations, but not in purely internal situations. However, the effect of the Court's ruling in *Guimont*-type cases is unclear. The fact that the national court requests a preliminary ruling shows that it is willing to follow the ECJ's interpretation and that it is willing to disapply the national measure, even though the case before it is a purely internal situation.[344]

146. In the light of these criticisms, especially the *Guimont* case law, and the *Dzodzi* case law less so, can be rejected. That is to say, while in *Dzodzi*-type cases the preliminary reference itself shows that national law or contracts render Union law applicable in the purely internal situation, in *Guimont*-type cases the ECJ does not require the national court to demonstrate that its national law prohibits reverse discrimination, nor does the ECJ examine this itself. Accordingly, it has been argued that this case law might constitute an illegitimate extension of the ECJ's jurisdiction.[345] However, as will be discussed in the following subsection, in the following case law, the ECJ has sought to limit the reach of its *Guimont* decision.

1.2.3.3. ECJ Puts 'Limited' Limits on the *Guimont* Line of Cases

147. In its *Omalet*, *Ordine degli ingegneri di Verona e provincial* and *Susisalo* judgments, the Court of Justice placed limits upon its *Guimont* line of cases. First, in *Omalet*, the *Guimont* judgment was confirmed in principle, but the Court ruled that it did not apply in the case at issue because the referring court itself pointed out that a judgment of the Belgian Constitutional Court regarding the contested rules revealed that Article 56 TFEU did not apply if the pending case was entirely situated within the Belgian legal system.[346] Since it is clear from the reference for a preliminary ruling that the referring court is not obliged to grant undertakings established in Belgium the same rights as undertakings falling under Union law and given the fact that the main proceedings related to a purely internal situation, the Court of Justice held that it did not have the

344 Lefevre, 'The Interpretation of Community Law by the Court of Justice in Areas of National Competence' (2004) 29 *ELRev* 501, 512, who argued that 'this jurisprudence in its current state may appear more confusing than helpful for national courts' and Ritter, 'Purely Internal Situations, Reverse Discrimination, Guimont, Dzodzi and Article 234' (2006) 31 *ELRev* 698 who argued that '[s]ince this is plainly wrong, the Court of Justice should say so, instead of responding to the question on the substance'.

345 Lefevre, 'The Interpretation of Community Law by the Court of Justice in Areas of National Competence' (2004) 29 *ELRev* 501, 509–13 and Ritter, 'Purely Internal Situations, Reverse Discrimination, Guimont, Dzodzi and Article 234' (2006) 31 *ELRev* 701.

346 ECJ case C-245/09 *Omalet* [2010] ECR I-13771, para 16.

jurisdiction to answer the questions referred for a preliminary ruling.[347] Hence, the ECJ regarded the request for a preliminary ruling in the *Omalet* case as being inadmissible – in other words it did not apply the *Guimont* principle – because the referring judge indicated that reverse discrimination was not prohibited by Belgian law.

148. The *Ordine degli ingegneri di Verona e provincia* judgment concerned the same legislation as that challenged in the ECJ's *Mosconi* order discussed above, that is to say, provisions on the reservation of work on classified heritage buildings to architects only.[348] In that order, the Court ruled that the principle of equal treatment under Union law cannot be invoked with respect to a purely internal situation and that it is up to the national court to decide whether national law prohibits reverse discrimination.[349] In response thereto, the regional administrative tribunal held that the contested legislation should be disapplied because it is incompatible with the principle of equal treatment as interpreted by the Italian Constitutional Court.[350] The provincial order of architects contested this judgment before the Italian Council of State who referred a question for preliminary ruling to the Court of Justice.

Against this background, the ECJ ruled that 'it is clearly in the European Union's interest that the Court interprets the provision of European Union law at issue', although the main proceedings clearly concerned a purely internal situation.[351] The Court reached this conclusion in two phases. First, the ECJ emphasised that the referring court explicitly considers that enabling reverse discrimination would infringe upon principles of national law.[352] Secondly, the Court referred to its *Guimont* case law according to which the interpretation of Union law requested might be useful to the referring court where national law grants the same rights to a national as those which a national of another Member State in the same situation would enjoy under European Union law.[353]

149. In *Susisalo*, the main proceedings concerned a purely internal situation and the referring court did not provide information as to the existence of a national prohibition on reverse discrimination. However, the ECJ ruled that it was not obvious that the interpretation of Union law provisions required was of no use to the referring court.[354] The Court based its jurisdiction in this case on the fact that 'at the hearing, the representative of the applicants in the main

347 Ibid paras 17–18.
348 Above nn 111–12.
349 ECJ case C-111/12 *Ordine degli ingegneri di Verona e provincia e.a.*, para 22.
350 Ibid para 24.
351 Ibid paras 34–35.
352 Ibid para 34.
353 Ibid para 35.
354 ECJ case C-84/11 *Susisalo*, paras 20–21.

proceedings argued that in Finnish administrative law there are rules which ensure that Finnish nationals do not suffer reverse discrimination'.

150. In *Crono Service* and *Airport Shuttle Express*, the main proceedings regarding car and driver hire services did not contain cross-border elements and the requests for a preliminary ruling did not make clear whether a requirement under national law to apply Article 49 TFEU could be relevant in the context of a purely domestic situation. In her joined Opinion, AG Kokott argued that it can be inferred from previous case law that the acceptance of a national prohibition of reverse discrimination primarily depends on the information supplied by the referring court.[355] The Advocate General observed that where the referring court has failed to provide such information, the Court has accepted the (undisputed) information provided by parties.[356] However, in the main proceedings, the referring court did not provide information on a national prohibition of reverse discrimination and the information provided by the parties was inconsistent.[357]

The ECJ recalled that 'according to the line of authority devolving from *Guimont*, the Court's answer to questions concerning fundamental freedoms of the European Union may, even in a purely internal situation, nevertheless be of use to the referring court, especially if its national law were to require it to allow a national to enjoy the same rights as those which a national of another Member State would derive from EU law in the same situation'.[358] Next, the ECJ itself assessed whether the answer to the questions could be useful for the referring court[359] and held that the interpretation of Article 49 TFEU on the freedom of establishment has no bearing on the disputes pending before the referring court.[360]

151. In sum, if it appears from the information provided to the Court of Justice that national law does not prohibit reverse discrimination, then the Court of Justice considers that is has no jurisdiction. By contrast, if either the referring court or the parties provide the Court of Justice the (undisputed) information that national law prohibits reverse discrimination, then the Court replies to the question referred for a preliminary ruling also where the main proceedings concern a purely internal situation.

However, if neither the referring court nor the parties provide undisputed information on the issue, it seems as if the ECJ assesses itself whether a reply

355 Opinion AG Kokott 26 September 2013 in C-162/12 and C-163/12, *Airport Shuttle Express* and joined cases C-419/12 and C-420/12, *Crono Service*, para 49.

356 Ibid para 50.

357 Ibid paras 45 and 51.

358 Ibid para 38.

359 Sevinga, 'Bevoegdheid van het Hof van Justitie: de ene interne situatie is de andere niet' (2014) *NTER* 196, 199.

360 ECJ joined cases C-162/12 and C-163/12 *Airport Shuttle Express*, para 49 and ECJ joined cases C-419/12 and C-420/12 *Crono Service*, para 43.

might be useful for the referring court.[361] The latter situation should be avoided because it entails the risk of an illegitimate extension of the ECJ's jurisdiction. In particular, the referring court has to take responsibility and should provide the ECJ with detailed and reliable information as to precisely which national situation must be treated on the same basis as which situation governed by European Union law pursuant to national law.[362]

2. THE PURELY INTERNAL SITUATION VERSUS SUFFICIENT CONNECTION WITH UNION LAW

152. It is self-evident that the interpretation of a sufficient link with Union law is crucial in the debate on reverse discrimination. In particular, the presence of such a connection with Union law determines whether or not a Union citizen can benefit from the more favourable treatment of the Treaty provisions on free movement and citizenship. That is to say, although Articles 9 TEU and 20 TFEU determine that every national of a Member State is a citizen of the Union, this is insufficient as such to rely on the Treaty provisions on free movement and citizenship. In order to fall within the scope of these provisions, a sufficient link with Union law is needed. Unfortunately, the precise conditions which need to be satisfied in order to establish such a link with Union law – in other words the personal scope of the Treaty provisions on free movement and citizenship – are hard to infer from the ECJ's case law.[363]

153. This section will disentangle the ECJ's interpretation of a sufficient connection with Union law. First, it will discuss the ECJ's traditional interpretation thereof, that is to say, the presence of a cross-border element comprising actual movement between Member States. Secondly, it will describe the evolution in the ECJ's interpretation of situations falling under Union law.

---

361 Sevinga, 'Bevoegdheid van het Hof van Justitie: de ene interne situatie is de andere niet' (2014) *NTER* 196, 199.

362 Opinion AG Kokott 26 September 2013 in C-162/12 and C-163/12, *Airport Shuttle Express* and joined cases C-419/12 and C-420/12, *Crono Service*, para 49; Opinion AG Wahl 5 September 2013 in C-159/12–C-161/12, *Venturini*, paras 44–45. See also Prechal, 'Interne situatie en prejudiciële vragen' (2015) 11 *SEW* 494, 494–96 who argues for a stricter assessment by the ECJ of request for preliminary ruling regarding a purely internal situation in the main proceedings.

363 No explicit definition of the personal versus the material scope of the Treaty provisions on free movement can be found in the ECJ's case law. See Spaventa, 'Seeing the Wood Despite the Trees? On the Scope of Union Citizenship and its Constitutional Effects' (2008) 45 *CMLRev* 13, 15.

2.1. TRADITIONAL INTERPRETATION OF SUFFICIENT LINK WITH UNION LAW: CROSS-BORDER ELEMENT AS ACTUAL MOVEMENT BETWEEN MEMBER STATES

154. This section discusses the requirements that need to be met in order to fall within the personal scope of the Treaty provisions on free movement and citizenship. Where the Treaty provisions on free movement are concerned, a sufficient link with Union law is considered to be at stake when a cross-border element and an economic activity are present. Where the Treaty provisions on Union citizenship are concerned, only a cross-border element is needed in order to fall under the scope of application of the aforementioned provisions.

2.1.1. Treaty Provisions on the Freedom of Movement

2.1.1.1. Treaty Provisions on Freedom of Movement: Cross-Border Element and Economic Activity

155. In order to fall within the scope of application of the Treaty provisions on free movement, the claimant should demonstrate the existence of both a cross-border element and an economic activity.[364] This has been inferred from the whole range of cases in which the ECJ ruled that a Union national who has been employed in another Member State falls within the scope of the Treaty provisions on free movement.[365]

The underlying rationale of these conditions can be explained in the context of the early EU – then the (E)EC – as an organisation with mainly economic aims and with the completion of the internal market in particular.[366] In this economic context, the distinction between citizens who make use of their right of free movement and those who do not, did not seem illogical.[367] According to this logic, only those people who pursue an economic activity in another Member State, other than the one for which they possess the nationality, contribute

---

364 See inter alia Spaventa, 'Seeing the Wood Despite the Trees? On the Scope of Union Citizenship and its Constitutional Effects' (2008) 45 *CMLRev* 13, 15–16.

365 See inter alia ECJ case C-419/92 *Scholz* [1994] ECR I-505, para 9 and ECJ case C-18/95 *Terhoeve* [1999] ECR I-345, paras 29 and 42. Specifically regarding the requirement of an economic activity see inter alia ECJ case C-363/89 *Roux* [1991] ECR I-273, para 9.

366 ECJ case 35/82 and 36/82 *Morson and Jhanjan* [1982] ECR 3723, para 15.

367 Dautricourt and Thomas, 'Reverse Discrimination and Free Movement of Persons Under Community Law: All for Ulysses, Nothing for Penelope?' (2009) 34 *ELRev* 454, 436; de Burca 'The Role of Equality in European Community Law' in Dashwood and O'Leary (eds), *The Principle of Equal Treatment in EC Law*, Sweet & Maxwell 1997, p 16; ECJ case C-363/89 *Roux* [1991] ECR I-273.

to the completion of the internal market and are, therefore, protected by the fundamental freedom provisions.[368]

2.1.1.2. Having Exercised His or Her Right of Free Movement

156. On the one hand, the condition of an economic activity is not particularly problematic since its presence in a specific case is normally quite easy to assess. On the other hand, a cross-border element was considered to be present where a national of a Member State actually moved between different Member States. Instead of mentioning these two conditions separately, the Court of Justice often considers whether or not a national of a Member State 'has exercised his right to freedom of movement'. If the answer is in the affirmative, the situation falls within the scope of application of the Treaty provisions on free movement.

157. The ECJ has articulated this clearly in, for instance, the *Scholz* judgment. Mrs Scholz, who is of German origin and acquired Italian nationality by marriage, participated in a recruitment drive for canteen staff at the University of Cagliari. She challenged the decision taken by the selection board because it refused to take into account, in accordance with the notice of competition, her previous employment in the German post office. The regional administrative court of Sardegna, before which the proceedings were instituted, referred a question for a preliminary ruling to the Court of Justice.

The Court of Justice held that 'any [Union] national who, irrespective of his place of residence and his nationality, has exercised the right to freedom of movement for workers and who has been employed in another Member State, falls within the scope of the [articles 18 and 45 TFEU]'.[369] The Court ruled that if a public body of a Member State, in recruiting staff for posts not falling under Article 45(4) TFEU, provides for account to be taken of the candidate's previous employment in the public service, Article 45 TFEU requires that that body may not make a distinction according to whether such employment was in the public service of that particular State or in the public service of another Member State.[370]

158. By contrast, a case regarding nationals of a Member State who have not made use of their right to free movement is, for instance, the *Morson and Jhanjan* case, discussed above.[371] Since the daughter and son of Mrs Morson

---

[368] Cambien, 'Mogen statische Unieburgers worden gediscrimineerd op het vlak van gezinshereniging? Enkele beschouwingen bij de arresten Ruiz Zambrano en McCarthy van het Hof van Justitie' (2011) 3 *T Vreemd* 241, 241 and Tryfonidou, *Reverse Discrimination*, Kluwer Law International 2009, p 166.

[369] ECJ case C-419/92 *Scholz* [1994] ECR I-505, para 9. See inter alia also ECJ case C-18/95 *Terhoeve* [1999] ECR I-345, para 27.

[370] ECJ case C-419/92 *Scholz* [1994] ECR I-505, para 12.

[371] See above nn 55–57.

and Mrs Jhanjan were Dutch nationals who were employed in the Netherlands and had never been employed in another Member State, Mrs Morson and Mrs Jhanjan could not benefit from rights derived from Union law. The ECJ held in this case that 'the Treaty provisions on freedom of movement for workers and the rules adopted to implement them cannot be applied to cases which have no factor linking them with any of the situations governed by [Union] law. Such is undoubtedly the case with workers who have never exercised the right to freedom of movement within the [Union].'[372]

159. However, factual situations are not always easy to interpret. The next section will discuss the evolution in the acceptance of a sufficient link with Union law by the Court of Justice extensively.[373] For now, it is sufficient to clarify that early on, the ECJ explained that 'a purely hypothetical prospect' of exercising the right to free movement 'does not establish a sufficient connection' with Union law in order to justify the application of Union provisions.[374] This can be seen in the *Moser* judgment.

Mr Moser was a German national who had always lived and resided in Germany. He was denied access to the vocational training necessary to enable him to become a teacher in primary and secondary education on the grounds of insufficient certainty of his loyalty to the Basic Law, by reason of his membership of the German communist party. In order to provide a connection with Union law, Mr Moser claimed that the application of the German legislation made it impossible for him to complete his training as a teacher, even in schools in other Member States.[375] However, the Court of Justice did not agree with this reasoning and ruled that 'a purely hypothetical prospect of employment in another Member State' did not establish a sufficient link with Union law to justify the application of Article 45 TFEU.[376]

2.1.2. *Treaty Provisions on Union Citizenship*

2.1.2.1. Treaty Provisions on Union Citizenship: Cross-Border Element

160. Following the introduction of EU citizenship with the Maastricht Treaty, the question arose as to whether the ECJ would hold on to its purely internal

372 ECJ case 35/82 and 36/82 *Morson and Jhanjan* [1982] ECR 3723, paras 16–17. This was the ECJ's initial position, however, see ECJ case C-403/03 *Schempp* [2005] ECR I-6421, discussed below.

373 See below nn 175 ff.

374 See inter alia ECJ case 180/83 *Moser* [1984] ECR 2539, para 18 and ECJ case C-299/95 *Kremzow* [1997] ECR I-2629, para 16.

375 ECJ case 180/83 *Moser* [1984] ECR 2539, para 17.

376 Ibid para 18.

situation doctrine. Whether the typical economic rationale, set out above, could still suffice in order to require a link with Union law in cases regarding Union citizenship was questioned.[377] The creation of the status of Union citizenship indicated that the EU's objectives clearly exceeded the purely economic ones.

Nevertheless, and as discussed previously,[378] the Court of Justice made clear that its purely internal situation doctrine also applies to the Treaty provisions on Union citizenship. In this regard, the *Uecker and Jacquet* judgment is often put forward. In this case, the ECJ explicitly considered that 'citizenship of the Union … is not intended to extend the scope *ratione materiae* of the Treaty also to internal situations which have no link with [Union] law'.[379]

161. A landmark case in the context of the personal scope of application of the Treaty provisions on Union citizenship is the *Martinez Sala* judgment.[380] The case concerned Mrs Martinez Sala, a Spanish national living in Germany where she held different jobs. Accordingly, she obtained various residence permits and extensions thereto. For a short period, she did not have a residence permit, but in that period she had applied for childcare allowance for her new-born child. This application was rejected by the German authorities because she did not have German nationality, a residence entitlement or a residence permit. In this factual context, the German judge stayed proceedings and referred different questions to the Court of Justice.[381]

162. According to the German government, the facts of the main proceedings fell neither within the scope *ratione materiae* nor within the scope *ratione personae* of Article 18 TFEU, prohibiting discrimination on the grounds of nationality.[382] The Court rejected the argument regarding the scope *ratione materiae* by referring to its replies to the previous question on the basis of which the childcare allowance in question in the main proceedings indisputably falls within the scope *ratione materiae* of Union law.[383]

Regarding the scope *ratione personae* of Article 18 TFEU, the ECJ held that if the referring court would not consider Mrs Martinez Sala to be a worker within the meaning of Article 45 TFEU, there is still Article 21(1) TFEU which determines that 'every citizen of the Union shall have the right to move and reside freely within the territory of the Member States, subject to the limitations and conditions laid down in the Treaties and by the measures adopted to give them

[377] See above n 78.
[378] See above nn 66–68.
[379] ECJ joined cases C-64/96 and C-65/96 *Uecker and Jacquet* [1997] ECR I-3171, para 23.
[380] ECJ case C-85/96 *Martinez Sala* [1998] ECR I-2691.
[381] The focus here is on the last question.
[382] Then Article 6 TEC.
[383] ECJ case C-85/96 *Martinez Sala* [1998] ECR I-2691, para 57.

effect'.[384] The Court pointed out that it was not necessary to examine whether Mrs Martinez Sala could rely upon Article 21(1) TFEU in order to obtain recognition of a new right to reside in Germany 'since it is common ground that she has already been authorised to reside there, although she has been refused issue of a residence permit'.[385] Hence, Mrs Martinez Sala came within the scope *ratione personae* of the Treaty provisions on EU citizenship '*as a national of a Member State lawfully residing in the territory of another Member State*'.[386]

Next, the Court considered that the right not to suffer discrimination on the grounds of nationality is attached to the status of a Union citizen.[387] Accordingly, the ECJ ruled that a Union citizen who is lawfully resident in a host Member State can rely on Article 21(1) TFEU in all situations which fall within the scope *ratione materiae* of Union law.[388] The Court ruled that the unequal treatment came within the Treaty and could not be justified since it was directly based upon the applicant's nationality and no justification whatsoever had been invoked before the Court.[389]

163. In *Baumbast*, the Court of Justice clearly articulated its position on the scope of application of the Treaty provisions on Union citizenship vis-à-vis the scope of application of the Treaty provisions on freedom of movement. Mr Baumbast, a German national, married a Colombian national in the UK in 1990. Between 1990 and 1993, Mr Baumbast pursued various economic activities in the UK. After his company failed, he was employed by German companies. Throughout the whole period, Mr and Mrs Baumbast owned a house in the UK and their daughters went to school there. In 1995, the family applied for indefinite leave to remain in the UK, but their application was refused. The Immigration Appeal Tribunal referred inter alia the question to the Court of Justice whether a Union citizen who no longer enjoys a right of residence as a migrant worker in the host Member State can enjoy a right of residence there on the basis of Article 21(1) TFEU.

164. The Court of Justice considered that 'although, before the Treaty on European Union entered into force, the Court had held that that right of residence, conferred directly by the EC Treaty, was subject to the condition

384 Ibid paras 58–59.
385 Ibid para 60.
386 Ibid para 61, emphasis added.
387 As enshrined in Article 18 TFEU. ECJ case C-85/96 *Martinez Sala* [1998] ECR I-2691, para 62.
388 ECJ case C-85/96 *Martinez Sala* [1998] ECR I-2691, para 63: '... including the situation where that Member State delays or refuses to grant to that claimant a benefit that is provided to all persons lawfully resident in the territory of that State on the ground that the claimant is not in possession of a document which nationals of that same State are not required to have and the issue of which may be delayed or refused by the authorities of that State'.
389 Ibid para 64.

that the person concerned was carrying on an economic activity within the meaning of [the Treaty provisions on free movement of workers, establishment and services], it is none the less the case that, since then, Union citizenship has been introduced into the EC Treaty and Article 18(1) EC [now article 21(1) TFEU] has conferred a right, for every citizen, to move and reside freely within the territory of the Member States'.[390] The Court added that in order to benefit from the Treaty provisions on Union citizenship, the Treaties do 'not require that citizens of the Union pursue a professional or trade activity, whether as an employed or self-employed person'.[391] In particular, Article 21(1) TFEU confers directly upon every Union citizen the right to reside within the territory of the Member States.[392] However, the Court recognised that this right is 'subject to the limitations and conditions laid down in the Treaties and by the measures adopted to give them effect'.[393] The Court of Justice stressed that those limitations and conditions must be applied in compliance with the general principles of Union law and, in particular, with the principle of proportionality.[394]

165. Regarding the case of Mr Baumbast, the Court considered that Mr Baumbast as a German national, and consequently a Union citizen, had the right to rely on Article 21(1) TFEU.[395] Directive 90/364 provides that Member States can require that the Union citizen and his family members be covered by sickness insurance and have sufficient resources to avoid becoming a burden on the social assistance system of the host Member State.[396] With respect to the application of the principle of proportionality to the case at issue, the Court made five observations on the case's circumstances.[397] First, it was undisputed that Mr Baumbast had sufficient resources. Secondly, he had worked and lawfully resided in the UK for several years. Thirdly, during that period his family resided in the UK and remained there even after his economic venture had collapsed. Fourthly, neither Mr Baumbast nor his family members had become burdens on the public system of the UK. Fifthly, Mr Baumbast and his family members had comprehensive sickness insurance in the UK. Under these circumstances, the Court held that a refusal of a right of residence of Mr Baumbast in the UK would be a disproportionate interference with the exercise of the right of residence conferred upon him by Article 21(1) TFEU.[398]

166. In sum, as AG Sharpston formulated it, 'with the introduction of EU citizenship in the Maastricht Treaty, nationals of a Member State acquired the

---

[390] ECJ case C-413/99 *Baumbast* 2002 [ECR] I-7091, para 81.
[391] Ibid para 83, emphasis added.
[392] Ibid para 84.
[393] Article 21(1) TFEU.
[394] ECJ case C-413/99 *Baumbast* 2002 [ECR] I-7091, para 91.
[395] Ibid para 84.
[396] Article 1(1) Directive 90/634.
[397] ECJ case C-413/99 *Baumbast* 2002 [ECR] I-7091, para 92.
[398] Ibid para 93.

right to move and reside freely within the territory of other Member States independently from the economic freedoms of movement and thus the pursuit of economic activity'.[399] However, the purely internal situation rule applies to the Treaty provisions regarding Union citizenship. This means that being a national of a Member State does not suffice, on its own, to benefit from the Treaty provisions on Union citizenship, but that some connection with Union law is still needed. This connection is considered to be present if the Union citizen can demonstrate a cross-border element. In the *Martinez Sala* judgment, the Court explicitly considered that Mrs Martinez Sala came within the scope *ratione personae* of the Treaty provisions on Union citizenship '*as a national of a Member State lawfully residing in the territory of another Member State*'.[400] The same approach can be seen in the *Baumbast* judgment, which clearly concerned a cross-border situation since Mr Baumbast, a German national, had resided with his family in the UK and he pursued an economic activity in the UK first and was subsequently employed by German companies.

2.1.2.2. Justifications for the ECJ's Application of the Purely Internal Situation Doctrine to the Treaty Provisions on Union Citizenship

167. As set out in Chapter 2, the ECJ's purely internal situation doctrine has been fiercely criticised in the light of the concept of Union citizenship – often in combination with the Union's principle of equality as enshrined in Article 18 TFEU.[401] Article 20 TFEU establishes Union citizenship. In this regard, it has been emphasised that it is settled case law of the ECJ that 'Union citizenship is destined to be the fundamental status of nationals of the Member States, enabling those who find themselves in the same situation to enjoy the same treatment in law irrespective of their nationality'.[402]

However, it is submitted that the ECJ's application of the purely internal situation to the Treaty provisions on Union citizenship should be supported. Several persuasive arguments lead to this conclusion.[403]

168. First, the argument based on Article 20 TFEU can be rebutted on the basis of the wording of Article 20 TFEU itself. In particular, it determines that 'citizenship of the Union shall be additional to and not replace national

---

399 Opinion AG Sharpston 12 December 2013 in C-457/12, *S*, para 47.

400 ECJ case C-85/96 *Martinez Sala* [1998] ECR I-2691, para 61.

401 Above nn 78–90.

402 ECJ case C-184/99 *Grzelczyk* [2001] ECR I-6193, para 31.

403 This section restates the arguments set out in Verbist, 'De invloed van het Unieburgerschap op zuiver interne situaties' [2011] *RW* 510, 525, with an additional argument put forward by Cambien (Cambien, 'Citizenship of the Union as a Cornerstone of European Integration', Dissertation, KU Leuven 2011, pp 253–55).

citizenship'. This reflects the Member State's unwillingness to have Union citizenship detract from national citizenship.[404] It can be read as a contra-indication to consider Union citizenship as such as a sufficient connection with Union law.

Moreover, although Article 21 TFEU itself does not explicitly require a cross-border element, it does determine that all Union citizens have the right to move and reside in the territory of the Member States 'subject to the limitations and conditions laid down in the Treaties and by the measures adopted to give them effect'. In particular, Article 3(1) of Directive 2004/38 confines its scope of application 'to all Union citizens who move to or reside in a Member State other than that of which they are a national'. From this perspective it can be argued that expanding the scope of application of the Treaty provisions on Union citizenship requires a prior amendment of Directive 2004/38.[405]

169. Secondly, proposals have been made to apply Article 18 TFEU to Union citizens who do not move, in other words, to prohibit discrimination against their own nationals in purely internal situations.[406] Contesting these proposals, AG Kokott recalled that the Court of Justice repeatedly considered that 'citizenship of the Union is not intended to extend the scope *ratione materiae* of EU law to internal situations which have no link with EU law'.[407] However, it should be pointed out that if the Court inferred a prohibition of discrimination against a Member State's own nationals from Article 18 TFEU, then it would not expand the material scope of application of the Treaty, but rather the personal scope of application. On the other hand, while Article 18 TFEU determines that discrimination on the grounds of nationality is forbidden 'within the scope of application of the Treaties', it does not determine it 'within the material scope of application of the Treaties'.

---

404 Shaw, 'Citizenship: Contrasting Dynamics at the Interface of Integration and Constitutionalism' in Craig and de Burca (eds), *The Evolution of EU Law*, Oxford University Press 2011, p 599.

405 Dautricourt and Thomas, 'Reverse Discrimination and Free Movement of Persons Under Community Law: All for Ulysses, Nothing for Penelope?' (2009) 34 *ELRev* 454, 450. It was earlier argued likewise more generally that prohibiting reverse discrimination at the Union level would require a Treaty amendment, see above n 97.

406 See inter alia Opinion AG Sharpston 30 September 2010 in C-34/09, *Ruiz Zambrano*, paras 139–50 and Spaventa, 'Seeing the Wood Despite the Trees? On the Scope of Union Citizenship and its Constitutional Effects' (2008) 45 *CMLRev* 13, 30–39.

407 Opinion AG Kokott 25 November 2010 in C-434/09, *McCarthy*, para 41 referring to ECJ joined cases C-64/96 to C-65/96 *Uecker and Jacquet* [1997] ECR I-3171, para 23; *Garcia Avello* [2003] ECR I-11613, para 26; ECJ case C-403/03 *Schempp* [2005] ECR I-6421, para 20; ECJ case C-212/06 *Flemish Care Insurance* [2008] ECR I-1683, para 39; and ECJ case C-499/06 *Nerkowska* [2008] ECR I 3993, para 25. On this case law see above nn 66–70.

170. Thirdly, the doctrine of purely internal situations regarding Treaty provisions on Union citizenship could not be rejected as a violation of the fundamental rights of Union citizenship in general. That is to say, the Charter on Fundamental Rights of the European Union explicitly provides that '[it] does not extend the field of application of Union law beyond the powers of the Union or establish any new power or task for the Union, or modify powers and tasks as defined in the Treaties'.[408]

171. Finally, it can be argued that the movement of non-economically active Union citizens may also still be required in the light of the Union's non-economic objectives. As explained above, historically, only those Union citizens who moved were protected by the provisions on free movement since they contributed to the completion of the internal market. At present, the requirement for the movement of non-economically active citizens can be justified in the light of other non-economic objectives, such as promoting social cohesion and European higher education.[409] Cambien points out that the criticisms of the purely internal situation rule regarding Treaty provisions on Union citizenship fail to recognise 'that the extension of the scope of beneficiaries of the free movement provisions was accompanied with an extension of or a shift in the purposes pursued by these provisions'.[410]

172. These non-economic objectives are acknowledged in primary and secondary Union law and in many important policy documents. Promoting social cohesion is mentioned as being one of the main objectives in Article 3(3) TEU.[411] Moreover, the preamble of Directive 2004/38 provides that 'enjoyment of permanent residence by Union citizens [and their family members] who have chosen to settle long term in the host Member State would strengthen the feeling of Union citizenship and is a key element in promoting social cohesion … in order to be a genuine vehicle for integration into the society of the host Member State in which the Union citizen resides, the right of permanent residence, once obtained, should not be subject to any conditions.'[412]

---

408 Article 51(2) Charter of Fundamental Rights of the European Union.

409 Cambien, 'Citizenship of the Union as a Cornerstone of European Integration', Dissertation, KU Leuven 2011, pp 253–55; Maas, *Creating European Citizens*, Rowman & Littlefield 2007, pp 102 and 105; and Communication from the Commission of 3 March 2010, 'Europe 2020: A Strategy for Smart, Sustainable and Inclusive Growth' COM (2010) 2020.

Cambien and Maas also argue that 'increased mobility within Europe will facilitate building a shared political community' (Maas, *Creating European Citizens*, Rowman & Littlefield 2007, p 102). However, this goal does not appear to be explicitly acknowledged in the Treaties or other texts of EU institutions.

410 Cambien, 'Citizenship of the Union as a Cornerstone of European Integration', Dissertation, KU Leuven 2011, pp 253–55.

411 See also Title XVIII of TFEU, entitled 'Economic, Social and Territorial Cohesion'.

412 Preamble Directive 2004/38, paras 17–18.

The objective of strengthening Europe's higher education is expressed in the Commission's Communication entitled: 'A Strategy for Smart, Sustainable and Inclusive Growth'.[413] The Commission considers that 'the aim is to enhance the performance and international attractiveness of Europe's higher education institutions and raise the overall quality of all levels of education and training in the EU, combining both excellence and equity, by promoting student mobility and trainees' mobility, and improve the employment situation of young people'.[414] For instance, the Commission will improve 'the EU's mobility, university and researchers' programmes (such as Erasmus, Erasmus Mundus, Tempus and Marie Curie) and link them up with national programmes and resources'.[415]

173. An example that demonstrates that the mobility of Union citizens not only promotes the economic objectives of the European Union, but also its non-economic objectives such as the strengthening of the system of European higher education, promotes social cohesion[416] within the EU and political integration. By contrast, the example of citizens staying in the Member State of which they are nationals does not promote these interests to the same extent.[417]

Imagine, for instance, a Belgian student who takes part in the Erasmus programme and studies at a German university for one year. The Belgian student will meet German students as well as other foreign students. Maybe friendships will grow that will last a lifetime, or maybe the student will meet his or her future partner in Germany. Moreover, the Belgian student's family and friends will come to Germany to visit. Perhaps, the Belgian student might even return to Germany after his or her graduation in order to work there. Residing in Germany, he or she would be able to take part, under certain conditions, in municipal elections.[418]

174. In sum, movement is still relevant in a European Union in which the objectives exceed purely economic ones. Accordingly, in order to be able to rely upon the Treaty provisions on Union citizenship, a Union citizen only

---

413 Communication from the Commission of 3 March 2010, 'Europe 2020: A Strategy for Smart, Sustainable and Inclusive Growth' COM (2010) 2020.

414 Ibid p 13.

415 Ibid.

416 Maas formulates it as follows: 'movers develop a sense of European loyalty and entitlement' (Maas, *Creating European Citizens*, Rowman & Littlefield 2007, p 105).

417 Cambien, 'Citizenship of the Union as a Cornerstone of European Integration', Dissertation, KU Leuven 2011, p 254. See also on the importance of citizen's mobility in the European project: Communication from the Commission of 20 April 2010 to the European Parliament, the Council, the European economic and social committee and the committee of the regions, Delivering an area of freedom, security and justice for Europe's citizens, Action Plan Implementing the Stockholm Programme, COM (2010) 171 final, in particular p 4.

418 Article 22(1) TFEU. See Cambien, 'Citizenship of the Union as a Cornerstone of European Integration', Dissertation, KU Leuven 2011, p 254 fn 236.

needs to demonstrate a cross-border element, but he or she does not need to demonstrate that he or she is economically active. Consequently, the pursuit of an economic activity has currently become less important in the Court's case law on purely internal situations and reverse discrimination. Since the most recent developments on the issue of reverse discrimination concern the freedom of movement for persons, particularly in the light of the status of Union citizenship, the focus will now be placed on the interpretation of the cross-border element, or in other words, the movement required of the Union citizen.[419]

2.2. EVER MORE GENEROUS INTERPRETATION OF A SUFFICIENT CONNECTION WITH UNION LAW BY THE ECJ?

175. The exact degree of connection with Union law that is required to fall within its scope is still unclear. This section explores the evolution in the interpretation of the connection required with Union law in the ECJ's case law. The heavy reliance upon the ECJ's case law results in this section being largely descriptive. This is inevitable in order to present the ways in which the ECJ determines whether or not a situation falls under Union law. This case law will, of course, be assessed critically.

176. It seems that the ECJ has come to accept an increasingly generous sufficient connection with Union law, bringing a situation within the scope of Union law as often as possible. In general it can be said the Court uses two 'techniques' in order to consider more and more situations as falling within the scope of Union law.

First, the Court interprets the existence of a cross-border element in an increasingly generous way. In other words, it stretches the notion of movement to its outer limits. Secondly, the Court has reduced the importance of movement in the light of Union citizenship. In particular, the ECJ has accepted a more abstract link with Union law, one which does not require any movement.

177. First, the criteria on the basis of which the evolution in the ECJ's interpretation of situations falling under Union law will be evaluated, are explained. On this basis, there is discussion of two types of issues which originate in the personal scope of application of the Treaty provisions on freedom of

---

419 By contrast, there will be no further discussion of the ECJ's interpretation of an economic activity. The ECJ generally accepts rather easily that an activity is an economic activity. See inter alia ECJ joined cases C-51/96 and C-191/97 *Deliège* [2000] ECR I-2549, paras 52–60, in particular para 56 in which the Court held that sporting activities may be an economic activity.

movement and citizenship which cause the perception that reverse discrimination is unjust. There will also be a brief discussion of the ECJ's restrictions approach. Although at first glance this has nothing to do with the purely internal situation doctrine of the Court, these two lines of case law have in common the fact that they regard the boundaries between the scope of application of Union law and that of national law. In particular, under the restrictions approach, all national measures 'which are capable of hindering, directly or indirectly, actually or potentially, intra-[Union] trade are to be considered as measures having an effect equivalent to quantitative restrictions'.[420] Accordingly, the restrictions approach is far more intrusive into national autonomy than the discriminations approach.

2.2.1. As a Preliminary Remark: Criteria of Evaluation

178. The evolution of the ECJ's interpretations of situations that fall under Union law can be evaluated from different perspectives. It is possible to take the perspective of the promotion of freedom of movement within the EU, which is essentially an economic perspective. This seems to be the ECJ's approach since, as will be explained later in this subsection, it readily accepts that a restriction to the freedom of movement is at stake. Since this perspective has a far-reaching effect upon the Member State's competences, this book will defend a narrower interpretation of restrictions to freedom of movement.

179. It is also possible to take the protection of the rights of Union citizens as a starting point. In particular, the ECJ tries to bring a situation within the scope of Union law as much as possible to allow the Union citizen to benefit from the more favourable treatment provided by Union law. However, the ECJ's generous approach to bringing situations within the scope of Union law can be considered as arbitrary and leading to divergent results which are difficult to justify. It is often unclear and hard to accept why Union citizen A is able to invoke Union law on the basis of a vague or an accidental link with Union law while Union citizen B in an almost identical situation without that particular element is not.

Obviously, it is important to protect the rights of Union citizens, but as already argued above, this is possible at levels beside the Union level.[421] The Member States also have to protect the fundamental rights of their citizens, both on the basis of the national Constitution and on the basis of the ECHR. Moreover, the presumption that the more favourable treatment of Union law, consisting of less requirements in order to benefit from a certain right, is in any case a better treatment is not necessarily correct, or at least not correct for everybody

---

420 ECJ case 8/74 *Dassonville* [1974] ECR I-837, para 5.

421 Above nn 100–02.

involved. The stricter rules for purely internal situations may, for instance, lead to a product with a higher quality or to a better informed consumer.

180. The criteria which will be decisive in further analysis are: legal certainty, a clear division of powers between the EU and the Member States and a broader perspective than a strictly economic one. Although the two first criteria are clearly inspired by the legal positivist school of thought, it is certainly not the intention here to focus too much on a formal application of legal rules without being aware of the substance of the issue and of the social implications involved.

In this author's opinion, extending the scope of Union law without a clear competence to do so, leads to a European Union which loses legitimacy and credibility. This is related to the issue of the so-called democratic deficit of the EU, about which entire libraries' worth of works have been written,[422] and runs the risk of alienating EU citizens from the project of the European Union.[423]

Finally, not granting a Union citizen a benefit or right on the basis of Union law, does not necessarily imply that this benefit or right is not justified; it simply implies that the right or benefit does not have to be granted on the basis of Union law by the ECJ. The right or benefit can be granted on the basis of Union law after a maximum harmonisation of the subject area at issue or the national authority can grant the right or benefit on the basis of national or international law.

2.2.2. *Precise Indications on How Much Movement and (Re)introduction of Causal Link*

181. In this subsection, we identify two problematic aspects of the ECJ's interpretation of a sufficient connection with Union law in order to fall within the scope of application of the Treaty provisions on freedom of movement and Union citizenship. Here, it will be explained how the ECJ should, in the

422 See inter alia MORAVCSIK, 'In Defence of the "Democratic Deficit": Reassessing Legitimacy in the European Union' (2002) 40 *JCMS* 603, 603–24; FOLLESDAL and HIX, 'Why There is a Democratic Deficit in the EU: A Response to Majone and Moravcsik' (2006) 44 *JCMS* 533, 533–62 and MENON and WEATHERILL, 'Democratic Politics in a Globalising World: Supranationalism and Legitimacy in the European Union' LSE, working papers 13/2007.

For an overview of the 'democratic deficit' debate see inter alia CRAIG, 'Integration, democracy and legitimacy' in CRAIG and DE BURCA (eds), *The Evolution of EU Law*, 2nd ed, Oxford University Press 2011, pp 13–40; HIX, *The Political System of the European Union*, 2nd edn, Palgrave Macmillan 2005, pp 177–80; and VERHOEVEN, *The European Union in Search of a Democratic and Constitutional Theory*, Kluwer Law International 2002, pp 57–74.

423 Craig identifies the 'distance issue' as being one of a number of different features of the concept of democratic deficit. In particular, he argues that 'democracy is also felt to be diminished because of the "distance issue"'. The EU entails a transfer of competence on many issues to Brussels, and away from the nation state, with the consequences that matters are becoming further removed from the citizen.

author's opinion, deal with these issues generally. While discussing specific ECJ judgments on the interpretation of a sufficient link with Union law, these two proposals will be applied and developed further.

2.2.2.1. Sufficient Connection with Union Law: How Much 'Movement' is Necessary?

182. The first problem is that the cross-border element required is less clear-cut than might appear at first glance. Initially, a trans-frontier element was considered to be present if a good or a person crossed a national frontier physically. In other words, some kind of actual movement was necessary. However, on a case-by-case basis, the ECJ relaxed its reading of the cross-border element necessary.

183. As early as 1986, Pickup criticised the ECJ's case law by arguing that 'the present need for a "linking factor" is an arbitrary distinction begging the question of what degree of connection is required'.[424] In the same vein, AG Sharpston argued in her Opinion in *Ruiz Zambrano* that 'if one insists on the premise that physical movement to a Member State other than the Member State of nationality is required before residence rights as a citizen of the Union can be invoked, the result risks being both strange and illogical'.[425] Hence, 30 years after Pickup's critique, the degree of connection which is required in order to fall under the Treaty provisions on free movement and Union citizenship remains uncertain. Or, as Van Elsuwege and Adam have remarked, it is 'not entirely clear what kind of movement should be exercised, when that exercise should have happened and for how long a cross-border element should exist'.[426]

184. It is submitted that this blurring of the dividing line between the scope of Union law and that of national law causes the perception that reverse discrimination is unfair and that it should be corrected. Or, in Tryfonidou's words: 'making it overly easy for a situation to fall within the scope of the fundamental freedoms provisions merely scratches the surface of the problem and, in fact, causes more problems than it solves'.[427] In the light of the principle of legal certainty and in order to delineate the scope of application of the Treaty

---

[424] Pickup, 'Reverse Discrimination and Freedom of Movement for Workers' (1986) 23 *CMLRev* 156, 154.

[425] Opinion AG Sharpston 30 September 2010 in C-34/09, *Ruiz Zambrano*, para 86. See also Opinion AG Geelhoed 27 April 2006 in C-1/05 *Jia*, para 75 and Nic Shuibhne, 'Free Movement of Persons and the Wholly Internal Rule: Time to Move on?' (2002) 39 *CMLRev* 771, 746 who criticise the 'arbitrariness'.

[426] Van Elsuwege and Adam, 'The Limits of Constitutional Dialogue for the Prevention of Reverse Discrimination' (2009) 5 *EuConst* 334. See also Cambien, 'Citizenship of the Union as a Cornerstone of European Integration', Dissertation, KU Leuven 2011, p 282.

[427] Tryfonidou, *Reverse Discrimination*, Kluwer Law International 2009, p 218.

provisions on freedom of movement and citizenship, the ECJ should give precise indications as to how much movement is needed in order to fall under the scope of these Treaty provisions and benefit from the rights granted thereby.

185. Moreover, with respect to the Treaty provisions on Union citizenship, movement (independently from an economic activity) has a paradoxical character. On the one hand, Union citizenship grants the nationals of the Member States the right to move to and to reside in another Member State than the Member State of nationality.[428] On the other hand, the rights that Union citizens infer from the Treaties – including the right from Article 21 TFEU – still depends on a cross-border element.[429] Or, more briefly, 'moving' is both a material right and a precondition that needs to be satisfied in order to rely on this right.[430] At present, it seems as though the Treaty does not grant the freedom of movement, but rather creates an obligation to move before one can rely on its right to move between the Member States.[431] Moreover, it seems as if the classic logic of the internal market in which one can only rely on fundamental freedoms and the principle of non-discrimination if one moves[432] collides with the logic of citizenship.[433]

428 Article 21 TFEU and Directive 2004/38.

429 Verbist, 'De invloed van het Unieburgerschap op zuiver interne situaties' [2011] *RW* 510, 519.

430 Spaventa, 'Seeing the Wood Despite the Trees? On the Scope of Union Citizenship and its Constitutional Effects' (2008) 45 *CMLRev* 13, 15: '[W]hilst the existence of a cross-border link is a precondition that needs to be satisfied in order to bring oneself within the personal scope of those provisions, the right to move is a right conferred upon individuals directly by the Treaty, and in that way it is correctly defined as part of the material scope of the treaty'. In this regard, it has been argued that the equal treatment of Union citizens should precede, irrespective of any transfrontier element. (See inter alia Spaventa, 'Seeing the Wood Despite the Trees? On the Scope of Union Citizenship and its Constitutional Effects' (2008) 45 *CMLRev* 13, 18 referring to Opinion AG Tizzano in ECJ case C-300/04, *Eman and Sevinger*, para 146: 'that persons possessing the nationality of a Member State are citizens of the Union and therefore, in principle and regardless of where they live, enjoy all rights available to such citizens under [Union] law, including naturally those provided for in the second part of the Treaty'.)

431 Dautricourt and Thomas, 'Reverse Discrimination and Free Movement of Persons Under Community Law: All for Ulysses, Nothing for Penelope?' (2009) 34 *ELRev* 454, 448 and Verbist, 'De invloed van het Unieburgerschap op zuiver interne situaties' [2011] *RW* 510, 524.

432 As discussed above, in order to fall within the scope of application of the Treaty provisions on free movement, one should have exercised his or her right of free movement, which implies both a cross-border element and an economic activity. See above nn 155–59.

433 Verbist, 'De invloed van het Unieburgerschap op zuiver interne situaties' [2011] *RW* 510, 524.

2.2.2.2. Causal Link Between the Exercise of Free Movement and the Right Protected by Union Law

186. The second issue concerns the causal link between the exercise of free movement – in order to come within the personal scope of the Treaty provisions, and the restriction to the right of free movement – the material scope of the Treaty provisions. According to AG Tesauro, there should be a link between them. He argued in his Opinion in the *Singh* case that 'the simple exercise of the right of free movement within the [Union] is not in itself sufficient to bring a particular set of circumstances within the scope of [Union] law; there must be some connecting factor between the exercise of the right of free movement and the right relied on by the individual'.[434]

187. The ECJ did not broach this issue in the *Singh* judgment, but it seemed to answer the question affirmatively half a year later in the *Werner* judgment. In this judgment, the Court considered that 'Mr. Werner is a German national who obtained his degrees and professional qualifications in Germany; he has always practiced his profession in Germany and is subject to German tax legislation. The only factor which takes his case out of a purely national context is the fact that he lives in a Member State other than that in which he practices his profession.'[435] The Court ruled that Article 49 TFEU does not preclude a Member State from imposing a heavier tax burden on its own nationals who work in its territory and receive their income there if they do not reside in that Member State.[436] Hence, the fact that he had his residence in the Netherlands was not considered to be a sufficient element to bring the heavier tax burden under the scope of the Treaty provisions on the freedom of establishment.[437]

188. However, in later judgments, the ECJ required a far less rigorous causal link to be established. The fiercely criticised *Carpenter* judgment is an example of this.[438] Mrs Carpenter, a Philippine national who was married to a British national, claimed that her deportation would restrict her husband's right to the free movement of services; that is to say, a significant part of Mr Carpenter's business consisted of providing services. Mr Carpenter sometimes needed to travel to other Member States in order to provide services abroad. During these

---

434 Opinion AG Tesauro 20 May 1992 in C-370/90, *Singh*, para 5. The Advocate General actually agreed with the Commission's remark in this case: 'it is true, as the Commission has correctly pointed out …'

435 ECJ case C-112/91 *Werner* [1993] ECR I-429, para 16.

436 Ibid para 17.

437 See also Tryfonidou, 'In Search of the Aim of the EC Free Movement of Persons Provisions: Has the Court of Justice Missed the Point?' (2009) 46 *CMLRev* 1591, 1593–94.

438 See inter alia Jadoul and Vanneste, 'Casenote on Case C-60/00 Carpenter' (2003) 9 *ColJourEurLaw* 447.

business trips, Mrs Carpenter took care of Mr Carpenter's two children from a previous marriage.

The Court of Justice ruled that Article 56 TFEU, read in the light of the fundamental right to respect for family life, precludes 'a refusal, by the Member State of origin of a provider of services established in that Member State who provides services to recipients established in other Member States, of the right to reside in its territory to that provider's spouse, who is a national of a third country'.[439] Hence, in *Carpenter*, the Court accepted the reasoning that Mr Carpenter, who used to travel to other Member States to provide services, would be restricted in his right to free movement of services if no residence permit was given to his spouse who took care of his children in his absence. However, the link between the exercise of free movement and the right relied upon is disputable. That is to say, it is doubtful whether the absence of Mrs Carpenter would actually deter Mr Carpenter from providing his services abroad.[440]

189. By contrast, in the *Jia* judgment, it seems that no such causal link can be found.[441] Ms Jia, a Chinese national who was financially dependent upon her son and daughter-in-law, claimed a residence permit in Sweden on the basis of Directive 73/148. Her daughter-in-law had German nationality and was self-employed in Sweden. Her son, also a Chinese national, held a residence permit in Sweden as a spouse of a Union citizen. The Swedish authorities rejected Ms Jia's application on the basis of insufficient proof of the situation of financial dependence.

The Court of Justice focused upon the interpretation of a 'dependent family member'. It can only be inferred that the Court implicitly accepted that Ms Jia was a family member of the spouse of a Union citizen who had exercised her right to free movement. The mere fact that her German daughter-in-law was self-employed in Sweden seemed to be sufficient for the ECJ. However, there is no link between the fact that the daughter-in-law exercised her right to free movement and the residence permit claimed by Ms Jia as a family member of a Union citizen. That is to say, the arrival of her mother-in-law from China seems to have had no impact whatsoever upon the exercise of the daughter-in-law's free movement; she was already exercising her right of free movement and she was not deterred from returning to Germany.

190. This evolution, in which the causal link between the exercise of free movement and the right claimed by the individual seems to weaken and even

---

439 ECJ case C-60/00 *Carpenter* [2002] ECR I-6279, para 46.

440 See also Jadoul and Vanneste, 'Casenote on Case C-60/00 Carpenter' (2003) 9 *ColJourEurLaw* 447, 450–53. Instead, it seems as though the ECJ considers it to be a breach on the right of family life, but the Court seems to avoid holding so straight away.

441 ECJ case C-1/05 *Jia* [2007] ECR I-1.

disappear over time, makes the presence of a cross-border element even more decisive.[442] However, at the same time, it becomes easier and easier to establish such a cross-border link, as will be explained in the following subsection. This issue is particularly visible in the area of family reunification and the so-called 'European routes'.[443] In these cases, a cross-border element is created with the sole purpose of falling under the more favourable protection of Union law.

191. The position that the Court of Justice should reintroduce this causal link between the exercise of free movement and the specific right invoked under Union law will be defended here. In the author's opinion, this should not only be required for the Treaty provisions on freedom of movement but also for the Treaty provisions on Union citizenship. Accordingly, it will be argued that a causal link should exist between the connection with Union law – traditionally interpreted as a cross-border element, but recently also as a more abstract connection with Union law – and the right invoked under Union law.

Reintroducing and reinforcing the causal link would result in a more precise dividing line between the scope of application of Union law and that of national law. This would lead to fewer situations in which Union law is beneficial and, accordingly, the possibility that more purely internal situations would be treated more strictly. Nevertheless, this would be easier to accept since the knowledge of why some situations can benefit from the rights under Union law would be more visible and understandable. It would reduce the aura of arbitrariness surrounding the ECJ's purely internal situations doctrine.

2.2.3. *The ECJ's Restrictions Approach*

192. After briefly explaining the ECJ's restrictions approach from the *Dassonville* judgment onwards, this section discusses the risks implied in this approach. The view will be defended here that a more limited interpretation of the restrictions to freedom of movement would provide an answer to the concerns identified.

2.2.3.1. *Dassonville* Case Law in the Area of Free Movement of Goods

193. Article 34 TFEU determines that 'quantitative restrictions on imports and all measures having equivalent effect shall be prohibited between Member

---

442 Nowak, 'Case Note, Case C-34/09, Gerardo Ruiz Zambrano v. Office national de l'emploi (ONEM) & Case C-434/09, Shirley McCarthy v. Secretary of State for the Home Department' (2011) 17 *ColJourEurLaw* 673, 7.

443 See inter alia Vanvoorden, 'Stelt het arrest Jia een einde aan de België route?' (2007) 2 *T Vreemd* 72–84.

States'. However, these restrictions can be justified on the grounds enumerated in Article 36 TFEU, in particular 'on grounds of public morality, public policy or public security; the protection of health and life of humans, animals or plants; the protection of national treasures possessing artistic, historic or archaeological value; or the protection of industrial and commercial property'.

194. Measures having equivalent effect have been given a broad interpretation by the Court of Justice, since its *Dassonville* judgment of 1974 particularly. The case concerned Belgian legislation prohibiting the importing of goods bearing a designation of origin in which these goods are not accompanied by an official document issued by the government of the exporting country. In particular, Mr Dassonville obtained Scotch whisky from France where it was in free circulation without being in possession of a certificate of origin from the British authorities. For Mr Dassonville, it was less easy to obtain this certificate than it was for importers who obtain it directly from the producer country.

The ECJ held that 'all trading rules enacted by Member States which are capable of hindering, directly or indirectly, actually or potentially, intra-[Union] trade are to be considered as measures having an effect equivalent to quantitative restrictions'.[444] Accordingly, the Court ruled that the contested Belgian legislation constituted a measure having an equivalent effect to a quantitative restriction, which is prohibited by the Treaty.[445]

195. It has become settled case law that Article 34 TFEU covers all those national measures which directly or indirectly, actually or potentially hinder the free movement of goods. A case which is often put forward to demonstrate the broad scope of this case law is the *Pistre* case. The case concerned French nationals who were prosecuted for marketing products under the label 'mountain', even though they were not authorised to use this denomination. They contested the French provisions at issue arguing that they were contrary to Article 34 TFEU. By contrast, the French government argued that the situation in the main proceedings did not fall within the scope of Article 34 TFEU, since it concerned French nationals and French products marketed on French territory.

The Court of Justice did not agree with the French government.[446] In particular, after citing the *Dassonville* case law,[447] it held that Article 34 TFEU 'cannot be considered inapplicable simply because all the facts of the specific case before the national court are confined to a single Member State'.[448] The Court considered that in a situation in which all the facts are confined to one Member State, the national measure may nevertheless also have effects on

444 ECJ case 8/74 *Dassonville* [1974] ECR I-837, para 5.
445 Ibid para 9.
446 ECJ joined cases C-321/94, C-322/94, C-323/94 and C-324/94 *Pistre* [1997] ECR I-2343, para 42.
447 Ibid para 43.
448 Ibid para 44.

the free movement of goods between Member States, 'in particular when the measure in question facilitates the marketing of goods of domestic origin to the detriment of imported goods'.[449] The Court held that 'in such circumstances, the application of the measure, even if restricted to domestic producers, in itself creates and maintains a difference of treatment between those two categories of goods, hindering, at least potentially, intra-[Union] trade'.[450]

196. This line of case law clearly has a considerable impact on national policy making because this broad definition of measures having equivalent effect 'takes in a complete range of legislative and administrative measures which are applicable without distinction to domestic and imported products, yet have a – sometimes minimal – effect on potential sales of imported products and hence on the free movement of goods'.[451] However, in the *Cassis de Dijon* judgment, the Court took into consideration public policy objectives other than those enumerated in Article 36 TFEU.[452] This case is known as 'the rule of reason' which can be an exception to the *Dassonville* case law of measures having an equivalent effect.[453] That is to say, if a Member State can demonstrate that its national measure that restricts trade also protects legitimate interests in a reasonable way, the measure is considered to be compatible with Article 34 TFEU.[454]

2.2.3.2. Extension of Restrictions Approach to Free Movement of Workers, Services and Establishment and to Union Citizenship

197. The ECJ's *Dassonville* case law, also known as the ECJ's restrictions approach,[455] has been extended to the other areas of free movement.[456]

---

449 Ibid para 45.

450 Ibid. However, it is strange that the ECJ uses the terms 'discriminates' and 'discriminatory in character' in its subsequent considerations, since its earlier considerations use the terminology of the restrictions approach (ibid paras 49 and 52 respectively).

451 Lenaerts and Van Nuffel, *European Union Law*, Sweet & Maxwell 2011, p 215. In the above-discussed *Guimont* judgment, the ECJ recognised that a rule such as that at issue in the main proceedings, which applies, according to its wording, without distinction to national and imported products and imposes marketing conditions, falls under Article 34 TFEU 'only in so far as it applies to situations that are linked to the importation of goods in intra-[Union] trade' (para 21). See above nn 139–41.

452 In particular the protection of consumers against unfair practices, but the Court considered that this could also be done by providing information on the packaging of products. See ECJ case 120/78 *Rewe* [known as *Cassis de Dijon*] [1979] ECR I-649, paras 8–13 (in particular 12 and 13).

453 See Craig and de Burca, *EU Law. Text, Cases, and Materials*, 6th ed, Oxford University Press 2015, pp 674–81.

454 See Lenaerts and Van Nuffel, *European Union Law*, Sweet & Maxwell 2011, p 218.

455 Barnard, *The Substantive Law of the EU: The Four Freedoms*, Oxford University Press 2013, p 463.

456 See inter alia Lenaerts and Van Nuffel, *European Union Law*, Sweet & Maxwell 2011, pp 245–47 and Daniele, 'Non-discriminatory Restrictions to the Free Movement of Persons' (1997) 22 *ELRev* 191, 192.

Although the wording of the Treaty provisions on free movement of workers and services seems to refer only to the prohibition on discriminatory measures,[457] the Court of Justice held that also non-discriminatory, but nonetheless restrictive rules infringe the free movement of workers, services and establishment.

198. The first extension of the *Dassonville* case law concerned the free movement of services, in particular in the *Säger* judgment.[458] The case concerned German legislation that reserved the activities of monitoring patents and renewing them by payment of fees on behalf of the patent-owners to lawyers and patent consultants. A firm that legally carried out these services in the UK would be prevented from carrying out the same activities in Germany because it did not satisfy the qualification required by German law.

In its judgment, the ECJ held that Article 56 TFEU 'requires not only the elimination of all discrimination against a person providing services on the ground of his nationality but also the abolition of any restriction, even if it applies without distinction to national providers of services and to those of other Member States, when it is liable to prohibit or otherwise impede the activities of a provider of services established in another Member State where he lawfully provides similar services'.[459] Here, the Court formulated its restrictions approach alongside its discrimination approach in a very clear-cut manner. Subsequently, the Court justified its restrictions approach by emphasising that a Member State may not 'deprive of all practical effectiveness' the freedom to provide services.[460] In other words, the Court made explicit that its restrictions approach is based on the '*effet utile*' argument of Union law.

Accordingly, the Court ruled that the contested legislation constituted a restriction to the freedom to provide services.[461] However, it subsequently examined whether the German legislation could be justified by 'imperative reasons relating to the public interest and which apply to all persons or undertakings pursuing an activity in the State of destination'.[462] Although the Court recognised that the aim of the protection of patent holders from legal advice from non-qualified persons is a public interest, it considered the contested legislation to be disproportionate.[463]

---

457 Article 45(2) TFEU determines that 'such freedom of movement shall entail *the abolition of any discrimination based on nationality* between workers of the Member States as regards employment, remuneration and other conditions of work and employment' (emphasis added). Article 57 TFEU determines that 'the person providing a service may, in order to do so, temporarily pursue his activity in the Member State where the service is provided, *under the same conditions* as are imposed by that State on its own nationals' (emphasis added).

458 ECJ case C-76/90 *Säger* [1991] ECR I-4221. Confirmed in several other judgments, for instance in ECJ case C-384/93 *Alpine Investments* [1995] ECR I-1141, paras 35–39.

459 ECJ case C-76/90 *Säger* [1991] ECR I-4221, para 12.

460 Ibid para 13.

461 Ibid para 14.

462 Ibid para 15.

463 Ibid paras 16–20.

199. In the *Kraus* judgment, the ECJ aligned its interpretation of the Treaty provisions on workers and establishment with its interpretation of the Treaty provisions on goods and services.[464] Mr Kraus, a German national, studied law in Germany and passed the first State examination. Subsequently, he obtained an LL.M. in the UK. Back in Germany, the national authorities required an administrative authorisation for using the UK-acquired academic title in Germany – whereas no such authorisation was required for the use of a diploma awarded by a German establishment.

Regarding the scope of application of Union law, the Court ruled that Mr Kraus was vis-à-vis his Member State of origin in a situation which may be assimilated to that of any other person enjoying the rights and liberties guaranteed by the Treaty.[465] Next, the Court considered that although the use of a postgraduate academic title in other Member States remains, in principle, a competence of the Member States since it has not been harmonised, Union law nevertheless sets limits upon the exercise of these competences.[466] In particular, the Court considered that Articles 45 and 49 TFEU 'preclude any national measure governing the conditions under which an academic title obtained in another Member State may be used, where that measure, even though it is applicable without discrimination on grounds of nationality, is liable to hamper or to render less attractive the exercise [of fundamental freedoms by Union] nationals, including those of the Member State which enacted the measure'.[467] However, such a measure can be justified if it pursues a reason of public interest and does not go beyond what is necessary for that purpose.[468]

The protection of the public against the abuse of academic titles was considered to be a legitimate interest to justifying a restriction.[469] Still, the Court emphasised that the procedure for administrative authorisations prior to using postgraduate academic titles obtained abroad had to fulfil certain conditions in order to be proportionate.[470]

200. Finally, the restrictions approach, which has been developed in the domain of free movement, has also been extended to the domain of Union citizenship. Accordingly, Union citizenship becomes 'a source of enforceable rights independent from the prohibition of discrimination on grounds of nationality, and giving protection against any unjustified restriction of free movement and residence'.[471]

---

[464] ECJ case C-19/92 *Kraus* [1993] ECR I-1663. As regards the free movement of workers, see inter alia also ECJ case C-415/93 *Bosman* [1995] ECR I-4921 and as regards the free movement of establishment, see inter alia also ECJ case C-55/94 *Gebhard* [1995] ECR I-4165.

[465] ECJ case C-19/92 *Kraus* [1993] ECR I-1663, paras 15–16.

[466] Ibid paras 27–28.

[467] Ibid para 32.

[468] Ibid.

[469] Ibid paras 33–36.

[470] Ibid paras 37–42.

[471] Comments, 'Two-speed European Citizenship? Can the Lisbon Treaty Help Close the Gap?' (2008) 45 *CMLRev* 1, 1.

201. An extension of the scope of application of the Treaty provisions on Union citizenship to non-discriminatory restrictions was first launched by AG Jacobs in the *Pusa* case. The case concerned Mr Pusa, a Finnish national residing in Spain. He received a Finnish invalidity pension and had outstanding debts in Finland. Consequently, on the basis of Finnish legislation, one third of Mr Pusa's pension was withheld for payment to the creditor. The amount which was withheld was calculated on the basis of Mr Pusa's gross, not net, pension, hence, it did not take into account the fact that Mr Pusa also paid 19 per cent tax in Spain. According to the Finnish authorities ruling on the case, this might conflict with the right of a citizen of the EU to move and to reside freely on the territory of the Member States as guaranteed. Therefore, it referred a question for a preliminary ruling to the Court of Justice.

202. In his Opinion, AG Jacobs argued that discrimination on the grounds of nationality is not necessary for the application of Article 21 TFEU.[472] In particular, he pointed out that it is not crucial to demonstrate that a national provision disadvantages nationals of other Member States more than its own nationals.[473] The Advocate General argued that the freedom of movement originally concerned workers, but 'has been extended and is now conferred by article [21 TFEU] on all citizens of the European Union'.[474] Moreover, Jacobs emphasised that originally, the freedom of movement was assured by a prohibition against discrimination on the grounds of nationality, but that it has been extended by a prohibition on non-discriminatory restrictions.[475] Next, the Advocate General pointed out that Article 18 TFEU determines that 'every citizen of the Union shall have the right to move and reside freely within the territory of the Member States, subject to the limitations and conditions laid down in the Treaties and by the measures adopted to give them effect'. He emphasised that the rights granted by Article 21 TFEU are not limited to a prohibition of discrimination.[476] Accordingly, AG Jacobs concluded that the right of a Union citizen to enter, reside in or leave a Member State can only be guaranteed if all measures which impose an unjustified restriction on those exercising it are abolished – then it is irrelevant whether or not nationals of other Member States are in a less favourable position than their own nationals.[477]

203. In its judgment in *Pusa*, the Court of Justice seemed to use the wording of its case law on returning citizens, rather than the wording which had been proposed by its Advocate General. That is to say, the Court considered in *Pusa*

472 Opinion AG Jacobs 20 November 2003 in C-224/02, *Pusa*, para 18.

473 Ibid.

474 Ibid para 19.

475 Ibid para 20, referring to ECJ case C-415/93 *Bosman* [1995] ECR I-4921, paras 103 and 104 of the judgment and ECJ case C-190/98 *Graf* [2000] ECR I-493, para 18.

476 Opinion AG Jacobs 20 November 2003 in C-224/02, *Pusa*, para 20.

477 Ibid paras 21–22.

that the freedom to move and to reside within the territory of the Member States 'could not be fully effective if a national of a Member State could be deterred from availing himself of them by obstacles raised to his residence in the host Member State by legislation of his State of origin penalising the fact that he has used them'.[478] Nowhere in the judgment is the term 'restriction' used. However, two years later, in particular in *Tas-Hagen*, the Court seemed to have adopted the restrictions approach in cases regarding Union citizenship.

204. The case concerned Mrs Tas-Hagen, who was born in the Dutch East Indies and who came to the Netherlands when she was 11 years old. She acquired Dutch nationality and after becoming incapable of working, she moved to Spain. She then applied for a benefit granted to civilian war victims, but her application was rejected on the grounds that she was not a resident in the Netherlands at the moment of submitting her application. Mrs Tas-Hagen challenged this decision and the Dutch authorities referred a question for preliminary ruling to the Court of Justice.

The Court of Justice held that Article 21 TFEU 'cannot be fully effective if a national of a Member State can be deterred from availing himself of them by obstacles raised to his residence in the host Member State by legislation of his State of origin penalising the fact that he has used them'.[479] Immediately afterwards, the Court considered that 'national legislation which places at a disadvantage certain of the nationals of the Member State concerned simply because they have exercised their freedom to move and to reside in another Member State is a restriction on the freedoms conferred by Article [21 TFEU] on every citizen of the Union'.[480]

Next, the Court examined whether the restriction could be justified. Although it considered that the aim of solidarity is an objective consideration of public interest, it held that the national legislation failed to comply with the principle of proportionality.[481] Accordingly, the Court ruled that the condition of residence in the national legislation is precluded by Article 21 TFEU.[482]

205. The Court confirmed its restrictions approach in subsequent case law on Union citizenship. In the *Morgan* case, in particular, the Court used the term 'unjustified restriction' for the first time.[483] In its subsequent case law, the Court

---

478 ECJ case C-224/02 *Pusa* [2004] ECR I-5763, para 19, referring to ECJ case C-224/98 *D'Hoop* [2002] ECR I-6191, para 31: 'Those opportunities could not be fully effective if a national of a Member State could be deterred from availing himself of them by obstacles raised on his return to his country of origin by legislation penalising the fact that he has used them (see, to that effect, Case C-370/90 Singh [1992] ECR I-4265, paragraph 23)'. Indeed, referring to the *Singh* judgment.

479 ECJ case C-192/05 *Tas-Hagen* [2006] ECR I-10451, para 30.

480 Ibid para 31.

481 Ibid paras 32–39.

482 Ibid para 40.

483 ECJ joined cases C-11/06 and C-12/06 *Morgan* [2007] ECR I-9161, para 28.

of Justice emphasised the assessment of proportionality.[484] This implies a case-by-case approach that insists upon the personal circumstances of the individual.[485] For instance in *Nerkowska*, the Court considered the residence requirement for a disability pension to be disproportionate: the fact that Ms Nerkowska had a Polish nationality and had lived in Poland for more than 20 years, during which she studied and worked, was sufficient to establish a connection between Poland and the recipient of the benefit, Ms Nerkowska.

2.2.3.3. Risks Implied in the Restrictions Approach – Confining the Concept of Restriction

206. Whereas only discriminatory national measures could be reviewed in the light of the Treaty provisions on freedom of movement previously, the ECJ considerably extended its supervisory power with the restrictions approach since the latter allows all measures which restrict intra-Union trade, even only indirectly and potentially, to be prohibited on the basis of an extensive interpretation of Article 34 TFEU. The significant impact on national regulatory autonomy by the *Dassonville* case law is precisely the reason why it is appropriate to discuss this case law.

207. In particular, the risk exists that the restrictions approach undermines legitimate national measures.[486] First, the restrictions approach is not subject to a minimum threshold; it is sufficient that a restriction is at stake, even if it is only minor.[487] Moreover, the meaning of the term 'restriction', or of 'obstacle' or 'hindrance' or 'impediment', is unclear. It can be understood in a very narrow or in a very broad sense.[488] The ECJ seems to choose the latter option; a judgment such as *Carpenter*[489] comes close to considering the mere existence of a national rule to be a restriction to free movement.[490]

---

484 Barnard, *The Substantive Law of the EU: The Four Freedoms*, Oxford University Press 2013, p 464.

485 Ibid pp 464–65.

486 Barnard, 'Restricting Restrictions: Lessons for the EU from the US?' (2009) 68 *CLJ* 575, 605.

487 See eg ECJ case C-49/89 *Corsica Ferries* [1989] ECR 4441, para 8: 'As the Court has decided on various occasions, the articles of the EEC Treaty concerning the free movement of goods, persons, services and capital are fundamental Community provisions and any restriction, even minor, of that freedom is prohibited'.

See also Barnard, *The Substantive Law of the EU: The Four Freedoms*, Oxford University Press 2013, p 265.

488 Spaventa distinguished three possible interpretations of restrictions to freedom of movement in Spaventa, 'From Gebhard to Carpenter: Towards a (Non-)economic European Constitution' (2004) 41 *CMLRev* 743, 757–59.

489 Above n 188.

490 Barnard, *The Substantive Law of the EU: The Four Freedoms*, Oxford University Press 2013, p 265. See also Barnard, 'Restricting Restrictions: Lessons for the EU from the US?' (2009) 68 *CLJ* 575, 593–94 referring to ECJ case C-98/01 *BAA* [2003] ECR I-4641.

208. In order to reduce the risk of undermining lawful national policy and legislation, it is suggested that the ECJ should introduce a specification, in a confining sense, of the concept of restriction. In this regard, we will discuss AG Tizzano's proposal in his Opinion in *Caixa Bank*[491] to adopt a non-discrimination approach together with a direct market access approach and Barnard's proposal that non-discriminatory national rules should benefit from a presumption of legality.[492]

209. In his Opinion in *Caixa Bank*, AG Tizzano thoroughly analysed the concept of restriction on the freedom of establishment. He started with the observation that 'the case-law of the Court on the freedom of establishment and, more generally, the freedom of movement of persons economically active in the internal market is not without ambiguity and therefore lends itself, as in this case, to different and even conflicting interpretations'.[493] Accordingly, the Advocate General examined that case law.

Since the *Kraus* judgment, the Court held that non-discriminatory national rules can also constitute a restriction to the freedom of movement of workers and establishment.[494] In particular, the national measure can already constitute a restriction 'by reason of its potential adverse repercussions on the *economic attractiveness of pursuing* certain occupations'.[495] According to the Advocate General, this test has been deemed necessary by the factual circumstances of the specific case involved.[496] Applying this in general would lead to a situation in which 'the State that enforces the most severe legislation automatically creates an impediment to the freedom of establishment of persons from other Member States'.[497]

However, in various other judgments, as in *Alpine Investments*, for instance, the Court only classified as prohibited restrictions on the freedom of movement for persons those measures 'that directly impede the taking-up of an economic activity or are by nature substantially discriminatory because they do not ensure equal conditions both in law and in fact as regards the taking-up and pursuit of an economic activity'.[498] In particular, in *Alpine Investments*, the Court held that

---

491 Opinion AG Tizzano 25 December 2004 in C-442/02, *Caixa Bank*.

492 Barnard, 'Restricting Restrictions: Lessons for the EU from the US?' (2009) 68 *CLJ* 575.

493 Opinion AG Tizzano 25 December 2004 in C-442/02, *Caixa Bank*, para 29.

494 Ibid para 33.

495 Ibid para 35, referring to ECJ case C-19/92 *Kraus* [1993] ECR I-1663, paras 21–22.

496 Opinion AG Tizzano 25 December 2004 in C-442/02 *Caixa Bank*, para 36. He argues that this can also be said for C-55/94 *Gebhard*, C-108/96 *Mac Quen* and C-79/01 *Payroll Data Services* (para 38).

497 Opinion AG Tizzano 25 December 2004 in C-442/02 *Caixa Bank*, para 45.

498 Ibid paras 47–48, also referring to C-177/94 *Perfili*, C-250/94 *Futura Participations* and joined cases C-397/98 and C-410/98 *Metallgeschellschaft*.

the national measure 'directly affect[ed] access to the market in services in the other Member State' and was hence 'capable of hindering intra-[Union] trade in services'.[499]

210. Against this background, AG Tizzano argued that considering a national measure which regulates the pursuit of an economic activity without directly affecting access to that activity and without discriminating between national and foreign operators to be a restriction incompatible with the Treaty because they reduce the economic attractiveness of that activity, contradicts both the system of powers set out in the Treaty as well as the purpose of the Treaty to create an internal market.[500] First, if no harmonisation has taken place on the basis of Article 53 TFEU, the Member States remain competent in regulating the pursuit of economic activities; the Union has no general power to regulate economic activities.[501] Secondly, it would lead to 'a market without rules ... except for those ... meeting imperative requirements in the public interest' because economic operators could fight each national measure regulating an economic activity.[502] Accordingly, AG Tizzano suggested that 'where the principle of non-discrimination is respected – and hence the conditions for the taking-up and pursuit of an economic activity are equal both in law and in fact – a national measure cannot be described as a restriction on the freedom of movement of persons unless, in the light of its purpose and effects, the measure in question directly affects market access'.[503]

211. As the Advocate General has pointed out, this interpretation has several advantages. First of all, it reconciles 'the objective of merging the different national markets into a single common market with the continuation of Member States' general powers to regulate economic activities'.[504] Moreover, it can be fitted into the existing case law on restrictions, with the *Alpine Investments* and *Graf* cases for instance.[505] Furthermore, it does not conflict with the *Kraus* line of cases according to the Advocate General.[506] In particular, AG Tizzano argued that the proposed interpretation 'merely specifies the scope of the concept of restriction propounded in those judgments, without calling the spirit of that

---

499 Opinion AG Tizzano 25 December 2004 in C-442/02, *Caixa Bank*, para 52, citing ECJ case C-384/93 *Alpine Investments* [1995] ECR I-1141, para 38. The Advocate General also referred in this regard to ECJ case C-415/93 *Bosman* [1995] ECR I-4921; ECJ case C-418/93 *Semeraro* [ECR] 1996 I-2975; ECJ case C-67/98 *Zenatti* [ECR] 1999 I-7289; ECJ case C-190/98 *Graf* [ECR] 2000 I-1287.

500 Opinion AG Tizzano 25 December 2004 in C-442/02 *Caixa Bank*, paras 58–63.

501 Ibid paras 59–61.

502 Ibid paras 62–63.

503 Ibid para 66.

504 Ibid para 68.

505 Ibid paras 70–73. Moreover, it would establish a test similar as the one in joined cases C-267/91 and C-268/91 *Keck and Mithouard* regarding the free movement of goods.

506 Opinion AG Tizzano 25 December 2004 in C-442/02, *Caixa Bank*, para 74.

concept into question. The tightening-up that I have proposed … is aimed solely at ensuring that too vague a formulation of that concept does not give rise to distorted readings of the freedom of movement of persons that lead to measures being classified as restrictions whose effects on the exercise of that freedom are merely hypothetical or entirely uncertain and indirect'.[507]

However, an important objection is that the notion 'market access' is not as straightforward as it might appear at first glance.[508] Accordingly, further clarification of the notion of something directly affecting market access is required.

212. Including AG Tizzano's proposal, Barnard further refines a narrower conception of restrictions to freedom of movement within the EU. Barnard starts with the example that, on the basis of the ECJ's current restrictions approach, BMW could challenge the 70mph speed limit on British motorways as comprising a restriction to the free movement of goods. The ECJ may find that the UK rules are restrictions to the freedom of movement and then the UK would have to justify the 70mph speed limit. Obviously, the UK could do so on the basis of road safety, but Barnard points out that the problem lies with proportionality. This example immediately illustrates that almost every national measure can be challenged as being a restriction to the freedom of movement within the EU, because almost every national measure has some effect upon intra-Union trade, even though this effect is often unintended and unforeseen at the moment of the national measure's creation. The question arises as to whether this economic perspective is always preferable. What if the national measures actually aim to protect social interests?[509]

213. Barnard argues that the ECJ's 'market access' or 'restrictions' approach, as applied at present, 'threatens to undermine legitimate national regulation and … recourse to the justification/proportionality formula is insufficiently sensitive to

---

507 Ibid para 75.

508 See more in Craig and de Burca, *EU Law. Text, Cases, and Materials*, 6th ed, Oxford University Press 2015, pp 692–95 and Snell, 'The Notion of Market Access: A Concept or a Slogan?' (2010) 47 *CMLRev* 437, 437–72.

509 See inter alia Craig who identifies 'the substantive imbalance issue' as being another one of the different features of the 'democratic deficit' in the EU. In particular, the priority of the economic over and above the social in the EU has been criticised (Craig, 'Integration, democracy and legitimacy' in Craig and De Burca (eds), *The Evolution of EU Law*, 2nd ed, Oxford University Press 2011, p 31, referring to Caporaso, 'The European Union and Forms of State: Westphalian, Regulatory or Post-modern' (1996) 34 *JCMS* 29, 48 and Scharpf, 'Economic Integration, Democracy and the Welfare State' (1997) 4 *JEPP* 18). See also Kelemen who observes that 'critics argue that the European Union undermines democracy because it shifts decision making further from the citizen and because it eliminates many national social rights and policies in the name of the free market' (Kelemen, *Eurolegalism. The Transformation of Law and Regulation in the EU*, Harvard University Press 2011, p 250).

local needs'.[510] She draws upon the US Supreme Court's approach to the 'dormant commerce clause' in order to propose a restrictive conception of restriction to freedom of movement within the EU.

214. Article 1, section 8, clause 3 of the US Constitution contains the so-called commerce clause and determines that 'the Congress shall have power ... to regulate commerce with foreign Nations, and among the several States'. This clause only gives the federal government the power to legislate with respect to commerce, but it does not prohibit restrictions on inter-state commerce. However, the Supreme Court has limited the State's competences in the context of inter-state commerce.[511] Under the so-called dormant commerce clause, the US Supreme Court analyses discriminatory state measures differently than non-discriminatory state measures. In particular, with respect to the non-discriminatory rules of the state, the Supreme Court set out a 'balancing approach' in *Pike v Bruce Church*.[512] Barnard admits that much uncertainty exists about the precise meaning of the *Pike* test, but this does not preclude us from drawing upon two aspects of it in order to argue '(1) that non-discriminatory ... rules which have only an incidental effect on free movement should also benefit from a presumption of legality; and (2) those that do have a substantial effect on free movement should be subject to a more genuine balancing'.[513]

215. Barnard describes how the ECJ should proceed in restricting its interpretation of non-discriminatory restrictions to the freedom of movement in detail.[514] First, she proposes that we presume that non-discriminatory national rules are legitimate. However, it would be possible to rebut this presumption by demonstrating that the national measure considerably impede access to the market. In particular, Barnard argues that 'the burden of proof for claimants would be a stiff one: their case would have to be more than simply that the host state rules are different ... and make life more expensive for the claimant than if they had not migrated'.[515] At this point, she includes AG Tizzano's proposal suggesting that 'the test for this might be that the national rules directly and substantially hinder market access: *i.e.* the national rules directly affects the claimants' ability to engage in their *specific economic activity* in the host state'.[516] Returning to the example of the British speed limit, she argues that BMW would not pass the test of direct and substantial hindrace to market access in its specific economic activity.

---

510 Barnard, 'Restricting Restrictions: Lessons for the EU from the US?' (2009) 68 *CLJ* 575, 605.
511 Tribe, *American Constitutional Law*, 3rd ed, Foundation Press 2000, p 1029.
512 *Pike v Bruce Church Inc.* 397 US 137 (1970).
513 Barnard, 'Restricting Restrictions: Lessons for the EU from the US?' (2009) 68 *CLJ* 575, 590.
514 Ibid 604–06. 515 Ibid 604. 516 Ibid.

216. Barnard proceeds by claiming that only if the claimants can show that their market access has been directly and substantially impeded, can the Treaty be engaged. Then the burden of proof shifts to the defendant State to justify the national rules. At this point, Barnard emphasises the need for 'a more nuanced approach to justification based on a true balance of competing interests'.[517] She argues that the national measure should only be considered to be incompatible with the Treaty provisions on freedom of movement if the justification is superficial or if the restrictive effects are excessive.

217. Finally, we can compare and evaluate AG Tizzano's and Barnard's proposals in the light of the criteria introduced above: legal certainty, the vertical division of powers between the EU and the Member States and a broader perspective than a purely economic one. Admittedly, the proposals to interpret restrictions in a more confining way are no easy exercise for which the outcome in particular cases might be predicted with certainty. However, legal certainty is not the only criterion that matters and the proposals have clear benefits in the light of criteria of the vertical division of competences between the EU and the Member States and the importance of other interests than purely economic ones.

218. Obviously, a more confining interpretation of restrictions to freedom of movement leaves more room for the regulatory autonomy of the Member States. It reduces the risk that valid national measures will become undermined on the basis of an all too extensive interpretation of the Treaty provisions on freedom of movement. Undermining legitimate national policy and legislation cannot have been the intention of the Treaty drafters and the Treaty provisions should not be used for a purpose for which they were not intended.[518]

219. Very important in Barnard's proposal especially is the genuine act of balancing competing interests. In particular, it leaves room for considerations and interests which are not purely economic in kind. As Barnard argues: 'the proposed approach ... recognises that there remain benefits, even in a single market, to maintaining a market with some national rules, particularly those which serve a social purpose. ... If the interpretation of the four freedoms leads to a reduction in the standard of living, due to the deregulatory effect of a blanket application of the restrictions approach, this is clearly not a result that the Treaty

517 Ibid.

518 See also Opinion AG Tizzano 25 December 2004 in C-442/02, *Caixa Bank*, paras 62–63 and Opinion AG Tesauro 27 October 1993 in C-292/92, *Hünermund*, para 1, questioning whether 'Article [34 TFEU is] a provision intended to liberalize intra-[Union] trade or is it intended more generally to encourage the unhindered pursuit of commerce in individual Member States?' AG Tesauro defended the first interpretation and this author could not agree more.

drafters envisaged. It is also an approach which also [sic] risks alienating EU citizens'.[519] This corresponds to the presumption that has been rebutted above that fewer requirements at Union level would lead to a better treatment of the Union citizen. In particular, it has been argued that fewer requirements, in order to benefit from a right on the basis of Union law, do not necessarily lead to a more favourable treatment of the Union citizens involved, or at least not for everybody involved. Stricter rules may actually lead to a better protection of citizens, socially for instance.

2.2.4. Stretching the Notion of Movement

220. After a rather long introduction spent (1) discussing the criteria with which to evaluate the ECJ's case law, (2) emphasising the need for precise indications on how much movement is required and for the (re)introduction of causal links and (3) analysing the ECJ's restrictions case law, we will now turn to the section's main subject; namely, the ECJ's generous interpretation of a sufficient connection with Union law. This subsection examines how much movement is required in order to invoke a certain right under Union law. The ECJ has challenged the limits of the interpretation of the traditional cross-border element.

221. First, we will discuss the ECJ's case law on so-called 'returning citizens'. Secondly, the question of whether mere residence in another Member State is sufficient in order to invoke a certain right under Union law will be examined. Thirdly, the section will analyse situations in which a Union citizen has exercised his right to free movement, without actually moving his residence to another Member State. In particular, the active and passive provision of services and the free movement of workers will be discussed.

222. In this subsection, emphasis will be placed on the need for limits on the interpretation of a sufficient connection with Union law. There will be particular emphasis on the need to assess the presence of a causal link between the cross-border element, which is the connection with Union law, and the specific right claimed on the basis of Union law. Reintroducing and reinforcing the causal link would result in a more precise dividing line between the scope of application of Union law and that of national law.

---

519 Barnard, 'Restricting Restrictions: Lessons for the EU from the US?' (2009) 68 *CLJ* 575, 606. Barnard repeatedly referred to the *Laval* (C-341/05) and *Viking* (C-438/05) cases in order to illustrate the importance of social interests (ibid eg 576 and 605).

2.2.4.1. 'Returning Citizens': Moving Back to Home Member State after Residing and Working in Another Member State

223. The idea that a Member State's national who has made use of his right of free movement cannot be disadvantaged afterwards by his own Member State has in fact been considered by the ECJ since the beginning of its case law regarding purely internal situations. That is to say, in *Knoors*[520] the Court ruled that Article 45 TFEU[521] applies to a Member State's own nationals when they have lawfully resided on the territory of another Member State where they have obtained a trade qualification which is recognised by Union law, since they are *'with regard to their Member state of origin in a situation which is similar to that of other persons enjoying the rights and liberties guaranteed by the Treaty'*.[522] In other words, the ECJ does not only interpret 'moving' as going to another Member State, but also as moving back to one's own Member State.

224. In the early nineties, this idea took on a new dimension in the area of family reunification. For the first time, in the *Singh* judgment, the ECJ ruled that the situation of a national of a Member State coming back to his Member State of origin with his family is to be equated with the situation of a national of a Member State going to another Member State in which he can be joined by his family members on the basis of Union law. The concept of 'returning citizen' is often used in this context.

225. However, an important difference can be noted between the early case law and the case law in the area of family reunification. For instance, in *Knoors* there was a direct link between the exercise of free movement and the right claimed under Union law. That is to say, Knoors was a Dutch national who had been working in Belgium as a plumbing contractor. Back in the Netherlands, however, the Dutch authorities refused his application to carry out the same trade in the Netherlands because he did not possess the necessary qualifications according to the Dutch legislation. The causal link between the exercise of free movement and the protection claimed under Union law is obvious in this case.[523]

By contrast, in cases of family reunification, the causal link between the exercise of free movement and the right to family reunification in the Member State of origin is less obvious and sometimes even seems to be lacking – where the Union citizen moves to another Member State with the sole aim of falling within the scope of the Union provisions on family reunification. Not surprisingly, the

---

520 See above Chapter 2.

521 Then Article 52 EEC Treaty.

522 ECJ case 115/78 *Knoors* [1979] ECR I-399, para 24, emphasis added.

523 See also ECJ case C-19/92 *Kraus* [1993] ECR I-1663. See above n 199.

intervening governments in these cases have questioned the risk of abuse of Union law.

i. First Cases on Returning Citizens: *Singh* and *Eind*

226. The first case concerned Mr Sing, an Indian national, who married a British national in the UK in 1982. From 1983 to 1985 Mr and Mrs Singh were employed in Germany. When they returned to the UK to open a business, Mr Singh was granted limited leave to remain in the UK as the husband of a British national. However, in 1987 he divorced from Mrs Singh and, therefore, the British authorities ended his leave to remain. In the proceedings against the deportation order, the national judge referred the question to the Court of Justice as to whether Article 49 TFEU and Directive 2004/38[524] oblige a Member State to give a residence permit to the spouse of an own national who, after going with that spouse to another Member State in order to work there, returns to his own Member State to establish him or herself.

227. As a preliminary remark, the Court of Justice observed that there were no indications that Mr and Mrs Singh arranged a marriage of convenience. Moreover, the fact that they divorced was not relevant for the question submitted, since the latter concerned Mr Singh's right of residence before the divorce.[525] Subsequently, the ECJ considered that a national of a Member State would be deterred from leaving his country of origin to pursue an economic activity in another Member State if, upon returning to his own Member State, his spouse and children were not also permitted to stay in his Member State of origin.[526] Therefore, a national of a Member State who has exercised his right to free movement and who then returns to his Member State of origin, has the right under Article 49 TFEU to be accompanied in his Member State of origin by his spouse, under conditions at least equivalent to those granted to him under Union law in another Member State.[527]

228. Moreover, it should be pointed out that the UK made the risk of fraud explicit in this case. In this regard, the ECJ only noted that 'the facilities created by the Treaty cannot have the effect of allowing the persons who benefit from them to evade the application of national legislation and of prohibiting Member States from taking the measures necessary to prevent such abuse'.[528]

---

524 Then respectively Article 52 TEEC and Directive 73/148/EEC.

525 ECJ case C-370/90 *Singh* [1992] ECR I-4265, para 12.

526 Ibid paras 19–20.

527 Ibid paras 21, 23 and 25.

528 Ibid para 24, referring inter alia to ECJ case 115/78 *Knoors* [1979] ECR I-399, para 25: 'it is not possible to disregard the legitimate interest which a Member State may have in preventing certain of its nationals, by means of facilities created under the Treaty, from attempting wrongly to evade the application of their national legislation as regards training for a trade'.

However, in the *Akrich* judgment, the ECJ considered the question of abuse more extensively. The Court held that the motives which may have prompted a national to seek employment in another Member State are not relevant; only the presence of an effective and genuine economic activity in another Member State is.[529] On the other hand, the Court held that if Union law is used in the context of a marriage of convenience, in order to circumvent national rules on residence of third country nationals, that this would be an abuse of Union law.[530]

These viewpoints in the ECJ's case law were later adopted in Directive 2004/38. In particular, Article 35 provides that: 'Member States may adopt the necessary measures to refuse, terminate or withdraw any right conferred by this Directive in the case of abuse of rights or fraud, such as marriages of convenience'.[531]

229. Thus, since the *Singh* judgment, the Court of Justice equates the situation of a national of a Member State going to another Member State with his family to the situation of a national of a Member State coming back to his Member State of origin with his family.[532] The Court grounds this in the presumption that a national of a Member State would be deterred from leaving his home Member State to exercise his rights of free movement if, upon returning to his own Member State, his family would not be permitted to stay in his home Member State. This is the so-called 'chilling effect'.[533]

Moreover, it should be noted that the Court of Justice decided this case on the basis of the freedom of establishment.[534] However, the idea of Union citizenship is clearly present in this judgment. This can be explained by the judgment's timing, July 1992. That is to say, at that moment, the Treaty of Maastricht, introducing the concept of Union citizenship, had already been signed (7 February 1992), but it had not yet entered into force (1 November 1993).

230. In the *Eind* judgment, the idea of Union citizenship was even more evident. The case concerned Mr Eind, a Dutch national who came to the UK to be economically active here. He was joined by his daughter who arrived directly

529 ECJ case C-109/01 *Akrich* [2003] ECR I-9607, para 55.

530 Ibid para 57.

531 See also para 28 of the preamble: 'To guard against abuse of rights or fraud, notably marriages of convenience or any other form of relationships contracted for the sole purpose of enjoying the right of free movement and residence, Member States should have the possibility to adopt the necessary measures'.

532 See inter alia Nowak, 'Case Note, Case C-34/09, Gerardo Ruiz Zambrano v. Office national de l'emploi (ONEM) & Case C-434/09, Shirley McCarthy v. Secretary of State for the Home Department' (2011) 17 *ColJourEurLaw* 673, 5 and Opinion AG Sir Gordon Slynn 6 October 1982 in 35/82 and 36/82 *Morson and Jhanjan.*

533 See inter alia Joined Opinion AG Sharpston 12 December 2013 in C-456/12 and C-457/12, *O and B* and *S and G*, para 94.

534 Article 49 TFEU and Directive 73/148. The Court also mentioned the freedom of movement for workers several times (Article 45 TFEU).

from Suriname. Mr Eind was no longer economically active when they went to the Netherlands. The question raised was whether Ms Eind could derive a right of residence in the Netherlands from Union law.

231. As a preliminary remark, the Court of Justice observed that the right conferred upon Union citizens by Article 21 TFEU, the right to reside in the territory of another Member State, is subject to the limitations and conditions imposed by the Treaty and by the measures adopted for its implementation.[535] However, since Mr Eind was a Dutch national, his right to reside in the Netherlands could not be made conditional or refused.[536] The Court of Justice considered that a national of a Member State could be deterred from leaving his Member State of origin in order to be economically active in another Member State 'if he does not have the certainty of being able to return to his Member State of origin, irrespective of whether he is going to engage in economic activity in the latter State'.[537] This effect could be derived from the prospect 'of not being able, on returning to his Member State of origin, to continue living together with close relatives'.[538] Accordingly, the Court held that Ms Eind had the right to settle with her father in the Netherlands, even if the latter was not economically active.[539] Hence, in light of Union citizenship, economic activity plays a less important role.[540]

ii. *Metock*: No Prior Lawful Residence is Required

232. After the *Singh* judgment, it was unclear whether or not the third country national family member of a Union citizen who has used his or her right of free movement should satisfy the condition of prior lawful residence in another Member State. The Court of Justice decided cases in opposing ways. That is to say, in *MRAX*, the Court ruled that 'a Member State is not permitted to refuse issue of a residence permit and to issue an expulsion order against a third country national who is able to furnish proof of his identity and of his marriage to a national of a Member State on the sole ground that he has entered the territory of the Member State concerned unlawfully'.[541] The Court held that the right of a third country national spouse of a Union citizen to enter the territory of the Member States derives from the family ties alone under Union law.[542] In

535 ECJ case C-291/05 *Eind* [2007] ECR I-10719, para 28.

536 Ibid para 31.

537 Ibid para 35.

538 Ibid para 36.

539 However, this is subject to the conditions in Regulation 1612/68 (amended by Directive 2004/38 and now repealed by Regulation 492/2011), paras 38–40.

540 See also Joined Opinion AG Sharpston 12 December 2013 in C-456/12 and C-457/12, *O and B* and *S and G*, para 109.

541 ECJ case C-459/99 *MRAX* [2002] ECR I-6591, para 80.

542 ECJ case C-459/99 *MRAX* [2002] ECR I-6591, para 59. Confirmed subsequently in inter alia ECJ case C-157/03 *Commission v Spain* [2005] ECR I-2911, para 28.

contrast, in *Akrich*, the Court decided that the condition of lawful residence has to be satisfied.[543]

233. Finally, with its judgment in *Metock*, the Court of justice took a clear position on the requirement of prior lawful residence in a Member State.[544] The case concerned Ms Ngo Ikeng, born a national of Cameroon, who acquired UK nationality. Mr Metock, a national of Cameroon, and Ms Ngo Ikeng met in Cameroon in 1994 and had a relationship from that time on. They had two children, one born in 1998 and the other in 2006. In June 2006, Mr Metock went to Ireland where he applied for asylum. However, the Irish authorities rejected his application. In the meantime, Ms Ngo Ikeng also went to Ireland where she resided and worked. In October, she married Mr Metock. Subsequently, Mr Metock applied for a residence card as a spouse of a Union citizen who has made use of her right of free movement. However, the Irish authorities refused the application on the basis that Mr Metock did not satisfy the condition of prior lawful residence in another Member State, as required by the Irish legislation. In the proceedings against this decision, the Irish judge referred the question to the Court of Justice as to whether the condition of prior lawful residence in another Member State is compatible with Directive 2004/38.

234. In the first place, the Court held that Directive 2004/38 does not make its application conditional upon the family members of a Union citizen previously having resided in a Member State.[545] The Court explicitly overruled its decision in *Akrich* and ruled that the benefit of the rights to family reunification 'cannot depend on the prior lawful residence of such a spouse in another Member State'.[546]

In the second instance, the Court ruled that this interpretation of Directive 2004/38 is consistent with the division of competences between the Member States and the Union.[547] The Court held that the Union is competent in establishing the measures by which to bring about the freedom of movement of Union citizens.[548] It held that if Union citizens were not permitted to live together, with their family in the host Member State, the exercise of the freedoms guaranteed by the Treaties would be seriously hindered.[549] Moreover, the Court

543 ECJ case C-109/01 *Akrich* [2003] ECR I-9607, para 61.

544 For a more extensive discussion of this judgment as well as the earlier case law on the matter, see Cambien, 'Citizenship of the Union as a Cornerstone of European Integration', Dissertation, KU Leuven 2011, pp 207–33, Costello, 'Metock: Free Movement and "Normal Family Life" in the Union' (2009) 46 *CMLRev* 587–662 and Peers, 'Free Movement, Immigration Control and Constitutional Conflict' (2009) 5 *EU Const* 173.

545 ECJ case C-127/08 *Metock* [2008] ECR I-6241, para 49.

546 Ibid para 58.

547 Ibid para 60.

548 Ibid para 61.

549 Ibid para 62.

ruled that it is irrelevant 'when and where their marriage took place and of how the national of a non-member country entered the host Member State' for the application of Article 3(1) Directive 2004/38.[550]

235. On the one hand, it has been argued that in its *Metock* judgment the Court of Justice balanced well the Member States' effective immigration control and the '*effet utile*' of the Union provisions on the freedom of movement for persons.[551] Moreover, the importance of strengthening the concept of European citizenship has been emphasised in the wake of the *Metock* judgment.[552] On the other hand, political reactions in the Member States were much less positive.[553] This can already be seen from the arguments of the intervening Member States in that case before the Court.[554] Following the ECJ's judgment, Denmark and the UK made clear that they were reluctant to give full effect to *Metock*.[555,556]

236. However, on the basis of Union law presently in force, the only thing a Union citizen must do in order to be able to rely on the right of family reunification under Union law is to move to another Member State or to return to his Member State of origin.[557] It is not required that the family members have previously legally resided in another Member State, nor is it relevant when and where the relationship was established.

---

550 Ibid para 99.

551 Cambien, 'Citizenship of the Union as a Cornerstone of European Integration', Dissertation, KU Leuven 2011, pp 232–33.

552 Lansbergen, 'Metock, Implementation of the Citizens' Rights Directive and Lessons for EU Citizenship' [2009] *Journal of Social Welfare and Family Law* 285, 295.

553 Currie has pointed out that 'there is a clear disjuncture ... between the view of *Metock* as a judgment which can be categorised as legally justified and the political reality (or perceived reality) which informs the application of national immigration law' (Currie, 'Accelerated Justice or a Step Too Far? Residence Rights of Non-EU Family Members and the Court's Ruling in Metock' (2009) 34 *ELRev* 310, 325).

554 ECJ case C-127/08 *Metock* [2008] ECR I-6241, paras 66 and 71 and 87–88.

555 See more in Currie, 'Accelerated Justice or a Step Too Far? Residence Rights of Non-EU Family Members and the Court's Ruling in Metock' (2009) 34 *ELRev* 310, 324–26; Lansbergen, 'Metock, Implementation of the Citizens' Rights Directive and Lessons for EU Citizenship' [2009] *Journal of Social Welfare and Family Law* 285, 290–93 and Shaw, 'Between Law and Political Truth? Member State Preferences, EU Free Movement Rules and National Immigration Law' [2015] *Cambridge Yearbook of European Legal Studies*, 24.

556 Moreover, in the context of the renegotiation of the UK's EU membership, the Commission Declaration states that it will make a proposal to amend Directive 2004/38 on this point, particularly by requiring prior lawful residence. This will be discussed further in the subsection on 'Abuse of Union law: a stricter notion of movement and real causal link'. Below nn 278–85.

557 See also Cambien, 'Citizenship of the Union as a Cornerstone of European Integration', Dissertation, KU Leuven 2011, p 232.

2.2.4.2. Residing in Another Member State

237. In this subsection, we will examine specifically whether mere residence in another Member State is a sufficient connection with Union law in order to claim a right under Union law. Does mere residence in another Member State constitute a sufficient cross-border element in order to fall within the scope of application of the Treaty provisions on free movement and citizenship as such, or is residence in another Member State a sufficient connection with Union law only under certain circumstances?

In the *Schempp* case, Mr Schempp tried to obtain a deduction on his income tax on the basis of Articles 18 and 21 TFEU. He argued that the sufficient connection with Union law existed in the movement of his ex-spouse to another Member State. In the *O and B* case, the claimants argued that the Union citizen's residence in another Member State was sufficient in order to derive a right of residence for a third country national in the Union citizen's home Member State.

i. Residence on the Territory of Another Member State by Ex-Spouse: *Schempp*

238. This case concerned Mr Schempp, a German national residing in Germany who, following his divorce, paid maintenance to his former spouse who resided in Austria. If his former spouse had been a resident in Germany, Mr Schemmp would have been able to deduct the total amount of the maintenance payments and the former Mrs Schempp would not have paid any tax on the maintenance received. However, in the case at hand, the German authorities refused Mr Schempp the deduction with respect to income tax because he did not provide a certificate from the Austrian tax authorities to demonstrate that his former spouse had been taxed in Austria on the maintenance. However, Mr Schempp could not have provided such a certificate because Austrian law excludes taxation of maintenance payments and does not allow them to be deducted. Mr Schempp challenged the German legislation in the light of the Articles 18 and 21 TFEU.

239. The Court of Justice considered that although direct taxation falls within the competence of the Member States, the latter must exercise this competence in accordance with Union law, particularly in accordance with the right of Union citizens to move and reside freely within the EU.[558] Next, the Court held that the fact that Mr Schempp, a Union citizen, had not made use of the right of freedom of movement he 'cannot, for that reason alone, be assimilated to a purely internal situation'.[559] The Court considered that although Mr Schempp had not exercised such a right, his former wife had undisputedly done so by establishing her

[558] ECJ case C-403/03 *Schempp* [2005] ECR I-6421, para 19.
[559] Ibid para 22, referring to ECJ case C-200/02 *Zhu and Chen* [2004] ECR I-9925, para 19.

residence in Austria.[560] Since the German legislation takes account of the fiscal treatment of the maintenance payments in the recipient's state of residence, the Court found that Mrs Schempp's exercise of her right to move and to reside freely in another Member State had an impact upon the deductibility of the maintenance paid by her former husband in Germany and, therefore, that the situation had a sufficient connection with Union law.[561] Since the situation was considered to fall within the scope of Union law, the Court assessed the case in the light of Articles 18 and 21 TFEU.

240. Regarding the principle of non-discrimination on grounds of nationality, the Court held that Article 18 TFEU 'is not concerned with any disparities in treatment, for persons and undertakings subject to the jurisdiction of the [Union], which may result from divergences existing between the various Member States, so long as they affect all persons subject to them in accordance with objective criteria and without regard to their nationality'.[562] Accordingly, the Court held that the payment of maintenance to a recipient in Germany could not be compared to the payment of maintenance to a recipient in Austria since these two recipients are subject to different tax systems, the German and Austrian ones respectively.[563] Therefore, the legislation such as at issue in the main proceedings does not establish discrimination within the meaning of Article 18 TFEU.[564]

241. Next, the Court examined whether Article 21 TFEU applied to Mr Schempp's situation. In this respect, the Court referred to its *Lindfors* judgment in which it held that 'the Treaty offers no guarantee to a citizen of the Union that transferring his activities to a Member State other than that in which he previously resided will be neutral as regards taxation'; hence, the use of a Union citizen's right to freedom of movement may either lead to an advantage in terms of taxation or not.[565] The Court ruled that this reasoning applies *a fortiori* to a situation in which the Union citizen concerned did not make use of his right of free movement, 'but claims to be the victim of a difference in treatment following the transfer of his former spouse's residence to another Member State'.[566] Accordingly, the Court ruled that Mr Schempp's unfavourable tax consequences were not precluded by either Article 18 or by Article 21 TFEU.[567]

242. For the present purposes, the most important aspect of this judgment is that Mr Schempp fell within the scope of Union law because his former wife had exercised her right to freedom of movement by establishing her residence

560 ECJ case C-403/03 *Schempp* [2005] ECR I-6421, para 23.
561 Ibid paras 24–25.
562 Ibid para 34.
563 Ibid para 35.
564 Ibid para 36.
565 Ibid para 45.
566 Ibid para 46.
567 Ibid para 47.

in Austria. Hence, movement is still relevant in the Court's interpretation of the scope of application of Union law. In this case it was not the Union citizen invoking a right under Union law who had moved, but his former wife; however, according to the Court this movement was relevant. In particular, the Court held that 'since the exercise by Mr. Schempp's former spouse of a right conferred by the [Union] legal order had an effect on his right to deduct in his Member State of residence, such a situation cannot be regarded as an internal situation with no connection with [Union] law'.[568] Although Mr Schempp's situation came within the personal scope of application of Articles 18 and 21 TFEU, these articles did not preclude Mr Schempp's unfavourable tax consequences.

ii. *O and B*: Genuine Residence and Creating/Strengthening Family Life

243. The pressing question of whether a Union citizen's residence in another Member State is sufficient in order to derive a right of residence for a third country national in the Union citizen's home Member State was at stake in the *O and B* case. In her Opinion in *O and B*, AG Sharpston explicitly invited the Court of Justice to provide 'clear and structured guidance as to the circumstances in which the third country national family member of an EU citizen who is residing in his home Member State but who is exercising his rights of free movement can claim a derived right of residence in the home Member State under EU law'.[569]

244. This case concerned Mr O, a Nigerian national, who married a Dutch national in 2006. From 2007 to 2010 Mr O lived in Malaga, Spain. He was in possession of a residence permit as a family member of a Union citizen, which was valid until 2014. Mr and Mrs O were registered at the same address in Malaga since 2009, even though Mrs O only resided with Mr O for two months because she could not find work in Spain. However, between 2007 and 2010, Mrs O regularly travelled from the Netherlands to Spain in order to spend time with Mr O. In the summer of 2010, Mr O moved to the Netherlands and was registered at the same address of Mrs O. His application for a residence permit in the Netherlands was rejected. The situation of Mr B, a Moroccan national and his partner Ms B, a Dutch national, was similar.[570] His application for a residence permit in the Netherlands was also rejected. The question was referred

568 Ibid para 25.

569 Joined Opinion AG Sharpston 12 December 2013 in C-456/12 and C-457/12, *O and B* and *S and G*, para 158.

570 In particular, in 2005 Mr B had to leave the territory of the Netherlands because of a two-month prison sentence he received for using a false passport. Therefore, Mr B moved to Belgium and lived in an apartment rented by Ms B who resided there every weekend. Since

for a preliminary ruling to the Court of Justice as to whether such a refusal of a right of residence for Mr O and Mr B is precluded by Directive 2004/38 and Article 21(1) TFEU.

245. The Court of Justice first recalled that third country nationals in situations such as those in the main proceedings are not entitled to derive a right of residence on the basis of Directive 2004/38 in the Member State of origin of their family member who is a Union citizen; therefore, the Court examined whether a right of residence could nevertheless be derived from Article 21(1) TFEU.[571] To begin with, the Court recalled the cases of *Singh* and *Eind* in which it ruled that if a Union citizen has resided with a family member who is a third country national in another Member State than the one of which he is a national and was employed there for a period exceeding 2.5 years and 1.5 years respectively, then that third country national must, when the Union citizen returns to his Member State of origin, be entitled to a derived right of residence in the latter State on the basis of Union law.[572] Otherwise, the Union citizen could be discouraged from exercising his rights of free movement.[573]

246. Next, the Court examined whether the *Singh* and *Eind* case law can be 'applied generally to family members of Union citizens who, having availed themselves of the rights conferred on them by Article 21(1) TFEU, resided in a Member State other than that of which they are nationals, before returning to the Member State of origin'.[574] The Court answered this question affirmatively since the removal of the same type of obstacle is concerned, that is to say, an obstacle to leaving the Member State of origin.[575]

Subsequently, the Court of Justice examined the conditions for granting a derived right of residence to a third country national who has resided in a host Member State with his family member a Union citizen when that Union citizen returns to his Member State of origin.[576] First of all, the Court noted that in principle, the conditions should not be stricter than those provided for by Directive 2004/38 for the situations falling within its scope.[577] According to the Court, even though Directive 2004/38 does not include a return such as that at issue in the main proceedings, 'it should be applied by analogy to the conditions for the residence of a Union citizen in a Member State other than that of which

Mr B was denied residence in Belgium, he returned to Morocco. Subsequently, Mr B married Mrs B and in 2009 Mr B moved to the Netherlands to reside there with Mrs B. His application for a residence permit in the Netherlands was rejected.

571 ECJ case C-456/12 *O and B*, para 44.

572 Ibid para 46, referring to ECJ case C-370/90 *Singh* [1992] ECR I-4265, paras 25 and 45.

573 ECJ case C-456/12 *O and B*, para 46.

574 Ibid para 48.

575 Ibid para 49.

576 Ibid paras 50 ff.

577 Ibid para 50.

he is a national, given that in both cases it is the Union citizen who is the sponsor for the grant of a derived right of residence to a third-country national who is a member of his family'.[578]

However, the Court immediately emphasised that an obstacle will only arise if the residence of the Union citizen in the host Member State has been 'sufficiently genuine so as to enable that citizen to create or strengthen family life in that Member State'.[579] Hence, not every residence by a Union citizen in a host Member State in which he is accompanied by a family member who is a third country national leads to a derived right of residence for the latter in the Member State of origin upon the Union citizen's return there.[580]

247. Next, the Court of Justice explained the requirement of genuine residence in the host Member State of the Union citizen and of the third country national, which is for the referring court to determine in the case at issue.[581] In particular, the ECJ defined genuine residence by referring to Articles 7 and 16 Directive 2004/38. Residence in the host Member State in conformity with the conditions in Articles 7 and 16 Directive 2004/38 constitutes sufficient evidence of genuine residence in principle.[582] The term 'genuine residence' means residence for more than three months upon the condition of either being a worker or self-employed person in the host Member State or having sufficient resources and a sickness insurance or studying in the host Member State and having a sickness insurance, or *a fortiori* having a permanent right of residence in the host Member State.[583]

In contrast, 'short periods of residence such as weekends or holidays spent in a Member State other than that of which the citizen in question is a national, even when considered together, fall within the scope of Article 6 of Directive 2004/38' and do not generate such a derived right of residence.[584] Moreover, the Court ruled that the mere fact that the third country national held a valid residence permit in the host Member State on the basis of Article 10 Directive 2004/38 does not force the Member State of origin of the Union citizen concerned to grant a derived right of residence to this third country national family member.[585]

248. If, during the genuine residence of the Union citizen in the host Member State, family life is created or strengthened in that Member State, then a right of residence to the family member who is a third country national can be derived from Article 21(1) TFEU.[586] Otherwise, the effectiveness of the rights conferred upon the Union citizen by Article 21 TFEU would be jeopardised, given that the Union citizen would be discouraged from leaving his Member State of origin, because it would be uncertain whether he would be able to continue a family

578 Ibid.
579 Ibid para 51.
580 Ibid.
581 Ibid paras 52–60.
582 Ibid paras 53–55.
583 Ibid paras 53–59.
584 Ibid paras 52 and 59.
585 Ibid para 60.
586 Ibid para 54.

life in his Member State of origin with his immediate family members which has been created or strengthened in the host Member State.[587]

249. Finally, the Court of Justice pointed out that 'the scope of Union law cannot be extended to cover abuses'.[588] In particular, the Court held that proof of an abuse of Union law requires both objective circumstances and a subjective element.[589] That is to say, a combination of 'objective circumstances in which, despite formal observance of the conditions laid down by the European Union rules, the purpose of those rules has not been achieved, and, secondly, a subjective element consisting in the intention to obtain an advantage from the European Union rules by artificially creating the conditions laid down for obtaining it'.[590]

250. The question at stake in the *O and B* case is under which circumstances a third country national can derive a right of residence from Union law. A right of residence in a host Member State can be derived from Directive 2004/38 if the Union citizen, of whom he is a family member, moves to another Member State than the one of which he is a national.[591] In *O and B*, the Court held that if the Union citizen returns to his Member State of origin after genuine residence in the host Member State in which he created or strengthened family life, a derived right of residence for the third country national in the Member State of origin can be derived from Article 21 TFEU.

251. First, it is remarkable that the Court of Justice used Directive 2004/38 as a reference point in its *O and B* judgment, whereas it explicitly held that 'Directive 2004/38 is … not intended to confer a derived right of residence on third-country nationals who are family members of a Union citizen residing in the Member State of which the latter is a national'.[592] According to Spaventa, most of the problems resulting from this judgment 'arise from the fact that the Court is bending the analogous application of Directive 2004/38 to situations which do not fit it, simply because the right of residence of a national returning home is fundamentally different from that of a non-national: the right to reside in one's own Member State is the corollary of nationality, and it is unconditional'.[593] There is certainly truth in this claim, but one should not lose sight of the attempts made by the Court of Justice in this judgment to clarify the inter-state element and to limit possible abuse.

---

587 Ibid para 54. 588 Ibid para 58. 589 Ibid. 590 Ibid.

591 Article 3(1) Directive 2004/38 determines that the Directive applies to 'all citizens who move to or reside in a Member State other than that of which they are a national'.

592 ECJ case C-456/12 *O and B*, para 43.

593 Spaventa, 'Family Rights for Circular Migrants and Frontier Workers: O and B, and S and G' (2015) 52 *CMLRev* 753, 774–75.

252. It is submitted that the Court of Justice took an important first step towards clarifying how much movement is required in order to derive a right of residence for a third country national family member on the basis of Article 21 TFEU.[594] The Court held that only genuine residence, that is to say only periods of residence of more than three months in another Member State by the Union citizen, can result in a derived right of residence in the Union citizen's home Member State for third country nationals family members. Hence, in contrast to AG Sharpston's Opinion, the Court considered the length of the residence in another Member State to be a decisive criterion. This choice can be defended by the attempt to guarantee a real causal link between the Union citizen's exercise of free movement and the third country national family member's right of residence in their home Member State. Accordingly, it is an attempt to restrict 'the possibility of "tourists" benefiting from EU-derived family reunification rights'.[595] Moreover, it is a clear indication for the national courts of 'how much movement' is required.

253. However, the Court's approach can also be described as being 'formalistic'[596] and 'simplistic'.[597] Why can a Union citizen who has lived for 3.5 months in another Member State in which he met his partner be joined by her when he returns to his Member State of origin and why is this not possible for the Union citizen who visits another Member State for a period of many consecutive years? The reality of family life can be rather complex and this is taken into account more in AG Sharpston's observations than in the Court's judgment. In particular, the Advocate General pointed out that 'the length of an EU citizen's stay in another Member State is (obviously) a relevant quantitative criterion'. However, it should not be applied as an absolute threshold, but instead as one of the decisive criteria for assessing who has or has not made use of his rights of residence and can, therefore, be joined or accompanied by his family members.[598] Furthermore, it can be questioned why 'genuineness is what truly distinguishes periods of residence of different duration' and whether it is the 'best adjective to capture that distinction' since it appears nowhere in the mentioned provisions of Directive 2004/38.[599]

---

594 See also Cambien, 'Cases C-456/12 O. and B. and C-457/12 S. and G Clarifying the Inter-state Requirement for EU Citizens?' (European Law Blog, 11 April 2014).

595 Spaventa, 'Family Rights for Circular Migrants and Frontier Workers: O and B, and S and G' (2015) 52 *CMLRev* 753, 776.

596 Cambien, 'Cases C-456/12 O. and B. and C-457/12 S. and G Clarifying the Inter-state Requirement for EU Citizens?' (European Law Blog, 11 April 2014).

597 Spaventa, 'Family Rights for Circular Migrants and Frontier Workers: O and B, and S and G' (2015) 52 *CMLRev* 753, 764.

598 Joined Opinion AG Sharpston 12 December 2013 in C-456/12 and C-457/12, *O and B* and *S and G*, para 111.

599 Nic Shuibhne, 'The "Constitutional Weight" of Adjectives' (2014) 39 *ELRev* 154.

254. Moreover, the Court of Justice could have given more guidance to the referring judge, particularly regarding the concept of creating or strengthening family life as well as regarding the question of whether the derived right of residence, on the basis of Article 21 TFEU, 'expire[s] if there is some (undefined) gap between the return of the EU citizen to his home Member State and the family member's arrival there?'[600] AG Sharpston examined this question and argued that the reason for the delay is immaterial, but 'what matters is that the decision to move in order to reside with an EU citizen is taken in the exercise of the right to a family life'.[601] She considered that 'the Court has held that Directive 2004/38 does not require family members of EU citizens to enter the host Member State at the same time as the EU citizen from whose status they derive rights'.[602] AG Sharpston has argued, more generally, that 'under Directive 2004/38, the host Member State cannot deny residence to a third country national on the basis of elapsed time'.[603]

In this author's view, the fact that it is not required that the third country national arrives at the same moment as the Union citizen in the *host* Member State does not imply that any lapse of time is immaterial when assessing whether a derived right of residence in the Member State *of origin* exists. Accordingly, it is submitted that the answer to the question of whether a derived right of residence in the home Member State expires on the basis of time elapsed should be affirmative if there is no causal link between the exercise of free movement and the right to family reunification invoked under Union law. Support for this interpretation can be found in the Court's consideration that if, during the genuine residence of the Union citizen in the host Member State, family life is created or strengthened in that Member State, a right of residence can be derived from Article 21(1) TFEU.[604] Depending on the circumstances of the case, a lapse of time may be decisive in order to refuse such a right of residence for a third country national family member, particularly if it is an (extra) indication that

600 Joined Opinion AG Sharpston 12 December 2013 in C-456/12 and C-457/12, *O and B* and *S and G*, para 138. See also Martin, 'Comments on Gouvernement de la Communauté française and Gouvernement wallon (Case C-212/06 of 1 April 2008) and Eind (Case C-291/05 of 11 December 2007)' (2008) 10 *EurJMigrL* 372.

601 Joined Opinion AG Sharpston 12 December 2013 in C-456/12 and C-457/12, *O and B* and *S and G*, para. 142.

602 Ibid para 141, referring to *Metock* (para 90) and *O and S* (para 54).

603 Joined Opinion AG Sharpston 12 December 2013 in C-456/12 and C-457/12, *O and B* and *S and G*, para 141.

604 ECJ case C-456/12 *O and B*, para 54. See also ECJ case C-138/02 *Collins* [2004] ECR I-2703, para 28 in which the Court held that 'Mr. Collins performed casual work in the United Kingdom, in pubs and bars and in sales, during a 10-month stay there in 1981. However, even if such occupational activity satisfies the conditions as set out in paragraph 26 of this judgment for it to be accepted that during that stay the appellant in the main proceedings had the status of a worker, no link can be established between that activity and the search for another job more than 17 years after it came to an end'.

there is no causal link between the exercise of free movement and the right invoked under Union law. It is submitted that a returning citizen should not be able to invoke rights under Union law for their lifetime since he exercised his rights of free movement once and then returned to his Member State of origin.[605]

2.2.4.3. Exercise of Free Movement without Moving Residence

255. The question that will be examined in this subsection is how the cross-border element is interpreted by the ECJ in cases in which Union citizens exercise their right of free movement without moving their residence to another Member State. In other words, under which circumstances is the exercise of the right of freedom of movement without moving one's residence to be considered as sufficient movement in order to invoke a certain right under Union law? In this regard, a distinction is made between the active exercise of the rights of free movement and the passive enjoyment of the rights of free movement (the latter in the context of the freedom to receive services especially). First to be discussed are cases that concern the active provisioning of services and the freedom of movement for workers. Next, we will discuss whether receiving services is enough for the Court to consider that the Treaty provisions on free movement and Union citizenship are engaged and to allow the citizen to benefit from the rights granted by them.

i. Active Provision of Services

256. The first situation which comes to mind as a cross-border situation of active provision of services is a situation in which the provider of services moves between Member States. However, it is possible that neither the provider nor the receiver cross borders of Member States, but that only the service itself does. These situations fall within the scope of application of Article 56 TFEU, enshrining the freedom to provide services. In these situations, Article 56 can be invoked against national measures which impede the provision of services, both measures laid down by the host Member State and measures laid down by the home Member State.

257. A remarkable case in which the provider of services moved between Member States and invoked Article 56 TFEU against his home Member State for restricting his freedom to provide services is the *Carpenter* case.[606] Mr Carpenter

---

605 See also Cambien who argued that 'it appears that "past" movement is not immediately relevant: third-country nationals who only became family members after the EU citizen had stopped exercising his free movement rights, cannot rely on EU law to derive such a right'. Cambien, 'Cases C-456/12 O. and B. and C-457/12 S. and G Clarifying the Inter-state Requirement for EU Citizens?' (European Law Blog, 11 April 2014)

606 ECJ case C-60/00 *Carpenter* [2002] ECR I-6279. See above n 188.

ran a business selling advertising space in medical and scientific periodicals and offered various administrative and publishing services to the editors of those periodicals. Both Mr Carpenter's business and the editors for which he sold advertising space were based in the UK. However, a lot of advertisers were established in other Member States and, for the purpose of his business, Mr Carpenter travelled to them. Mrs Carpenter, a Philippine national, took care of the household and, in particular, of Mr Carpenter's two children from a previous marriage. She claimed that her deportation would be a restriction to her husband's right to free movement of services.

The Court of Justice held that the provision of services by Mr Carpenter came within the scope of Article 56 TFEU 'both in so far as the provider travels for that purpose to the Member State of the recipient and in so far as he provides cross-border services without leaving the Member State in which he is established'.[607] The Court of Justice affirmed Mrs Carpenter's reasoning and held that Article 56 TFEU precluded a refusal by the British authorities of a right of residence for Mrs Carpenter in the UK.[608]

258. The application of Article 56 TFEU seems artificial because the main issue did not concern a protectionist national rule that impedes the exercise of the freedom to provide services, but the right to respect for family life.[609] The fact that Mr Carpenter provided cross-border services seems accidental in respect to the deportation of Mrs Carpenter.[610] Accordingly, the causal link between the exercise of free movement and the restriction to free movement seems highly tenuous. In other words, it could be argued that the freedom to provide services was instrumentalised in order to protect the right to respect for family life.[611] This judgment will be compared with the *S and G* judgment in the following subsection.[612]

259. The Court of Justice has also held that Article 56 TFEU applies when neither the provider nor the recipient of the service moves between the Member States, but only the service itself moves. The *Alpine Investments* judgment can be discussed in this regard.[613]

---

607 ECJ case C-60/00 *Carpenter* [2002] ECR I-6279, para 29.

608 Ibid para 46.

609 Acierno, 'The Carpenter Judgment: Fundamental Rights and the Limits of the Community Legal Order' (2003) 28 *ELRev* 398, 405.

610 Editorial comment, 'Freedoms Unlimited? Reflections on Mary Carpenter v. Secretary of State' (2003) 40 *CMLRev* 537, 541.

611 Acierno, 'The Carpenter Judgment: Fundamental Rights and the Limits of the Community Legal Order' (2003) 28 *ELRev* 398, 541.

612 Below n 265.

613 ECJ case C-384/93 *Alpine Investments* [1995] ECR I-1141. See also ECJ case 352/85 *Bond* [1988] ECR 2085 and ECJ joined cases C-34/95 to C-36/95 *De Agostini* [1997] ECR I-3843.

Alpine Investments is a company that calls individuals without their prior consent in order to offer them different financial services. This practice is known as 'cold calling'. The company is established in the Netherlands, but it has clients in different Member States. Eventually, however, the Dutch Minister for Finance imposed a general prohibition on cold calling. Alpine Investments challenged this prohibition in the light of Article 56 TFEU.

The Court of Justice examined whether the Treaty provisions on the free movement of services cover offers of services made by telephone by a provider established in one Member State to a potential recipient established in another Member State, whereby none of them moves to another Member State than the one in which they have been established.[614] The Court held that 'it follows from the express terms of the article [56 TFEU]' that this kind of services are covered within the meaning of this provision.[615] The Court ruled that 'rules of a Member State which prohibit providers of services established in its territory from making unsolicited telephone calls to potential clients established in other Member States in order to offer their services constitute a restriction on freedom to provide services'.[616]

ii. Exercise of Free Movement of Workers

260. If a Union citizen works in another Member State without moving his residence to that Member State, he can rely on Article 45 TFEU in order to challenge the host Member State's measures on employment rights. This would be a classic situation in which a worker is protected by the Treaty provisions concerning the freedom of movement for workers. In *S and G*, the question arose as to whether the fact that a Union citizen works in another Member State without moving his residence to that host Member State can lead to a derived right of residence in his home Member State for third country national family members.

261. The case concerned Ms S, a Ukrainian national who wanted to obtain a right of residence in the Netherlands with her son-in-law, a Netherlands national. Ms S took care of her grandson, her son-in-law's child. Her son-in-law resided in the Netherlands, but spent one third of his weekly working time on

---

614 ECJ case C-384/93 *Alpine Investments* [1995] ECR I-1141, paras 20–21.

615 Ibid. Other cases in which the Court accepted a potential recipient or provider of services in another Member State is a sufficient link with Union law in order to fall under the scope of Article 56 TFEU are: ECJ case C-405/98 *Gourmet International* [2001] ECR I-1795 and ECJ case C-355/00 *Freskot* [2003] ECR I-5263 (see Spaventa, 'Seeing the Wood Despite the Trees? On the Scope of Union Citizenship and its Constitutional Effects' (2008) 45 *CMLRev* 13, 16).

616 ECJ case C-384/93 *Alpine Investments* [1995] ECR I-1141, para 39.

preparing and making business trips to Belgium. He travelled to Belgium at least once a week.

The other case concerned Ms G, a Peruvian national who married a Dutch national and with whom she had a daughter. Her husband travelled daily between the Netherlands and Belgium for his work. Referring to *Carpenter*, the court in the main proceedings referred the question for preliminary ruling to the Court of Justice as to whether Ms S and Ms G could invoke a right of residence on the basis of Article 45 TFEU.

262. The Court of Justice recognised that the 'interpretation of Article 56 TFEU in *Carpenter* is transposable to Article 45 TFEU'.[617] However, the Court considered that a derived right of residence for a third country national in the Member State of nationality of his family member who is a Union citizen is justified by the fact that a refusal would run the risk of interfering with the exercise of the right to freedom of movement of workers of that Union citizen.[618] The referring court has to make this assessment.[619]

The Court of Justice pointed out that the fact that 'the third-country national in question takes care of the Union citizens' child may, as is apparent from the judgment in *Carpenter*, be a relevant factor to be taken into account'.[620] However, the Court held that although in *Carpenter* it was decisive that the child in question was being taken care of by the third country national who is the Union citizen's spouse, it is not sufficient as such that 'it might appear desirable that the child be cared for by the third-country national who is the direct relative in the ascending line of the Union citizen's spouse'.[621]

Accordingly, the Court held that 'Article 45 TFEU must be interpreted as conferring on a third-country national who is the family member of a Union citizen a derived right of residence in the Member State of which that citizen is a national, where the citizen resides in that Member State but regularly travels to another Member State as a worker within the meaning of that provision, if the refusal to grant such a right of residence discourages the worker from effectively exercising his rights under Article 45 TFEU, which it is for the referring court to determine'.[622]

263. Spaventa has argued that the reference to *Carpenter* is misguiding since in that judgment, the Court 'focused exclusively on the connection between the right to movement and the right to family life; at no point did the Court demand that such family included children, or even worse that the rights of the spouse might be dependent upon their caring role within the family'.[623] She argued that

617 ECJ case C-457/12 *S and G*, para 40.
618 Ibid para 41.
619 Ibid para 42.
620 Ibid para 43.
621 Ibid.
622 Ibid para 44.
623 Spaventa, 'Family Rights for Circular Migrants and Frontier Workers: O and B, and S and G' (2015) 52 *CMLRev* 753, 765–66.

since the *S and G* judgment, the Union citizen has to show the presence of 'a more precise link of causation between the denial of a residence permit and her exercise of the right to move'.[624] According to Spaventa, derived rights of residence for third country family members 'become purely instrumental to the achievement of the internal market – in a way they are demoted from rights of the person (family life) to instruments of integration'.[625]

264. However, AG Sharpston's analysis of the situation of a Union citizen moving to another Member State as a worker, but without moving residence seems more convincing.[626] She argued that the derived right of residence in the home Member State of the Union citizen of which she is a family member is dependent upon three criteria.[627] That is to say: 'the family connection with the EU citizen; the EU citizen's exercise of rights of free movement and the causal link between the residence of the third country national and the EU citizen's exercise of rights of free movement'.[628] AG Sharpston has emphasised that the assessment of these elements does not lead to a simple answer being given regarding the derived right of residence.[629] For instance, the closeness of the family relation may play an important role. Sharpston has argued that a restriction of the choice of whether or not to use the right of free movement exists if refusing residence to the third country national would 'cause the EU citizen to move, to cease to move or to abandon the real prospect of moving'.[630] The Advocate General pointed out that the Court of Justice did not consider in *Carpenter* whether the refusal of a right of residence for Mrs Carpenter in the UK would in fact cause Mr Carpenter to stop his activities abroad.[631]

265. It is submitted that the causal link, which Spaventa rejects as being instrumental, is crucial in order to respect the division of competences between the EU and the Member States and to draw an acceptable and clear division line between the scope of application of Union law and that of national law. It is further submitted that this causal link is much more disputable in the *Carpenter* case than it is in the *S and G* case. That is to say, Mr Carpenter only occasionally (in the *Carpenter* case) went abroad to provide services. By contrast, the family members of Ms S and Ms G in Belgium work on a regular basis. The fact that the third country national takes care of the Union citizen's child may be relevant in order to derive a right to residence. However, there is a big difference between searching for someone to take care of the children of the Union citizen (in the *Carpenter* case) only occasionally, or, by contrast, on a regular basis (in the case of Ms S and Ms G). Whether the *Carpenter* case can be regarded as 'good

624 Ibid 768.

625 Ibid.

626 Joined Opinion AG Sharpston 12 December 2013 in C-456/12 and C-457/12, *O and B* and *S and G*, paras 119–23.

627 Ibid para 122.

628 Ibid.

629 Ibid para 123.

630 Ibid.

631 Ibid para 117.

case law' can be questioned. The link between occasionally providing services and a derived right of residence for a third country national taking care of the Union citizen's child(ren) is much weaker than the link between regularly working abroad and a derived right of residence for a third country national taking care of the Union citizen's child(ren).

iii. Passive Exercise of Free Movement: Receiving Services

266. Although Articles 56 and 57 TFEU only expressly mention rights for the providers of services, the Court of Justice held in *Luisi and Carbone* that the freedom to travel to receive services from a provider of services established in another Member State is the 'necessary corollary' of the freedom to actively provide services.[632] In particular, the Court held that the freedom to provide services includes the freedom, for the recipients of services, to go to another Member State in order to receive services regarding tourism, medical treatment and education.[633]

Enjoying services in another Member State has become readily accessible. Many Union citizens spend their holidays in another Member State or order products from other Member States online, etc. The question has arisen as to whether receiving services from a host Member State is enough to invoke rights under Union law. It is contended that this depends upon whether or not a causal link exists between the exercise of free movement and the specific right invoked under Union law.

267. The *Cowan* and *Bickel and Franz* cases are illustrations of a clear causal link. The *Cowan* case concerned a British citizen who was assaulted at the exit of a metro station during a brief stay in Paris.[634] Since his offenders could not be identified, Mr Cowan applied to the French Treasury for compensation for his injuries. However, according to the French Treasury, Mr Cowan did not satisfy the conditions for such compensation since the French criminal legislation only provided this for French nationals or foreign nationals who are either a national of a State which has concluded a reciprocal agreement with France or who are holders of a residence permit. The question for a preliminary ruling was referred to the ECJ as to whether the prohibition on the grounds of nationality, now Article 18 TFEU, precludes such national legislation as that at stake in the main proceedings.

The ECJ recalled its judgment of 31 January 1984 in which it ruled that 'the freedom to provide services includes the freedom for the recipients of services

632 ECJ joined cases 286/82 and 26/83 *Luisi and Carbone* [1984] ECR 377, para 10.
633 Ibid para 16.
634 ECJ case 186/87 *Cowan* [1989] ECR 195.

to go to another Member State in order to receive a service there, without being obstructed by restrictions, and that tourists, among others, must be regarded as recipients of services'.[635] The Court held that the protection from harm in the host Member State is a corollary of the freedom of movement. Therefore, the prohibition of discrimination on grounds of nationality applies to the recipients of services as regards the right to obtain as the victim of an assault financial compensation provided for by national law.[636]

268. The *Bickel and Franz* judgment regards similar facts and a similar reasoning by the Court of Justice.[637] Mr Bickel, an Austrian lorry driver and resident in Austria, was charged with driving while under the influence of alcohol in the Trentino-Alto Adige Region of Italy. Mr Franz, a German national resident in Germany, was visiting this region as a tourist when he was found to be in possession of a prohibited type of knife. Mr Bickel and Mr Franz declared before the court in Bolzano that they had no knowledge of Italian and requested that the proceedings be conducted in German – the German-speaking citizens of the province of Bolzano are entitled to use German in relation to the judicial administrative authorities. The question as to whether the rules of procedure applicable to the citizens of the Province of Bolzano should be extended to nationals of other Member States visiting the province was referred for a preliminary ruling to the Court of Justice.

The Court held that Article 56 TFEU 'covers all nationals of Member States who … visit another Member State where they intend or are likely to receive services'. On the basis of the prohibition of discrimination on grounds of nationality, the Court ruled that individuals such as Mr Bickel and Mr Franz are entitled 'to treatment no less favourable than that accorded to nationals of the host State so far as concerns the use of languages which are spoken there'.[638]

269. In sum, it can be inferred from the *Cowan* and *Bickel and Franz* cases that receiving services in another Member State is sufficient to bring the Treaty provisions into play. However, it should be emphasised that in these cases a clear causal link exists between the exercise of free movement and the right claimed

---

635 Ibid para 15, referring to ECJ joined cases 286/82 and 26/83 *Luisi and Carbone v Ministero del Tesoro* [1984] ECR 377.

636 ECJ case 186/87 *Cowan* [1989] ECR 195, para 17. The Court recognised that in principle, criminal legislation is the responsibility of each Member State. However, on the other hand, Union law sets limits to their powers. That is to say, these legislative provisions cannot constitute a discrimination nor a restriction of fundamental freedoms of persons protected by Union law. Ibid para 19.

637 ECJ case C-274/96 *Bickel and Franz* [1998] ECR I-7637.

638 Ibid para 16. The Court made the same comment on criminal legislation as in the *Cowan* case (ibid para 17).

under Union law.[639] In fact, the causal link cannot be demonstrated more obviously than in these cases. That is to say, they were exercising their right to free movement when something occurred that made them invoke a right under Union law.[640]

270. When receiving a service in another Member State than the Member State of nationality is sufficient in order to establish a connection with Union law, then it is not difficult at all to fall within the scope of Union law.[641] This is precisely what the defendants claimed in the *Angonese* case.

271. In this case, Mr Angonese, an Italian national resident in the province of Bolzano, went to study in Austria from 1993 to 1997. In August 1997, he wished to apply for a job with a private banking institution in Bolzano. One of the conditions for application was possession of a type-B certificate of bilingualism (in Italian and German). Mr Angonese did not possess such a certificate, but was able to demonstrate his bilingualism by means of various other documents. However, he was not permitted to apply because he had not provided the specific type-B certificate.

272. In this factual context, the defendants argued that there was no connection with Union law. They argued that study abroad can only be taken into account 'if it results in a relevant diploma or recognised training – a condition not satisfied in the present case, as the applicant's studies in Vienna had no connection with banking and could not be relied upon by him in the competition. Otherwise, short educational exchanges or even periods of as little as one day spent abroad as a tourist could, quite arbitrarily, enable a person to invoke [Union]-law rights against his own Member State'.[642] By contrast, the Commission observed that a connecting factor with Union law could be found

639 See above.

640 In this author's opinion, the *Deliège* case can also be put in this category (ECJ joined cases C-51/96 and C-191/97 *Deliège* [2000] ECR I-2549). Ms Deliège was a several-time Belgian judo champion, as well as European and world champion. She maintained that the officers of the Belgian and French-speaking judo federations frustrated her career development by not selecting her for various European and world championships.

The Court of Justice held that sporting activities may be an economic activity (paras 52–60, in particular para 56). It ruled that 'a degree of extraneity may derive in particular from the fact that an athlete participates in a competition in a Member State other than that in which he is established' (para 58). It is submitted that a link exists between the exercise of Ms Deliège's right of free movement and the alleged restriction thereof. However, the Court decided that the selection rules in themselves did not constitute a restriction on the freedom to provide services (para 69).

641 See also Cambien, 'Citizenship of the Union as a Cornerstone of European Integration', Dissertation, KU Leuven 2011, p 284.

642 See Opinion AG Fennelly, 25 November 1999 in C-281/98, *Angonese*, para 9.

in 'the applicant's exercise of his right of free movement as a student to follow a course of vocational training abroad, and from the fact that he wished to take up employment in Bolzano at the end of his studies'.[643]

273. However, the Court of Justice did not follow the reasoning of the defendant nor that of the Commission.[644] In this respect, the Court only considered that it is for the national court alone to decide both on the need for a preliminary ruling and the relevance of the questions which it submits to the Court of Justice.[645] Moreover, the Court held that it is far from clear that the interpretation of Union law has no actual relation to the case in the main proceedings.[646] Hence, unlike AG Fennelly,[647] the Court did not address the question of whether a sufficient connection with Union law was at stake.[648]

274. It may be regarded as something of a missed opportunity that the Court of Justice did not openly deal with the question of whether receiving services is sufficient in order to invoke a right under Union law.[649] It is no surprise that the question has recently been raised again. In particular, it has risen in connection with a derived right of residence for a third country national family member of a Union citizen in the home Member State of the latter.

275. In her Opinion in *O and B* and *S and G*, AG Sharpston specifically reflected upon the possible consequences of 'the "passive" freedom to receive services in another Member State without moving there'.[650] She argued that when a Union

---

643 See ibid para 10. According to the Commission, the duration of the study abroad and the interval of time between the end of those studies and the invocation of Union law rights were not problematic (see ibid). It is unclear why Mr Angonese did not obtain such a certificate at the end of his secondary school studies (which is apparently common in Bolzano, see ibid para 6). Can this be explained by the fact that he was studying in Austria? If the answer is affirmative, it is arguable that a sufficient link with the Union is obvious. See also above the remark on the real link in *Cowan* and *Bickel and Franz*.

644 ECJ case C-281/98 *Angonese* [2000] ECR I-4139, para 17.

645 Ibid para 18.

646 Ibid para 19.

647 Opinion AG Fennelly 25 November 1999 in ibid para 43.

648 Lane and Nic Shuibhne, 'Case Note on Case C-281/98, Angonese' (2000) 37 *CMLRev* 1237, 1242–43.

649 In the *Angonese* case, the right invoked under Union law was the access to employment on the basis of Article 45 TFEU. It could be argued that the Court implicitly answered the question in an affirmative sense by assessing the case in the light of Article 45 TFEU.

650 Joined Opinion AG Sharpston 12 December 2013 in C-456/12 and C-457/12, *O and B* and *S and G*, paras 124–31. See, three years earlier, Opinion AG Sharpston 30 September 2010 in C-34/09, *Ruiz Zambrano*, para 86. In particular, AG Sharpton hypothesised about a friendly neighbour who had taken Diego and Jessica on a visit or two to Parc Astérix in Paris, or to the seaside in Brittany. They would then have received services in another Member State. She asked how many visits would have sufficed and whether a day trip would be enough, or whether, by contrast, an overnight stay would be needed.

citizen goes to another Member State in order to receive services there, he or she falls within the scope of application of Union law.[651] Next, AG Sharpston emphasised that this does not imply that every passive form of receiving services in another Member State leads to derived rights of residence for third country nationals, 'because not every denial of residence constitutes a barrier to family reunification such as to restrict an EU citizen's fundamental right to move'.[652]

276. In particular, AG Sharpston observed that Union citizens increasingly cross borders in order to enjoy services, such as holidays, or that they enjoy cross-border services, by ordering books online, for instance.[653] Although these activities are undoubtedly exercises of economic freedom, 'in most circumstances, derived rights of residence for family members ... are not necessary for an EU citizen to enjoy a service which is essentially temporary'.[654] She argued that the fact that receiving services in another Member State would be more pleasant together with a family member is, as such, insufficient to create a restriction on the right of free movement of services of the Union citizen.[655]

However, AG Sharpston considered that in exceptional circumstances a refusal of a derived right of residence for a third country national who is a family member in the home Member State of the Union citizen might be a restriction on the free movement of services.[656] In particular, this could happen if the Union citizen becomes dependent upon the third country national family member 'due to the very circumstances that cause him to cross borders in order to enjoy services in another Member State'.[657]

277. In the *O and B* judgment, which was described in detail in the previous subsection,[658] the Court of Justice acted upon the request of AG Sharpston to provide clear and structured guidance regarding the circumstances in which a third country national can benefit from a derived right of residence in the

---

651 Joined Opinion AG Sharpston 12 December 2013 in C-456/12 and C-457/12, *O and B* and *S and G*, para 125, referring to ECJ case C-221/11 *Demirkan*, paras 35–36.

652 Ibid para 125, referring to Opinion AG Tesauro 20 May 1992 in C-370/90, *Singh*, point 5.

653 Ibid para 126.

654 Ibid paras 128–29.

655 Ibid para 130.

656 Ibid para 131.

657 Ibid, in which she gave an illustration: 'For example, suppose a German national residing in Germany and married to a Chinese national who has not been authorised to reside there becomes ill and requires long-term treatment. He decides, for medical reasons, to receive that treatment in Belgium. He has no intention of changing his residence and settling there. He does however require assistance to travel regularly to Belgium. He also needs help to take care of other things that he can no longer do for himself. He becomes dependent upon a carer. Understandably, he would like that carer to be his Chinese wife. That decision belongs to the sphere of his private and family life; but at the same time it is connected to the conditions in which he exercises rights of free movement.'

658 Above nn 243–54.

home Member State of the Union citizen of whom they are a family member.[659] In particular, the Court of Justice held that 'short periods of residence such as weekends or holidays spent in a Member State other than that of which the citizen in question is a national, even when considered together' do not generate derived rights of residence from Article 21(1) TFEU for third country nationals family members of the Union citizen in the home Member State.[660]

2.2.4.4. Abuse of Union Law: A Stricter Notion of Movement and Real Causal Link

278. In this section on stretching the notion of movement, several cases have been discussed in which the parties or the intervening Member States have argued that the abuse of Union law was at stake.[661] Cambien has identified three different types of abuse in the context of derived rights for family members of Union citizens.[662] First, fraud in the sense of a false representation of facts can be stake, for instance when a false birth certificate is used. In this case, Member States can deny rights in favour of those Union citizens.[663]

Secondly, it may happen that family relationships are fraudulently established, marriages of convenience in particular. In this regard, Article 35 Directive 2004/38 determines that 'Member States may adopt the necessary measures to refuse, terminate or withdraw any right conferred by this Directive in the case of abuse of rights or fraud, such as marriages of convenience'.[664]

Thirdly, an artificial link with another Member State may be established in order to fall within the scope of Union law. However, it is remarkable that the ECJ is very reluctant to accept this type of abuse of Union law. This type of abuse will be discussed in more detail in the following paragraphs.

---

659 Joined Opinion AG Sharpston 12 December 2013 in C-456/12 and C-457/12, *O and B* and *S and G*, para 158.

660 ECJ case C-456/12 *O and B*, paras 59 and 61.

661 ECJ case C-370/90 *Singh* [1992] ECR I-4265; ECJ case C-109/01 *Akrich* [2003] ECR I-9607; ECJ case C-200/02 *Zhu and Chen* [2004] ECR I-9925; and ECJ case C-456/12 *O and B*.

662 Cambien, 'Citizenship of the Union as a Cornerstone of European Integration', Dissertation, KU Leuven 2011, pp 228–29.

663 Sørensen, 'Abuse of Rights in Community Law: A Principle of Substance or Merely Rhetoric?' (2006) 43 *CMLRev* 431, referring to ECJ case C-285/95 *Kol* [1997] ECR I-309, para 28.

664 In ECJ case C-202/13 *McCarthy II*, the Court held that measures adopted by the national authorities on the basis of Article 35 Directive 2004/38 have to be based on an individual assessment of the specific circumstances (para 52). Such measures cannot be 'founded on considerations of general prevention, to the exclusion of any specific assessment of the conduct of the person concerned himself' (para 55). However, Nic Shuibhne pointed to the different approach in ECJ case C-333/13 *Dano*. See more in Nic Shuibhne, 'Limits Rising, Duties Ascending: The Changing Legal Shape of Union Citizenship' (2015) 52 *CMLRev* 889, 911–12.

279. The Court of Justice has repeatedly held that the reason why a Union citizen moves to another Member State is immaterial.[665] For the Court it is only relevant whether an effective and genuine economic activity or genuine residence in another Member State is present.[666] In *O and B*, the ECJ elaborated a little further on the issue considering that proof of an abuse of Union law requires both objective circumstances and a subjective element.[667] That is to say, a combination of 'objective circumstances in which, despite formal observance of the conditions laid down by the European Union rules, the purpose of those rules has not been achieved, and, secondly, a subjective element consisting in the intention to obtain an advantage from the European Union rules by artificially creating the conditions laid down for obtaining it'.[668]

280. The ECJ's reluctance to consider an artificial link with Union law as abuse of Union law can probably be explained by the fact that an overly broad interpretation of the abuse of Union law would undermine Union law since it would imply that rights conferred by Union law would be denied in these cases.[669] However, this type of abuse of Union law could be remedied by reintroducing limits to the notion of movement and also reintroducing a real causal link between the actual movement and the restriction to the right of free movement. It might be that the Court of Justice is aware of this and is already opting for this direction. That is to say, after an evolution of 25 years in which the ECJ stretched the notion of movement, it seems that the ECJ has established limits to this broad interpretation. In particular, in the *O and B* judgment, the ECJ attempted to give clear guidelines to the referring court. Moreover, as explained in the previous subsection, the idea of a causal link might also be present in the *O and B* judgment.[670] Finally, in the *Bogendorff von Wolffersdorff* judgment, which will be discussed in the next section, the ECJ seems to open the way for taking the reasons of a Union citizen's actions into account.[671]

---

665 See inter alia ECJ case 53/81 *Levin* [1982] ECR 1035, para 23; ECJ case C-109/01 *Akrich* [2003] ECR I-9607, para 55 and ECJ case C-200/02 *Zhu and Chen* [2004] ECR I-9925, paras 34–36.

666 ECJ case C-109/01 *Akrich* [2003] ECR I-9607, para 55 and ECJ case C-456/12 *O and B*, para 56.

667 ECJ case C-456/12 *O and B*, para 58.

668 Ibid.

669 Sørensen has argued that 'Member States cannot be entirely free to combat what they consider to be abuse, as this would seriously undermine EU law. Were the Member States free to deny the exercise of [Union] rights as they see fit, EU law would be applied very differently in the different Member States' (Sørensen, 'Abuse of Rights in Community Law: A Principle of Substance or Merely Rhetoric?' (2006) 43 *CMLRev* 431). See also Triantafyllou, 'L'interdiction des abus de droit en tant que principe général du droit communautaire' (2002) 38 *CDE* 2002, 613–15.

670 Above nn 275–77.

671 ECJ case C-438/14 *Bogendorff von Wolffersdorff*, below nn 296–98.

281. However, a more explicit and systematic assessment by the Court of Justice would be welcome. It is submitted that the Court of Justice should openly and systematically examine whether there is a link between the exercise of free movement and the right invoked under Union law in each case. Specifically, the ECJ could follow AG Sharpston's proposal in her Opinion in *O and B* and *S and G* that 'a restriction of the choice whether or not to use the right of free movement exists if refusing residence to the third country national would cause the EU citizen to move, to cease to move or to abandon the real prospect of moving'.[672] This requires an individual assessment of a real causal link for each case. In so doing, the Court of Justice has to manage the difficult balancing act between a sufficient level of abstraction and a useful reply for the referring court.[673] That is to say, the interpretation of Union law is the Court of Justice's competence and the application to the case in the main proceedings is the competence of the national referring judge.[674]

282. An objection to requiring a stricter interpretation of movement and a causal link might be that only those Union citizens who receive good advice and have sufficient resources can benefit from Union law.[675] However, it seems that this objection is even more reasonable if it would be extremely easy to benefit from Union law. This author believes that the provision of a better and stricter demarcation line between the scope of Union law and that of national law would make the possible existence of reverse discrimination less arbitrary and hence more acceptable.

283. The issue of the abuse of derived rights for family members on the basis of Union law was especially topical in the context of the renegotiation of the UK's EU membership. The deal of 19 February 2016 consisted of seven legal texts; specifically a Decision of the Member States' Heads of State and Government (the main draft decision), a Statement of the Heads of State and Government, a Declaration by the European Council and four declarations of the European Commission. If the main draft decision had entered into force,[676] the Commission would have had a political commitment to propose certain amendments to the EU Citizenship Directive, the EU Regulation on free movement of workers

---

672 Joined Opinion AG Sharpston 12 December 2013 in C-456/12 and C-457/12, *O and B* and *S and G*, para 123.

673 Nowak, 'Case Note C-93/12 ET Agrokonsulting' (2014) 3 *SEW* 144, 147.

674 Craig and de Burca, *EU Law. Text, Cases, and Materials*, 6th ed, Oxford University Press 2015, pp 496–99.

675 Spaventa, 'Seeing the Wood Despite the Trees? On the Scope of Union Citizenship and its Constitutional Effects' (2008) 45 *CMLRev* 13, 38.

676 However, this did not happen since the referendum of 23 June 2016 resulted in 51.6% of voters voting in favour of leaving the EU.

and the EU Regulation on social security. Here, we will examine only the EU Citizenship Directive regarding the admission of non-EU family members.

284. In his speech of November 2014, David Cameron announced the will to impose the same strict conditions that apply to UK citizens regarding the admission of non-EU family members upon Union citizens. However, the legislative amendment of the draft deal proposed did not go quite this far. In particular, the Commission Declaration stated that it would make a proposal to amend Directive 2004/38: 'to exclude, from the scope of free movement rights, third country nationals who had no prior lawful residence in a Member State before marrying a Union citizen or who marry a Union citizen only after the Union citizen has established residence in the host Member State. Accordingly, in such cases, the host Member State's immigration law will apply to the third country national'.[677] As discussed earlier,[678] the issue of prior lawful residence in a Member State has already been the subject of ECJ case law. While the Court held in *Akrich* that Member States were allowed to require prior lawful residence of non-EU family members in 2003, it overruled this decision in 2008 in *Metock*. In other words, this amendment would have been a codification of the ECJ's *Akrich* case law have been.[679,680]

285. It is submitted that this amendment to Directive 2004/38 would have led to fewer cases of abuse of Union law regarding the admission of non-EU family members. That is to say, it would have addressed marriages 'with third country nationals for the purpose of making use of free movement as a route for regularising unlawful stay in a Member State or for bypassing national immigration rules applying to third country nationals'.[681]

However, some issues would have still remained unclear.[682] That is to say, when exactly would the condition of lawful residence have been considered to have been satisfied? For instance, the question would have arisen as to how the situation of a pending asylum application should be qualified. Moreover, what would have been the exact consequences of the application of the host Member State's

---

677 European Council meeting (18 and 19 February 2016) conclusions, annex 7, p 35.

678 Above nn 232–36.

679 Obviously upon the condition that the proposal would have been adopted. That is to say, the Commission's proposal would have had to be approved by the Council (by a qualified majority of the Member States) and the European Parliament (by a majority of the vote).

680 The facts in the pending case of *Lounes* (C-165/16) allow the ECJ to reassess its case law on the issue and, possibly, to reverse its *Metock* case law.

681 European Council meeting (18 and 19 February 2016) conclusions, annex 1, section D, p 21.

682 Two of the six points which Steve Peers examined regarding this legislative amendment are discussed. See more in Peers, 'EU Law Analysis: The Draft Renegotiation Deal: EU Immigration Issues', <http://eulawanalysis.blogspot.be/2016/02/the-draft-renegotiation-deal-eu.html>. According to Peers, there is some possibility that the amended rules would be incompatible with EU free movement law. By contrast, he argued that it is unlikely that it would be a violation of the EU Charter right to family life.

immigration law? In particular, the question would have arisen as to whether the family member would be excluded from the scope of Directive 2004/38 forever, such as for access to possible social benefits in the host Member State.

2.2.5. *Reducing the Importance of Movement in the Light of Union Citizenship*

286. The Court of Justice has not only extended its interpretation of movement, it has also reduced the importance of movement. The Court of Justice has been doing so since the long-settled case law of *Dassonville*, discussed above,[683] according to which not only is discrimination forbidden, but so too are restrictions on the freedom of movement. In particular, on the basis of the *Dassonville* case law, all national provisions which are capable of obstructing directly or indirectly, actually or potentially, intra-Union trade are considered as measures having equivalent effect. Even in a situation in which all the facts are confined to a single Member State, the national measure may also have effects on free movement between Member States.

287. This section discusses the impact of Union citizenship on the interpretation of the required link with Union law. As mentioned previously, it is the ECJ's settled case law that 'citizenship of the Union … is not intended to extend the scope *ratione materiae* of the Treaty also to internal situations which have no link with [Union] law'.[684] Although the ECJ initially acted as though Union citizenship had no effect upon the purely internal situation doctrine, it cannot be denied that the impact Union citizenship has had upon the interpretation of the purely internal situation rule has been remarkable.[685] In particular, in the light of Union citizenship, the Court of Justice interprets the required link with Union law in an increasingly abstract way, one which reduces the importance of movement.

2.2.5.1. External Element Other than Movement Between Member States: Nationality of One Member State and Resident in Another Member State

i. *Garcia Avello*

288. In the *Garcia Avello* case, the Court of Justice did not look for any cross-border element in the traditional sense, but took its inspiration for a sufficient

[683] ECJ case 8/74 *Dassonville* [1974] ECR I-837, above nn 193–96.

[684] See inter alia ECJ joined cases C-64/96 and C-65/96 *Uecker and Jacquet* [1997] ECR I-3171, para 23 and *Garcia Avello* [2003] ECR I-11613, para 26, and ECJ case C-403/03 *Schempp* [2005] ECR I-6421, para 20.

[685] See inter alia Craig and de Burca, *EU Law. Text, Cases, and Materials*, 6th ed, Oxford University Press 2015, pp 865–71 and Verbist, 'De invloed van het Unieburgerschap op zuiver interne situaties' [2011] *RW* 510.

link with Union law from the concept of Union citizenship. The case concerned Mr Garcia Avello, a Spanish national, and Ms Weber, a Belgian national, who were married in Belgium and resided there. In particular, the case concerned their children, Esmeralda and Diego, who had dual (Belgian and Spanish) nationality. On the basis of Belgian law, the children had the father's surname, that is to say, Garcia Avello's surname. However, the parents requested that the surname be changed to Garcia Weber, in accordance with Spanish law in which the surname of a child consists of the first surname of the father followed by that of the mother. The children were registered with the Spanish embassy under the name Garcia Weber. After refusal by the Belgian authorities to change their name in Belgium to Garcia Weber, the parents of Esmeralda and Diego brought an application for annulment of that decision before the Council of State, which decided to refer a question for preliminary ruling to the Court of Justice.

289. AG Jacobs observed in his Opinion that the Court could have opted for a traditional cross-border element regarding the connection required with Union law. That is to say, AG Jacobs argued that the refusal to change his children's surname concerned Mr Garcia Avello, who acted as a parent and legal representative of his minor children.[686] Since Mr Garcia Avello was a Spanish national who had exercised his rights of free movement, by working and residing in Belgium, his situation fell within the sphere of Union law.[687]

290. However, the Court of Justice decided to make a different assessment in order to determine whether or not the situation fell under the scope of Union law. First, the Court considered that although the rules governing a person's surname is a Member State competence, the latter must exercise that competence in accordance with Union law, in particular with the right to move and to reside freely in the territory of the Member States.[688] Next, the Court held that the situation in the main proceedings contained a link with Union law since Esmeralda and Diego were nationals of one Member State and lawfully resident in another Member State.[689] The Court emphasised that this 'cannot be invalidated by the fact that the children involved in the main proceedings also have the nationality of the Member State in which they have been resident since their birth'.[690]

Hence, the Court assessed the decision by the Belgian authorities to reject the application for a change of surname in the light of the Articles 18 and 20 TFEU.[691] The Court considered that Esmeralda and Diego, having both Spanish

686 Opinion AG Jacobs 22 May 2003 in C-148/02, *Garcia Avello*, para 50.
687 Ibid para 51.
688 ECJ case C-148/02 *Garcia Avello* [2003] ECR I-11613, para 25.
689 Ibid para 27. 690 Ibid para 28. 691 Ibid paras 29 ff.

and Belgian nationality and therefore different surnames under the two legal systems, were in a different situation from those individuals who have Belgian nationality alone.[692] Since this discrepancy in surnames could cause serious inconvenience for the children at both the professional and private levels, the Court rejected the justifications put forward by the Belgian government.[693] Accordingly, the Court held that Articles 18 and 20 TFEU preclude a Member State from refusing a change of name in circumstances such as in the main proceedings.[694]

ii. *Zhu Chen*

291. In his Opinion in *Zhu and Chen*, AG Tizzano referred to the *Garcia Avello* judgment in order to argue that the situation at issue was not purely internal. In particular, the case concerned Mr and Mrs Chen, both of Chinese nationality, who wanted to have a second child, but were not entitled to do so under Chinese law. Therefore, Mrs Chen went to the UK when she was six months' pregnant. She went to Belfast to give birth to a daughter, Catherine, and they currently resided in the UK. Catherine acquired Irish nationality on the basis of the *ius soli* principle enshrined in Ireland's nationality legislation, which means that every person born on the Irish territory becomes an Irish citizen.[695]

292. AG Tizzano argued on the basis of the *Garcia Avello* judgment that Catherine's Irish nationality was sufficient to establish a link with Union law.[696] However, the Court of Justice did not explicitly consider this in the *Zhu and Chen* judgment. The Court merely held that 'the situation of a national of a Member State who was born in the host Member State and has not made use of the right to freedom of movement cannot, for that reason alone, be assimilated to a purely internal situation'.[697]

293. In its assessment of whether Catherine and her family members might have the right to long-term residence under Article 21 TFEU and under Directive

[692] Ibid para 35. [693] Ibid paras 36–44. [694] Ibid para 45.

[695] Section 6(1) Irish Nationality and Citizenship Act of 1956.

[696] Opinion AG Tizzano 18 May 2004 in C-200/02, *Zhu and Chen*, paras 32–34.

[697] ECJ case C-200/02 *Zhu and Chen* [2004] ECR I-9925, para 19, referring to *Garcia Avello*, paras 13 and 27. However, analysing the *Zhu Chen* judgment, Carlier argued that 'referring to the previously cited *Garcia Avelo* case, and already to a lesser extent the *Carpenter* case, it can be noted that the condition of movement is becoming a fiction, the person does not have to move physically, it is sufficient for his or her nationality to move' (Carlier, 'Case Note on C-200/02, Zhu Chen' (2005) 42 *CMLRev*, 1126–27). See also Vanvoorden, 'Case Note on C-200/02, Zhu Chen' (2005–06) 12 *ColJEurL* 305, 312, arguing that 'it also seems now firmly established that another sufficient condition is having the nationality of a Member State other than the one you are residing in'.

90/364,[698] the Court considered that Catherine had both sickness insurance and sufficient resources, provided by her mother, in order not to become a burden upon the social assistance system of the host Member State.[699] The objection that Catherine did not personally possess these resources was rejected by the Court on the basis that Directive 90/364 does not determine what the origin of these resources need to be.[700]

Moreover, the Court of Justice rejected the UK's argument that Mrs Chen abused Union law since she gave birth to her child in Belfast solely in order to make it possible to acquire Irish nationality for her child.[701] Although Mrs Chen's purpose was certainly to obtain a long-term residence permit in the UK for herself and Catherine, the Court stressed that Catherine had acquired Irish nationality in a perfectly legal way.[702]

The Court held that Article 21 TFEU and Directive 90/364 'confer on a young minor who is a national of a Member State, is covered by appropriate sickness insurance and is in the care of a parent who is a third-country national having sufficient resources for that minor not to become a burden on the public finances of the host Member State, a right to reside for an indefinite period in that State'.[703] Furthermore, the Court decided that even though the Directive entitles only ascendants who are dependent upon a Union citizen to join the latter in another Member State, a parent of a minor Union citizen who is that minor's primary carer should also be entitled to do so.[704]

iii. Subsequent Case Law on Surnames: *Grunkin and Paul*, *Sayn-Wittgenstein* and *Bogendorff von Wolffersdorff*

294. In 2008, in particular in the *Grunkin and Paul* case, the Court explicitly considered whether having the nationality of one Member State and residing in another Member State is a sufficient connection with Union law. The case concerned Leonhard Matthias Grunkin-Paul, who was born in Denmark, the child of Paul and Grunkin, who both had German nationality. Leonhard

---

698 Directive 90/364/EEC of 28 June 1990 was repealed by Directive 2004/38.

699 ECJ case C-200/02 *Zhu and Chen* [2004] ECR I-9925, para 28.

700 Ibid paras 29–30.

701 Ibid paras 34–35, referring to ECJ case C-212/97 *Centros* [1999] ECR I-1459.

702 ECJ case C-200/02 *Zhu and Chen* [2004] ECR I-9925, paras 36 and 38. In this respect the Court referred to the *Centros* judgment in which it held that 'the fact that a national of a Member State who wishes to set up a company chooses to form it in the Member State whose rules of company law seem to him the least restrictive and to set up branches in other Member States cannot, in itself, constitute an abuse of the right of establishment. The right to form a company in accordance with the law of a Member State and to set up branches in other Member States is inherent in the exercise, in a single market, of the freedom of establishment guaranteed by the Treaty' (ECJ case C-212/97 *Centros* [1999] ECR I-1459, para 27).

703 ECJ case C-200/02 *Zhu and Chen* [2004] ECR I-9925, para 41.

704 Ibid paras 42–46.

Matthias possesses German nationality and has lived in Denmark since his birth. Pursuant to Danish law, his surname is Grunkin-Paul. However, the German authorities refused to recognise this surname as German law does not allow a child to bear a double-barrelled surname composed of both the father and the mother's surnames.

295. The Court of Justice held that the situation of Leonhard Matthias Grunkin-Paul falls within the scope of the Treaty.[705] In particular, the Court recalled that 'such a link with [Union] law does exist in regard to children who are nationals of one Member State and are lawfully resident in the territory of another Member State'.[706] The Court ruled that 'in circumstances such as those of the case in the main proceedings, [article 21 TFEU] precludes the authorities of a Member State, in applying national law, from refusing to recognise a child's surname, as determined and registered in a second Member State in which the child – who, like his parents, has only the nationality of the first Member State – was born and has been resident since birth'.[707] The Court of Justice confirmed this position in the name case *Sayn-Wittgestein*.[708]

296. Another recent name case is *Bogendorff von Wolffersdorff*. The case concerned a German national who moved to the UK where he pursued the profession of insolvency advisor in London. During his stay in London, he acquired British nationality. Moreover, he changed his name according to English law. After a couple of years, on account of his wife's pregnancy, he moved back to Germany where his daughter was born. The German authorities refused to register his daughter, holding dual German and British nationality, under her British name.

297. In the Opinion in *Bogendorff von Wolffersdorff*, AG Wathelet argued that Mr Bogendorff von Wolffersdorff, who holds British nationality and is lawfully resident in Germany, was able to rely on a connection with Union law in his relations with Germany; the applicability of Union law is not precluded by his German nationality.[709] Moreover, the AG added that 'the cross-border nature of the case at issue is even more relevant if account is taken of the fact that Mr Bogendorff von Wolffersdorff had, according to English law and during a period of lawful residence in England, acquired the forenames and surname

[705] ECJ case C-353/06 *Grunkin and Paul* [2008] ECR I-7639, para 15.

[706] Ibid para 17, referring to *Garcia Avello* [2003] ECR I-11613, para 27.

[707] ECJ case C-353/06 *Grunkin and Paul* [2008] ECR I-7639, para 39.

[708] ECJ case C-208/09 *Sayn-Wittgenstein* [2010] ECR I-13693, paras 37–42.

[709] Opinion AG Wathelet 14 January 2016 in C-438/14, *Bogendorff von Wolffersdorff*, paras 32 and 29–31, referring to *Garcia Avello* [2003] ECR I-11613, paras 27–28.

whose recognition he seeks to obtain in Germany by exercising the right to freedom of movement conferred on him by Articles 20 TFEU and 21 TFEU'.[710]

298. In the *Bogendorff von Woflffersdorff* judgment, the ECJ followed its Advocate General and explicitly considered why a sufficient connection with Union law was present. In particular, it held that 'the applicant in the main proceedings holds the nationality of two Member States and, as a citizen of the Union, exercises his freedom to move and reside in a Member State other than his Member State of origin in accordance with Article 21 TFEU'.[711]

iv. The Reinterpretation of *Garcia Avello* in *McCarthy*

299. Following the *Garcia Avello* judgment, it has been argued that since citizens with the nationality of one Member State are lawfully resident in another Member State were considered as having a connection with Union law, then people having a dual nationality from two Member States can also always demonstrate a sufficient link with Union law.[712] However, in 2011 in *McCarthy* the Court of Justice made clear that dual nationality – or the nationality of another Member State than the one in which the Union citizen has resided his or her entire life – in itself is not enough to establish a sufficient link with Union law.[713] In this author's view, the Court reinterpreted[714] its *Garcia Avello* judgment when it considered in *McCarthy* that 'what mattered was not whether the discrepancy in surnames was the result of the dual nationality of the persons concerned, but the fact that that discrepancy was liable to cause serious inconvenience for the Union citizens concerned that constituted an obstacle to freedom of movement that could be justified only if it was based on objective considerations and was proportionate to the legitimate aim pursued'.[715]

300. Rather surprisingly, the Court referred here to its *Grunkin and Paul* judgment, and not to paragraph 17 which was considered above, but to the

710 Opinion AG Wathelet 14 January 2016 in C-438/14, *Bogendorff von Wolffersdorff*, para 33.

711 ECJ case C-438/14, *Bogendorff von Wolffersdorff*, para 33.

712 See Ackermann: 'This link being derived from the grant of the nationality of another Member State than the State of residence, Union citizens with dual nationality can never be found in an internal situation if they have their place of residence anywhere within the EU' (Ackermann, 'Case Note on C-148/02, Garcia Avello' (2007) 44 *CMLRev* 146).

713 The *McCarthy* judgment will be discussed in the following subsection. Below nn 311–17.

714 Verbist, 'De invloed van het Unieburgerschap op zuiver interne situaties' [2011] *RW* 510, 518–19. See also Nowak, 'Case Note, Case C-34/09, Gerardo Ruiz Zambrano v. Office national de l'emploi (ONEM) & Case C-434/09, Shirley McCarthy v. Secretary of State for the Home Department' (2011) 17 *ColJourEurLaw* 673, 19.

715 ECJ case C-434/09 *McCarthy* [ECR] I-3375, para 52.

subsequent paragraphs in which it held that regarding children with a dual nationality, 'discrepancy in surnames is liable to cause serious inconvenience for those concerned at both professional and private levels'.[716] This serious inconvenience caused by the discrepancy in surnames can either be caused by dual nationality or by a situation such as that of the main proceedings.[717] Finally, the Court referred in *McCarthy* to its consideration in *Grunkin and Paul* according to which 'an obstacle to freedom of movement such as that resulting from the serious inconvenience described in paragraphs 23 to 28 of this judgment could be justified only if it was based on objective considerations and was proportionate to the legitimate aim pursued'.

301. It seems that two things are getting mixed up: on the one hand, the question of whether a situation has a sufficient connection with Union law and, on the other hand, whether a national provision constitutes a restriction of free movement of Union citizens. This concerns the tension between movement as a precondition and a right at the same time.[718] That is to say, on the one hand, that Union citizenship confers to the nationals of the Member States a right to move and to reside in another Member State than the Member State of which they possess the nationality. On the other hand, the rights that Union citizens derive from the Treaties are still dependent upon a link with Union law, traditionally a cross-border element.

In the *McCarthy* judgment, the Court seems to have reinterpreted[719] *Garcia Avello*, that is, not the issue of dual nationality as such, but future movement constituted a sufficient link with Union law.[720] Hence, the future movement is a precondition in order to fall within the scope of the Treaties, precisely in order to enjoy the right of freedom of movement granted by the Treaties. The question arises as to whether the future movement should be understood as a

716 ECJ case C-353/06 *Grunkin and Paul* [2008] ECR I-7639, para 23.

717 Ibid para 24. The Court made the same observations in ECJ case C-208/09 *Sayn-Wittgenstein* [2010] ECR I-13693, paras 66–67.

718 Verbist, 'De invloed van het Unieburgerschap op zuiver interne situaties' [2011] *RW* 510, 519. Above n 185.

719 See also Nowak, 'Case Note, Case C-34/09, Gerardo Ruiz Zambrano v. Office national de l'emploi (ONEM) & Case C-434/09, Shirley McCarthy v. Secretary of State for the Home Department' (2011) 17 *ColJourEurLaw* 673, 691 and 703 and Cambien, 'Mogen statische Unieburgers worden gediscrimineerd op het vlak van gezinshereniging? Enkele beschouwingen bij de arresten Ruiz Zambrano en McCarthy van het Hof van Justitie' (2011) 3 *T Vreemd* 241, speaks about a 'new, more narrow interpretation'.

720 Verbist, 'De invloed van het Unieburgerschap op zuiver interne situaties' [2011] *RW* 510, 519 and see also Nic Shuibhne, '(Some of) the Kids are All Right: Comment on McCarthy and Dereci' (2012) 49 *CMLRev* 369; Nowak, 'Case Note, Case C-34/09, Gerardo Ruiz Zambrano v. Office national de l'emploi (ONEM) & Case C-434/09, Shirley McCarthy v. Secretary of State for the Home Department' (2011) 17 *ColJourEurLaw* 673, 694 and Van Elsuweghe and Adam, 'Situations purement internes (2008) *CDE* 680 (who describe the cross-border element in *Garcia Avello* as '*hypothétique*').

purely hypothetical issue or as something which is highly probable. A part of the answer can be found in the *Iida* judgment, which will be discussed below, in which the ECJ recalled that 'the purely hypothetical prospect of exercising the right of freedom of movement does not establish a sufficient connection with European Union law to justify the application of that law's provisions'.[721] Admittedly, in the case of *Garcia Avello* it seems not to be a purely hypothetical matter that the children will move to or reside in Spain for a certain period in their lives since they probably have family over there.[722]

2.2.5.2. Intrinsic Connection with Union Law Introduced in *Rottmann* and *Ruiz Zambrano*

i. *Rottmann*

302. The first case in which the Court of Justice openly opted for an abstract interpretation of the required link with Union law is the *Rottmann* case of 2010. Mr Rottmann was an Austrian citizen by birth. He transferred his residence to Germany in which he started a naturalisation procedure, without mentioning the criminal proceedings for fraud which had been initiated against him in Austria. He was granted German nationality which caused him to lose his Austrian nationality. When the German authorities found out that a warrant had been issued in Austria for Mr Rottmann, they wanted to withdraw the naturalisation with retroactive effect. The federal administrative court of Bayern referred the question for preliminary ruling to the Court of Justice of whether this withdrawal of German nationality, which would render Mr Rottmann stateless, was compatible with Article 20 TFEU.

303. The Court held that, although it is a Member State competence to determine the conditions for the acquisition and loss off nationality, the national rules must have due regard to Union law.[723] Subsequently, the Court held that it is obvious that the situation of a Union citizen 'in a position capable of causing him to lose the status conferred by Article [20 TFEU] and the rights attaching thereto falls, by reason of its nature and its consequences, within the ambit of European Union law'.[724] Accordingly, the Court held that it was competent to rule on the question referred 'which concern the conditions in which a citizen of the Union may, because he loses his nationality, lose his status of citizen of the Union and thereby be deprived of the rights attaching to that status'.[725]

---

721 ECJ case C-40/11 *Iida*, para 77, referring to ECJ case C-299/95 *Kremzow* [1997] ECR I-2629.

722 However, that the children have family in Spain is not made explicit in the case, it is only an assumption.

723 ECJ case C-135/08 *Rottmann* [2010] ECR I-1419, paras 39–41.

724 Ibid para 42.

725 Ibid para 46.

304. Next, the Court recognised that a decision withdrawing naturalisation because of deception corresponds to a reason relating to the public interest and that it is legitimate that a Member State wants 'to protect the special relationship of solidarity and good faith between it and its nationals and also the reciprocity of rights and duties, which form the bedrock of the bond of nationality'.[726] The Court stressed that this reason of public interest remains valid, in principle, when the consequences of the withdrawal are that the citizen in question loses not just the nationality of the Member State of naturalisation but also citizenship of the Union.[727] However, it is for the national court to determine, before the decision of withdrawal takes effect, that the principle of proportionality is respected in the light of both European Union law and national law.[728] Accordingly, the Court ruled that Article 20 TFEU does not preclude a Member State from withdrawing the nationality of that State acquired by naturalisation from a Union citizen when that nationality has been obtained by deception, if the decision of withdrawal is compatible with the principle of proportionality.[729]

305. Without doubt, the *Rottmann* case is an important landmark in the Court's case law on purely internal situations.[730] It should be noted that the Court could have opted for an approach in which it found a sufficient connection with Union law in the exercise by Mr Rottmann of his rights of free movement.[731] Instead, the Court's remark in paragraph 42 is decisive, in which it held that the situation fell 'by reason of its nature and its consequences, within the ambit of European Union law'. Here, the Court explicitly found a link with Union law in an abstract element. That is to say, the loss of the status of Union citizenship is such a vital issue for the Court that it falls under Union law because of the nature and the consequences of the situation. As Barnard pointed out, this paragraph in *Rottman* 'paved the way for the momentous and highly controversial decision in *Ruiz Zambrano*' of March 2011.[732]

---

726 Ibid para 51.

727 Ibid para 54.

728 Ibid paras 55–58.

729 Ibid para 59.

730 See inter alia Barnard, *The Substantive Law of the EU: The Four Freedoms*, Oxford University Press 2013, pp 476–77; Cambien, 'Mogen statische Unieburgers worden gediscrimineerd op het vlak van gezinshereniging? Enkele beschouwingen bij de arresten Ruiz Zambrano en McCarthy van het Hof van Justitie' (2011) 3 *T Vreemd* 241, 243 and Kochenov, 'Case Note on C-135/08, Rottmann' (2010) 47 *CMLRev* 1831, 1836.

731 AG Poiares Maduro argued in this way, see Opinion AG Poiares Maduro 30 September 2009, C-135/08, *Rottmann*, paras 11–13. See also Kochenov, 'Case Note on C-135/08, Rottmann' (2010) 47 *CMLRev* 1831, 1841.

732 Barnard, *The Substantive Law of the EU: The Four Freedoms*, Oxford University Press 2013, p 477. See also Cambien, 'Mogen statische Unieburgers worden gediscrimineerd op het vlak van gezinshereniging? Enkele beschouwingen bij de arresten Ruiz Zambrano en McCarthy van het Hof van Justitie' (2011) 3 *T Vreemd* 241, 243. Kostakopoulou describes the judgment in *Ruiz Zambrano* as 'revolutionary' (Kostakopoulou, 'Co-creating European Union Citizenship: Institutional Process and Crescive Norms' (2012–13) 15 *Cambridge Yearbook of European Legal Studies* 267).

ii. *Ruiz Zambrano*

306. This case concerned Mr Zambrano, a Colombian national, who arrived with his family in Belgium in 1999. He immediately submitted an application for asylum, but this was rejected. Because of the civil war in Colombia, the order to leave Belgium included a non-refoulement clause. Subsequently, Mr Zambrano submitted several applications in order to regularise his situation, but they were rejected each time. Accordingly, Mr and Mrs Zambrano could not obtain a long-term residence permit on the basis of the Belgian Aliens Act.

During their stay in Belgium, Mrs Zambrano gave birth to their second and third children. These children acquired Belgian nationality because of the interplay between the Colombian and Belgian legislation concerning nationality. In particular, the relevant Colombian legislation determines that a child of parents of Colombian nationality which is born outside the territory of Colombia does not automatically acquire Colombian nationality, but only after the registration of the child at the Colombian embassy abroad.[733] The Zambranos neglected to do this, since the Belgian legislation determined that 'any child born in Belgium who, at any time before reaching the age of 18 or being declared of full age, would be stateless if he or she did not have Belgian nationality, shall be Belgian'.[734]

307. Ruiz Zambrano argued that he derived a right of residence directly by virtue of Union law, or at least a derived right of residence since he is the parent of two EU citizens.[735] The Brussels Labour Court referred the question for preliminary ruling to the Court of Justice whether the provisions on Union citizenship confer on a third country national with dependent minor children, who are Union citizens, a right of residence in the Member State of which they are nationals and in which they reside.

However, according to the intervening governments and the European Commission, Union law did not apply in the case at issue because the main proceedings concern a purely internal situation since the second and third children of Ruiz Zambrano, Belgian citizens and hence Union citizens, never left Belgium. The Court of Justice gave no response at all to this remark.[736]

308. To begin with, the Court of Justice held that Directive 2004/38 does not apply to the situation in the main proceedings.[737] Next, the Court grounded

---

733 Article 96 Colombian Constitution, as amended by Legislative Act 01 of 25 January 2002, *Official Journal* No 44693 of 31 January 2002.

734 Article 10(1) Belgian Nationality Code, *Moniteur belge*, 12 July 1984, p 10095.

735 In this respect, Mr Zambrano referred to the *Zhu and Chen* case, see above n 293.

736 ECJ case C-34/09 *Ruiz Zambrano* [2011] ECR I-1177, para 37.

737 Ibid para 39.

its argument on the basis of Article 20 TFEU, the Treaty provision which creates Union citizenship. Referring to paragraph 42 of its *Rottmann* judgment, the Court stressed that Article 20 TFEU 'precludes national measures which have the effect of depriving citizens of the Union of the genuine enjoyment of the substance of the rights conferred by virtue of their status as citizens of the Union'.[738] The Court held that a refusal to grant a right of residence and a work permit to a third country national with dependent minor children who are Union citizens has such an effect because the children would have to leave the territory of the Union together with their parents.[739] Accordingly, the Court ruled that Article 20 TFEU precludes a Member State from refusing a right of residence and a work permit to a third country national with minor children who are Union citizens 'in so far as such decisions deprive those children of the genuine enjoyment of the substance of the rights attaching to the status of European Union citizen'.[740]

309. If the Court of Justice had followed its previous case law on purely internal situations – and hence followed the argument of the intervening governments and the European Commission – it would have declared the question inadmissible. However, the Court decided otherwise and moreover, required only seven paragraphs to decide the case. Accordingly, this judgment has given rise to more questions than it has answered.[741] The two most important questions in the wake of this judgment were: has the Court of Justice abandoned its purely internal situation doctrine and what does 'deprival of the genuine enjoyment of the substance of the rights conferred by virtue of their status as citizens of the Union' actually mean?

2.2.5.3. In the Aftermath of *Ruiz Zambrano*

310. In the *McCarthy* judgment of May 2011, the Court of Justice already provided some clarification to the questions which had arisen in the aftermath of the *Ruiz Zambrano* judgment.[742] Indeed, all the following judgments which will be discussed here – *McCarthy*, *Dereci*, *Iida*, *O and S*, *Ymeraga* and *Alokpa*

---

[738] Ibid para 42. [739] Ibid paras 43–44. [740] Ibid para 45.

[741] See inter alia HAILBRONNER and THYM, 'Case Note on Case C-34/09, Ruiz Zambrano' (2011) 48 *CMLRev* 1253–70; NIC SHUIBHNE, 'Seven Questions for Seven Paragraphs' (2011) 36 *ELRev* 161; and VAN EIJKEN and DE VRIES, 'A New Route into the Promised Land? Being a European Citizen After Ruiz Zambrano' (2011) 36 *ELRev* 704–21. By contrast, Van Elsuwege argued that the *Ruiz Zambrano* judgment '*clarifies* the constitutional relationship between primary EU law, secondary EU legislation and Member State competence' (VAN ELSUWEGE, 'Shifting the Boundaries? European Union Citizenship and the Scope of Application of EU Law' (2011) 38 *LIEI* 263, 275).

[742] However, many aspects still remained unclear. See inter alia DANIELE, 'La Corte di Giustizia rompe il vaso di pandora della cittadinanza europea' [2012] *Giornale Dir Amm* 39.

– can be seen as (limiting) explanations of the *Ruiz Zambrano* judgment.[743] All these cases concern the right of residence for a third country national family member of a Union citizen. The central question is whether the situation of the Union citizen has a sufficient connection with Union law in order to derive such a right of residence for a third country national family member.

i. The Purely Internal Situation Doctrine Confirmed: *McCarthy*

311. The *McCarthy* case concerned Mrs McCarthy, who possessed British and Irish nationality. She was born and had always lived in the UK. Her Jamaican husband had no right to reside in the UK under British Immigration Rules. Mrs McCarthy tried to obtain a right to reside in the UK for her Jamaican husband on the basis of Union law.

312. The Court of Justice first examined the applicability of Directive 2004/38.[744] It held that Directive 2004/38 did not apply to the case at issue since the Directive is not applicable to a Union citizen, who has always resided in a Member State of which he is a national.[745] The fact that the citizen also possesses the nationality of another Member State does not alter this conclusion.[746] Although Directive 2004/38 confers derived rights to family members of beneficiaries, Mrs McCarthy's husband could not invoke the Directive since Mrs McCarthy herself did not fall within the beneficiaries in the sense of the Directive.[747]

313. Secondly, the Court ruled upon the applicability of Article 21 TFEU. In that respect, the Court recalled its settled case law according to which the Treaty provisions on free movement for persons cannot be applied to activities which have no link with any of the situations governed by Union law and of which all the relevant elements can be situated within the internal sphere of one single Member State.[748] Hence, in the aftermath of the *Ruiz Zambrano* case, the Court

---

743 Nic Shuibhne has argued that 'McCarthy exhibits the beginnings of a more wide-scale and sustained recent shift from predominantly rights-opening to predominantly rights-curbing assessments of citizenship rights. The intensity of academic but also political reaction to Ruiz Zambrano is an important factor internal to citizenship law when thinking about motivations that may have produced this shift.' Nic Shuibhne, 'Limits Rising, Duties Ascending: The Changing Legal Shape of Union Citizenship' (2015) 52 *CMLRev* 889, 902. See also Tryfonidou, '(Further) Signs of a Turn of the Tide in the CJEU's Citizenship Jurisprudence, Case C-40/11, *Iida*' (2013) 20 *MJ* 302.

744 ECJ case C-434/09 *McCarthy* [ECR] I-3375, paras 30–43.

745 Ibid para 39.

746 Ibid para 40. Next, the Court considered: 'Indeed, the fact that a Union citizen is a national of more than one Member State does not mean that he has made use of his right of freedom of movement' (para 41).

747 Ibid para 42.

748 Ibid para 45.

made immediately clear in *McCarthy* that it still holds on to its purely internal situation doctrine.

314. Next, the Court added that a Union citizen, like Mrs McCarthy, who has not exercised her right of free movement, cannot on that ground alone be assimilated to a purely internal situation.[749] However, the Court held that no element of Mrs McCarthy's situation indicates that the British Immigration Rules result in 'depriving her of the genuine enjoyment of the substance of the rights associated with her status as a Union citizen, or of impeding the exercise of her right to move and reside freely within the territory of the Member States, in accordance with Article 21 TFEU'.[750] The Court distinguished the *McCarthy* case from the *Ruiz Zambrano* and *Garcia Avello* cases precisely on this ground.[751]

As opposed to the situation of Ruiz Zambrano's children, the British Immigration Rules did not have the effect of obliging Mrs McCarthy to leave the territory of the European Union since on the basis of her British nationality, she had an unconditional right of residence in the UK under international law.[752] The Court also distinguished the *McCarthy* case from the *Garcia Avello* judgment. In the *McCarthy* judgment, the Court clarified that what mattered in the *Garcia Avello* case was not that the discrepancy in surnames resulted from the dual nationality of Mr Garcia Avello's children, but that this discrepancy could cause serious inconvenience, and in particular, could represent an obstacle to the freedom of movement to the Union citizens concerned.[753]

315. Next, the Court held that the fact that Mrs McCarthy had the nationality of two Member States was not sufficient in itself for finding a sufficient link with Article 21 TFEU.[754] The Court explicitly classified Mrs McCarthy's situation as being a purely internal one to which Union law does not apply.[755] Accordingly, the Court held that Article 21 TFEU was not applicable to a situation such as that in the main proceedings.[756]

316. In general, the *McCarthy* judgment clarified some important issues which had arisen after the *Ruiz Zambrano* judgment. In particular, it can be concluded that although the purely internal situation doctrine remains applicable in principle, in two cases no link with Union law in the sense of a cross-border element is necessary.[757] First, if a Union citizen is deprived of the genuine enjoyment of the substance of the rights conferred by virtue of the status of

749 Ibid para 46.
750 Ibid para 49.
751 Ibid para 53.
752 Ibid para 50.
753 Ibid para 52.
754 Ibid para 54.
755 Ibid para 55.
756 Ibid para 56.
757 Verbist, 'De invloed van het Unieburgerschap op zuiver interne situaties' [2011] *RW* 510, 521.

Union citizen. Secondly, if a Union citizen is impeded in the exercise of his right of free movement and residence within the territory of the Member States.

Of course, this raises the question of what the difference is between an impairment of the genuine enjoyment of the substance of the rights derived from Union citizenship and other possible obstacles to Union citizenship, such as the right to move and to reside. According to AG Sharpston, the 'core right' of Union citizenship is precisely the right to move and to reside freely on the territory of other Member States.[758] However, the Court of Justice seems to consider the cases in which a deprivation of the genuine enjoyment of the substance of the rights derived from Union citizenship as comprising a distinct category.[759] Hereafter, this will be referred to as the *Ruiz Zambrano* criterion or the genuine enjoyment criterion.

317. It seems that the situation of Garcia Avello's children falls within the scope of Union law as the second situation that the Court puts forward in its dictum in *McCarthy*. Although the Garcia Avello children are not (yet) in a cross-border situation, an obstacle to move and reside on the territory of the Member States exists which falls within the scope of Article 21 TFEU.[760] In other words, as argued above, the connection with Union law seems to lie in the future movement of the children to Spain – which seems not to be a purely hypothetical matter, but is rather probable given that fact that their father is a Spanish national. If they go to Spain, the discrepancy in their surnames will impede their right of free movement.

ii. *Dereci: Ruiz Zambrano* Criterion is Exceptional and the Right to Respect for Family Life Should be Taken into Account

318. In November 2011, the Grand Chamber of the Court of Justice decided again upon questions for preliminary ruling in the field of family reunification. Mr Dereci was a Turkish national who entered Austria illegally and married an Austrian national who had never exercised her right of free movement. Together they had three children who are Austrian citizens, and still minors at the time of the hearing. Mr Dereci had been subject to an expulsion order and was trying to obtain a right of residence on the basis of European Union law, in particular on the basis of the provisions regarding citizenship.

---

758 Opinion AG Sharpston 30 September 2010 in C-34/09, *Ruiz Zambrano*, para 80.

759 By contrast, Van Elsuwege and Kochenov argue that 'the new "genuine enjoyment" and the traditional "cross-border situation" test overlap' (Van Elsuwege and Kochenov, 'On the Limits of Judicial Intervention: EU Citizenship and Family Reunification Rights' (2011) 13 *EJML* 433, 451).

760 Verbist, 'De invloed van het Unieburgerschap op zuiver interne situaties' [2011] *RW* 510, 518–19 and 522.

319. In its *Dereci* judgment, the Court of Justice subsequently examined the applicability of Directives 2003/86 and 2004/38, the applicability of the Treaty provisions on Union citizenship and the applicability of the right to respect private and family life. First, the Court considered that the Directives were not applicable.[761]

320. Secondly, the Court examined the applicability of the Treaty provisions on Union citizenship. In particular, it referred to the *Ruiz Zambrano* judgment and clarified that 'the criterion relating to the denial of the genuine enjoyment of the substance of the rights conferred by virtue of European Union citizen status refers to situations in which the Union citizen has, in fact, to leave not only the territory of the Member State of which he is a national but also the territory of the Union as a whole'.[762] The Court added that this criterion 'is specific in character' and applies only 'exceptionally'.[763] Moreover, the Court made clear that mere economic reasons or a desire to keep the family together on the territory of the Union is not sufficient in order to fall under the aforementioned criterion.[764] Accordingly, the Court held that the Treaty provisions on Union citizenship do not preclude a Member State from refusing a right of residence to a third country national who is a family member of a Union citizen, 'provided that such refusal does not lead, for the Union citizen concerned, to the denial of the genuine enjoyment of the substance of the rights conferred by virtue of his status as a citizen of the Union, which is a matter for the referring court to verify'.[765]

321. Thirdly, the Court considered that it might be that a right of residence cannot be refused on the basis of other criteria.[766] In this respect, the Court examined the applicability of the right to respect private and family life. In particular, the Court of Justice held that 'if the referring court considers, in the light of the circumstances of the disputes in the main proceedings, that the situation of the applicants in the main proceedings is covered by European Union law, it must examine whether the refusal of their right of residence undermines the right to respect for private and family life provided for in Article 7 of the Charter. On the other hand, if it takes the view that that situation is not covered by European Union law, it must undertake that examination in the light of Article 8(1) of the ECHR.'[767]

---

761 ECJ case C-256/11 *Dereci*, paras 47 and 57. In particular, Directive 2003/86 does not apply to family members of a Union citizen. Moreover, Directive 2004/38 does not apply to Union citizens who have never exercised their right of free movement and have always resided in the Member State of which they are nationals.

762 ECJ case C-256/11 *Dereci*, para 66.

763 Ibid para 67.

764 Ibid para 68.

765 Ibid para 74.

766 Ibid para 69.

767 Ibid para 72. The Court refers on the one hand to Article 51 of the Charter which determines that the Charter only applies to the Member States when they are implementing Union law

322. Hence, in *Dereci*, the Court of Justice clarified the *Ruiz Zambrano* criterion. In particular, the Court of Justice made clear that this criterion 'is specific in character' and applies only 'exceptionally'.[768] The Court held that it refers to a de facto obligation for a Union citizen to leave the territory of the Union as a whole.[769] By contrast, mere economic reasons or the desire to keep the family together on the territory of the Union are not sufficient in order to fall under the aforementioned criterion.[770]

It seems that Mr Dereci's situation did not fall within the *Ruiz Zambrano* criterion, even though the Court of Justice did not explicitly say as much and considered that it is up to the referring court to verify this. In this regard, AG Mengozzi observed in his Opinion that 'the citizenship of the Union held by Mrs Dereci could, paradoxically, be seen as a factor which checks and/or defers family reunification'.[771] In particular, both the situation of the Dereci family and that of the Ruiz Zambrano family involve young children who are Union citizens.[772] Unlike the Ruiz Zambrano couple, Mrs Dereci and her children had the right to reside in Austria. Moreover, 'the family life of the three young children of the Dereci couple is, in practice, subject to their mother exercising one of the freedoms of movement laid down in the TFEU and therefore, in all likelihood, to her movement to a Member State other than Austria'.[773]

323. The Court's additional consideration, concerning the right to respect for family life, might seem helpful at first glance, but actually raises even more questions.[774] That is to say, if the referring court considers that Mr Dereci's situation is covered by EU law, then it must examine the case in the light of Article 7 of the Charter. However, it is unclear how Mr Dereci's situation can fall within the scope of Union law. As always, we have to look at the Union citizen of which he is a family member: Mrs Dereci is an Austrian citizen who has always lived in Austria and has never exercised her right of free movement. Hence, at first glance, there is no link with Union law. Next, it seems that the situation of Mr Dereci does not fall under the *Ruiz Zambrano* criterion since neither Mrs Dereci nor her children would be forced to leave the territory of the Union if Mr Dereci were to be deported. Accordingly, nothing in the facts of the situation

---

and that the Charter does not extend the field of application of Union law (ibid para 71). On the other hand, the Court considers that all the Member States are parties to the ECHR which contains the right to respect family life in Article 8 (ibid para 73).

768 Ibid para 67. 769 Ibid para 66. 770 Ibid para 68.

771 Opinion AG Mengozzi 29 September 2011 in C-256/11, *Dereci*, para 45.

772 This is unlike the *McCarthy* case. This explains why Mrs McCarthy did not fall within the *Ruiz Zambrano* criterion. That is to say, if her Jamaican husband was deported to Jamaica, Mrs McCarthy would not have to leave the territory of the Union.

773 Opinion AG Mengozzi 29 September 2011 in C-256/11, *Dereci*, para 45.

774 Adam and Van Elsuwege, 'Citizenship Rights and the Federal Balance Between the European Union and its Member States: Comment on Dereci' (2012) 37 *ELRev* 185.

has a sufficient connection with Union law; hence, Article 7 of the Charter does not apply.[775] However, the Court of Justice did not openly take this position and instead passed the problem on to the national referring court.

324. In sum, the ECJ avoided declaring that neither the Treaty provisions on Union citizenship – by lack of a cross-border element and of a *Ruiz Zambrano* style situation – nor the Charter apply to the main proceedings in *Dereci*. A plausible explanation for 'the restraint of the ECJ might be a compromise between diverging standpoints within the Grand Chamber on the sensitive issue of the scope and limits of the innovation in *Ruiz Zambrano*'.[776] Although many questions remained unanswered, the *Dereci* judgment emphasises the right to respect for family life for all Union citizens, whether or not they fall within the scope of Union law.[777] That is, if Article 7 of the Charter does not apply, Article 8 ECHR is applicable.

iii. Explicit Position by ECJ in *Iida* and *Ymeraga*: No Derived Right of Residence, Neither on the Basis of Article 20 TFEU Nor on the Basis of Article 7 Charter

325. Whereas in *Dereci*, the Court of Justice refrained from giving clear guidance as to how Union law should be interpreted in the case in the main proceedings, it felt no similar restraint in *Iida* and *Ymeraga*. In both cases, the Court of Justice used the same three-fold structure as in *Dereci* and it took the clear position that there was no sufficient connection with Union law in the situation in the main proceedings in order to derive a right of residence for a third country national family member.

326. In November 2012, the Court of Justice decided upon the *Iida* case. Mr Iida, a Japanese national, married a German national in the US. Their daughter Mia, born in the US, had German, American and Japanese nationalities. A year later, the family moved to Germany. Two years after that, Mr Iida's wife started working full-time in Vienna and eventually the couple were permanently separated, although they were not divorced. Their daughter resided in Vienna where she went to school. The relationship between father and daughter was

---

775 See also Opinion AG Sharpston 12 December 2013 in C-456/12 and C-457/12, *O and B*, para 60: 'the Charter does not apply to an internal situation, such as that of Mrs McCarthy' and Eijken, 'Ruiz Zambrano the aftermath: de impact van artikel 20 VWEU op de Nederlandse rechtspraak' (2012) *NTER* 47.

776 Adam and Van Elsuwege, 'Citizenship Rights and the Federal Balance Between the European Union and its Member States: Comment on Dereci' (2012) 37 *ELRev* 185, 184.

777 Kostakopoulou, 'Co-creating European Union Citizenship: Institutional Process and Crescive Norms' (2012–13) 15 *Cambridge Yearbook of European Legal Studies* 267, 271 and 275.

very good. In this factual context, Mr Iida applied for a right of residence as a family member of a Union citizen. However, his application was rejected by the German authorities.

327. The Court of Justice held first that Mr Iida's situation did not fall within the scope of Directive 2003/109[778] or Directive 2004/38.[779] Secondly, the Court of Justice considered whether the situation had an 'intrinsic connection with the freedom of movement of a Union citizen'.[780] In this regard, the Court considered that Mr Iida had always resided in that Member State in accordance with national law, 'without the absence of a right of residence under European Union law having discouraged his daughter or his spouse from exercising their right of freedom of movement by moving to Austria'.[781] Accordingly, the Court explicitly held that the refusal to grant Mr Iida a right of residence on the basis of Union law neither had the effect of denying Mr Iida's spouse and daughter from the genuine enjoyment of the substance of the rights conferred upon them by their status of Union citizen nor did it impede Mr Iida's spouse and daughter from exercising their right to move and reside freely within the territory of the European Union.[782] Moreover, the Court added that 'the purely hypothetical prospect of exercising the right of freedom of movement does not establish a sufficient connection with European Union law'.[783]

328. Finally, the Court assessed whether the fundamental rights as enshrined in the Charter applied. Compared to the *Dereci* judgment, the *Iida* judgment gives much more guidance to the referring court. In particular, the Court held that the German authorities' refusal to grant Mr Iida a right of residence as a family member of a Union citizen 'does not fall within the implementation of European Union law within the meaning of article 51 of the Charter, so that its conformity with fundamental rights cannot be examined by reference to the rights established by the Charter'.[784] The Court considered in this regard that although the relevant German provisions intend to implement EU law, the

[778] He has since voluntarily withdrawn his application (para 48). Moreover, Mr Iida's right to reside in Germany is renewable and in principle he can be granted the status of long-term resident under Directive 2003/109 (ECJ case C-40/11 *Iida*, para 75).

[779] Since he did not accompany nor join his wife or daughter in Austria (ibid para 65).

[780] Ibid para 72.

[781] Ibid para 74.

[782] Ibid para 76.

[783] Ibid para 77, referring to Case C-299/95 *Kremzow* [1997] ECR I-2629, para 16. Arguably, the Court of Justice is simply recalling its *Kremzow* case law here. (See, by contrast, TRYFONIDOU, '(Further) Signs of a Turn of the Tide in the CJEU's Citizenship Jurisprudence, Case C-40/11, *Iida*' (2013) 20 *MJ* 302, 307(–13).) However, it is not clear why the Court added this consideration since it held in the previous paragraph that Articles 20 and 21 did not apply to the case in the main proceedings. Moreover after the consideration of 'purely hypothetical prospects', the Court proceeds to consider fundamental rights.

[784] ECJ case C-40/11 *Iida*, para 81.

case is not governed by European Union law since Mr Iida did not satisfy the conditions of Directive 2004/38 and he did not apply for a long-term residence on the basis of Directive 2003/109.

329. Probably, the fact that Mr Iida has always had a right of residence under German law which was renewable and the fact that he withdrew his application for a long-term residence on the basis of Directive 2003/109 caused the Court to take such an explicit position in the case.[785] That is to say, other remedies were available for Mr Iida whereas for Ruiz Zambrano, for instance, a right of residence on the basis of Union citizenship was his only chance to stay in Europe.

330. The *Ymeraga* judgment of May 2013 concerned Mr Ymeraga, a citizen of Kosovo, who arrived in Luxembourg as a 15-year-old in 1999, to live with his uncle, a Luxembourg national, who became his legal guardian. After his studies, he found regular employment in Luxemburg and he had resided there since 1999. Between 2006 and 2008, his parents and two brothers arrived in Luxembourg. Their applications to obtain a residence permit on grounds of asylum and family reunification were rejected. In the meantime, Mr Ymeraga obtained Luxembourg nationality. The subsequent application for a residence permit for his parents and brothers as family member of a Union citizen were rejected.

331. First, the Court of Justice noted that the applicants in the main proceedings did not qualify for the protection granted by Directives 2003/86 and 2004/38.[786] In particular, Directive 2003/86 does not apply to family members of a Union citizen and Directive 2004/38 does not apply to a Union citizen who has never exercised his right of free movement and who has always resided in the same Member State of which he is a national.

332. Secondly, the Court considered whether a right of residence could be derived from Article 20 TFEU.[787] Article 20 TFEU could not be relied upon since the refusal to grant such a right of residence would not have the effect of denying Mr Kreshnik Ymeraga the genuine enjoyment of the substance of the rights conferred by virtue of his status as citizen of the Union.[788]

---

785 However, not everyone seems convinced that Mr Iida's right of residence in Germany is assured. In particular, Tryfonidou has argued that if the German authorities refuse to grant Mr Iida a right of residence in Germany in the future, this will lead to a violation of the rights his daughter Mia derives from Articles 7 and 24 Charter and Article 8 ECHR (Tryfonidou, '(Further) Signs of a Turn of the Tide in the CJEU's Citizenship Jurisprudence, Case C-40/11, *Iida*' (2013) 20 *MJ* 302, 318–19).

786 ECJ case C-87/12 *Ymeraga*, paras 24–33.

787 Ibid paras 34–39.

788 Ibid para 39.

333. Thirdly, the Court examined the situation in the light of the fundamental rights mentioned by the referring court. First of all, the Court emphasised that, on the basis of Article 51 of the Charter, the provisions thereof are addressed to the Member States only when they are implementing Union law and that the Charter does not extend the powers of the European Union.[789] The Court pointed out that in order to determine whether the refusal by the Luxembourg authorities falls within the scope of the Charter, the following issues should be taken into account: does the national legislation at issue implement Union law, what is the character of the legislation and which objectives are pursued by it?[790] In particular, the Court of Justice considered that 'while the Law on freedom of movement is indeed intended to implement European Union law, it is none the less the case that the situation of the applicants in the main proceedings is not governed by European Union law, since Mr. Kreshnik Ymeraga cannot be regarded as a beneficiary of either Directive 2004/38 or, as regards the applications at issue in the main proceedings, Directive 2003/86, and the refusal to confer a right of residence on Mr. Kreshnik Ymeraga's family members does not have the effect of denying him the genuine enjoyment of the substance of the rights conferred by virtue of his status as citizen of the Union'.[791]

334. Accordingly, the Court held that the refusal by the Luxembourg authorities to grant a residence permit to Mr Ymeraga's family members 'is not a situation involving the implementation of European Union law within the meaning of Article 51 of the Charter, so that its conformity with fundamental rights cannot be examined in the light of the rights established by the Charter'.[792] Finally, the Court added that the situation in the main proceedings can still be judged in the light of the provisions of the European Convention for the Protection of Human Rights and Fundamental Freedoms.[793]

335. It is remarkable that in the *Iida* and the *Ymeraga* cases the ECJ explicitly held that there was no sufficient connection with Union law in the main proceedings in order to derive a right of residence for a third county national family member of the Union citizen. This might be a response to the criticisms following the *Dereci* judgment, according to which the Court of Justice did not provide enough guidance to the referring court in order to decide on the case in the main proceedings.[794] Admittedly, it is a difficult balancing act for the Court of Justice between an overly abstract interpretation of Union law and all too

789 Ibid para 40.
790 Ibid para 41.
791 Ibid para 42.
792 Ibid para 43.
793 Ibid para 44.
794 See inter alia Adam and Van Elsuwege, 'Citizenship Rights and the Federal Balance Between the European Union and its Member States: Comment on Dereci' (2012) 37 *ELRev* 185, 185.

concrete guidance, since the referring court has to decide the case in the main proceedings.[795]

336. In any event, *Iida* and *Ymeraga* confirm the reading of *Dereci* according to which Article 7 of the Charter did not apply to the main proceedings in the latter case. More generally, it can be concluded that the Court of Justice clarified in the *Iida* and *Ymeraga* judgments the scope of application of the fundamental rights enshrined in the Charter. That is to say, if the Union citizen is not a beneficiary of Directive 2004/38 or Directive 2003/86 and the *Ruiz Zambrano* criterion is not satisfied, the situation at stake does not involve the implementation of Union law within the meaning of Article 51 of the Charter. Accordingly, in such a situation no right of residence for a third country national family member of a Union citizen can be derived from Article 7 of the Charter.

As AG Sharpston argued in her Opinion in *O and B*, the Charter does not enhance 'free-standing' rights, but only applies them where Union law applies.[796] In particular, AG Sharpston argued that Articles 20 and 21 TFEU are 'not simply a basis for residence status separate from Article 7 of the Charter', enshrining the right to respect for private and family life, they must be interpreted in a 'Charter-compliant' manner.[797] She emphasised that this approach does not violate the division of competences between the EU and the Member States, given that it merely respects the principle that all the relevant law is taken into account when interpreting a measure of that legal order.[798]

337. Spaventa has argued that 'it is possible that we are witnessing a shift so that national rules are subject first and foremost to the national and ECHR standards, the Charter being relevant only in those cases where there is a more direct connection between EU law and the national implementing measure. Be that as it may, it would be good for some clarity to be brought in this matter.'[799] This interpretation seems to comply with Article 51 of the Charter, delimiting the scope of application of the Charter.[800]

---

795 Article 267 TFEU. Lenaerts, Maselis and Gutman, *EU Procedural Law*, Nowak (ed), Oxford University Press 2014, pp 65, 82–86 and Opinion AG Sharpston 12 December 2013 in C-456/12 and C-457/12, *O and B*, para 66.

796 Opinion AG Sharpston 12 December 2013 in C-456/12 and C-457/12, *O and B*, paras 60–61.

797 Ibid para 62.

798 Ibid para 63.

799 Spaventa, 'Family Rights for Circular Migrants and Frontier Workers: O and B, and S and G' (2015) 52 *CMLRev* 753, 774.

800 Unfortunately, the precise meaning of Article 51 Charter is still open to discussion. See more in Sanchez, 'The Court and the Charter: The Impact of the Entry into Force of the Lisbon Treaty on the ECJ'S Approach to Fundamental Rights' (2012) 49 *CMLRev* 1565, 1590.

338. Moreover, it should not make a difference to the individual in the main proceedings whether the assessment is based on Article 7 Charter or under Article 8 ECHR. AG Sharpston has pointed out that if Article 7 of the Charter applies, then it should be interpreted in a manner that takes the case law of the European Court of Human Rights into account, particularly regarding Article 8 ECHR.[801] Sharpston has argued that 'it should be immaterial whether one considers whether application of a particular national measure would breach Article 7 of the Charter or Article 8 ECHR'.[802] She argues that since the standard being applied is the same, so should be the conclusion.[803] This interpretation certainly finds support in Article 52(3) of the Charter which provides that 'in so far as this Charter contains rights which correspond to rights guaranteed by the Convention for the Protection of Human Rights and Fundamental Freedoms, the meaning and scope of those rights shall be the same as those laid down by the aforementioned Convention. This provision shall not prevent Union law providing more extensive protection'.

iv. Further Guidance on the *Ruiz Zambrano* Criterion in *O and S*

339. Another relevant case in this list is the *O and S* case, again concerning family reunification and the right of residence. Ms S, a national of Ghana and resident in Finland on the basis of a permanent residence permit, married a Finnish national. The couple had a child, who acquired Finnish nationality and who has always lived in Finland. When the couple divorced, Ms S was awarded sole custody of the child. Three years later, Ms S married Mr O, a national of the Côte d'Ivoire. They had a child together who has Ghanaian nationality. Mr O's application for a residence permit on the basis of the marriage was rejected.[804] In this factual context, the question arose as to whether the Treaty provisions on Union citizenship preclude a Member State from refusing a third country national, such as Mr O, a right of residence.[805]

340. The Court of Justice recalled that the fact that children of Finnish nationality have not used their right of free movement does not automatically lead to the conclusion that they are in a purely internal situation.[806] In this respect, the Court recalled the *Ruiz Zambrano* case.[807] In particular, the Court emphasised that it is for the national judge to establish whether the refusal of the residence permit for Mr O led in the circumstances at issue to 'a denial of the

---

801 Opinion AG Sharpston 12 December 2013 in C-456/12 and C-457/12, *O and B*, para 64.
802 Ibid para 65. 803 Ibid.
804 I only described the facts of Case C-356/11.
805 Case C-357/11 concerns Ms L and Mr M whose situation is almost identical with that of Ms S and Mr O, only the dates and nationalities differ.
806 ECJ joined cases C-356/11 and C-357/11, *O and S*, para 43.
807 Ibid paras 45 ff.

genuine enjoyment of the substance of the rights' conferred upon the Finnish children by their status of Union citizen.[808] When making this assessment, the referring court must examine all the circumstances in the case.[809] In this regard, the Court of Justice indicated which elements are decisive or not.[810]

341. On the one hand, the Court recalled that the fact that it might be desirable for economic reasons or in order to preserve the family unit in the EU is in itself not sufficient in order to bring the case within the *Ruiz Zambrano* criterion.[811] Moreover, it is not decisive whether the person for whom a right of residence is sought lives together with the Union citizen of which he is a family member.[812] Next, the Court emphasised that although the *Ruiz Zambrano* criterion only applies in exceptional circumstances, its application is not confined to situations in which there is a blood relationship between the third country national for whom a right of residence is sought and the Union citizen who is a minor from whom that right might be derived.[813]

342. On the other hand, it should be taken into account that the mother of the Union citizen has a permanent residence permit in Finland, so in law there is no obligation for them or for the minor Union citizen to leave Finland or the territory of the EU.[814] Moreover, it is relevant that the mother has sole custody over the minor child who is a Union citizen and that the latter is part of a reconstituted family.[815] Next, the Court emphasised that what matters is the relationship of dependency between the minor Union citizen and the third country national since that dependency would lead to the Union citizen being obliged, in fact, to leave the territory of the European Union as a whole.[816]

343. The Court considered that on the basis of the information available to it no legal, financial or emotional dependency existed between the minor Union citizen and the third country national for whom a right of residence was sought.[817] Accordingly, the Court held that Article 20 TFEU does not preclude 'a Member State from refusing to grant a third country national a residence permit on the basis of family reunification where that national seeks to reside with his spouse, who is also a third country national and resides lawfully in that Member State and is the mother of a child from a previous marriage who is a Union citizen, and with the child of their own marriage, who is also a third country national, provided that such a refusal does not entail, for the Union citizen concerned, the

[808] Ibid para 49.
[809] Ibid para 53.
[810] Ibid paras 50–57.
[811] Ibid para 52.
[812] Ibid para 54.
[813] Ibid para 55.
[814] Ibid para 50.
[815] Ibid para 51.
[816] Ibid para 56, referring to Opinion AG Bot 27 September 2012 in C-356/11 and C-357/11, para 44.
[817] ECJ joined cases C-356/11 and C-357/11, *O and S*, paras 56–57.

denial of the genuine enjoyment of the substance of the rights conferred by the status of citizen of the Union, that being for the referring court to ascertain'.[818]

344. Finally, the Court of Justice examined the situation in the main proceedings in the light of Directive 2003/86 although the referring court did not refer a question for preliminary ruling concerning that Directive specifically.[819] Not surprisingly, the Court held that 'applications for residence permits on the basis of family reunification such as those at issue in the main proceedings are covered by Directive 2003/86'.[820] Hence, the Court offered a solution for the specific situation of Mr O on its own motion.

345. Although guidance has been given as to decisive elements required to bring a case within the *Ruiz Zambrano* criterion, questions regarding specific factual circumstances continue to exist. For instance, would a Union citizen fall within the *Ruiz Zambrano* criterion if his spouse has a disability or if his parent is ill? The answer probably depends on the precise circumstances of the case, but the answer seems to be in the affirmative generally. In *O and S*, the Court of Justice emphasised that the relationship of dependency between the Union citizens and the third country national is crucial in order to fall under the criterion of being denied the substance of the rights conferred by the status of Union citizenship. In particular, this dependency may be of a legal, financial or economic nature. The Court of Justice even referred to the Opinion of the Advocate General in this regard, in particular to point 44.

In the subsequent point, AG Bot argued precisely that those situations may also concern 'adult children on whom a parent is dependent because of an illness or a disability'.[821] AG Mengozzi had already expressed the same thought in his view in *Dereci*.[822] Moreover, AG Bot underlined that the 'third-country nationals who exercise no responsibility, either parental or financial, over the Union citizen' are not concerned, because otherwise a right of residence for third country nationals on the sole basis of Article 20 TFEU, and outside the provisions of secondary law, risks being founded.[823]

v. *Alokpa*: Combining *Zhu Chen* and *Ruiz Zambrano*

346. The *Alokpa* case builds upon the *Zhu and Chen* and *Ruiz Zambrano* cases. The case concerned Mrs Alokpa, a citizen of Togo, who applied for asylum in

[818] Ibid para 58.
[819] Ibid paras 60–61.
[820] Ibid para 82.
[821] Opinion AG Bot 27 September 2012 in C-356/11 and C-357/11, *O and S*, para 45.
[822] View AG Mengozzi 29 September 2011 in C-256/11, *Dereci*, paras 47–48.
[823] Opinion AG Bot 27 September 2012 in C-356/11 and C-357/11, *O and S*, para 45.

Luxembourg. Her application was rejected, but she was granted discretionary leave to remain because in Luxembourg she had given birth to twins who required medical care due to their premature birth. Mrs Alokpa's children were recognised by Mr Moudoulou, a French national; therefore, they acquired French nationality. However, the children never enjoyed a family life with their father, who only declared their birth and enabled them to acquire French nationality. Mrs Alokpa applied for a residence permit as a family member of Union citizens, although it is undisputed that the latter had not exercised their right of free movement.

347. In its assessment, the Court of Justice first observed the situation in the main proceedings in the context of Directive 2004/38.[824] At first glance, Mrs Alokpa does not fall under the definition of family member, in the meaning of Article 3(1) of Directive 2004/38, since she is not an ascendant who is dependent uon a Union citizen. Quite on the contrary, her two sons, Union citizens, are dependent upon her.[825] However, in this respect, the Court of Justice recalled its *Zhu Chen* judgment. In particular, it held that in a situation in which 'a Union citizen was born in the host Member State and had not made use of the right to free movement', Article 7(1)(b) of Directive 2004/38 must be interpreted in the sense that it suffices that sufficient resources are available to the Union citizens, the origins of those resources are not relevant.[826] Next, the Court ruled that 'a refusal to allow a parent … who is the carer of a minor child who is a Union citizen to reside with that child in the host Member State would deprive the child's right of residence of any useful effect, since enjoyment by a young child of a right of residence necessarily implies that the child is entitled to be accompanied by the person who is his primary carer'.[827] Accordingly, the Court held that a minor child who is a Union citizen and satisfies the conditions of Article 7(1)(b) of Directive 2004/38 enjoys a right of residence in the host Member State on the basis of Article 21 TFEU and Directive 2004/38 and that the same provisions allow the parent who is the minor's primary carer to reside with the latter in the host Member State.[828] It was emphasised that it is for the referring court to assess whether in the case of the main proceedings Mrs Alokpa's children satisfy the conditions set out in Article 7(1)(b) of Directive 2004/38.[829]

348. Next, the Court considered that if the referring court rules that Article 21 TFEU does not preclude Mrs Alokpa from being refused a right of residence in Luxembourg, it should still ascertain whether such a right of residence should,

---

824 ECJ case C-86/12 *Alokpa*, paras 24 ff.
825 Ibid para 26.
826 Ibid para 27.
827 Ibid para 28.
828 Ibid para 29.
829 Ibid para 30.

nevertheless and exceptionally, be granted in the light of Article 20 TFEU.[830] That is to say, if a refusal would result in Mrs Alokpa's children being obliged to leave the territory of the European Union and hence, denying them the genuine enjoyment of the substance of the rights conferred by their status of Union citizen.[831] In this respect, the Court of Justice left no room for interpretation for the referring court and held that Mrs Alokpa, as the mother and sole carer of her two sons with a French nationality, had a right to reside in France.[832] Consequently, the Luxembourg authorities' refusal to grant Mrs Alokpa a right of residence does not result in obliging her children to leave the territory of the European Union altogether.[833] In spite of this clear assessment, the Court of Justice added that it is, however, up to the referring court to determine whether this is in fact the case in the light of all elements of the main proceedings.[834]

349. As emerges from recurring requests for preliminary rulings regarding the interpretation of the *Ruiz Zambrano* judgment, the precise scope of that judgment is still not entirely clear. For instance, the pending *Rendon Marin* case concerns the interpretation and scope of Article 20 TFEU in the light of the *Zhu Chen* and *Ruiz Zambrano* judgments when, in particular, the applicants in the main proceedings have a criminal record.[835]

2.2.5.4. The Clear Impact of Union Citizenship on the Connection Required with Union Law – Recent Limits

350. Since *Rottmann* and *Ruiz Zambrano*, in contrast to the Treaty provisions on free movement, a connection with Union citizenship can exist that lacks a cross-border element.[836] Accordingly, at present, a sufficient connection with Union law can exist in the presence of a cross-border element – in which some kind of movement (generously accepted by the ECJ) brings the situation within the scope of application of Union law – or in the presence of an intrinsic connection with Union law – in which more abstract elements bring the situation within the scope of application of Union law.

351. In the aftermath of *Ruiz Zambrano* – in *McCarthy, Dereci, Iida, O and S, Ymeraga and Alokpa* – the ECJ has restrictively interpreted this intrinsic

830 Ibid paras 32–33.

831 Ibid para. 3.

832 Ibid para 34 and referring to Opinion AG Mengozzi 21 March 2013 in ibid paras 54–55. He pointed out that the two sons of Mrs Alokpa have an unconditional right to enter France and reside there on the basis of Article 21 TFEU and as a principle of international law.

833 Ibid para 35.

834 Ibid. However, this addition seems rather pro forma.

835 ECJ pending joined cases C-165/14 and C-304/14, *Rendon Marin*. See already Opinion AG Szpunar 4 February 2016 in ibid.

836 Lenaerts, '"Civis europaeus sum": From the Cross-border Link to the Status of Citizen of the Union' [2011] *Online Journal on Free Movement of Workers within the European Union* 6, 17–18.

connection with Union law, which is a positive development since otherwise the division of competences between the EU and the Member States would be disturbed.[837] Although these judgments definitely emphasise the role of the Union citizen's status, the ECJ has not recognised, at least not in general, Union citizenship in itself as a sufficient link with Union law.[838] Neither has the Court recognised 'the right to stay where one is' or a general 'free-standing right of residence',[839] although this would have had the advantage that most situations of reverse discrimination would disappear because nationals could rely in a purely internal situation on Article 21 TFEU,[840] recognising that a free-standing right of residence would be too intrusive upon the Member States' competences. Nevertheless, the genuine enjoyment criterion or the *Ruiz Zambrano* criterion can be seen as a free-standing right of residence in specific and exceptional situations. For these particular situations, the paradox between moving as a precondition and as a material right at the same time has been solved.

352. It seems that recently the Court of Justice has increasingly emphasised the limits on the rights conferred by the status of Union citizenship. As Nic Shuibhne has observed in general, 'case law trends also ebb and flow – expansive decisions follow restrictive decisions; and vice versa'.[841] However, she has argued that the *McCarthy* judgment 'exhibits the beginnings of a more wide-scale and sustained recent shift from predominantly rights-opening to predominantly rights-curbing assessments of citizenship rights'.[842] A probable explanation lies in the intense academic and political reactions to the *Ruiz Zambrano* judgment.[843] The current author shares this view. In the first place, this is clear regarding the interpretation of the purely internal situation rule since *McCarthy*. As has been argued above, the *McCarthy, Dereci, Iida, O and S,*

---

837 Ibid 873.

838 This has been defended by inter alia O'Leary, *The Evolving Concept of Community Citizenship. From the Free Movement of Persons to Union Citizenship*, Kluwer Law International 1996, p 278; Spaventa, 'Seeing the Wood Despite the Trees? On the Scope of Union Citizenship and its Constitutional Effects' (2008) 45 *CMLRev* 13, 30 and also Dautricourt and Thomas, 'Reverse Discrimination and Free Movement of Persons Under Community Law: All for Ulysses, Nothing for Penelope?' (2009) 34 *ELRev* 454, however, arguing that the Union legislator should take this step, 447–50.

839 See inter alia D'Oliveira, 'Is Reverse Discrimination Still Possible Under the Single European Act?' in *Forty Years On: The Evolution of Postwar Private International Law in Europe: Symposium in Celebration of the 40th Anniversary of the Centre of Foreign Law and Private International Law, University of Amsterdam, on 27 October 1989*, Kluwer 1990, pp 85–86 and Opinion AG Sharpston 30 September 2010 in C-34/09, *Ruiz Zambrano*, paras 84 and 100–01.

840 Cambien, 'Citizenship of the Union as a Cornerstone of European Integration', Dissertation, KU Leuven 2011, p 253.

841 Nic Shuibhne, 'Limits Rising, Duties Ascending: The Changing Legal Shape of Union Citizenship' (2015) 52 *CMLRev* 889, 902.

842 Ibid.

843 Ibid.

Ymeraga and *Alokpa* judgments can be seen as limiting explanations of the *Ruiz Zambrano* judgment. Moreover, this 'rights-curbing' perspective on Union citizenship rights seems to be confirmed in the ECJ's case law concerning the access to benefits in a host Member State, in particular in the *Dano* and *Alimanovic* judgments.[844]

[844] Verbist, 'Case Note on C-67/14, Alimanovic' (2016) 5 *SEW* 233–236. See also Peers, 'EU Law Analysis: Free Movement and Social Benefits for Economically Inactive EU Citizens: The Dano Judgment in Historical Context' (<http://eulawanalysis.blogspot.be/2014/11/free-movement-and-social-benefits-for.html>) and 'EU Law Analysis: EU Citizens' Access to Benefits: The CJEU Clarifies the Position of Former Workers' (<http://eulawanalysis.blogspot.be/2015/09/eu-citizens-access-to-benefits-cjeu.html>) (last accessed 4 April 2016).

CONCLUSION PART I

1. REVERSE DISCRIMINATION AS A SIDE EFFECT OF THE SCOPE OF APPLICATION OF UNION LAW

353. According to settled case law of the ECJ, the Treaty provisions on free movement and citizenship do not apply to purely internal situations, in which all of the relevant aspects are confined to one single Member State. Therefore, a Member State may treat its own nationals in purely internal situations less favourably than persons falling within the scope of application of Union law. Hence, the limited scope of application of the Treaty provisions on free movement and citizenship may lead to a situation of reverse discrimination. In particular, reverse discrimination can be considered to be a side effect of the fact that national law and Union law are applicable to the same territory; however, each of them with its own limited scope of application.

354. It is settled case law of the Court of Justice that situations of reverse discrimination are not prohibited by Union law. Accordingly, situations of reverse discrimination fall within the scope of law of the Member States and they have to deal with it. It has been argued above that the ECJ's traditional approach remains valid since reverse discrimination has to be considered as a possible side effect of the limited scope of application of Union law which is based on the division of competences between the EU and the Member States as governed by the principle of conferral of powers.

355. It was argued that a general prohibition of reverse discrimination at Union level would only be possible by changing primary law; that is to say, by a Treaty amendment of the Treaty provisions on freedom of movement and Article 18 TFEU. However, this seems not only to be politically unfeasible in the near future, it also seems to be unnecessary and undesirable. First, the supposition that a general prohibition on reverse discrimination at Union level would lead to better protection of Union citizens in all cases has been challenged. The more favourable conditions for those who fall within the scope of Union law often impose fewer requirements in order to benefit from a certain right. However, the stricter conditions for purely internal situations can not only be seen to be a less favourable treatment of purely internal situations, but also as a way to achieve higher standards of quality and protection.

Secondly, a general prohibition on reverse discrimination at the Union level would imply that policy decisions actually pass from national level to the EU. However, national institutions seem to be better suited to assess situations of reverse discrimination than EU institutions[845] because they are familiar with the national rules, principles and interests which are at stake.

Finally, it has been emphasised that already-existing remedies for reverse discrimination are available at both the Union and national levels. Correcting reverse discrimination at the Union level is possible by way of maximum harmonisation of legislation in a specific domain. In the absence thereof, the Member States can correct the situation of reverse discrimination, as Part II will go on to analyse.

2. THE ECJ'S INTERPRETATION OF A PURELY INTERNAL SITUATION

356. The extent to which reverse discrimination falls within the scope of law of the Member States depends upon the interpretation of what a purely internal situation is. It is the Court of Justice that ultimately interprets whether a situation is purely internal or whether it falls within the scope of application of Union law.

357. The ECJ accepts a sufficient connection with Union law very generously, bringing a situation as often as possible within the scope of Union law. We have distinguished two techniques that the ECJ uses in order to consider increasingly greater numbers of situations as falling within the scope of Union law. First, the Court stretches the notion of movement to its outer limits – a cross-border element as actual movement between Member States is far from a necessary condition. Secondly, the Court reduces the importance of movement in the light of Union citizenship by accepting more abstract elements inherent to the situation as a sufficient link with Union law.

358. Although the precise degree of connection with Union law which is required to fall within its scope remains opaque, some indications can be inferred from recent case law. It is remarkable that the most significant element of recent developments in the Court's case law on a sufficient link with Union law

---

845 Hanf, '"Reverse Discrimination" in EU Law: Constitutional Aberration, Constitutional Necessity, or Judicial Choice?' (2011) 18 *MJ* 29, 57; Poiares Maduro, 'The Scope of European Remedies: The Case of Purely Internal Situations and Reverse Discrimination' in Kilpatrick, Novitz and Skidmore (eds), *The Future of European Remedies*, Hart Publishing 2000, p 137 and Ritter, 'Purely Internal Situations, Reverse Discrimination, Guimont, Dzodzi and Article 234' (2006) 31 *ELRev* 702.

concerns derived rights of residence for third country nationals, who are family members of Union citizens, in the home Member State of the Union citizen.

359. In the *O and B* case, the Court of Justice gave some further guidance on how much movement is required in order to derive a right of residence for a third country national family member on the basis of Article 21 TFEU. In particular, the Court held that only genuine residence, understood as periods of residence by the Union citizen of more than three months in another Member State and during which family life has been created or strengthened, can result in a derived right of residence in the Union citizen's home Member State for third country national family members. Moreover, the Court of Justice held that weekends or holidays spent in another Member State do not generate such a derived right of residence from Article 21 TFEU, not even when all the short periods are considered together.

360. The *Ruiz Zambrano* judgment is of particular importance regarding the reduction of the importance of movement. Since Ruiz Zambrano's children, Belgian citizens and hence Union citizens, had never left Belgium, it was argued that Union law did not apply in the case at issue because the main proceedings concerned a purely internal situation. The Court of Justice gave no response to this remark and held that national measures 'which have the effect of depriving citizens of the Union of the genuine enjoyment of the substance of the rights conferred by virtue of their status as citizens of the Union' are incompatible with Article 20 TFEU.

The two main questions following this judgment were: had the Court of Justice abandoned its purely internal situation doctrine and what does 'deprival of the genuine enjoyment of the substance of the rights conferred by virtue of their status as citizens of the Union' actually mean? The Court of Justice answered these questions in subsequent cases, providing an explanation of the *Ruiz Zambrano* judgment that confined its application to very specific cases.

361. The first question was answered two months later in the *McCarthy* judgment in which the Court of Justice confirmed its purely internal situation doctrine. In *Dereci*, the Court of Justice clarified that the *Ruiz Zambrano* criterion is specific in character and applies only exceptionally. The Court held that it refers to a de facto obligation for a Union citizen to leave the territory of the Union as a whole. By contrast, merely economic reasons or a desire to keep the family together on the territory of the Union are not sufficient in order to bring the circumstances within the aforementioned criterion. In *O and S*, the Court emphasised that the relationship of dependency – be it legal, financial or economic – between the Union citizen and the third country national is decisive, given that that dependency would lead to the Union citizen being obliged, in fact, to leave the territory of the European Union as a whole.

362. The demarcation line between the scope of application of the Treaty provisions on free movement (and citizenship) and the scope of application of national law coincided, at first, with cross-border situations and purely internal situations respectively. However, this no longer applies. Either a cross-border element or an intrinsic connection with Union law can constitute a sufficient connection with Union law in order to fall within the scope of application of the Treaty provisions on freedom of movement and citizenship. Accordingly, the boundaries between the scope of application of EU law and national law have been shifted in favour of the former.

3. DISTINGUISHING PROBLEMATIC AND UNPROBLEMATIC CASES OF REVERSE DISCRIMINATION – REDEFINING THE SCOPE OF APPLICATION OF UNION LAW

363. As argued above, our starting point is that reverse discrimination has to be considered to be a side effect of the limited scope of application of Union law which is based on the division of competences between the EU and the Member States as governed by the principle of conferral of powers. However, this does not imply that some situations of reverse discrimination should not be considered to be problematic. This raises the question of which situations of reverse discrimination require a solution and which do not. In this author's opinion, this is related to the demarcation line between the scope of application of Union law and that of national law. In particular, the ECJ's interpretation of the boundaries between the scope of application of Union law and that of national law can be criticised as being arbitrary.

3.1. PROPOSALS IN LITERATURE DISTINGUISHING PROBLEMATIC CASES FROM UNPROBLEMATIC CASES OF REVERSE DISCRIMINATION

364. This section discusses the position of two scholars, Spitaleri and Tryfonidou, who after arguing that reverse discrimination should be remedied at the Union level, have specified that not all situations of reverse discrimination are problematic at Union level. This book's approach is different in the sense that it starts from the idea that reverse discrimination is a side effect of the limited scope of application of Union law, based on the division of competences between the EU and the Member States which should be accepted as a starting point, but that in some circumstances the reverse discrimination should be remedied.

365. Spitaleri has argued that not every situation of reverse discrimination should be considered to be illegitimate at the Union level, but only those most serious forms of reverse discrimination which cannot be justified in the light of the fundamental goals of the Union.[846] In these cases, the Union principle of equality should prohibit the reverse discrimination.[847] On the other hand, Spitaleri has argued that 'the less serious' cases of reverse discrimination could still be remedied at national level.[848]

366. Of course, the question arises of when a stricter treatment of purely internal situations is unjustified in the light of the fundamental goals of the European Union. In this regard, referring to the *Lancry* judgment, Spitaleri has argued that subjecting only national products to heavier burdens can be prohibited because it brings the unity of the common market at risk.[849] He argued likewise that the position of workers who have never exercised their right of free movement could be protected because the lack of attributing to them the rights which are granted in identical situations to citizens falling under Union law can be perceived as a privilege without motivation, creating in this way sentiments of hostility vis-à-vis the EU integration which could stop its evolution.[850] On the other hand, he submitted that the situation is different if the less favourable treatment of national products does not prejudice the primary goals of the Union legal order, but responds instead to reasonable national needs, for instance, the will of a Member State to safeguard the high qualitative standards of national products.[851] In this case, the different treatment can be judged to be compatible with the general principle of equality as enshrined in Union law.[852]

367. If Spitaleri can be interpreted as arguing that reverse discrimination has to be remedied where it undermines the legitimacy of the EU, then it is submitted he is right. However, where he seems to suggest that the solution lies in extending the scope of application of Union law in some situations, it is submitted instead that the solution lies in a more limited interpretation of the scope of application of Union law than that currently adopted by the ECJ.

For instance, Spitaleri has argued that not attributing certain rights to workers who have never exercised their right of free movement can lead to hostility towards the EU project. He argues that in such cases, reverse discrimination should be considered illegitimate at the Union level. This author agrees that

846 Spitaleri, *Le discriminiazioni alla rovescia nel diritto comunitario*, Università di Trieste 2005, pp 157 and 160. See also Lenaerts, 'L'égalité de traitement en droit communautaire. Un principe unique aux apparences multiples' [1991] *CDE* 41, 19. Above n 70.

847 Spitaleri, *Le discriminiazioni alla rovescia nel diritto comunitario*, Università di Trieste 2005, pp 157 and 160.

848 Ibid p 157.

849 Ibid.

850 Ibid pp 157–58.

851 Ibid p 158.

852 Ibid.

granting rights to Union citizens in identical situations depending on whether or not they can demonstrate a sufficient connection with Union law entails the risk of alienating Union citizens from the project of EU integration. However, it seems that the perception of the injustice of reverse discrimination is due to the unpredictability with which the Court of Justice accepts a sufficient connection with Union law. The problem seems to be exacerbated by the ECJ's increasingly generous interpretation of a sufficient connection with Union law. Therefore, it is contended that the most logic solution lies in a more straightforward and a more limited interpretation of the scope of application of the Treaty provisions on free movement and citizenship.

368. Against the background of the post-Maastricht developments, Tryfonidou has argued that the EU should provide a solution to the problem of reverse discrimination. That is to say, in the light of the internal market, she is of the opinion that 'reverse discrimination may amount to a violation of the [Union] principle of equality'.[853] It is only in her concluding chapter that Tryfonidou argues that 'not all instances of reverse discrimination are problematic from the point of view of [Union] law'.[854]

In particular, Tryfonidou has argued that the distinction between problematic and non-problematic instances of reverse discrimination actually depends upon whether the situations are similar and, therefore, must be treated in a like manner.[855] That is to say, reverse discrimination originally arose as a side-effect of European economic integration. The European Community aimed at achieving substantive equality by having recourse to positive action.[856] In this context, the more favourable treatment was a compensation for the disadvantage they would have suffered as a result of exercising one of the fundamental freedoms. In these cases of reverse discrimination, one could say that the different situations are treated differently. However, it is problematic if reverse discrimination arises 'as a result of the overcompensation of a disadvantage; or when it involves the provision of more favourable treatment in situations where no disadvantage would have been suffered as a result of exercising one of the fundamental freedoms'.[857] According to Tryfonidou, these situations of reverse discrimination concern the different treatment of similar situations.

369. Tryfonidou has illustrated this difference in instances of reverse discrimination on the basis of specific cases brought before the ECJ. In the domain of freedom of movement for persons, Tryfonidou has discussed a 'paradigmatic'

853 Tryfonidou, *Reverse Discrimination*, Kluwer Law International 2009, pp 218–20.
854 Ibid p 220. She defends the choice to only point this out at the end of her book because she 'did not wish to add an extra layer of perplexity to the analysis'.
855 Ibid.
856 Ibid.
857 Ibid p 221.

situation of reverse discrimination regarding occupational or educational qualifications.[858] The *Aubertin* case, in particular, concerned nationals of other Member States who had already complied with one set of regulations, while nationals of the host State were only regulated by the host Member State. Tryfonidou has argued that such instances of reverse discrimination do not constitute discrimination.[859]

On the other hand, she referred to *Hurd* as being an unacceptable instance of reverse discrimination. The case concerned teachers in a European school situated in Britain, and in particular the (exemption from) income tax on their 'European supplement'. While the European supplement of British teachers was subjected to British income tax, the European supplement of non-British teachers was exempted from British income tax. According to Tryfonidou, this exemption constituted an overcompensation for persons who had exercised their right of free movement because they had not already paid income tax in their state of origin. She considered that since the non-British teachers were in a similar situation to that of British nationals, they should be treated in the same way.[860]

370. Moreover, Tryfonidou referred to the area of family reunification as being an example 'of an area where instances of reverse discrimination that used to be acceptable because they achieved substantive equality, have now been transformed to unacceptable instances of reverse discrimination that must be targeted for resolution'.[861] That is to say, while the EC initially wanted to ensure that migrant workers would not lose their right to family life when exercising their right of free movement, now 'extra rights [are] given to some Member State nationals just because they are lucky enough to be able to point to a link with [Union] law (even an entirely artificial one!)'.[862] Accordingly, Tryfonidou has argued that this form of reverse discrimination has gone from 'positive action' to 'blatant discrimination'.[863]

371. Tryfonidou has also provided some examples in the area of trade. She argued that an instance of acceptable reverse discrimination regarding production requirements was at stake in *Drei Glocken*. In particular, pasta produced in Italy was only subjected to Italian rules, where imported pasta also had to comply with the production requirements in their State of origin. Subjecting the latter to the Italian production requirements imposed a double

---

858 Ibid.

859 Ibid p 222 discussing ECJ joined cases C-29/94 to C-35/94 *Aubertin* [1995] ECR I-301.

860 Tryfonidou, *Reverse Discrimination*, Kluwer Law International 2009, pp 222–23, discussing ECJ case 44/84 *Hurd* [1986] ECR 29. For a description of the facts, see above n 60.

861 Tryfonidou, *Reverse Discrimination*, Kluwer Law International 2009, p 223.

862 Ibid p 224.

863 Ibid.

regulatory burden upon them. Accordingly, the ECJ held that Union law precluded the application of the Italian rules to imported pasta. In Tryfonidou's opinion, this is a justified form of reverse discrimination since Union law merely compensates for the disadvantage of goods moving between Member States.[864]

By contrast, in *Franzén*, she pointed out that the marketing rules constituted unjustified discrimination. Since imported alcoholic drinks were not subjected to a similar wholesale licence in their Member State of origin, no double regulatory burden existed. Accordingly, disapplying the wholesale licence only for imported products would lead to reverse discrimination which is unjustified since domestic and imported drinks are in the same position.[865]

372. Tryfonidou concluded that reverse discrimination 'should now be considered an unjustified difference in treatment that is contrary to the [Union] principle of equality'[866] – presumably she meant situations of reverse discrimination resulting from an overcompensation by Union law. She argued that when a situation of reverse discrimination is challenged before the Court of Justice, the latter may hold that the stricter treatment of purely internal situations violates the Union principle of equality. Moreover, this principle should have direct effect in order that Union citizens can invoke it as well.[867]

373. As will be explained below, the distinction that Tryfonidou makes between compensation and overcompensation by Union law will be used to distinguish unproblematic cases of reverse discrimination from problematic ones. Whereas Tryfonidou introduced the concept and discussed it on the basis of ECJ cases, this book will further develop the concept and will also go on to apply it to the national level in Parts II and III.

3.2. REDEFINING THE SCOPE OF APPLICATION OF THE TREATY PROVISIONS ON FREE MOVEMENT AND CITIZENSHIP

374. As has been argued above, reverse discrimination has to be considered to be a side effect of the limited scope of application of Union law which is based on the division of competences between the EU and the Member States.

---

864 Ibid, discussing ECJ case 407/85 *Drei Glocken* [1988] ECR 4233. Above n 11.

865 Ibid p 225, discussing ECJ case C-189/95 *Franzén* [1997] ECR I-5909.

866 Ibid p 231.

867 Ibid, relying on the Opinion AG Poiares Maduro 6 May 2004 in C-72/03, *Carbonati Apuani*. See also POIARES MADURO, 'The Scope of European Remedies: The Case of Purely Internal Situations and Reverse Discrimination' in KILPATRICK, NOVITZ and SKIDMORE (eds), *The Future of European Remedies*, Hart Publishing 2000, p 138 where Poiares Maduro argued that Union law should give the national judges 'the means to provide the adequate remedies'.

Nevertheless, reverse discrimination is often perceived of as being unfair and as a problem that should be solved. It is submitted that it is the lack of clarity in the dividing line between the scope of application of Union law and that of national law that causes this perception. Accordingly, redefining the scope of application of the Treaty provisions on free movement and citizenship in a clear and acceptable manner, particularly in respecting the vertical division of competences between the EU and Member States as governed by the principle of conferral, could alter this perception. After all, in the context of the (E)EC the distinction between citizens who make use of their right of free movement, and those who do not, seems illogical and possible situations of reverse discrimination are considered to be sustainable.[868]

375. It is suggested that the scope of application of the Treaty provisions on free movement and citizenship be redefined in a more narrow way. Accordingly, fewer situations would benefit from the more favourable treatment of Union law, but it would be clear and acceptable as to why they fall within the scope of Union law and why other situations are purely internal and fall under the scope of application of national law. Following the more limited redefinition of the scope of application of the Treaty provisions on free movement and citizenship, the remaining situations of reverse discrimination would be required to be accepted as disparities, as a by-product of the multi-levelled structure of the European Union.

376. This suggestion is obviously challenging to realise in practice. Accordingly, this section will distinguish three ways in which to redefine the scope of application of the Treaty provisions on free movement and citizenship in a more limited way.

377. First, a narrower interpretation of 'restriction to the freedom of movement' fits within this aim. In this regard, we have discussed AG Tizzano's proposal in his Opinion in *Caixa Bank* to adopt a non-discrimination approach together with a direct market access approach and Barnard's proposal that non-discriminatory national rules should benefit from a presumption of legality. Although the section concerning tightening up the concept of restrictions to freedom of movement was only a brief digression in Part I, it actually deserves more research. In particular, more proposals could be analysed and it would be interesting to apply them to the cases discussed in Part I.

868 See inter alia Dautricourt and Thomas, 'Reverse Discrimination and Free Movement of Persons Under Community Law: All for Ulysses, Nothing for Penelope?' (2009) 34 *ELRev* 454, 436; de Burca 'The Role of Equality in European Community Law' in Dashwood and O'Leary (eds), *The Principle of Equal Treatment in EC Law*, Sweet & Maxwell 1997, p 16 and Tryfonidou, *Reverse Discrimination*, Kluwer Law International 2009, pp 166 and 220.

378. Secondly, it was emphasised in Part I that the ECJ should further elaborate on considerations as to the presence of a sufficient connection with Union law. Moreover, it has been argued here that the ECJ should systematically and openly assess whether a causal link is present between this connection with Union law and the right invoked under Union law. Only if both a sufficient connection with Union law and a causal link are present does the situation fall within the scope of application of the Treaty provisions on free movement and citizenship. In this way, legal certainty would be enhanced. Moreover, it would prevent the occurrence of a significant form of abuse of Union law in which an artificial connection with Union law is created. That is, situations involving artificial connections with Union law would be revealed and would not be allowed to benefit from Union law.

It may be that the ECJ is already aware of these concerns and is taking them into account in its recent case law, for instance in the recent name case *Bogendorff von Wolffersdorf*.[869] For one thing, the ECJ explicitly considered why the situation had a sufficient link with Union law.[870] Moreover, in this case, it may be that the ECJ is opening the way for taking the reasons for a Union citizen's actions into account.[871]

379. Thirdly, the concept of compensation and overcompensation can help to redefine the scope of application of Union law vis-à-vis the scope of application of national law and to distinguish unproblematic cases of reverse discrimination from problematic ones. The working hypothesis employed will be explained, based on the distinction between compensation and overcompensation by Union law, in the following subsection.

3.3. WORKING HYPOTHESIS BASED ON COMPENSATION/ OVERCOMPENSATION BY UNION LAW

3.3.1. The Distinction between Compensation and Overcompensation by Union Law

380. The idea of compensation is that if Union law only compensates for a disadvantage, resulting from the use of free movement, a mere difference in

---

[869] See also the *O and B* judgment, above nn 243–54, 275–77, 359.

[870] ECJ case C-438/14 *Bogendorff von Wolffersdorff*, para 33: 'the applicant in the main proceedings holds the nationality of two Member States and, as a citizen of the Union, exercises his freedom to move and reside in a Member State other than his Member State of origin in accordance with Article 21 TFEU'.

[871] Ibid para 58: 'the refusal to recognise the British name of the applicant in the main proceedings cannot be justified by the mere fact that the change of name was made at his own initiative, without account being taken of the reasons for the change'.

treatment and no discrimination is at stake. In this case, the purely internal situations and the situation with a sufficient connection with Union law are considered as being different situations which can be treated differently. Union law creates substantive equality. The situation of reverse discrimination is not considered to be problematic.

381. By contrast, if it appears that Union law grants more rights than necessary in order to compensate for a disadvantage suffered as a result from the exercise of free movement or when rights are granted where no disadvantage would have resulted from the use of the fundamental freedoms, then an overcompensation by Union law is at stake. In that case, the reverse discrimination is problematic because similar situations are treated differently.

382. Hence, the distinction between overcompensation and mere compensation is a way through which to assess whether the situations are similar or different respectively.[872] If they are similar, they should be treated alike; if they are different, they can be treated differently.

The application of the principle of equality requires a balancing act. First of all, comparing two persons or things, requires 'a common standard of measurement' in each particular case.[873] It is important to explicitly identify this 'common standard of measurement' or 'tertium comparationis'[874] or 'relevant reference framework'[875] in order to apply the principle of equality in a transparent way. Regarding reverse discrimination and the principle of equality, the question arises as to whether purely internal situations and cross-border situations are comparable. Accordingly, it can be argued that the concept of (over)compensation constitutes this common standard of measurement in order to assess whether the two components of the reverse discrimination are similar or different, as the first step in the application of the principle of equality. The concept can help in making the assessment of cases of reverse discrimination more transparent, in making implicit assumptions explicit.

383. If a situation of reverse discrimination is a result of an overcompensation by Union law, the question arises as to the level of governance at which a solution for the reverse discrimination should be provided. It is contended that in case of overcompensation by Union law, the reverse discrimination should

---

872 See also Tryfonidou, *Reverse Discrimination*, Kluwer Law International 2009, p 220.

873 Westen, *Speaking of Equality*, Princeton University Press 1990, pp 13–38.

874 Spitaleri, *Le discriminiazioni alla rovescia nel diritto comunitario*, Università di Trieste 2005, p 181.

875 Opinion AG Trstenjak 3 February 2009 in C-428/07, *Horvath*, paras 102–08.

be remedied in the first place at Union level. Both the Union legislator – by way of harmonisation – and the Court of Justice can take steps in order to prevent reverse discrimination resulting from overcompensation. In the event of a lack of Union action in cases of overcompensation, the national authorities should remedy the situation of reverse discrimination.

3.3.2. *Interpretation of '(Over)Compensation' and 'Disadvantage Resulting from Exercise of Free Movement'*

384. The working hypothesis is based upon the distinction between compensation and overcompensation by Union law for a disadvantage resulting from the exercise of rights of free movement within the EU. The first question that raises is what precisely a disadvantage resulting from the exercise of free movement might be. Although this question may seem easy to answer at first glance, in fact, it is not always so clear. Accordingly, it is useful to give some more specific examples of disadvantages resulting from the exercise of free movement. Inspiration has been drawn from the EU citizenship report of 2010 by the Commission in which the latter listed 25 obstacles that Union citizens may confront living and/or working in another EU Member State and 25 actions proposed to improve the daily life of EU citizens.[876] Some of these are as follows: Union citizens may encounter 'cumbersome and costly formalities regarding cross-border recognition of civil status documents and difficult cross-border access to justice', 'taxation problems in cross-border situations, in particular regarding registration of cars', 'European citizens do not fully benefit from cross-border healthcare', and 'burdensome and uncertain procedures for recognition of academic diplomas and professional qualifications'. Hence, the disadvantages often concern obstacles of a financial and administrative nature.

385. It is important to emphasise that the disadvantage resulting from the exercise of free movement should be assessed in each particular case. In line with the view presented here of a narrower interpretation of restrictions to the freedom of movement, the presence of a disadvantage should not be accepted too easily. This assessment is closely related to the following question of whether the compensation meets the disadvantage in a proportional manner; if only a small disadvantage is at stake, and for which only a small compensation is granted, there is no problem.

876 COM (2010) 603, 4–28.

386. By contrast, if Union law goes too far in compensating a disadvantage, a case of overcompensation arises. The proportionality of compensating is easier to observe at the European level than at the national level. This applies in particular to the Court of Justice because it has to decide in specific cases. For instance in the *Carpenter* case, the Court of Justice arguably overcompensated the disadvantage suffered by Mr Carpenter and his family.

387. It is admitted that the concepts of (Over)compensation, disadvantage suffered from the exercise of free movement and proportionality are open to discussion. In order to indicate guiding principles, and to interpret these concepts, it is helpful to refer back to the starting point that reverse discrimination has to be considered to be a side effect of the limited scope of application of Union law which is based on the division of competences between the EU and the Member States. It has been argued above that the opaque scope of application of the Treaty provisions on freedom of movement and citizenship causes the perception that reverse discrimination is unjust and has to be solved. In this respect, we have suggested redefining the scope of application of the Treaty provisions on free movement and citizenship in a clear and acceptable manner, in particular respecting the vertical division of competences between the EU and Member.

Accordingly, the first principle that comes into play is the principle of conferral, as enshrined in Article 5(2) TEU. That is to say, the EU can only take action if this forms part of the competences conferred upon it by the Treaties. Two complementing principles of the principle of conferral are the principle of proportionality and the principle of subsidiarity, as enshrined in Article 5(3)(4) and Protocol Number 2 on the application of the principles of subsidiarity and proportionality.[877] According to the principle of subsidiarity, the EU should only act if the tasks cannot be performed effectively at a lower level in areas of shared competences, namely, by the Member States at central, regional or local level. According to the principle of proportionality, 'the content and form of

[877] Van Gerven, *The European Union. A Polity of States and Peoples*, Stanford University Press 2005, pp 138–41. See also Craig and de Burca, *EU Law. Text, Cases, and Materials*, 6th ed, Oxford University Press 2015, pp 172–74, Dashwood, 'The Relationship between the Member State and the European Union/European Community' (2004) 41 *CMLRev* 355, 366–69 and Weatherill, 'Competence Creep and Competence Control' (2004) 23 *YEL* 1, 1–55. In particular on the concept of subsidiarity, see Walker, 'Subsidiarity and the Deracination of Political Community: The EU and Beyond', Edinburgh School of Law Research Paper Series 2015/31. Walker argued that despite the possible criticisms of the concept of subsidiarity, we should preserve and develop it in our political discourse because it is an 'attractive solution concept' in a political context marked by 'differentiation of forms, partiality of authority and overlapping and interfering jurisdictions. … It offers a general allocative principle applicable across a range of different species of political authority' (p 7).

Union action shall not exceed what is necessary to achieve the objectives of the Treaties'.[878]

388. Finally, it should be pointed out that the open character of the concept of (over)compensation cannot just be seen as a weakness, but also a strength, particularly because of its flexibility. That is, and as will be explained further in the following subsection, although overcompensation by Union law is currently seen mainly in the area of family reunification, we cannot predict whether or not there will be another area in the future in which the EU will do the same thing and overcompensate. Nevertheless, this formula will remain applicable because it allows for evolution over time.

3.3.3. *Illustration: Reverse Discrimination in the Area of Family Reunification*

3.3.3.1. Family Reunification Directive 2003/86 and Citizenship Directive 2004/38

389. In its first proposal for the Family Reunification Directive 2003/86, the Commission proposed regulating family reunification both with third country nationals and with Union citizens, even if the latter do not make use of their rights to free movement. In particular, the Commission submitted that 'the family reunification of Union citizens who do not exercise their right to freedom of movement for persons has hitherto been subject solely to national rules. This situation generates an unwarranted difference in treatment between the family of Union citizens who have not exercised their right to free movement and have stayed in the country of their nationality and those who have exercised their right to free movement. National law in some circumstances regulates the family reunification of its own nationals more restrictively than [Union] law. As Union citizenship is indivisible, the gap must be filled. This Article accordingly allows the family members of Union citizens to enjoy the benefit of the relevant provisions of [Union] law in matters of family reunification.'[879] In other words, the Commission proposed the prevention of situations of reverse discrimination.

390. However, this proposal encountered strong objections, from the Netherlands and Germany in particular, who wanted to maintain the sovereignty to regulate their own citizens' situations.[880] Consequently, no rules

---

878 Article 5(4) TEU.

879 COM (1999) 638, 1 December 1999, article 4, p 14.

880 Strik, *Besluitvorming over asiel- en migratierechten*, Boom Juridische Uitgevers 2011, pp 86–87.

were proposed for this group of Union citizens in later drafts of the Family Reunification Directive 2003/86.[881]

391. Finally, family reunification with Union citizens has been governed by the Citizenship Directive 2004/38,[882] but only if the Union citizens are in a cross-border situation.[883] In particular, Article 3(1) Directive 2004/38 determines that 'this Directive shall apply to all Union citizens who move to or reside in a Member State other than that of which they are a national, and to their family members as defined in point 2 of Article 2 who accompany or join them'. By contrast, family reunification with Union citizens who have not exercised their right to free movement is subject to national rules. Consequently, situations of reverse discrimination may arise here.

392. In the following, we will not delve further into the Family Reunification Directive, but will focus instead on the Citizenship Directive. As noted in the introductory chapter, the basis of the research for this book focuses upon Union citizens and their family members, not on third country nationals and their family members.[884]

3.3.3.2. The Evolution from Compensation to Overcompensation by Union Law in the Area of Family Reunification

393. On the basis of the case law discussed in Part I, it will be explained that the right to family reunification on the basis of Union law has evolved from a compensation to an overcompensation. Initially, the EC wanted to guarantee that a migrant worker would not lose his right to family life when exercising his right of free movement. This could certainly deter a national of a Member State from leaving his own Member State to exercise his rights of free movement.

394. Since the time of the *Singh* judgment, the Court of Justice has equated the situation of a national of a Member State going to another Member State with

---

881 Ibid p 86, referring to COM (2002) 225, 2 May 2002.

882 See more on the legislative history in Cambien, 'Citizenship of the Union as a Cornerstone of European Integration', Dissertation, KU Leuven 2011, pp 294–95 and Nic Shuibhne, 'Limits Rising, Duties Ascending: The Changing Legal Shape of Union Citizenship' (2015) 52 *CMLRev* 895–98.

883 Directive 2004/38/EC of the European Parliament and of the Council of 29 April 2004 on the right of citizens of the Union and their family members to move and reside freely within the territory of the Member States amending Regulation (EEC) No 1612/68 and repealing Directives 64/221/EEC, 68/360/EEC, 72/194/EEC, 73/148/EEC, 75/34/EEC, 75/35/EEC, 90/364/EEC, 90/365/EEC and 93/96/EEC.

884 Accordingly, regarding family reunification, the focus is on the Citizenship Directive 2004/38, not on Directives 2003/86 and 2003/109 which concern third country nationals.

his family to the situation of a national of a Member State coming back to his Member State of origin. It is submitted that this case law on returning citizens can still be regarded as compensation by Union law on the condition that a real causal link exists between the exercise of free movement, or in other words, the cross-border element, and the restriction to free movement. That is, if the Union citizen moves to another Member State with the sole aim of falling within the scope of the Union provisions on family reunification, this could be considered an abuse of Union law.

395. At a later stage, the Court of Justice accepted an accidental or occasional cross-border element as comprising a sufficient connection with Union law in order to derive residence rights for family members. For instance, in the *Carpenter* case, it was enough for the Court that Mr Carpenter only occasionally went abroad to provide services, in order for it to reach the conclusion that Mrs Carpenter's deportation would be a restriction to her husband's right to the free movement of services.

Moreover, since the *Metock* judgment, it is settled case law that it is not required that the third country national family member of the Union citizen has previously legally resided in another Member State, nor is it relevant when and where the relationship was established. Hence, the Union citizen only has to move to another Member State or to return to his Member State of origin in order to be able to rely upon the right of family reunification. This strengthens the perception that an artificial cross-border element suffices in order to rely on Union law for a right of residence for a third country national family member.[885] Granting rights to family reunification on the basis of Union law in these cases with a very weak or even artificial link with Union law can be qualified as an overcompensation by Union law.

396. As argued above, overcompensations by Union law should be remedied in the first place at the Union level. In particular, the most coherent and acceptable solution for the delicate area of family reunification – touching upon the emotional and highly important right to live together with one's family – would be to harmonise the law in this area. That is, to determine the conditions under which a Union citizen has the right to family reunification whether or not he can demonstrate a connection with Union law. The further harmonisation of national immigration law could solve reverse discrimination in the area of family reunification. In particular, harmonisation could be achieved by a

[885] Admittedly, in *O and B*, the ECJ tried to give some more specific guidance by requiring genuine residence in a host Member State during which time family life has been created or strengthened (ECJ case C-456/12 *O and B*).

bridging construction on the basis of Article 79 TFEU.[886] This could be done by a new directive stating that the provisions of Directive 2004/38 also apply to static Union citizens.[887] However, broad political support for this approach seems to be lacking.[888]

397. Another solution for the overcompensation by Union law can be offered by the ECJ itself. In particular, it has been argued in Part I that in order to alter the perception of an arbitrary connection with Union law being sufficient, the ECJ should openly and systematically examine whether there is a real causal link between the exercise of free movement and the right invoked under Union law in each case. Although this would lead to fewer Union citizens, and their family members, benefitting from the more favourable conditions under Union law, it is not intended to imply that the rights of immobile Union citizens and their family members should not be protected. Instead, it only implies that these rights should not be granted by over-stretching the scope of application of the Treaty provisions on free movement and the Citizenship Directive. The individual Member States still have to protect the rights of their own nationals in purely internal situations.

---

886 Directive 2003/86 is based on Article 79 TFEU. However, extending this directive to static Union citizens would not solve the situation of reverse discrimination because Directive 2003/86 grants less rights than Directive 2004/38, based on the Treaty provisions of freedom of movement, applying to Union citizens who have made use of their rights to free movement.

887 Verschueren, 'Reverse Discrimination: An Unsolvable Problem?' in Minderhoud and Trimikliniotis (eds), *Rethinking the Free Movement of Workers: The European Challenges Ahead*, Wolf Legal Publishers 2009, p 199.

888 Strik, *Besluitvorming over asiel- en migratierechten*, Boom Juridische Uitgevers 2011, pp 86–87.

PART II

REVERSE DISCRIMINATION FROM NATIONAL PERSPECTIVES

398. According to the ECJ, as discussed in the previous Part, Union law does not prohibit reverse discrimination and the Member States must decide individually whether or not to remedy it. Since it is up to the Member States to deal with the issue, their perspectives are a crucial part of research into reverse discrimination. Hence, in this Part, reverse discrimination will be examined from a variety of national perspectives.

399. Whereas previous monographs on reverse discrimination have focused on the perspective of only one Member State,[889] the approach taken here is to compare the perspectives of five Member States. Alongside cases in the author's home country of Belgium, cases of reverse discrimination from France, Italy, Germany and Austria are also discussed. The choice of these five particular Member States has been explained in the section concerning methodology in the book's general introduction.[890]

1. DIFFERENT NATIONAL AUTHORITIES AND DIFFERENT PRINCIPLES AND RULES

400. In general, it can be stated that a Member State has a choice between either treating its own nationals in purely internal situations more severely than 'mobile' Union citizens, or tackling the reverse discrimination by extending the more favourable treatment provided by Union law to its own nationals in purely

---

889 Cals discusses examples in French law (Cals, *La discrimination à rebours et le droit communautaire*, Université de Toulouse 2001); Epiney discusses examples in German law (Epiney, *Umgekehrte Diskriminierungen*, Carl Heymans Verlag KC 1995) and Spitaleri discusses examples in Italian law (Spitaleri, *Le discriminiazioni alla rovescia nel diritto comunitario*, Università di Trieste 2005).

890 Above n 31.

internal situations.[891] This choice can be made by different actors at the national level and they may use different principles and rules in order to assess any given situation of reverse discrimination.

401. In particular, both the legislative, the executive and judicial powers may be in the position to decide whether or not to remedy a situation of reverse discrimination. First, the national (or regional) legislator can take the initiative to remedy reverse discrimination by extending the more favourable treatment, provided by Union law, to their own nationals in purely internal situations. This will be called 'autonomous legislative alignment'.[892] Conversely, when the legislator leaves the reverse discrimination untouched – often implicitly and simply by not extending the more favourable EU provisions to purely internal situations – it is possible that the national courts may assess the situation of reverse discrimination in the light of the principles and rules enshrined in national law. Finally, the executive power is also able to make a choice for or against reverse discrimination in some areas.

402. These different national authorities may use different principles and rules in order to assess a situation of reverse discrimination. First, Member States can assess a situation of reverse discrimination in the light of the principle of equality as enshrined in national law. Secondly, Member States can assess this situation in the light of a substantial right, such as the right to respect for family life or the freedom to choose an occupation. Thirdly, Member States can assess the situation in the light of rules concerning the division of competences, both between the EU and the Member States and the internal division of competences within one Member State. Finally, and rather surprisingly, national authorities

---

891 The other option to avoid reverse discrimination would be to apply to everyone, (im)mobile own nationals and other Union citizens, the less favourable treatment. However, if the more favourable treatment is obliged by Union law within its scope of application, such a Member State's response would clearly entail a violation of its obligations under Union law.

892 See Hanf, '"Reverse Discrimination" in EU Law: Constitutional Aberration, Constitutional Necessity, or Judicial Choice?' (2011) 18 *MJ* 29, 49, who uses this term. See also Cals, *La discrimination à rebours et le droit communautaire*, Université de Toulouse 2001, p 114 who speaks of '*l'alignement de la réglementation interne sur la réglementation communautaire*'.

Often, however, this is called 'spontaneous harmonisation'. This author prefers not to use this denomination because neither the term 'spontaneous' nor the term 'harmonisation' seems to fully capture the idea of remedying reverse discrimination by way of legislative action. It is obvious that if the national legislation is generally amended after a judgment of the ECJ finding an infringement of Union law, it can hardly be called 'spontaneous'. Nor is 'harmonisation' appropriate here, since in the European context this term presumes a harmonisation between different Member States, or in other words between various national legislative provisions (Lenaerts and Van Nuffel, *European Union Law*, Sweet & Maxwell 2011, pp 292 ff), whereas here one Member State is concerned which decides to align its national legislation with the European rules.

sometimes do not assess a situation of reverse discrimination on the basis of national law, but instead on the basis of Union law.

2. THE STRUCTURE OF PART II

403. The structure of Part II has been prompted by research findings regarding a variety of national perspectives on reverse discrimination. Throughout the course of the research undertaken for this book, different structures were considered and disregarded as inadequate.

2.1. NEITHER BY THE ASSESSMENT'S RESULT NOR BY THE MEMBER STATE

404. First, an attempt was made to divide the cases into two parts depending on whether or not they remedy reverse discrimination. This approach was not selected because only Italian cases remedy reverse discrimination in a consistent manner.[893] In contrast, the other four Member States under analysis seem to adopt an ad hoc approach, which sometimes results in remedying reverse discrimination in some cases and allowing it in other cases. This is also the reason why the second possible structure, by which to examine the cases Member State by Member State, was not chosen.

2.2. NOT BY PRINCIPLE OR RULE

405. Next, an approach whereby cases were examined by principle or rule was considered.[894] That is, first, all of those cases in which national authorities have assessed reverse discrimination in the light of the principle of equality, then in the light of a substantial right, such as the right to respect for family life, and finally in light of the rules concerning the division of competences. However, the cases concern very divergent matters and the decisions go either way, for or

[893] In Italy, the following evolution can be seen: from an initial underestimation of the problem, to recognition of the issue and a prohibition on reverse discrimination in a specific area to a general prohibition of reverse discrimination (see Spitaleri, *Le discriminiazioni alla rovescia nel diritto comunitario*, Università di Trieste 2005, pp 215–17).

[894] Epiney considered German examples in this way. In particular, the assessment of reverse discrimination in the light of Article 12 Basic Law focuses on the measure's restriction of the personal freedom to choose an occupation. The assessment in the light of Article 3 Basic Law focuses on the permissibility of discriminatory or unequal treatment caused by reverse discrimination. Epiney, *Umgekehrte Diskriminierungen*, Carl Heymans Verlag KC 1995.

against reverse discrimination. Hence, no general conclusion can be drawn by principle or rule: the use of a particular principle or rule does not predict the outcome of the national authorities' assessment of a specific situation of reverse discrimination.

406. In particular, the application of the principle of equality, as enshrined in national law, to a situation of reverse discrimination can, in theory, lead to three different sorts of judgments. The first possibility is to consider a purely internal situation, on the one hand, and a situation that falls within the scope of Union law, on the other hand, to be incomparable. The assessment in the light of the principle of equality stops right there. There is no discrimination, but rather a different treatment of different situations involved. The second possibility is to consider the situations to be comparable, but to conclude that the difference in treatment is justified in the circumstances of the case. In that case there is likewise no discrimination, but rather a lawful difference in treatment. Finally, it is possible to consider the situations to be comparable and to conclude that there is no sufficient justification for the difference in treatment. Then, the situation of reverse discrimination is a violation of the constitutional principle of equality and should be remedied. The application of substantial rights and rules concerning division of competences as enshrined in national law can also go either way.

407. For the sake of completeness, it should be added that, rather surprisingly, national authorities do not always assess situations of reverse discrimination in the light of national law. This is remarkable given the settled case law of the ECJ that 'any discrimination which nationals of a Member State may suffer under the law of that State fall within the scope of that law and must therefore be dealt with within the framework of the internal legal system of that State'.[895] Although one would expect that a Member State, confronted with a situation of reverse discrimination, would deliberately choose for or against the reverse discrimination in the light of national rules, principles and policies, examples can be found of national authorities assessing situations of reverse discrimination on the basis of Union law.

In particular, national authorities have based the assessment of reverse discrimination on the primacy of Union law. Moreover, national authorities interpreted the scope of application of Union law in a very extensive manner in order to include situations which were actually purely internal.

408. Finally, it should be noted that Member States dealing with a situation of reverse discrimination often do not make the underlying reason explicit.

---

[895] See inter alia ECJ joined cases C-64/96 and C-65/96 *Uecker and Jacquet* [1997] ECR I-3171, para 23 and ECJ case C-253/01 *S.A. Krüger* [2004] ECR I-1191, para 36.

Numerous examples can be found of a general amendment or extension of national legislation after an ECJ judgment finding an infringement of Union law or after an action of the Commission without, however, ever explicitly determining whether this also applies to purely internal situations and whether this was done so deliberately in order to avoid reverse discrimination.[896] The ECJ's judgment or the Commission's action are often only merely referred to, without further explanation.[897]

It is submitted that this evasive approach to reverse discrimination is clearly inadequate. By contrast, national authorities should recognise the issue of reverse discrimination at stake and make a clear assessment in the light of legal criteria enshrined in national law.

2.3. STRUCTURE BY SUBJECT AREA

409. Finally, the structure which has been selected is by subject area into which the cases can be situated. In particular, cases regarding the free movement of goods are discussed first. Next, cases regarding the freedom of movement for persons are examined, and these are subdivided into cases on classic economic free movement rights and on family reunification.

410. This structure was chosen mainly because 'there is an argument against a global approach which treats goods and persons in a similar manner because they concern very different technological, economic and social situations'.[898] In particular, 'the freedom of movement for persons has always been an area of

---

896 Of course, it is also possible that no further explanation is given if, after an ECJ judgment or action of the Commission, the national legislation is only adapted for cases falling within the scope of Union law and, hence, reverse discrimination continues to exist.

897 The French rules on the (prohibition of) payment of remuneration on sight accounts offer an example in this regard. Upon a question referred for a preliminary ruling by the French Council of State, the Court of Justice ruled that 'Article [49 TFEU] precludes legislation of a Member State which prohibits a credit institution which is a subsidiary of a company from another Member State from remunerating sight accounts in euros opened by residents of the former Member State' (ECJ case C-442/02 *Caixa Bank* [2004] ECR 15). Although this judgment clearly determines that it only relates to credit institutions which are subsidiary of companies which are established in other Member States, the French Minister of Economy decided to abrogate the prohibition to remunerate sight accounts in euros for all companies (Order of 8 March 2005 [Arrêté du 8 Mars 2005 relatif à l'abrogation des textes réglementaires interdisant la rémunération des comptes de dépôts à vue]). Hence, a situation of reverse discrimination was prevented, however without explicitly arguing so. (Moreover, the Annual Report (2005) of the Comité consultatif de la législation et de la réglementation financières' (pp 19 and 53) also merely refers to the ECJ's *Caixa Bank* judgment.)

898 Barnard, *The Substantive Law of the EU: The Four Freedoms*, Oxford University Press 2013, p 56.

greater sensitivity than the free movement of goods. People raise security and welfare implications in a way that goods do not.'[899] Moreover, cases discussed in one particular area deal with similar questions and the broader underlying interests at stake are often similar. For instance, regarding goods, the quality of products, unfair competition and consumer protection often come into play. Regarding family reunification, the right to family life is often balanced against the control of migration flows.

411. However, it should be emphasised that differences also exist within an area between types of reverse discrimination and the impact of the stricter conditions. For instance, not having the right of family reunification with your parents or grandparents is different from being subjected to having to demonstrate sufficient income. Although a person can, at least in theory, change the latter situation – by searching for a job and proving financial independence, he cannot change the first situation – parents are not entitled to join him whether or not they are taken care of and whether or not they are a burden upon the Belgian social security, for instance.

3. THE AIM OF PART II

412. In Part II, the grounds upon which the Member States decide whether they allow reverse discrimination to exist or whether they require the same treatment for purely internal situations are examined. It should be noted that it is not the intention of this Part to give an exhaustive overview of examples of reverse discrimination and their potential remedies in each of these five Member States.

413. Moreover, the aim is to add to the answer to this book's third research question: should reverse discrimination be considered as a problem that requires a solution in each case? And if a solution is required, who should provide this solution: the EU, the Member States, regions or several levels of government in interaction?

This research question was partially answered in Part I. In particular, it was concluded in Part I that not all cases of reverse discrimination require a solution, since not all cases of reverse discrimination are problematic. If it appears that Union law only compensates for a disadvantage resulting from the use of free movement, a mere difference in treatment, and not discrimination, is at stake. By contrast, if it appears that the EU has gone further than merely compensating

899 Ibid p 231.

a disadvantage resulting from the exercise of free movement – which is called an overcompensation by Union law – the reverse discrimination is perceived as being unjust and is deemed problematic.

It has been argued in Part I that an overcompensation by Union law should be remedied at the Union level in the first place; either by the Union legislator or the Court of Justice.

414. In Part II, the question of whether the working hypothesis based on the concept of compensation and overcompensation can be applied to the assessment of reverse discrimination by national authorities will be considered. That is, if a national authority has to deal with a situation of reverse discrimination, it is suggested that it should examine whether a mere compensation or an overcompensation arises. On the basis of this assessment, a different approach by the national authority is suggested.

415. In particular, in cases of compensation by Union law, a mere difference in treatment is at stake according to our working hypothesis. The same holds if the overcompensation has been remedied at the Union level. Reverse discrimination can be seen as a side effect of the EU's multilayered structure of government and, accordingly, the national review can stop right there. The division of competences between the EU and the Member States can be accepted as a conclusive argument.

Nevertheless, the national authority is still able to assess the purely internal situation as such – not as a reverse discrimination – in the light of national law. It seems that the principle of equality as enshrined in national law is not an appropriate instrument for the assessment since the purely internal situation is the only one remaining to be assessed under national law. That is, in cases of compensation by Union law, according to the working hypothesis applied here, the purely internal situation and the situation falling under Union law are not comparable situations. Accordingly, other principles and rules are required in order to make the assessment. In particular, substantial rights, such as the right to respect for private and family life and the right to economic freedom, seem appropriate in order to assess a situation of reverse discrimination which is the result of a mere compensation by Union law.

416. By contrast, in cases of overcompensation by Union law, the principle of equality as enshrined in national law seems the most appropriate instrument for the national authority to assess a case of reverse discrimination resulting from an overcompensation by Union law. That is, it allows for the comparison of purely internal and cross-border situations and it allows for the justifications and the impact of the stricter conditions for purely internal situations to be balanced.

This approach does not imply prohibiting all situations in which reverse discrimination is a result of overcompensation by Union law at the national level. However, it is suggested that the national authority does not accept justifications for reverse discrimination which are the result of overcompensation by Union law too easily. That is, cases of compensation by Union law and, hence, mere differences in treatment are already filtered out.

CHAPTER 4

REVERSE DISCRIMINATION WITH RESPECT TO GOODS

417. The reverse discrimination of goods often occurs in regulations on food and drinks. In particular, a lot of Member States have established some form of regulation in order to protect the reputation of specific regional products. These products must meet certain standards before they are allowed to use a specific denomination, such as containing certain ingredients or being made through a specific production process. This type of regulation not only aims to protect the reputation of the products, but it also aims to guarantee these products' quality and to avoid consumers being misled.

In a lot of cases the strict conditions imposed upon products are incompatible with the Treaty provisions on free movement because they create a restriction to free movement within the EU. Accordingly, these rules cannot be applied to cross-border situations, but they may remain applicable to purely internal situations. National producers selling these goods in their home Member State might challenge this situation of reverse discrimination, by claiming, for instance, that it leads to unfair competition and an unjustified difference in treatment.

418. The recent changes in the Belgian legislation on mayonnaise illustrate the awareness of the competing interests which are at stake in a situation of reverse discrimination of goods. That is to say, Belgian mayonnaise had to contain at least 80 per cent fat and 7.5 per cent egg yolk.[900] By contrast, other EU Member States had aligned their legislation with the code of good practice adopted in 1991 by the *Fédération des Industries Condimentaires au niveau européen* which provides 70 per cent fat and 5 per cent egg yolk for mayonnaise.[901] Belgian producers of mayonnaise complained about the stricter rules for producing mayonnaise in Belgium.

In 2005, the Belgian competent advisory body argued in favour of the stricter Belgian legislation and pointed out that lowering the requirements on fat and egg yolk implies that additives such as water, milk and sugar as well as

900 Decision of 12 April 1955 [*Koninklijk Besluit betreffende de handel in mayonaise en soortgelijke producten*].

901 *Raad voor het Verbruik*, Opinion 344, Brussels 30 November 2005.

preservatives may be added, which leads to a mayonnaise of inferior quality.[902] However, in the summer of 2015, the issue was raised again and the Minister for Consumer Affairs reconsidered the legislation. In particular, the Decision of 26 May 2016 reduces the fat percentage for mayonnaise from 80 per cent to 70 per cent and the egg yolk percentage from 7.5 per cent to 5 per cent.[903] This enhances the competitiveness of Belgian producers of mayonnaise with regard to foreign producers. Moreover, the Decision introduces the denomination 'traditional mayonnaise' which still has to contain 80 per cent fat and 7.5 per cent egg yolk.[904] In this way, the specific taste and quality of traditional Belgian mayonnaise is ensured.

1. ASSESSMENT BY NATIONAL COURTS OF REVERSE DISCRIMINATION WITH RESPECT TO GOODS

419. This section examines the assessment by national courts of four cases of the reverse discrimination of goods. In particular, we discuss two French cases on ethyl alcohol and emmenthal, a German case on the purity of beer and an Italian case on industrially dried pasta. Analysis will be provided on the national authority's reasoning and the working hypothesis based on the concept of compensation and overcompensation will be applied to each case.

1.1. THE FRENCH COUNCIL OF STATE ON ETHYL ALCOHOL

420. In its judgment of 27 July 1979, the French Council of State assessed a situation of reverse discrimination in the legislation concerning ethyl alcohol.[905] The French State has a monopoly on the national production and marketing of ethyl alcohol.[906] The *Service des Alcools* may, however, allow producers, if they so request, to dispose freely of certain alcohol reserved to the State upon payment of a cash adjustment, or '*soulte*'.[907] The *Syndicat national des fabricants de spiritueux consommées à l'eau* complained that its members were obliged to

[902] *Raad voor het Verbruik*, Opinion 344, Brussels 30 November 2005, 4–5.

[903] Article 3 Decision 26 May 2016 [*Koninklijk Besluit betreffende mayonaise*] *BS* 10 June 2016.

[904] Article 5 ibid.

[905] Conseil d'Etat 27 July 1979 no 09664, *Syndicat national des fabricants de spiritueux consommés à l'eau* in which the annulment of Decree no 77/842 of 25 July 1977 was requested, as well as the annulment of two orders of the Minister of Economy and Finances of 25 July 1977.

[906] Article 358 Code Général des Impôts (CGI). The French State leaves the production to private undertakings whilst retaining the property in the production which it buys and markets itself (Article 358 *juncto* 370 CGI).

[907] Article 269 of Annex II CGI.

pay a 'cash adjustment' on the 'freed' alcohol which they produce, while similar alcohol produced in another Member State was not subject to this charge.[908] In other words, a situation of reverse discrimination had arisen.[909]

421. The Council of State ruled that the decree contested violated neither Articles 258 and 285 of the Code Général des Impôts (CGI), nor the principle of equality in bearing public burdens (*principe d'égalité devant les charges publiques*). Without any further explanation, the Council of State decided that the situation of reverse discrimination was not forbidden on the basis of the provisions and principles of the French legal system.

Next, the Council of State recalled that in order to contest the legislation on ethyl alcohol, the *Syndicat national* also invoked the Rome Treaty of 1957 and, more specifically, those provisions that prohibit 'each discrimination on grounds of nationality' and 'each discrimination between nationals of the Member States'. According to the Council of State, it is clear that these provisions have no other goal than to eliminate discrimination which is unfavourable to the nationals of other EU Member States and that they would, in no event, limit the national authorities' competences regarding their own nationals.[910] In other words, the Council of State refused to apply the EU Treaties to purely internal situations in order to end a situation of reverse discrimination.

422. It is remarkable that the Council of State did not refer to the ECJ's *Peureux* judgment concerning exactly this legislation.[911] The ECJ ruled in this case that 'since … it is open to a Member State to impose on a national product internal taxation in excess of that imposed on a similar imported product, whether or not it is a national product coming under a commercial monopoly in that Member State, it is a fortiori open to it to impose on a national product internal taxation in excess of that imposed on a similar product in another Member State. The disparities arise from the power of the Member States in the matter of taxation and are not affected either by article [110 TFEU and Article 37 TFEU].'[912]

423. When applying the working hypothesis to this case, the first step is to consider whether compensation or overcompensation is at stake. It can be argued that the case concerned a mere compensation by Union. That is to say, requiring the charge for alcohol imported from other Member States would be

908 Articles 1–3 of Decree no 77/842 of 25 July 1977.

909 See inter alia Drago, Note de jurisprudence, Conseil d'Etat 27 juillet 1797, RDP 1980, 214.

910 The author's translation of: [*les stipulations du traité de Rome ne sauraient en aucun cas limiter les pouvoirs dont les autorités nationales sont investies à l'égard de leurs propres ressortissants*].

911 ECJ case 86/78 *Peureux* [1979] ECR 897, which concerned precisely the provisions contested in this case before the Council of State, para 27b.

912 Then Articles 95 and 37 EEC Treaty. ECJ case 86/78 *Peureux* [1979] ECR 897, paras 39–40.

incompatible with Article 37 TFEU.[913] According to the working hypothesis applied here, this implies that a mere difference in treatment exists and that the national authority can stop its assessment right there. This is precisely what the French Council of State did: it held that the reverse discrimination at issue was not a problem and it allowed it to continue to exist.

1.2. THE FRENCH COURT OF CASSATION ON EMMENTHAL

424. The Commercial Chamber of the French Court of Cassation ruled on a situation of reverse discrimination in the *Entremont* case.[914] The company Entremont accused certain manufacturers of making and selling cheese under the denomination 'emmenthal' in violation of Decree 88/1206 reserving this denomination to cheese with 'a hard, dry rind of a colour between golden yellow and light brown'.[915] After being condemned by the Court of Appeal of Paris, these manufacturers, the BSA companies, challenged the case before the Commercial Chamber of the Court of Cassation.

425. The BSA companies argued that the Court of Appeal of Paris violated the principle of primacy of Union law *juncto* Article 34 TFEU.[916] In this respect, they invoked the ECJ's *Guimont* judgment, in which the ECJ ruled that Article 34 TFEU 'precludes a Member State from applying to products imported from another Member State, where they are lawfully produced and marketed, a national rule prohibiting the marketing of a cheese without rind under the designation emmenthal in that Member State'.[917] According to the BSA companies, by reserving the denomination 'emmenthal' only to a cheese with a 'hard, dry rind of a colour between golden yellow and light brown' without distinguishing on the basis of the origin of the cheese and the country of the producer, the Decree 88/1206 violated Article 34 TFEU since it directly or potentially hinders intra-Union trade.

426. Moreover, the BSA companies argued that the Court of Appeal violated the principle of legal equality since French nationals were condemned for infringements in France that Union law, integrated into the internal legal order, does not consider

---

913 This was initially provided by Decree 74/91 of 6 February 1974. However, the Commission argued that this was incompatible with Article 37 TFEU (referring to ECJ case 47/95 *Rewe* [1976] ECR 569 and ECJ case 91/75 *Miritz* [1976] ECR 217). After an exchange of views between the Commission and the French government, the latter adopted Decree 77/842 of 25 July 1977. See ECJ case 86/78 *Peureux* [1979] ECR 897, paras 20–22.

914 French Court of Cassation Commercial Chamber 3 May 2006 no 03–14.171.

915 Decree 88/1206 of 30 December 1988, *JO* 31 December 1988.

916 Then Article 28 TEC.

917 ECJ case C-448/98 *Guimont* [2000] ECR I-10663, para 35.

to be infractions with respect to nationals of other Member States acting in the national territory. They contested that the judgment created a situation of reverse discrimination that was detrimental to national products by applying the Decree 88/1206, which was declared incompatible with Union law, to purely internal situations. According to the BSA companies, the Court of Appeal of Paris disregarded the spirit and reach of the decree, since the decree was indistinctly applicable to national and imported products and it assured an equal treatment for French and foreign producers and distributors of emmenthal in the national territory.

427. The Court of Cassation recognised that, in *Guimont*, the ECJ ruled that Article 34 TFEU precludes that a Member State prohibits the marketing of a cheese without rind, imported from another Member State, under the denomination 'emmenthal'.[918] It also recalled, however, that the ECJ's consideration that 'that article is not designed to ensure that goods of national origin enjoy the same treatment as imported goods in every case, and a difference in treatment as between goods which is not capable of restricting imports or of prejudicing the marketing of imported goods does not fall within the prohibition contained in that article'.[919] The Court of Cassation emphasised that the ECJ had responded to the preliminary reference in a case in which all the specific facts of the main proceedings were confined to one single Member State; the ECJ considered that its reply regarding the interpretation of Union law 'might be useful' to the national court 'if its national law were to require, in proceedings such as those in this case, that a national producer must be allowed to enjoy the same rights as those which a producer of another Member State would derive from [Union] law in the same situation'.[920]

In this context, the Court of Cassation concluded that the Court of Appeal rightly ruled that neither Union law nor French law prohibits national products from being submitted to more stringent conditions than imported products since it was not demonstrated that the application of the national measure, which was only declared incompatible with Union law as far as imported products were concerned, could have an effect of the intra-Union trade. The Court of Cassation ruled that the Court of Appeal did not violate the principle of legal equality.[921]

918 Ibid. 919 Ibid para 15. 920 Ibid para 23.

921 French Court of Cassation Commercial Chamber 3 May 2006 no 03-14.171: [*que c'est donc à bon droit que la cour d'appel, qui n'a pas violé le principe de l'égalité devant la loi, sans application dès lors que ne sont concernés que des produits, a retenu que ni le droit communautaire ni le droit français n'interdisent de soumettre les produits nationaux à des exigences plus sévères que les produits d'importation, lorsqu'il n'est pas démontré que l'application de la mesure nationale, qui n'avait été déclarée incompatible avec le droit communautaire qu'en ce qui concerne les produits importés, pourrait avoir des effets sur la libre circulation des marchandises entre Etats membres, notamment en favorisant la commercialisation des marchandises d'origine nationale au détriment des marchandises importées ; que le moyen n'est pas fondé*].

428. The decision by the French Court of Cassation's Commercial Chamber that the reverse discrimination at issue was not a violation of the principle of equality as enshrined in French law can be supported on a double basis. First, in *Guimont*, the ECJ ruled that the interpretation of Union law 'might be useful' for the national judge, which leaves the room for the French Court of Cassation to rule differently in purely internal situations. The French Court of Cassation certainly did not follow the ECJ's suggestion of applying the Union interpretation – of not requiring rind for cheese under the denomination 'emmenthal' for purely internal situations as well.

429. Secondly, the French Court of Cassation's judgment of fits into the working hypothesis applied here. In particular, it can be argued that a mere compensation by Union law is at stake here. That is to say, emmenthal imported from another Member State already has to comply with its host Member State's production and marketing requirements.[922] The imported emmenthal should not be subjected to production and marketing legislation in France, because this would impose a double burden on the imported emmenthal.[923] By contrast, emmenthal produced in France is only regulated by French rules. Instead of only holding that the principle of equality was not violated, the French Court of Cassation could have added that the principle, as enshrined in French law, was not violated because a mere difference in treatment was at stake or that the two situations at hand are not comparable. According to our working hypothesis, and according to the French Court of Cassation, the reverse discrimination is not problematic and can continue to exist.

1.3. THE GERMAN FEDERAL ADMINISTRATIVE COURT ON THE PURITY REQUIREMENT FOR BEER

430. In 2005, the German Federal Administrative Court assessed a situation of reverse discrimination in the light of *das Grundrecht der Berufsfreiheit*, the German fundamental right to choose an occupation.[924] The case concerned the German beer legislation.[925] According to Article 9(1) Beer Act, only malt, hops, yeast and water can be used for the production of bottom-fermented beer. This is the so-called 'purity requirement' for beer. On the basis of Article 9(7) Beer Act, on request, authorisation to derogate from Article 9(1) Beer Act may be granted in individual cases for the production of special beers.

922 ECJ case C-448/98 *Guimont* [2000] ECR I-10663, para 35.
923 Tryfonidou, *Reverse Discrimination*, Kluwer Law International 2009, p 224.
924 German Federal Administrative Court 24 February 2005, no 3 C. 5.04.
925 *Vorläufigen Biergesetzes* of 21 December 1992 (hereafter the Beer Act).

However, on the basis of the ECJ's judgment of 1987, this legislation does not apply to beers imported from other Member States. In particular, the ECJ held that 'in so far as the German rules on additives in beer entail a general ban on additives, their application to beers imported from other Member States is contrary to [Article 34 TFEU prohibiting measures having equivalent effect]'.[926]

431. In the case before the German Federal Administrative Court, the applicant brewed a bottom-fermented dark beer in which malt, hops, yeast and water were used and to which filtration sugar syrup was added thereafter, for taste reasons. When her request for the authorisation of the production derogated from the purity requirement and for marketing the drink under the name 'beer' was rejected, the applicant challenged the German legislation on the basis of two grounds.[927] First, she asserted that her fundamental right to choose a profession was violated. Secondly, she claimed that the legislation violates the general principle of equal treatment because similar drinks that are produced in another Member State could be put on the market in Germany under the name 'beer'.[928] However, her drink could not because it was produced in Germany.

432. The Federal Administrative Court assessed the case in the light of Article 12(1) Basic Law, the freedom to choose an occupation. First, the Court examined the claim for the authorisation to produce a special beer in the sense of Article 9(7) Beer Act. The Court held that it is controversial whether the purity requirement for beer, described above, can be constitutionally justified since it regulates the practice of a profession and hence restricts the fundamental right of Article 12(1) Basic Law.[929] The Court considered that this legislation's justification cannot be found in the interest of public health, but only in the maintenance of a cultural tradition of German brewing and guaranteeing a certain quality level of the product. However, the Court considered that the present case did not require taking a definitive position on the constitutional concerns identified.[930]

The Court ruled that, in any event, it is incompatible with Article 12(1) Basic Law to subject the production of beer without any exception to the purity requirement. In particular, the Federal Administrative Court held that the purity requirement for beer can be justified as a rule if exceptions can be allowed. This condition was considered to be satisfied by Article 9(7) Beer Act which provides

926 ECJ case 178/84 *Commission v Germany* [1987] ECR 1227, paras 53–54.
927 German Federal Administrative Court 24 February 2005, no 3 C. 5.04, p 2.
928 On the basis of the ECJ case 178/84 *Commission v Germany* [1987] ECR 1227.
929 German Federal Administrative Court 24 February 2005, no 3 C. 5.04, p 5.
930 Ibid: [*Der vorliegende Fall erfordert icht, zu den aufgezeigten verfassungsrechtlichen Bedenken abschliessend Stellung zu nehmen*].

the possibility of exceptions, which should be generously authorised according to the Court.

The Court concluded that the applicant produced a special beer, in the sense of Article 9(7) Beer Act, and was hence entitled to the authorisation to derogate from Article 9(1) Beer Act.[931] The Court recognised that Article 9(7) Beer Act grants the competent authority a margin of discretion, but immediately added that Article 12(1) Basic Law requires that the authorisation must be granted if there is no risk of abuse or another overriding reason of public interest.

433. Secondly, the Federal Administrative Court assessed the applicant's claim to put her drink on the market under the name 'beer'.[932] The Court considered that labelling law regulates the practice of profession and should therefore be measured in the light of Article 12(1) Basic Law.[933] The Court recognised that the aim of the labelling legislation, the protection of consumers against deception, is a legitimate public interest. Since the Court considered that the measure was neither necessary nor appropriate to attaining the aim pursued, it held that it is no longer justified the denial of the denomination 'beer' to legally produced special beers. The Court concluded that the decision to grant an authorisation pursuant to Article 9(7) Beer Act does not only affect the production, but also the marketing of a product as 'beer'.

At the end of the judgment, the Federal Administrative Court raised the issue of the aforementioned ECJ judgment[934] and rather vaguely held that within the present practice of labelling legislation the principle of equal treatment must be protected.[935]

434. The facts in the German purity of beer case are similar to the facts in the French emmenthal case. In particular, it can be argued that in the German case a mere compensation by Union law was also at stake; namely that the purely internal situation and the cross-border situation were not comparable. That is to say, only German beers are subjected to the German purity of beer requirement. By contrast, imported beers are not because they are considered to have been lawfully produced and marketed in their Member State of origin. Imposing the purity requirement upon the latter would impose a double burden

931 Ibid p 7. 932 Ibid pp 7 ff. 933 Ibid p 11.

934 ECJ case 178/84 *Commission v Germany* [1987] ECR 1227, para 35.

935 German Federal Administrative Court 24 February 2005, no 3 C. 5.04, p 12: [*Wird dem Hersteller eines besonderen Bieres auf diesem Wege eine besondere Kennzeichnung auferlegt, so darf dies keine negative Einschätzung des Produkts zur Folge haben (vgl. EuGH, Urteil vom 12. März 1987, ... Rn. 35) und muss auch innerhalb der gegenwärtigen Handhabung des Kennzeichnungsrechts bei Bier den Gleichbehandlungsgrundsatz wahren*].

on the imported emmenthal. This would be incompatible with Article 34 TFEU prohibiting measures having equivalent effect.[936]

435. Although the circumstances in the German beer and French emmenthal cases were similar, the French and German courts decided upon the cases differently, on the basis of different principles and rules and with different results. Specifically, the French Court of Cassation simply held that the principle of equality was not violated – without further explanation – and hence, the reverse discrimination could continue to exist.

By contrast, the German Federal Administrative Court refrained from reviewing the reverse discrimination in the light of the principle of equality as enshrined in national law. Instead, the German Court made an elaborate assessment of the case in the light of the fundamental right to choose a profession as enshrined in Article 12(1) Basic Law. In particular, the Court decided that Article 12(1) Basic Law requires a (more) generous implementation of the exception of the purity requirement for beer and held that it is no longer justified to deny the denomination 'beer' to legally produced special beers.

436. This assessment of the German Federal Administrative Court corroborates our working hypothesis in the case of a mere compensation by Union law. In particular, the German Court did not use the principle of equality, as enshrined in German law, to assess the situation of reverse discrimination resulting from a compensation by Union law, but instead it assessed the purely internal situation in the light of the substantial right to choose an occupation. The Court examined the purely internal situation as such in the light of German law exclusively. Moreover, this case demonstrates that our working hypothesis in the case of mere compensation by Union law does not necessarily lead to the result of allowing reverse discrimination. That is to say, thanks to the more generous interpretation of the exception to the purity of beer requirement, fewer cases of reverse discrimination will arise in the future.

1.4. THE ITALIAN CONSTITUTIONAL COURT ON DRIED PASTA

437. In December 1997, the Italian Constitutional Court banned a situation of reverse discrimination on the basis of the Italian principle of equality. The facts in the case at issue concerned the legislation of industrially dried pasta. It was determined that dried pasta could only contain those ingredients that

936 See ECJ case 178/84 *Commission v Germany* [1987] ECR 1227, paras 53–54.

were expressly permitted by that law. The regulation only applied to national producers who produced and sold such pasta in Italy.

438. The Italian Constitutional Court recognised explicitly that the case concerned reverse discrimination.[937] It defined reverse discrimination as situations of inequality to the detriment of nationals or companies of a Member State which occur as an indirect effect of the application of Union law.[938] Although the Court considered that 'the Union approach towards situations of reverse discrimination was not of interest',[939] it pointed out that in the ECJ's *Zoni* judgment, which concerned exactly the law that was being contested before the Constitutional Court, in which the ECJ confirmed 'that [Union] law does not require the legislature to repeal the law as far as pasta producers established on Italian territory are concerned'.[940] The Court considered – in line with the settled case law of the Court of Justice – that 'a possible tolerant attitude' towards reverse discrimination falls, for Union law, under the choices which the Member States are allowed to make.[941] The Court, however, emphasised that this area of sovereignty, which Union law leaves to the Italian State, should not be used in an arbitrary manner, but should be based on constitutional principles; namely the principles of equality and freedom of economic initiative.[942]

439. The Constitutional Court considered that while the difference in treatment between undertakings depending on whether their activities occur in a national context exclusively or in a cross-border context is irrelevant for Union law, it is not for Italian law.[943] If a constitutionally grounded justification is lacking, the only alternative for the legislator is, according to the Constitutional Court, to equate the legislation of national undertakings with the legislation of other Member States in which no such restrictions on the production and commercialisation exist as the

---

937 Italian Constitutional Court 30 December 1997, no 443/1997, para 5.

938 Ibid: [*situazioni di disparità in danno dei cittadini di uno Stato membro, o delle sue imprese, che si verificano come effetto indiretto dell'applicazione del diritto comunitario*]. This definition has since been confirmed by the Italian Constitutional Court in 2007 (Italian Constitutional Court 8 October 2007, no 341/2007).

939 Italian Constitutional Court 30 December 1997, no 443/1997, para 5: [*Va chiarito che in questa sede non interessa accertare quale sia il regime comunitario di simili discriminazioni*].

940 ECJ 90/86 *Zoni* [1988] ECR 4285, para 25.

941 Italian Constitutional Court 30 December 1997, no 443/1997, para 5: [*Un eventuale atteggiamento di tolleranza nei confronti delle 'discriminazioni a rovescio' rientrerebbe, insomma, per il diritto comunitario, tra le scelte consentite agli Stati membri, interamente rimesse alla loro libera autodeterminazione di Stati sovrani]*.

942 Enshrined in Articles 3 and 41 of the Constitution; Italian Constitutional Court 30 December 1997, no 443/1997, para 5.

943 Italian Constitutional Court 30 December 1997, no 443/1997, para 6. Author's own translation of [*La disparità di trattamento tra imprese nazionali e imprese comunitarie, seppure è irrilevante per il diritto comunitario, non lo è dunque per il diritto costituzionale italiano*].

ones in force in Italy.[944] The Court ruled that in the absence of uniform legislation at Union level, the principle of non-discrimination between undertakings demands that 'national undertakings' are not burdened with more charges, constraints and prohibitions than 'Union undertakings'.[945] The Constitutional Court emphasised that in the assessment of the principle of equality which is entrusted to it, it cannot ignore the discriminatory effects that the application of Union law is capable of causing.[946] The Court concluded that contested legislation on industrially dried pasta was incompatible with the constitutional principle of non-discrimination.

440. The Italian Constitutional Court's judgment contains a well-elaborated reasoning on reverse discrimination. First of all, it made the issue of reverse discrimination explicit and provided a full definition of the term. Secondly, the Court considered that although reverse discrimination falls outside the scope of application of Union law, it is relevant from the perspective of Italian law and it should be assessed in the light of the Italian principle of equality. The Court ruled that in the light of the principle of equality it cannot ignore the discriminatory effects, which the application of Union law might possibly entail. Accordingly, cross-border situations and purely internal situations should be treated equally, unless the difference in treatment can be constitutionally justified. Hence, the Italian Constitutional Court assesses in principle each situation of reverse discrimination under the Italian principle of equality and only where a sufficient constitutional justification is present, can that situation of reverse discrimination be considered a mere difference in treatment that can continue to exist.

441. Spitaleri has argued that this judgment not only provides a valid control in order to prohibit situations of reverse discrimination, but also for all the unjustified differences in treatment which are caused in the internal legislation by the impact of Union law more generally.[947] He highlighted that the Court stated, *in general*, that in its assessment of the principle of equality, it cannot ignore the discriminatory effects that the application of Union law might

---

944 Ibid.

945 Ibid: [*In definitiva, in assenza di una regolamentazione uniforme in ambito comunitario, il principio di non discriminazione tra imprese che agiscono sullo stesso mercato in rapporto di concorrenza, opera, nella diversità delle discipline nazionali, come istanza di adeguamento del diritto interno ai principii stabiliti nel trattato agli artt. 30 e seguenti; opera, quindi, nel senso di impedire che le imprese nazionali siano gravate di oneri, vincoli e divieti che il legislatore non potrebbe imporre alla produzione comunitaria: il che equivale a dire che nel giudizio di eguaglianza affidato a questa Corte non possono essere ignorati gli effetti discriminatori che l'applicazione del diritto comunitario è suscettibile di provocare*].

946 Ibid.

947 Spitaleri, *Le discriminiazioni alla rovescia nel diritto comunitario*, Università di Trieste 2005, pp 187 ff.

possibly cause.[948] In his view, these effects are not only at stake in cases of reverse discrimination, but also in the lack of the horizontal effect of unimplemented directives[949] as well as in procedural disharmonies depending upon whether they derive from a Union or national source.[950] In sum, Spitaleri considers that the Italian principle of equality, in the way it was used by the Constitutional Court in its judgment 443/1997, is an effective instrument in the elimination of all unjustified differences in treatment which Union law causes in the internal legislation.[951]

442. When applying our working hypothesis to the Italian case of industrially dried pasta, it could be argued that a mere compensation by Union law was at stake. That is, the situation of imported pasta is different from pasta produced and sold in Italy. Whereas pasta imported from another Member State is considered to have been lawfully produced according to the rules established in the Member State of origin, Italian pasta has to comply with the Italian regulation of not containing certain ingredients.

However, the Italian Constitutional Court seems to be willing to apply the Italian principle of equality to each situation of reverse discrimination and it seems to presume that purely internal situations and cross-border situations will always be comparable. In other words, it seems to consider each case of reverse discrimination as one resulting from an overcompensation by Union law. In the case of industrially dried pasta, the Italian Constitutional Court considered that a burden existed for national producers without a sufficient constitutional justification, thus the Court ended the situation of reverse discrimination. However, at least in principle, it seems that reverse discrimination can be allowed if a constitutional justification is at stake.[952]

2. REVERSE DISCRIMINATION OF GOODS: RARE CASES?

443. According to Barnard, situations of the reverse discrimination of goods are quite rare because 'given the broad scope of the *Dassonville* formula ... it is relatively easy for a trader to argue that a national measure has at least "potential"

[948] Ibid pp 187–88. [949] Ibid pp 187–92.

[950] Ibid pp 192–97. Spitaleri found confirmation of this approach in the Constitutional Court's judgment no 114/2000 (Italian Constitutional Court 21 April 2000, no 114/2000).

[951] Spitaleri, *Le discriminiazioni alla rovescia nel diritto comunitario*, Università di Trieste 2005, pp 197 and 219.

[952] However, see the Italian legislation of 2005 and 2009 prohibiting reverse discrimination in general.

effect on trade'.[953] In this respect, the author refers to the *Pistre* judgment in which Mr Pistre was prosecuted for having marketed meat under a label with the term 'mountain' when he was not authorised, in relation to those products, to make specific reference to mountain areas. Mr Pistre argued that by requiring prior administrative authorization before products could be put on sale the French legislation was incompatible with Article 34 TFEU.[954] By contrast, the French government and the Commission argued that the prosecutions have been brought against French nationals and concern French products marketed on French territory, and hence are confined to French territory.[955] Although AG Jacobs argued that there was no need to examine the rule in the light of Article 34 TFEU, because a purely internal situation was at stake,[956] the Court of Justice decided otherwise. Referring to the *Dassonville* judgment, the Court held that Article 34 TFEU 'cannot be considered inapplicable simply because all the facts of the specific case before the national court are confined to a single Member State'.[957] The Court considered that 'the measure in question facilitates the marketing of goods of domestic origin to the detriment of imported goods'. Therefore, the Court continued, the measure created a difference of treatment between domestic and imported products, 'hindering, at least potentially, intra-[Union] trade'.[958]

444. Although it certainly seems easy to argue that a national measure potentially hinders the free movement of goods, this does not necessarily result in fewer cases of reverse discrimination in the area of free movement of goods. The four examples discussed above seem to confirm this. First, in *Peureux*, the ECJ held that it is open to a Member State 'to impose on a national product internal taxation in excess of that imposed on a similar product in another Member State. The disparities arise from the power of the Member States in the matter of taxation and are not affected either by article [110 TFEU and Article 37 TFEU].'[959] Secondly, in *Commission v Germany*, the ECJ ruled that 'in so far as the German rules on additives in beer entail a general ban on additives, their application to beers imported from other Member States is contrary to [Article 34 TFEU prohibiting measures having equivalent effect]'.[960] The purity requirement for beer can continue to apply after this judgment, creating a situation of reverse

953 Barnard, *The Substantive Law of the EU: The Four Freedoms*, Oxford University Press 2013, p 89.
954 ECJ joined cases C-321/94, C-322/94, C-323/94 and C-324/94 *Pistre* [1997] ECR I-2343, para 6.
955 Ibid para 41.
956 Opinion AG Jacobs in ibid para 42.
957 Ibid paras 43–44.
958 Ibid para 45. Barnard refers here also to ECJ case C-293/02 *Jersey Produce* [2005] ECR I-9543.
959 Then Articles 95 and 37 EEC Treaty. ECJ case 86/78 *Peureux* [1979] ECR 897, paras 39–40.
960 ECJ case 178/84 *Commission v Germany* [1987] ECR 1227, paras 53–54.

discrimination. Thirdly, in *Zoni*, the ECJ explicitly held 'that [Union] law does not require the legislature to repeal the law as far as pasta producers established on Italian territory are concerned'.[961] Finally, in *Guimont*, Article 34 TFEU 'is not designed to ensure that goods of national origin enjoy the same treatment as imported goods in every case, and a difference in treatment as between goods which is not capable of restricting imports or of prejudicing the marketing of imported goods does not fall within the prohibition contained in that article'.[962] Although the ECJ considered that its reply, regarding the interpretation of Union law, 'might be useful' to the national court, 'if its national law were to require, in proceedings such as those in this case, that a national producer must be allowed to enjoy the same rights as those which a producer of another Member State would derive from [Union] law in the same situation',[963] it leaves room to the national authorities to decide differently.

While the three first judgments could be rejected as dated – from 1978, 1987 and 1988 respectively – and therefore overruled by *Pistre*, this cannot be said for the *Guimont* judgment. Both cases concern purely internal situations and the Court of Justice replied to the reference for preliminary ruling. In *Pistre*, the Court ruled in the first case that Article 34 TFEU prohibits the national rule at issue – without saying 'in so far products imported from another Member State are concerned'. In *Guimont*, the Court held that Article 34 TFEU 'is not designed to ensure that goods of national origin enjoy the same treatment as imported goods in every case, and a difference in treatment as between goods which is not capable of restricting imports or of prejudicing the marketing of imported goods does not fall within the prohibition contained in that article'.[964] Moreover, the Court added that its interpretation of Union law 'might be useful' to the national court if national law prohibits reverse discrimination. From this it may be inferred that where national law does not prohibit reverse discrimination, the national authority is free to decide otherwise for purely internal situations which may result in a situation of reverse discrimination.

961 ECJ case 90/86 *Zoni* [ECR] 1988 4285, para 25.

962 ECJ case C-448/98 *Guimont* [2000] ECR I-10663, para 15.

963 Ibid para 23.

964 Ibid para 15.

CHAPTER 5
REVERSE DISCRIMINATION OF PERSONS

446. Classic free movement rights of persons is discussed separately from family reunification, the latter based on Directive 2004/38 or on Articles 20 and 21 TFEU on Union citizenship, even though it has been argued that 'the Court appears to be moving towards a convergence of approach under articles 45, 49, 56 and now article 21(1) TFEU on citizenship'.[965] Two main reasons relating to the nature of family reunification justify this decision. First, family reunification concerns derived rights for third country nationals who are family members of Union citizens while classic economic free movement rights concern Union citizens directly. Secondly, family reunification is one of the main sources of immigration to the EU,[966] and immigration is traditionally a competence of the sovereign State, which makes it a delicate issue politically.[967]

1. CLASSIC ECONOMIC FREE MOVEMENT RIGHTS OF PERSONS

447. Reverse discrimination in the area of the classic economic free movement of persons often occurs in the area of employment. In particular, a lot of cases concern professional qualifications. For instance, Member States sometimes reserve certain jobs for persons with a very specific education or diploma. This kind of regulation aims to guarantee a high quality of work. However, it is often incompatible with the Treaty provisions on free movement because it creates a restriction to free movement within the EU, perhaps because the

---

965 Barnard, *The Substantive Law of the EU: The Four Freedoms*, Oxford University Press 2013, p 244, referring to ECJ case C-19/92 *Kraus* [1993] ECR I-1663, para 32.

966 COM (2008) 610, 3.

967 See inter alia Barnard, *The Substantive Law of the EU: The Four Freedoms*, Oxford University Press 2013, p 538; Strik, *Besluitvorming over asiel- en migratierechten*, Boom Juridische Uitgevers 2011, p 87; Walter, *Reverse Discrimination and Family Reunification*, Wolf Legal Publishers 2008, pp 60 and X., Editorial comments, 'The EU as an Area Of Freedom, Security and Justice: Implementing the Stockholm Programme' (2010) 47 *CMLRev* 2010, 1307. For a theoretical assessment of the concept of sovereignty see MacCormick, *Questioning Sovereignty*, Oxford University Press 1999.

education or diploma may not exist in that form in other Member States, for instance. Moreover, a lot of cases of reverse discrimination concern employment conditions such as less favourable wage-setting mechanisms or fixed-term contracts instead of contracts of an indeterminate duration.

448. Reverse discrimination in the area of the classic economic freedom of movement for persons also occurs regarding the rights of persons acquiring goods. For instance, some Member States impose authorisation procedures on the acquisition of buildings and land, or they subject the right of heirs to cumbersome modes of evidence of their status and/or rights. Since these strict conditions are often considered to comprise restrictions to free movement within the EU, they only remain applicable to purely internal situations and hence situations of reverse discrimination arise.

1.1. PROFESSIONAL QUALIFICATIONS

1.1.1. The Austrian Constitutional Court on the Exemption from Proof of Qualification on the Basis of Previous Professional Activity in Another EEA Member State

449. An Austrian photographer and an Austrian architect challenged the Austrian legislation that established that in order to benefit from an exemption of a proof of qualification only relevant professional activities in another EEA Member than Austria were sufficient, whilst similar professional activities in Austria could not suffice. Implementing Directive 75/368, the Austrian legislation did not distinguish on the basis of nationality, but on the basis of the location in which the professional activities were exercised.[968] The citizens that were mostly affected by this legislation were Austrians working in Austria, including the plaintiffs. Although the term 'reverse discrimination' (in German '*Inländerdiskriminierung*') is used by the federal government and is mentioned as a keyword of the judgment, the Austrian Constitutional Court itself did not use it in its reasoning.

450. The Austrian Constitutional Court assessed this legislation in the light of the Austrian constitutional principle of equality.[969] The Court did not consider

968 Article 5(1) Council Directive 75/368/EEC of 16 June 1975 on measures to facilitate the effective exercise of freedom of establishment and freedom to provide services in respect of various activities (ex ISIC Division 01–85) and, in particular, transitional measures in respect of those activities.

969 Austrian Constitutional Court 9 December 1999, no 15 683, VI, 2.

whether the difference in treatment concerned comparable situations, but it immediately considered whether or not the difference in treatment could be justified.

451. First, the Austrian Constitutional Court ruled that the transposition of a European Union Directive is not a sufficient justification for the difference in treatment contested.[970] The Court held that if the Austrian legislator treats Austrian citizens in a purely internal situation less favourably than citizens falling within the scope of application of the Union Directive, this should be in accordance with the Austrian Constitution and, in particular, with the principle of equality.

452. Secondly, according to the Austrian Constitutional Court, the goal of the conservation of a high level of commercial activity in Austria cannot justify the contested difference in treatment. The Court considered that although the goal is legitimate, it cannot justify the rules according to which the acquisition of a relevant education abroad and a corresponding activity in a managerial position abroad are suited to exemption from the requirement of qualification, whereas the same training and the same activities in Austria are not. By contrast, the Austrian Constitutional Court was of the opinion that an appropriate training and a corresponding activity in each industry in Austria, with respect to the provision of a proof of qualification for the commercial legal requirements, is better-suited rather than worse-suited to achieving the desired level of commercial activity and the necessary qualifications.[971] Finally, the Court ruled that the fact that the rules on recognition and proof of qualification are not harmonised for different kinds of jobs does not justify the contested distinction.[972] After rejecting all of the possible justifications, the Austrian Constitutional Court concluded that the situation of reverse discrimination was a violation of the Austrian principle of equality.[973]

453. It could be argued that the situation at issue was a case of compensation by Union law and that the alleged reverse discrimination was a mere difference in treatment that does not have to be compared with the situations falling under Union law. That is, Directive 75/368 aims at facilitating the effective exercise of freedom of establishment and freedom to provide services with respect to various activities. Accepting the evidence of previous professional activities, instead of a proof of qualification, certainly facilitates the access to jobs in other Member States.

---

970 Ibid 3 c).
971 Ibid.
972 Ibid.
973 Ibid 3 d).

The Austrian Constitutional Court could have assessed the purely internal situation as such in the light of a substantial right as enshrined in national law, such as the right to choose a profession.[974] This assessment could have led either to allowing the exemption for a proof of qualification for previous professional experience in Austria or to confirming the legality of the difference in treatment between purely internal situations and cross-border situations. However, the Austrian Constitutional Court decided differently. Without considering that the purely internal situation and cross-border situation were comparable, it held that the reverse discrimination was a violation of the principle of equality as enshrined in Austrian law.

1.1.2. The French Council of State on Tourist Guides and Architects

1.1.2.1. The French Council of State on Proof of Good Behaviour for Tourist Guides

454. The *Association professionnelle des guides interprètes* challenged the order of the Minister of Trade of 8 August 1979[975] before the Council of State, laying down the conditions for issuing and delivering the licence of guide-interpreter since they were more constraining for French citizens than for 'foreigners residing outside France'.[976,977] In particular, for French citizens or foreigners residing in France[978] the licence is obtained depending on the results of a morality survey. Conversely, for foreigners outside France, nationals of another EU Member State or of a country with which France has signed a convention of reciprocity, the licence is obtained after an individual produces an excerpt of their criminal record, or by default, after delivery of an equivalent document by a competent judicial or administrative authority of the country of origin. Upon receipt of one of these documents, they can obtain a provisional authorisation to work as a guide which is valid for a maximum of nine months. The association challenged the Minister's order in the light of Treaty provisions prohibiting discrimination on grounds of nationality.

---

974 Article 18 Basic Law of 21 December 1867 *juncto* Article 149 of the Austrian Constitution. The Austrian Constitution contains no bill of rights, but in Article 149 it determines that the Basic Law of 21 December 1867 is to be regarded as constitutional law.

975 Modified by the order of 8 November 1984.

976 Author's translation of: [*les étrangers résidant hors de 'rance*].

977 Council of State 3 June 1987, *Association professionnelle des guides interprètes*, no 65228.

978 At first glance, this is not a situation of reverse discrimination in the strict sense, since foreigners who reside in France are also subjected to the more constraining conditions. However, do they not also fall within the scope of Union law and should they not be eligible for the more favourable treatment as well? Then a situation of reverse discrimination in the strict sense would be at stake.

455. The Council of State considered that the Treaty provisions that prohibit 'discrimination on grounds of nationality' have no other goal than eliminating discrimination detrimental to the nationals of other EU Member States and that they do not under any circumstances limit the powers of the national authorities with regard to their own nationals.[979] The Council of State decided that the applicant association could not rely on these Union provisions in order to ask for the annulment of the Minister of Trade's order which is more restrictive for French citizens than it is for foreigners residing outside France.[980]

456. Next, the Council of State assessed the case in the light of French law. It rejected the argument made by the applicant that the Minister of Trade exceeded the powers he held on the basis of the Articles 65 and 69 of the Decree of 28 March 1977.[981] Since the Council of State rejected the alleged violations of Union law and French law, it ruled that the request for annulment of the order was unfounded. Hence, the situation of reverse discrimination was allowed to exist.

457. In the light of our working hypothesis, it can be argued that a mere compensation by Union law was at stake. That is, in order to take the morality survey, candidates have to see an administrative authority in the department in which they are domiciled. For citizens residing outside France, this poses a practical problem. If they have to go to Paris, for instance, the morality survey would clearly be an extra burden for them. Therefore, providing an excerpt of their criminal records, instead of taking a morality survey, constitutes a compensation for citizens residing abroad that means they are not prevented from benefitting from the provisions on free movement of workers and services.

Unfortunately, the French Council of State's judgment does not contain any such considerations. It basically held that neither Union law nor French law was violated and, accordingly, the stricter treatment of purely internal situations was not considered to be a problem.

---

979 Council of State 3 June 1987, *Association professionnelle des guides interprètes*, no 65228: [*Considérant qu'il ressort clairement des stipulations du traité instituant la communauté économique européenne en date du 25 mars 1957 qui interdisent 'toute discrimination exercée en raison de la nationalité' qu'elles n'ont d'autre objet que d'éliminer les discriminations défavorables aux ressortissants des autres Etats membres de la communauté et qu'elles ne sauraient, en aucun cas, limiter les pouvoirs dont les autorités nationales sont investies à l'égard de leurs propres ressortissants*].

980 Ibid: [*qu'ainsi l'association requérante ne peut utilement se prévaloir de ce que les dispositions précitées de l'arrêté du 8 août 1979 seraient plus contraignantes pour les citoyens français que pour les étrangers résidant hors de France pour soutenir que les stipulations du traité instituant la Communauté économique européenne auraient été méconnues*].

981 The Council of State considered that the circumstance that the contested order did not envisage the situations of French citizens residing abroad has no influence on the legality.

1.1.2.2. The French Council of State on the Restoration of Classified Historic Monuments by a Specific Type of Architect

458. In 2008, the French Council of State condemned a situation of reverse discrimination in the light of the principle of equality for the very first time. The case concerned legislation regarding the restoration of classified historic monuments.[982] In France, classified historic monuments cannot be destroyed, moved or be the object of restoration works, reparation or modification of any nature without authorisation by the administrative authority.[983] The categories of professionals under whose control these works can proceed are specified in a decree. By virtue of the Decree of 20 November 1980,[984] one group of architects effectively exercised a monopoly on restoration works of historic classified monuments – whether these belonged to the State or not. This quasi monopoly led to a reasoned Opinion by the European Commission of 4 April 2006,[985] which considered that this legislation was not compatible with the Union principle of free movement of establishment and services (Articles 49 and 56 TFEU).

459. In order to avoid proceedings before the ECJ, the French government decided to reform the French regime concerning the restoration of historic monuments. The Decree of 28 September 2007 determines that the control of the restoration works of classified historic monuments has to be assured by the group of architects responsible for historical monuments with respect to monuments belonging to the State.[986] Regarding those classified historic monuments not belonging to the State, the restoration works can be undertaken by those architects or by a national of another EU Member State or a State party to the European Economic Area (EEA) if they are not established in France (complying with the conditions required for the competition and to be registered at the roll of the order of architects).[987] Article 2 of the Decree of 28 September 2007 provides that is also open to nationals of other Member States or State Parties to the EEA to join the association of architects responsible for historical monuments.

---

982 Council of State 6 October 2008, no 310146.

983 Article L. 621-9 du Code du Patrimoine.

984 Decree no 80-911, 20 November 1980 [*Statut particulier du corps des architectes en chef des monuments historiques*] *JO* 21 November 1980.

985 As referred to by Iliopoulou and Jauréguiberry, 'La première condamnation d'une discrimination à rebours. A propos de l'arrêt du Conseil d'Etat du 6 octobre 2008' [2009] *RFDA* 132, 133.

986 Article 3 Decree no 2007-1405 of 28 September 2007 [*portant statut particulier du corps des architectes en chef des monuments historiques et adaptation au droit communautaire des règles applicables à la restauration des immeubles classés*] *JO* 30 September 2007.

987 Article 3 *juncto* 9 Decree no 2007-1405.

460. The association of architects responsible for historical monuments challenged the Decree of 28 September 2007, because it created a situation of reverse discrimination since it continued to exclude architects – other than the specialised architects responsible for historical monuments – who are established in France from the restoration of classified historic monuments not belonging to the State.

461. The Council of State reviewed the legality of the contested provisions in the light of the general principle of equality.[988] First, the Council of State considered in general that the principle of equality does not preclude that different situations be regulated differently, nor that the legislator derogates from an equal treatment for reasons of general interest, provided that the resulting difference in treatment is suited to obtaining the goal pursued and is not disproportionate.[989]

462. Next, the Council of State ascertained that the Decree had the effect of excluding architects established in France from heading the restoration works of those classified historic monuments not belonging to the French State. According to the Council of State, the difference of treatment between French professionals and nationals from other EU Member States or State Parties to the EEA instituted by the Decree, depending on whether they are established in France or in another EU Member State or State Party to the EEA, was not in line with the goal of Article 9 of the contested Decree of 28 September 2007. In particular, its goal is to make it possible to entrust the restoration of those monuments to other categories of professionals than the architects responsible for historical monuments. Since the Council of State ruled that there is no

---

988 Since no reference is made to specific legislation, it may be supposed that the principle of equality was considered here as a general principle of law. See Cluzel-Métayer, 'Le principe d'égalité et de non-discrimination dans la jurisprudence du Conseil d'Etat et de la Cour de cassation: analyse comparée dans le domaine de l'emploi' [2010] *RFDA* 309, 309: [*L'égalité, affirmée à plusieurs reprises dans le bloc de constitutionnalité (à l'article 1er de la Constitution de 1958, à l'article 6 de la Déclaration des droits de l'homme et du citoyen et aux alinéas 3 et 5 du Préambule de la Constituion de 1946) est depuis longtemps érigée en principe: principe général du droit et même principe à valeur constitutionnelle*].

989 French Council of State 6 October 2008, no 310146: [*Considérant que le principe d'égalité ne s'oppose pas à ce qui l'autorité investie du pouvoir réglementaire règle de façon différente des situations différentes ni à ce qu'elle déroge à l'égalité pour des raisons d'intérêt général, pourvu que la différence de traitement qui en résulte soit, dans l'un comme l'autre cas, en rapport avec l'objet de la norme qui établit et ne soit pas manifestement disproportionnée au regard des différences de situations susceptibles de la justifier*]. Iliopoulou and Jauréguiberry pointed out that this formula is settled case law of the Council of State and has been inspired by the case law of the Constitutional Council (Iliopoulou and Jauréguiberry, 'La première condamnation d'une discrimination à rebours. A propos de l'arrêt du Conseil d'Etat du 6 octobre 2008' [2009] *RFDA* 132, 137).

general interest ground justifying the discriminatory treatment suffered by French professionals established in France, it concluded that the principle of equality was violated to the extent that it excludes professionals established in France from its field of application.

463. Moreover, the French Council of State not only annulled Article 9 of the Decree of 28 September 2007 to the extent that it excluded professionals established in France from its scope of application, it also ordered the French government to issue a decree in order to make the provisions conform with the principle of equality.

464. Although neither the French Council of State nor the parties used the term 'reverse discrimination' ('*discrimination à rebours*'), it was generally stated that this was the Council's first condemnation of a reverse discrimination.[990] According to Iliopoulou and Jauréguiberry, this judgment is more than a solution for the specific problem of the case at issue.[991] They argued that the principle of equality could function as a yardstick for the French legislative and executive power when addressing reverse discrimination in the future.[992] They do not consider this to be a 'mechanic operation'; the consideration in a specific case can either lead to the abandonment or to the creation or maintenance of the stricter national legislation.[993]

465. In the light of our working hypothesis, it could be argued that a compensation by Union law was at stake. Most likely, the title 'architect responsible for historical monuments' does not exist in each Member State. Excluding nationals from these Member States from heading the restoration works of classified historic monuments directly impedes their access to that activity and, hence, constitutes a restriction to the free movement of workers. Accordingly, not requiring this title for non-French nationals can be considered as compensating for a disadvantage resulting from the exercise of free movement. Therefore, the French Council of State could have ruled that this was a simple

990 See eg Cluzel-Métayer, 'Le principe d'égalité et de non-discrimination dans la jurisprudence du Conseil d'Etat et de la Cour de cassation: analyse comparée dans le domaine de l'emploi' [2010] *RFDA* 309, 313 and 321 and Iliopoulou and Jauréguiberry, 'La première condamnation d'une discrimination à rebours. A propos de l'arrêt du Conseil d'Etat du 6 octobre 2008' [2009] *RFDA* 132. See also the French journal, *Actualité juridique Droit Administratif* which published the full text of the judgment under the title '*Condamnation d'une discrimination à rebours*' [2008] *AJDA* 1919.

991 Iliopoulou and Jauréguiberry, 'La première condamnation d'une discrimination à rebours. A propos de l'arrêt du Conseil d'Etat du 6 octobre 2008' [2009] *RFDA* 132, 139.

992 Ibid.

993 Ibid 138 and 139.

difference in treatment. It could still have assessed the situation, in the light of the right to employment for instance.[994]

466. After the judgment of the Council of State, the French legislator amended the Decree.[995] Article 9 has been abrogated entirely and the Decree no longer contains the category of classified historic monuments not belonging to the State; restoration works concerning these monuments, hence, seem to be open to all architects without further conditions. Conversely, classified historic monuments belonging to the State continue to be entrusted exclusively to the architects responsible for historical monuments.[996] The question then arises as to whether that legislative choice is compatible with Union law. France could invoke the public service exception of Article 45(4) TFEU in order to justify the different treatment of classified historic monuments depending on whether or not they belong to the State.[997]

1.1.2.3. The French Council of State on Attestation of Professional Qualifications for Tourist Guides

467. In 2010, the French Council of State took a different approach when ruling on a case regarding the order of 30 May 2008 implementing Directive 2005/36

---

994 Article 6 of the Declaration of Human and Civil Rights of 26 August 1789 determines that 'The Law is the expression of the general will. All citizens have the right to take part, personally or through their representatives, in its making. It must be the same for all, whether it protects or punishes. All citizens, being equal in its eyes, shall be equally eligible to all high offices, public positions and employments, according to their ability, and without other distinction than that of their virtues and talents.' The preamble of the French Constitution provides that 'The French people solemnly proclaim their attachment to the Rights of Man and the principles of national sovereignty as defined by the Declaration of 1789, confirmed and complemented by the Preamble to the Constitution of 1946, and to the rights and duties as defined in the Charter for the Environment of 2004.'

995 Amendment by Decree no 2009-749 of 22 June 2009.

996 Article 3 of Decree no 2007-1405 as modified by Decree no 2009-749 of 22 June 2009.

997 Article 45(4) TFEU provides that the principles of free movement of workers and non-discrimination on the ground of nationality do not apply to 'employment in the public service'. This derogation presumes 'the existence of a special relationship of allegiance to the State and reciprocity of rights and duties which form the foundation of the bond of nationality' (ECJ case C-392/05 [2007] ECR I-3505, para 70 and ECJ case C-47/02 [2003] ECR I-10447, para 20). In general, the ECJ interprets this exception narrowly, but in case 149/79 *Commission v Belgium*, the Court ruled that local authority posts for architects, supervisors and night watchmen did fall within the exception of Article 45(4) TFEU (ECJ case 149/79 *Commission v Belgium* [1982] ECR 1845, para 8; see Barnard, *The Substantive Law of the EU: The Four Freedoms*, Oxford University Press 2013, pp 500–02). Although Articles 51 and 62 TFEU contain a similar provision regarding the freedom of establishment and services, it is doubtful whether the ECJ would still consider this to be 'good law', especially in the light of ECJ's case law regarding notaries. In particular, see ECJ case C-47/08 *Commission v Belgium* [2011] ECR I-4105, para 123 and ECJ case C-50/08 *Commission v France* [2011] ECR I-4195, para 106.

on the recognition of professional qualifications.[998] Whereas tourist guides who are established in France where they practice a usual and regular activity are obliged to submit a declaration of professional qualifications, tourist guides who are established in another EU Member State providing temporary and occasional services on the French territory, are exempted from the obligation of declaration since they fall under the Union provision on free movement of services. The parties invoked a violation of the principle of equality because the order subjected those residing in France to stricter rules regarding recognition of the professional qualification.

The French Council of State ruled that 'this difference in treatment finds its justification in the difference between the situations'.[999] Therefore, it decided that the argument based on the violation of the principle of equality must be dismissed.[1000]

468. In the light of our working hypothesis, it can be concluded that the French Council of State considered that a compensation by Union law and, hence, a mere difference in treatment was at stake. Two possible explanations may be given as to why the Council of State considered the situations to be incomparable. Either, it is possible that the Council of State considered the situation to be different because it focused on the criterion of residence. Or, it may also be that the Council of State made a distinction between the freedom of movement of services on the one hand and the freedom of movement of establishment on the other.[1001]

1.1.3. The German Federal Constitutional Court on Skilled Trades Order

469. The German Federal Constitutional Court ruled in 2000, and subsequently in 2005, on situations of reverse discrimination in the context of the German Skilled Trades Order.[1002] The Skilled Trades Order provides that only natural or legal persons or associations of persons who are entered on the Skilled Trades

[998] French Council of State 23 July 2010, no 318932. Directive 2013/55/EU of the European Parliament and of the Council of 20 November 2013 amending Directive 2005/36/EC on the recognition of professional qualifications and Regulation (EU) no 1024/2012 on administrative cooperation through the Internal Market Information System.

[999] French Council of State 23 July 2010, no 318932: [*cette différence de traitement trouve sa justification dans la différence de situation*].

[1000] French Council of State 23 July 2010, no 318932: [*par suite, le moyen tiré de la méconnaissance du principe d'égalité doit être écarté*].

[1001] The ECJ distinguishes the freedom of services from the freedom of establishment on the basis of temporary nature. See Lenaerts and Van Nuffel, *European Union Law*, Sweet & Maxwell 2011, p 75 and references to the ECJ's case law there.

[1002] '*Handwerksordnung*'.

Register[1003] are authorised to pursue a skilled trade activity in an independent capacity. This registration corresponds to the granting of an authorisation to carry out that activity.[1004] Any person who has passed the master's examination in the skilled trade, to be carried out by him or in a related craft or trade, shall be entered on the Skilled Trades Register.[1005] Lower requirements apply to EU craftsmen.[1006]

470. In its judgment of 31 March 2000, the German Federal Constitutional Court ruled upon the interpretation and application of Article 3 Skilled Trades Order.[1007] In particular, paragraphs 2 and 3 thereof provide that registration is not necessary when the skilled trade activity is negligible (if it does not exceed the average working time of a full-time business, without assistants, in the skilled trade branch concerned during one year) nor when the skilled trade activity is only a dependent, auxiliary service.

471. The case concerned an electrician who operated an electrical retail store, which was open five days a week, but for only three hours each day. The complainant delivered the goods sold and afterwards, where necessary, he repaired the electrical installations. Due to seriously declining sales, he started working as a warehouseman on the side. He was ordered to pay a fine for independently exercising a skilled trade business without being entered on the Skilled Trades Register. The complainant challenged this decision on the basis of Articles 3(1) and 12(1) of the Constitution as well as on the basis of the freedom of establishment under European law.[1008]

472. The German Federal Constitutional Court held that the question of whether the requirements of the master's examination were still justified in view of the lower requirements for EU craftsmen could remain undecided here.[1009]

1003 '*Handwerksrolle*'.

1004 Article 1(1) Skilled Trades Order.

1005 First sentence of Article 7(1) Skilled Trades Order.

1006 Verordnung über die für Staatsangehörige der Mitgliedstaaten der Europäischen Union oder eines anderen Vertragsstaates des Abkommens über den Europäischen Wirtschaftsraum oder der Schweiz geltenden Voraussetzungen der Eintragung in die Handwerksrolle (EU/EWR-Handwerk-Verordnung – EU/EWR HwV) Vom 4. August 1966 (BGBl. I S. 469) zuletzt geändert durch Art. 4 der Verordnung über den Erlass und die Änderung handwerksrechtlicher Verordnungen vom 22. Juni 2004 (BGBl. I S. 1314).

1007 German Federal Constitutional Court 31 March 2000, 1 BvR 608/99.

1008 Ibid para 5. He also referred to Articles 2(1) Constitution, the free development of personality, and 20(1) Constitution, determining that the Federal Republic is a democratic and social federal State. These grounds were not addressed by the Court.

1009 German Federal Constitutional Court 31 March 2000, 1 BvR 608/99, para 15.

The Court based its conclusion on the complainant's contentions that his activities did not constitute the exercising of a particular skilled trade, but rather were exercised as an auxiliary service and thus registration on the Skilled Trade Register was unnecessary. The Court pointed out that, although the complainant fulfilled the requirements of the EU regulation, he did not assert that he was an 'EU craftsman'.

473. Next, the Federal Constitutional Court ruled that the contested decision did not meet the standard of Article 12(1) Basic Law.[1010] The Court considered that the relevant provisions of the Skilled Trade Order comply with the requirements of Article 12(1) Basic Law insofar as the risk exists that in a business which is designated as a retail business, in reality it is not trade that is exercised, but rather artisanal work is being carried out.[1011] The Court pointed out that the legislator seeks to take the realities of economic life into account, in particular the transition between branches, by establishing thresholds below which a proof of qualification is not required.[1012] The Federal Constitutional Court pointed out that, in compliance with the constitutionally guaranteed right of the freedom of occupation, it distinguished the core business of skilled trade from auxiliary services in numerous decisions.[1013]

474. The Court stressed that the question of whether or not Article 1 Skilled Trade Order is applicable needs to be grounded on a factual assessment of the case at issue; however, the contested decision failed to do so.[1014] The Federal Constitutional Court ruled that if the contested decision had interpreted the Skilled Trades Order, which interferes with the freedom of independent professional practice (a sensitive issue), in conformity with the Constitution, then it would have attached the appropriate weight to the exceptions of Article 3 Skilled Trades Order and made its decision to impose a fine based on the facts of the case.[1015] Accordingly, the Court held that the contested decision violated Article 12 Basic Law.[1016]

475. In its judgment of 5 December 2005, the Federal Constitutional Court had to interpret Article 7 Skilled Trades Order, which determines that any person who has passed the master's examination in the skilled trade carried on by him or in a related craft or trade shall be entered on the Skilled Trades Register. Pursuant to Article 8, in exceptional cases, authorisation to be entered on the Skilled Trades Register is granted if the applicant is able to demonstrate the knowledge and skill required to pursue the skilled trade to be carried on by him independently.

1010 Ibid para 29.
1011 Ibid para 30.
1012 Ibid.
1013 Ibid para 31.
1014 Ibid paras 32–37.
1015 Ibid para 38.
1016 Ibid paras 38–39.

476. The case concerned a carpenter who, after successfully completing his education, worked in the business of his education for a couple of years. Afterwards, the complainant started his own business in trade and installation of doors and wooden ceilings. After a master carpenter had been hired as a manager in the company, the business had been entered on the Skilled Trade Register. However, after the master carpenter's departure, the registration was deleted. The applicant was subsequently registered with the business 'installation of standardised prefabricated construction' in the Skilled Trades Register; however, the additional registration requested for carpentry work was rejected due to the lack of a master's examination.

477. The complainant challenged this decision on the basis of Articles 12(1) and 3(1) Basic Law. He asserted that the restriction of the choice of profession by the master's examination is no longer justifiable since it is neither appropriate nor necessary to guarantee the quality of artisanal work. Moreover, he pointed out that for EU foreigners lighter conditions for market access for crafts apply and he contested this '*Inländerdiskriminierung*'[1017] as being an unjustified unequal treatment in the light of Article 3(1) Basic Law.

478. The German Federal Court ruled that interference with the freedom of choice of occupation is only permitted on the basis of a statutory provision which is justifiable by reasons of public interest and is consistent with the principle of proportionality.[1018] In particular, the Court considered that changes in economic and legal circumstances have led to doubts as to whether the legislation on the compulsory master's examination still meets the principle of proportionality.[1019] In this respect, the Court recognised the legislation's two main objectives, to ensure a high level of proficiency and efficiency and to guarantee the education of young people, as important public interest grounds.[1020]

479. First, the Court considered whether the significant technical and financial requirements of the master's examination were still reasonable to meet the objective of maintaining the level of quality and efficiency of crafts.[1021] In this connection, the Court considered that at least in border areas, German craftsmen face serious competition from craftsmen from other EU countries who are not required to pass the master's examination.[1022] According to the Court, Articles 1 and 7 Skilled Trades Order were no longer appropriate to ensuring the quality of craft services, since they failed to reach the providers from other EU countries.[1023] Moreover, the Court ruled that the more stringent conditions

[1017] The German Federal Constitutional Court, however, did not use this term.
[1018] German Federal Constitutional Court, 5 December 2005, 1 BvR 1730/02, para 17.
[1019] Ibid para 18.
[1020] Ibid para 19.
[1021] Ibid para 20.
[1022] Ibid para 21.
[1023] Ibid para 22.

for market access for Germans were no longer proportionate to the increasingly blurred aim of guaranteeing quality.[1024]

480. Secondly, the Court examined the proportionality of the requirement of a master's examination in the light of the objective of good education.[1025] The Court ruled that the requirement was not proportional since this aim could also be achieved in an equally effective, but less intrusive, way.[1026] Hereby, the Court referred to the Skilled Trades Order as applicable since 2004. Although it was not applicable in the case at issue, it demonstrates that the objective of ensuring education does not necessarily entail the condition that only craftsmen that have passed a master's examination can provide professional training. The new legislation determines that professionally experienced individuals, who also have their names entered on the Skilled Trades Register can do so when they can demonstrate their professional and educational knowledge.[1027]

481. Finally, the Court held that the concerns on the proportionality of the interference with the freedom of choice of occupation, analysed above, reaffirmed the necessity to generously apply the exemptions of Article 8 Skilled Trades Order in the light of the meaning and scope of the fundamental right of the complainant under Article 12(1) Basic Law.[1028]

However, the Court emphasised that administrative practice does not sufficiently use the possibility of exemptions provided for in Article 8 Skilled Trades Order.[1029] In particular, administrative practice seems to require a comparative examination of knowledge and skills in order to apply Article 8, rather than also using it in favour of professionally experienced individuals.[1030] The Court ruled that a generous interpretation and application of Article 8 Skilled Trades Order is possible given the open wording of the provision[1031] and is necessary in the light of Article 12(1) Basic Law.[1032]

482. These two judgments by the German Federal Constitutional Court in 2000 and 2005 concerning the German Skilled Trades Order are discussed together because they have a lot in common. First of all, in both cases, the applicants based their claim on both Article 3(1), enshrining the principle of equality, and Article 12(1) Basic Law, enshrining the fundamental right to choose a profession. The Federal Constitutional Court refrained from reviewing the cases in the light of the principle of equality and instead decided the case on the basis of Article 12 Basic Law. The Court's reasoning comes down to the fact that restrictions on Article 12 Basic Law should be interpreted strictly, the requirement of a master's

---

1024 Ibid.
1025 Ibid para 23.
1026 Ibid para 24.
1027 Ibid.
1028 Ibid para 25.
1029 Ibid para 27.
1030 Ibid.
1031 Ibid paras 26–27.
1032 Ibid para 25.

examination in particular. Exceptions to these requirements should in turn be interpreted generously. De facto, these decisions lead to fewer situations of reverse discrimination.[1033]

483. This reasoning fits perfectly into our working hypothesis because it can be argued that a compensation by Union law was at stake. In particular, in order to become a master craftsman in Germany one should follow an education including theoretical and practical training in the craft as well as business and legal training and, finally, one should pass the master's examination. If craftsmen from other EU Member States had to comply with these demanding German standards, their access to exercise a craft in Germany would be impeded. Accordingly, requiring lower standards for EU craftsmen could be seen as being a compensation for the disadvantage of making use of the rights of free movement within the EU.

The German court has exclusively assessed the purely internal situation in the light of national law, in particular, the right to choose an occupation. In both judgments of 2000 and 2005, the Court's ruling led to fewer situations of reverse discrimination.

1.1.4. Intermezzo: *Compensation by Union Law: Assessment of a Purely Internal Situation in the Light of National Law, but Union Rules May be Inspiration*

484. In our working hypothesis, it is suggested that in case of reverse discrimination resulting from compensation by Union law, the national authority is still able to assess the purely internal situation as such – not as reverse discrimination – in the light of national law. Since the purely internal situation is the only one remaining to be assessed under national law, the principle of equality as enshrined in national law is not conceptually appropriate for further assessment, given that the purely internal situation and the situation falling under Union law are not comparable situations. Accordingly, other principles and rules are required in order to make the assessment. In particular, substantial rights, such as the right to respect for private and family life and the right to economic freedom, seem appropriate in order to assess a situation of reverse discrimination which is the result of a mere compensation by Union law. However, it is submitted that this does not prevent the national authority from considering the Union rules for cross-border situations as comprising an inspiration or an additional argument by which to treat purely internal situations differently (less strictly) in

1033 The same analysis applies to the judgment of the German Federal Administrative Court of 2005 on purity of beer (German Federal Administrative Court 24 February 2005, no 3 C. 5.04), discussed above nn 430–36.

the future. In order to illustrate this, some examples will be discussed, starting with the judgment of the German Federal Constitutional Court discussed in the previous subsection.

485. In 2005, the German Federal Constitutional Court assessed the Skilled Trades Order in the light of the right to choose an occupation. In particular, the case regarded the registration in the Skilled Trades Register, in principle on the basis of the master's examination (Article 7) and exceptionally by demonstrating knowledge and skill (Article 8).

In its judgment, the Court referred to the distinct treatment of craftsmen from other EU Member States providing services in Germany, in particular to border areas. However, it was on the basis of the open wording of Article 8 Skilled Trades Order[1034] that the Court decided that a generous interpretation and application of Article 8 was possible; moreover it considered this necessary in the light of Article 12(1) Basic Law.[1035] In other words, the German Court decided the case on the basis of national law, but took the Union rules for cross-border situations into account as one of the relevant factors in its assessment of the case at issue.

486. Our second example will outline an alternative reasoning for the Austrian Constitutional Court's judgment regarding the exemption of proof of qualification of previous professional activity in another EEA State, discussed above.[1036] In that judgment, the Austrian Constitutional Court, without considering the comparability of the purely internal situation and the cross-border situation, held that the reverse discrimination at issue was a violation of the principle of equality as enshrined in Austrian law. According to the Austrian Constitutional Court, the aim of guaranteeing a high level of commercial activity in Austria could not justify the rules according to which the acquisition of a relevant education abroad and a corresponding activity in a managerial position abroad are appropriate to exemption from the requirement of qualification, whereas the same training and the same activities in Austria are not.

487. However, an alternative reasoning may be suggested based upon the working hypothesis as it is being developed in this subsection. First, as has been argued above, the Austrian Constitutional Court could have assessed the purely internal situation as such in the light of the right to choose a profession as protected by Austrian law.[1037] Secondly, it could have referred to the way in

1034 German Federal Constitutional Court, 5 December 2005, 1 BvR 1730/02, paras 26–27.

1035 Ibid para 25.

1036 Above nn 449–53.

1037 Article 18 Basic Law of 21 December 1867 *juncto* Article 149 Austrian Constitution. The Austrian Constitution contains no bill of rights, but Article 149 Austrian Constitution determines that the Basic Law of 21 December 1867 has to be regarded as constitutional law.

which situations falling under the scope of Directive 75/368 are regulated as one of the arguments that should be taken into account in order to come to a conclusion in the case.

In fact, this alternative reasoning is not at all that far from the actual judgment of the Austrian Constitutional Court as might appear at first glance. That is to say, an assessment in the light of the right to choose an occupation may also lead to the result of ending the situation of reverse discrimination – as the judgment of the German Federal Constitutional Court described above demonstrates. Moreover, the inspiration from Union law can be found in the actual judgment's assessment of the justification for the difference in treatment.

This demonstrates that our working hypothesis does not aim to completely alter the assessment of reverse discrimination at the national level, but it does aim to provide a clear and logically structured framework through which to assess a situation of reverse discrimination. In order to achieve that objective, it is important that the national authority adequately substantiates the different steps in its reasoning.

488. As a final example, the position Goossens holds regarding the Belgian authentic instruments regarding succession will be briefly discussed.[1038] In particular, the heirs, legatees, executors of the will or administrators of the estate should be able to demonstrate their status and/or rights and power easily. Traditionally, in this regard, authentic instruments based on witness statements were used. That is, in this notarised document, the witness makes a statement regarding the identity and claims of the heirs based on general awareness or on their personal knowledge. However, in our modern society, this authentic instrument grounded on witness statements has reached its limits. In 2009, the Belgian legislator introduced another authentic instrument based on their own observations of the notary.[1039] However, this only applies in the context of the release of funds in bank accounts.

By contrast, in cross-border successions, it is possible to rely on the European Certificate of Succession. In particular, this creates a third party protection with a general scope for the proof of status and rights in matters of succession.[1040] Consequently, this raises the issue of reverse discrimination of Belgian successions.

1038 Goossens, 'Pleidooi voor de veralgemeende invoering van de Europese erfrechtverklaring in het Belgisch recht' [2013] *Not.Fisc.M.* 204.

1039 Article 1240*bis* Burgerlijk Wetboek.

1040 Article 69 Regulation (EU) no 650/2012 of the European Parliament and of the Council of 4 July 2012 on jurisdiction, applicable law, recognition and enforcement of decisions and acceptance and enforcement of authentic instruments in matters of succession and on the creation of a European Certificate of Succession.

489. Goossens has argued for the introduction in Belgium of an authentic instrument of a general scope for demonstrating status and rights in the domain of succession. She bases this on a threefold argument: by clarifying the legislative history and *ratio legis* of the instrument introduced in 2009 (national component), by comparing the Belgian instrument of 2009 to functional equivalents abroad (comparative component), and by reflecting upon the introduction and implications of the European Certificate of Succession (European Union component).[1041] The consideration of Union rules for cross-border situations is only one of three arguments that Goossens puts forward in support of an amendment of the Belgian legislation concerning authentic instruments regarding succession, in particular establishing a third party protection with a general scope. Such an amendment of the Belgian legislation would end the situation of reverse discrimination in demonstrating status and rights in matters of succession.[1042]

1.2. ACQUIRING IMMOVABLE PROPERTY: THE AUSTRIAN CONSTITUTIONAL COURT

490. In March 2004, the Austrian Constitutional Court had to rule upon the Austrian legislation, which subjected the acquisition of immovable property to a prior authorisation procedure.[1043] In particular, the acquirer had to show that the land would, within a reasonable timeframe, be put to use.[1044]

491. First, the Austrian Constitutional Court referred to its settled case law according to which the harsher treatment of Austrian citizens in relation to foreigners has to be assessed in the light of the principle of equality and, therefore requires an objective justification.[1045] This also applies, according to the Court, to so-called situations of reverse discrimination.[1046] In this respect,

1041 Goossens, 'Pleidooi voor de veralgemeende invoering van de Europese erfrechtverklaring in het Belgisch recht' [2013] *Not.Fisc.M.* 204.

1042 Ibid 210–11.

1043 Austrian Constitutional Court 1 March 2004, no 17 150, II.

1044 See ECJ case C-300/01 *Salzmann II* [2003] ECR I-4899, para 9.

1045 Austrian Constitutional Court 1 March 2004, no 17 150, II, 2.1: [*Der Verfassungsgerichtshof judiziert in ständiger Rechtsprechung, daß eine Schlechterstellung österreichischer Staatsbürger im Verhältnis zu Ausländern am Gleichheitssatz zu messen ist und daher einer sachlichen Rechtfertigung bedarf* (vgl. VfSlg. 13084/1992, 14863/1997, 14963/1997)].

1046 Austrian Constitutional Court 1 March 2004, no 17 150, II, 2.1: [*Diesen Gedanken hat der Verfassungsgerichtshof – unter Hinweis auf die 'doppelte Bindung' des Gesetzgebers bei der Umsetzung von Gemeinschaftsrecht – auch auf die sogenannte 'Inländerdiskriminierung' übertragen* (VfSlg. 14863/1997, 14963/1997, 15683/1999)].

the Court pointed out that this does not concern discrimination on the basis of nationality, but the disadvantageous position of purely internal situations in relation to situations falling within Union law; therefore, Austrian citizens are the most affected by it.[1047]

492. Secondly, the Austrian Constitutional Court considered that the harsher treatment of purely internal situations does not directly result from the national provisions itself in the case under analysis.[1048] Instead, it follows from the primacy of Union law. In particular, the ECJ held, specifically in the context of the contested Austrian legislation, that the freedom of movement of capital precludes a prior authorisation procedure for the acquisition of a building plot.[1049] The Austrian Constitutional Court explicitly stated that the ECJ's judgment only applies to situations that have a connection with Union law, hence, essentially for the legal transactions whereby a Union or an Austrian citizen acquires immovable property in Austria using capital from another Member State.[1050]

493. Finally, the Court considered that there was no objective justification for the fact that the acquisition of building plots in purely internal situations is subjected to a prior authorisation procedure and is, therefore, treated more strictly than a similar acquisition which has a connection with Union law.[1051] Accordingly, the Austrian Constitutional Court held that the contested decision violated the constitutionally guaranteed right of equality of all citizens.[1052]

494. The Austrian Constitutional Court did name specifically and clarify the issue of reverse discrimination. The Court specified that the reverse discrimination at issue resulted from the consequences of the ECJ's judgment – the prior authorisation procedure of the Austrian legislation could no longer be required for cross-border situations – and the Austrian legislation which continued to be applied to purely internal situations. Subsequently, the Austrian Constitutional Court decided, in only one paragraph, that no objective justification was apparent for treating purely internal acquisitions of immovable property worse than acquisitions of immovable property that have a Union connection. Without further elaborating upon this, the Court held that the constitutional principle of equality was violated.

1047 Austrian Constitutional Court 1 March 2004, no 17 150, II, 2.1.
1048 Ibid 2.4.
1049 ECJ case C-300/01 *Salzmann II* [2003] ECR I-4899, para 57.
1050 Austrian Constitutional Court 1 March 2004, no 17 150, II, 2.4.
1051 Ibid 2.5.
1052 Ibid.

495. In the light of our working hypothesis, it can be argued that a compensation by Union law and, hence, a mere difference in treatment was at stake. That is, requiring that the acquirer shows that the land will be put to use, seems a clear restriction to their free movement within the EU. Not surprisingly, the ECJ held in *Salzmann* that this condition cannot apply to cross-border situations. Accordingly, the Austrian Constitutional Court could have stopped its assessment of reverse discrimination right there. Or, it could have assessed the purely internal situation as such in light of Austrian law in the light of the freedom of movement or the right to own property for instance, as enshrined in Articles 4 and 5 Basic Law of 21 December.[1053]

1.3. EMPLOYMENT CONDITIONS

1.3.1. Wage-Setting Mechanisms: Changing Approach of the French Court of Cassation's Social Chamber

496. In 2002, the French Court of Cassation's Social Chamber had to rule upon the situation of the Goethe Institute of Lille's French secretary of the board who claimed to be the victim of discrimination on grounds of nationality regarding the salary she received.[1054] She claimed an amount of money corresponding to the difference between the salary that she received and that received by an employee of German nationality exercising the same function and responding to the same criteria of seniority, civil status and education.

497. The Court of Cassation considered that Article 18 TFEU[1055] and Article 45 TFEU[1056] have direct effect and have primacy over each national measure that is contrary to them. Pursuant to these Treaty provisions, the Court of Appeal of Douai had ruled that the Goethe Institute could not have adopted a different salary regime in France, according to the nationality of the staff, since that would constitute forbidden discrimination with respect to the French employees. The

[1053] Articles 4 and 5 Basic Law of 21 December 1867 *juncto* Article 149 Austrian Constitution. The Austrian Constitution contains no bill of rights, but Article 149 Austrian Constitution determines that the Basic Law of 21 December 1867 has to be regarded as constitutional law.

[1054] Cour de Cassation Chambre Sociale 10 December 2002, no 00–42.158.

[1055] [Then Article 12 TEC], which prohibits in a general way discrimination on grounds of nationality.

[1056] [Then Article 39 TEC], which applies the principle of non-discrimination by providing in its second paragraph that the freedom of movement of workers entails the abolition of any discrimination based on nationality between workers of the Member States as regards employment, remuneration and other conditions of work and employment.

Court of Cassation shared this view since it concluded that the Court of Appeal of Douai had legally justified its decision.

498. In other words, the Court of Cassation applied the above-mentioned Treaty provisions to a purely internal situation on the basis of primacy of Union law. It is submitted that the use of the primacy argument, in order to apply Union law to purely internal situations, is an incorrect application of Union law. Nevertheless, if national authorities want to apply the same treatment to purely internal situations, they should base their reasoning on national law, possibly in combination with Union law, but not on Union law solely.

499. We can only speculate on the reasons why a national authority would opt for such an interpretation of Union law. Do the national authorities want to grant the same treatment to purely internal situations as they do to situations falling under Union law, but do not have the courage to base their reasoning on national law because they fear being criticised by other national actors? In other words, are they hiding behind Union law in a certain sense?[1057]

500. However, in its judgment of 17 April 2008, the Social Chamber of the Court of Cassation seems to have reconsidered its evaluation of reverse discrimination, since it refused to apply Union law to the purely internal situation in this case.[1058] In particular, the Social Chamber of the Court of Cassation had to rule upon the rejection of the expatriation allowance claimed by a French employee of the European Synchrotron Radiation Facility, an international organisation established in Grenoble.[1059] The internal rules of the organisation reserved the payment of an allowance of expatriation to employees with a foreign nationality.[1060] According to the French employee, the expatriation allowance, which was only paid to foreign employees and was independent of the fact that the latter are effectively expatriated, constituted discrimination on grounds of nationality which is forbidden by Article L. 122-45 of the Labour

[1057] See also above n 145.

[1058] The case law of the Criminal Chamber of the Court of Cassation evolved in the same way, but the reasoning in these judgments is more vague and complex than in the judgments of the Social Chamber of the Court of Cassation. The Criminal Chamber first prohibited reverse discrimination on the basis of the EU free movement provisions (Court of Cassation, Criminal Chamber, 16 June 1983, no 81-92.532, no 81-92.316, no 81-93.140). Subsequently, the Criminal Chamber did not apply this line of jurisprudence, precisely by referring to an ECJ judgment stating that the Treaty provisions do not apply to purely internal situations (ECJ case 355/85 [1986] ECR 3231, para 12 and Court of Cassation, Criminal Chamber, 20 April 1988, 87–81.851).

[1059] Cour de Cassation Chambre Sociale 17 April 2008, no 06-45.270.

[1060] Article 50 of the Corporate Convention of 1993 [Convention d'Entreprise] 18 June 1993.

Code,[1061] Article 14 ECHR and Articles 18 and 45 TFEU.[1062] He also argued that the principle of 'equal work, equal salary',[1063] which is enshrined in those same Articles, was violated.

501. To begin with, the Social Chamber of the Court of Cassation considered that the principle of non-discrimination on grounds of nationality provided for in Article 18 TFEU is intended to apply only to situations governed by Union law. Likewise, in the area of employment, Article 45 TFEU aims to guarantee the free movement of workers. Consequently, these provisions cannot be invoked by an employee who has not exercised his freedom of movement to work in another Member State.

Next, the Court of Cassation considered that it follows from, inter alia, Article 50 of the Corporate Convention and the preamble of the Convention of Paris of 16 December 1988 regarding the construction and the exploitation of a European Synchrotron facility that the expatriation allowance is destined to compensate the drawbacks resulting from the expatriation of the employee and his family and to contribute to 'the creation of a scientific international centre of excellence'.[1064] The Court of Cassation ruled that the deprivation of this advantage for French employees rests on an objective and pertinent ground that does not constitute a forbidden discrimination and is proportional to the legitimate purpose pursued by the contracting States.[1065]

502. This case fits perfectly with our working hypothesis, according to which situations of reverse discrimination in which the European Union grants more favourable treatment to Union citizens falling within the scope of Union law merely in order to compensate for the disadvantages resulting from having made use of the right of free movement, do not constitute discrimination, but rather

1061 [Code du travail].

1062 Then Articles 12 and 39 TEC.

1063 [*à travail égal, salaire égale*].

1064 Cour de Cassation Chambre Sociale 17 April 2008, no 06-45.270: [*Attendu, ensuite, qu'il résulte des dispositions combinées du préambule de la Convention de Paris du 16 décembre 1988 relative à la construction et à l'exploitation d'une installation européenne de rayonnement synchrotron, de la résolution n°2 jointe à l'acte final, des articles 12 et 25 des statuts de la société Installation européenne de rayonnement synchrotron et 50 de la convention collective d'entreprise précitée*, que la prime d'expatriation, prévue par les statuts annexés à la convention, est destinée à compenser les inconvénients résultant de l'expatriation du salarié et de sa famille et à contribuer à la création d'un pôle d'excellence scientifique international]. Emphasis added.

1065 Cour de Cassation Chambre Sociale 17 April 2008, no 06-45.270: [*que la privation de cet avantage pour les salariés français repose ainsi sur une raison objective, pertinente, étrangère à toute discrimination prohibée et proportionnée à l'objectif légitimement poursuivi par les Etats contractants; que le moyen n'est pas fondé*].

a mere difference in treatment. The Social Chamber of the Court of Cassation considered that the expatriation allowance was intended as a compensation for the drawbacks consequential on the expatriation of the employee and his family. Accordingly, it concluded that there was no discrimination.

1.3.2. Duration of Contracts: Extensive Interpretation of Link with Union Law by the Italian Constitutional Court

503. In 1995, the Italian Constitutional Court ruled on a situation of reverse discrimination for the first time, specifically, on the limited duration of contracts between Italian universities and foreign language assistants.[1066] Before discussing this judgment, it should be emphasised that chronologically it precedes the judgment of 1997 on industrially dried pasta.

504. In particular, a situation of discrimination arose as a result of the ECJ's *Allué and Coonan* judgment. The ECJ ruled in this judgment that Article 45 TFEU 'does not preclude a Member State from concluding contracts of employment with foreign-language assistants for a limited period if it appears, at the time of the appointment, that the teaching requirement will not exceed that period. However, contracts which are intended to meet continuous needs for teaching, as where the study of a particular language is compulsory or is known to be especially in demand, must be concluded for an indeterminate period in the same way as the employment relationship of other teachers fulfilling such needs.'[1067]

505. On the basis of the *Allué and Coonan* judgment, the Italian Decree could no longer be applied to citizens of other EU Member States working in Italian universities. By contrast, this judgment did not touch upon the situation of citizens falling outside the scope of Union law. Consequently, Italian foreign language assistants were treated less favourably by Italian universities than their colleagues who possessed the nationality of another EU Member State.

506. This discriminatory effect on Italian citizens was questioned before the Italian Court of Cassation.[1068] The latter ruled that 'given the scope of the ECJ's

---

1066 Article 28 Decree of the President of the Republic 11 July 1980, no 382: [*Riordinamento della docenza universitaria, relativa fascia di formazione, nonché sperimentazione organizzativa e didattica*] *GU* no 209, 31 July 1980.

1067 ECJ joined cases C-259/91, C-331/91 and C-332/91 *Allué and Coonan* [1993] ECR I-4309, paras 16–17.

1068 Italian Court of Cassation 21 March 1994, 2659/1994.

Allué and Coonan judgment and its immediate effect in the national legislation', the Italian rules should not only be set aside for citizens of another EU Member State, but also for Italian citizens.[1069] Hence, the Court of Cassation did not even consider the requirement of a link with Union law, but seemed to base the application of Union law on the direct effect of Union law.[1070]

507. Following the judgment of the Court of Cassation, however, the position of third country national foreign language assistants remained uncertain. Their position was questioned before the Constitutional Court.[1071] According to the referring judge, third country national assistants were in a worse position than Union assistants falling within Article 45 TFEU.[1072] The referring judge argued that this difference in treatment was incompatible with Articles 3 and 10 of the Italian Constitution.[1073]

508. At first glance, the Italian Court did not have to rule on a 'typical' situation of reverse discrimination in which Italian citizens who have never used their right of free movement were treated worse than other Union citizens making use of their right of free movement within the EU in this case. The Italian Constitutional Court, however, dealt with this issue as well since it considered the position of citizens of other Member States first, then the position of Italian

---

1069 Spitaleri, *Le discriminiazioni alla rovescia nel diritto comunitario*, Università di Trieste 2005, p 164 and references there.

1070 According to Spitaleri, The Court of Cassation – erroneously – based its reasoning on the fact that Italian citizens are Union citizens and therefore they can rely on the Treaty provisions on free movement (Spitaleri, *Le discriminiazioni alla rovescia nel diritto comunitario*, Università di Trieste 2005, p 164). However, this does not actually appear in the text of the judgment.

1071 Italian Constitutional Court 16 June 1995, no 249/1995. For more on this judgment see inter alia Zoppi, 'Le discriminazioni a rovescio' (2006) 4 *Diritto comunitario e degli scambi internazionali* 795 and Spitaleri, *Le discriminiazioni alla rovescia nel diritto comunitario*, Università di Trieste 2005, pp 162–67 and more references in fn 286.

1072 Then Article 48 TEEC.

1073 Article 3 Italian Constitution: 'All citizens have equal social dignity and are equal before the law, without distinction of sex, race, language, religion, political opinion, personal and social conditions. It is the duty of the Republic to remove those obstacles of an economic or social nature which constrain the freedom and equality of citizens, thereby impeding the full development of the human person and the effective participation of all workers in the political, economic and social organisation of the country.'

Article 10 Italian Constitution: 'The Italian legal system conforms to the generally recognised principles of international law. The legal status of foreigners is regulated by law in conformity with international provisions and treaties. A foreigner who, in his home country, is denied the actual exercise of the democratic freedoms guaranteed by the Italian constitution shall be entitled to the right of asylum under the conditions established by law. A foreigner may not be extradited for a political offence.'

citizens – where the issue of reverse discrimination arises – and finally, the position of third country nationals.

509. After setting out the ECJ's *Allué and Coonan* judgment, the Italian Constitutional Court ruled that this judgment applies to all foreign language assistants working in Italian universities, no matter which nationality they have.[1074] The Constitutional Court referred back to the conclusion of the Court of Cassation in the higher mentioned judgment.

Unlike the Court of Cassation, however, the Constitutional Court explicitly referred to the ECJ's settled case law concerning the inapplicability of the free movement provisions to purely internal situations of a Member State, in which every connecting factor to one of the situations envisaged by Union law is lacking.[1075] The Italian Constitutional Court found this connecting factor in the Article 28 Decreto Presidente Repubblica (DPR) 382/1980 itself.[1076] In particular, Article 28 DPR 382/1980 refers to *all* foreign language assistants, independently of their nationality.[1077]

Therefore, the Court considered that the reach of the *Allué and Coonan* judgment should be extended to foreign language assistants with Italian nationality, precisely in order to avoid an irrational discrimination at Union level.[1078] The Constitutional Court emphasised that it does not matter whether the Italian citizens have ever exercised their right of free movement. What does matter, according to the Constitutional Court, is that Italian law treats Italian citizens in the same way as foreign language assistants from other Member States, taking their different job titles and their type of teaching activity into account.[1079] Accordingly, the Italian Constitutional Court concluded that Article 28 of the Decree should also be set aside for foreign language assistants with Italian nationality.[1080]

510. Finally, the Italian Constitutional Court assessed the position of those assistants who are third country nationals. The Court considered that Article 1

1074 Italian Constitutional Court 16 June 1995, no 249/1995, '*Ritenuto in diritto 3*'.

1075 Ibid. 1076 Ibid.

1077 Ibid: [*nella specie il collegamento è dato dal riferimento dell'art. 28 del D.P.R. n. 382 del 1980 ai lettori di madre lingua straniera, indipendentemente dal loro stato di cittadinanza, in ragione del titolo, per tutti idéntico, che li abilita al lettorato di una lingua straniera*].

1078 Italian Constitutional Court 16 June 1995, no 249/1995, '*Ritenuto in diritto 3*': [*Perciò la sentenza 2 agosto 1993 della Corte di giustizia, proprio per evitare una irrazionale discriminazione a livello del diritto comunitario, non può non estendere la sua portata anche ai lettori di madre lingua straniera aventi la cittadinanza italiana, fin dalla nascita (si pensi al caso di un altoatesino di lingua madre tedesca) o per acquisizione successiva*].

1079 Ibid: [*ció che importa è che la legge li accomuna ai lettori cittadini di altri Stati membri, in considerazione dell'identità del loro titolo e del tipo di attività di insegnamento esercitata*].

1080 Ibid '*Ritenuto in diritto 4*'.

Law 943/1986 guarantees the same treatment and full equality of rights compared to Italian workers to third country nationals.[1081] This provision, together with the Court's conclusion that Article 28 DPR 382/1980 is not applicable to Italian foreign language assistants, resulted in the disapplication of Article 28 to foreign language assistants who are third country nationals as well.[1082] Therefore, the Constitutional Court concluded that the question concerning the compliance of Article 28 DPR 382/1980 with the Constitution was irrelevant and, thus, inadmissible given the inapplicability of this norm.[1083]

511. In this analysis of the Italian Constitutional Court's judgment, the position of assistants who are third country nationals will not be considered, since in this connection reverse discrimination is not at stake. First, I would like to point out that although the Italian Constitutional Court recognised the purely internal doctrine of the ECJ, it interpreted it completely differently than the ECJ. According to the Italian Constitutional Court, the criterion of having made use of free movement rights is not relevant to making a distinction between purely internal and cross-border situations. Decisive for the Italian Constitutional Court in this regard was the fact that the Italian legislation did not make a distinction on the basis of nationality. The Court considered this to be sufficient as a required link with Union law.[1084]

It is on the basis of Union law then, 'in order to avoid an unlawful discrimination at Union level', that the Italian Constitutional Court decided to apply the ECJ's *Allué and Coonan* judgment to foreign language assistants with Italian nationality as well. Hence, the Court came to this conclusion on the basis of the Union principle of equality, not on the basis of the Italian principle of equality.[1085]

512. Furthermore, it should be noted that the intervening parties had considered that the question referred to the Constitutional Court presupposed the exact determination of the link between the national provision, Article 28 DPR 382/1980, and Article 45 TFEU.[1086] They had argued that, since

1081 Ibid. 1082 Ibid. 1083 Ibid.

1084 Spitaleri applied a slightly different analysis. He argued that the Italian Court started from an erroneous premise: that the Treaty provisions on free movement also apply to 'domestic workers' and consequently the Court considered that the ECJ's judgment should be extended to purely internal situations (Spitaleri, *Le discriminiazioni alla rovescia nel diritto comunitario*, Università di Trieste 2005, p 215).

1085 See also Adinolfi, 'The Judicial Application of Community Law in Italy' (1998) 35 *CMLRev* 1313, 1326. See, however, for the current general approach of the Italian legal system towards reverse discrimination, above nn 437–42 and below 585–94.

1086 Italian Constitutional Court 16 June 1995, no 249/1995, '*Ritenuto in fatto 2*'.

the interpretation of the scope of application of Article 45 TFEU is reserved to the Court of Justice, the referring judge, instead of raising the question of constitutionality before the Constitutional Court, should have referred a question for a preliminary ruling to the Court of Justice.[1087] Therefore, the intervening parties argued that the question raised before the Constitutional Court was inadmissible.[1088] It is certainly striking that the Italian last instance court seemed to interpret the scope of an ECJ judgment – and the scope of Article 45 TFEU indirectly – without referring a question for a preliminary ruling on the basis of Article 267 TFEU.[1089]

513. Given the fact the Court of Justice has always held that reverse discrimination is not forbidden by Union law,[1090] it is not surprising that the reasoning of the Constitutional Court in this judgment has been severely criticised.[1091] Nevertheless, the judgment is instructive, since it indicates the Italian Constitutional Court's intention to avoid situations of reverse discrimination.[1092]

2. FAMILY REUNIFICATION WITH A UNION CITIZEN

2.1. INTRODUCTION

514. In Part I, it was argued that the right to family reunification on the basis of Union law had evolved from a compensation to an overcompensation.[1093] In the light of our working hypothesis, the national authority should assess the situation of reverse discrimination in this area as comprising a case of overcompensation by Union law. The national authority cannot make the assessment of compensation or overcompensation *in abstracto*, even though a

---

1087 Ibid. 1088 Ibid.

1089 Adinolfi, 'The Judicial Application of Community Law in Italy' (1998) 35 *CMLRev* 1313, 1326: 'Furthermore, it seems rather surprising that the Constitutional Court (without even suggesting that a preliminary reference should be made under article 177) deemed to have the power of interpreting the scope of a principle stated in a ruling of the Court of Justice.'

1090 See above nn 58–62.

1091 See amongst others Adinolfi, 'The Judicial Application of Community Law in Italy' (1998) 35 *CMLRev* 1313, 1326: 'If one may approve the conclusion reached by the Court, its reasoning is clearly incorrect'; and Della Chà, 'Challenge of Internal Rules on Grounds of Reverse Discrimination: An Open Issue' (2002) 16 *Diritto del commercio internazionale* 145, 160: 'The constitutional court, although not with a completely satisfactory reasoning, ruled for the application of Community law also to Italian lecturers, stating that there was a "connection" with that law.'

1092 See in the same vein Spitaleri, *Le discriminiazioni alla rovescia nel diritto comunitario*, Università di Trieste 2005, pp 166–67 and 215.

1093 Above nn 393–97.

mere compensation by Union law is at stake in some cases. Since the risk of overcompensation definitely exists, it is most logical to start, at national level, from the hypothesis that an overcompensation is at stake. Accordingly, the principle of equality, as enshrined in national law, is appropriate to make the assessment of the situation of reverse discrimination. In this context, the Member States should critically assess the stricter conditions for purely internal situations in the light of the right to respect for private and family life, as enshrined in their national Constitution and in Article 8 ECHR.

2.2. FAMILY REUNIFICATION: AN EMOTIVE AND POLITICALLY SENSITIVE SUBJECT

515. As explained in Part I, reverse discrimination in the area of family reunification can be solved by harmonisation on the basis of Article 79 TFEU.[1094] However, political will in this respect seems to be lacking. The important question arises as to why the Member States are so reluctant to harmonise the rules on family reunification.

516. In general, it can be argued that migration is 'a highly emotive, politically sensitive subject'.[1095] Migration touches upon fundamental questions as to the control of state borders and membership in a community, these issues affect the state in its sovereign self-determination.[1096]

In the last two decades, migration has become one of the central issues in the politics of liberal democratic states.[1097] In this period, a kind of globalisation of migration has occurred whereby individuals move intercontinentally.[1098] This has created the fear that a growing number of people will move to the world's prosperous states.[1099]

1094 Above n 396.

1095 Barnard, *The Substantive Law of the EU: The Four Freedoms*, Oxford University Press 2013, p 538.

1096 Joppke, 'Immigration Challenges the Nation State' in Joppke (ed), *Challenge to the Nation-State: Immigration in Western Europe and the United States*, Oxford University Press 1998, pp 5–46.

1097 Freeman, 'The Decline of Sovereignty? Politics and Immigration Restriction in Liberal States' in Joppke (ed), *Challenge to the Nation-State: Immigration in Western Europe and the United States*, Oxford University Press 1998, pp 86.

1098 Gibney, *The Ethics and Politics of Asylum, Liberal Democracy and the Response to Refugees*, Cambridge University Press 2004, p 4.

1099 Ibid.

517. Four major groups of entrants in Western States can be distinguished: refugees, asylum seekers, economic migrants and family migrants.[1100] The situation of the latter group is considered to be the most complicated group of migrants.[1101] Moreover, in its report on the application of Directive 2003/86, the Commission considered that 'for the past 20 years family reunification has been one of the main sources of immigration to the EU. In many Member States today, family reunification accounts for a large (and still increasing) share of legal migration. Discussions on how to manage more effectively the large inflow of migrants under family reunification led to a number of policy changes, many restrictive in nature, in some Member States.'[1102]

518. In each of the Member States under analysis, at a certain moment, the national legislator made the choice to treat family reunification with own nationals in a purely internal situation more strictly than family reunification with Union citizens falling under the scope of Union law. These stricter conditions can take different forms: being subjected to an evaluation and formation, being obliged to obtain a residence permit from abroad, being subjected to demonstrate sufficient resources, being denied the right to family reunification with ascendants, etc. The following sections discuss the assessments of judicial instances in France, Germany, Austria, Belgium and Italy of situations of reverse discrimination in the area of family reunification.

2.3. INCOMPARABLE SITUATIONS ACCORDING TO FRENCH AND GERMAN COURTS

2.3.1. The French Council of State on Family Reunification

519. In its judgment of 19 May 2010, the French Council of State had to rule upon reverse discrimination against family members of French citizens regarding family reunification.[1103] In particular, Article L. 211-2-1 of the Code on entrance and residence of foreigners and the right to asylum and the Articles 4 and 5 of Decree 2008-1115[1104] provide, to family members of French citizens, a procedure for the evaluation of and training analogous to that provided to applicants of family reunification with third country nationals.

1100 Ibid 5.
1101 Ibid 14.
1102 COM (2008) 610, 2.
1103 French Council of State 19 May 2010, no 323758.
1104 Decree 2008-1115 of 30 October regarding the preparation and integration in France of foreigners aiming at a permanent right of residence.

520. The French Council of State considered that, on the basis of Directive 2004/38, family members of Union citizens having made use of their right of free movement are not subjected to the procedure of evaluation and formation. Moreover, the provisions of this directive cannot be invoked against the contested Decree, the aim of which is only to regulate the purely internal situation of the family members of French citizens.

The French Council of State held that, given the objective of the contested provisions of learning the French language and given the aim of the applicants to become French citizens, family members of French citizens are not in the same situation as family members of Union citizens who have made use of their right to free movement. Accordingly, the French Council of State held that the creation of a specific provision for evaluation and formation for family members of French citizens does not violate Articles 8 and 14 ECHR, the general principles of Union law, the principle of equality or international treaty provisions on the prohibition of racial discrimination.

521. In sum, the French Council of State allowed this situation of reverse discrimination in the area of family reunification because it considered purely internal situations and cross-border situations to be different and different situations may be treated differently. In the light of our working hypothesis, this assessment is what could be expected in the case of compensation by Union law. However, as has been argued in the introduction to this section, Union law overcompensates in the area of family reunification in certain cases.

Accordingly, an alternative reasoning fitting into the working hypothesis could be that the situations were comparable in the light of the principle of equality. The Council of State could have retained the considerations regarding knowledge of the French language and becoming French citizens as part of the justification's assessment for the difference in treatment. At that point in the reasoning, the Council of State could also have explained why Article 8 ECHR, enshrining the right to respect for private and family life, was not violated.

2.3.2. *German Administrative Courts on Family Reunification*

2.3.2.1. Administrative Appeal Court of Hesse 2006

522. In its judgment of 23 October 2006, the Administrative Appeal Court of Hesse took a firm position on reverse discrimination in the light of the principle of equality as enshrined in the German Basic Law.[1105] The case concerned the

[1105] Administrative Appeal Court of Hesse 23 October 2006, 7 TG 2317/06.

German provision that foreign family members of German citizens must obtain a residence permit from abroad if they do not fulfil the general preconditions for a residence permit of Article 5 '*Aufenthaltsgesetz*'.[1106] By contrast, no such restrictive prerequisites for granting a residence permit are allowed on the basis of Directives 2004/38 and 2003/86 for the spouses of Union citizens who move to or reside in a Member State other than that of which they are a national and for the spouses of third country nationals. The applicant, inter alia, invoked a violation of the principle of equality, as enshrined in Article 3(1) Basic Law.

523. The Administrative Appeal Court ruled that no unequal treatment, in the sense of Article 3(1) Basic Law, was at stake.[1107] The Court considered that the material scope of application of Article 3(1) Basic Law presupposes a different treatment of two comparable situations.[1108] The Court specified that this only occurs if the two cases which are treated differently by an authority, are based on essentially equal situations.[1109] Furthermore, the Court added that an unequal treatment in the sense of Article 3(1) Basic Law is only present when the comparable situations can be attributed to the same authority.[1110] This is lacking when the two situations are created by two different public authorities.[1111] The principle of equality only binds each public authority within its specific jurisdiction.[1112]

524. Next, the Administrative Appeal Court considered that the European institutions have provided for residence permits for foreigners and their family members in different directives.[1113] By contrast, the EU leaves it up to the Member States to regulate the residence rights of family members of their own nationals autonomously.[1114] This can lead to a situation in which the latter group of persons, on the basis of national provisions of residence law, must fulfil

---

1106 Ibid: [*dass die ausländischen Ehegatten von deutschen Staatsangehörigen die Erteilung einer Aufenthaltserlaubnis vom Ausland aus verfolgen müssen, wenn sie die allgemeinen Erteilungsvoraussetzungen des §5 AufenthG nicht erfüllen*].

1107 Ibid paras 8 and 10.

1108 Ibid para 9: [*Der sachliche Anwendungsbereich des Art. 3 Abs. 1 GG setzt eine unterschiedliche Behandlung zweier vergleichbarer Sachverhalte voraus*].

1109 Ibid para 9: [*Diese liegt nur dann vor, wenn die Fälle, die von einer Behörde unterschiedlich behandelt worden sind, auf wesentlich gleichen Sachverhalten beruhen*].

1110 Ibid para 9: [*Eine Ungleichbehandlung im Sinne des Art. 3 Abs. 1 GG liegt ferner nur dann vor, wenn die Vergleichsfälle der gleichen Stelle zuzurechnen sind*].

1111 Ibid para 9: [*Daran fehlt es, wenn die beiden Sachverhalte von zwei verschiedenen Trägern öffentlicher Gewalt gestaltet werden*].

1112 Ibid para 9: [*Der Gleichheitssatz bindet nämlich jeden Träger öffentlicher Gewalt allein in dessen konkretem Zuständigkeitsbereich*].

1113 Ibid para 10, referring to Directives 2003/86 and 2004/38.

1114 Ibid para 10: [*Demgegenüber überlässt die Europäische Union es ihren Mitgliedsstaaten, die Aufenthaltsrechte der Familienangehörigen ihrer eigenen Staatsangehörigen eigenständig zu regeln*].

more demanding requirements to obtain a residence permit than the family members of foreigners whose residence rights are laid down in the European directives.[1115] Since two different public authorities – the German Bundestag and the Council – establish the residence right of foreign family members, no unequal treatment in the sense of Article 3(1) Basic Law occurs.[1116]

2.3.2.2. German Federal Administrative Court 2011

525. The German Federal Administrative Court shares the same view. In its judgment of 22 June 2011, it provided an extensive legal assessment on the scope of application of the freedom of movement rights within the EU in the light of the recent case law of the ECJ (*Ruiz Zambrano*, *McCarthy*, *Dereci*).[1117] The case concerned a citizen of Togo who claimed a visa in Germany on the basis of family reunification with his German spouse. Subsequently, several authorities rejected the request because of serious doubts as to whether the spouses really lived as a couple.[1118]

526. The Federal Administrative Court ruled, first of all, that the Court of Appeal had rightly assessed the claim in the light of the '*Aufenthaltsgesetz*'.[1119] This law applies because the legal position of the complainants is not recognised by the '*Freizügigkeitsgesetz*'. The Federal Administrative Court considered that the latter only regulates the entrance and residence of citizens of other Member States of the EU, but not the entrance and residence of family members of German citizens. Next, the Federal Administrative Court considered that Directive 2004/38 also did not apply since Article 3 determines that the Directive applies 'to all Union citizens who move to or reside in a Member State other than that of which they are a national, and to their family members'.[1120] According to the Federal Administrative Court, the ECJ's case law on so-called 'returning

---

1115 Ibid para 10: [*Dies kann dazu führen, dass der zuletzt genannte Personenkreis nach den nationalen Regeln des Aufenthaltsgesetzes weitergehende Voraussetzungen für ein Aufenthaltsrecht zu erfüllen hat als die Familienangehörigen von Ausländern, deren Aufenthaltsrechte in den europäischen Richtlinien festgelegt worden sind*].

1116 Ibid para 10: [*Da es sich bei den Normgebern des Deutschen Bundestages und des Rates der Europäischen Union um zwei verschiedene Träger öffentlicher Gewalt handelt, die das Aufenthaltsrecht von ausländischen Familienangehörigen gestalten, liegt keine Ungleichbehandlung im Sinne von Art. 3 Abs. 1 GG vor*].

1117 German Federal Administrative Court 22 June 2011, 1 C 11.10.

1118 First by decision of 28 April 2006 of the embassy in Brussels, then confirmed by the Verwaltungsgericht and subsequently confirmed by judgment of 23 April 2010 of the Oberverwaltungsgericht of Berlin-Brandenburg.

1119 German Federal Administrative Court 22 June 2011, 1 C 11.10, para 7.

1120 Ibid para 8.

citizens'[1121] could also not be applied as the German spouse of the complainant certainly did not durably make use of her right of free movement through her three short visiting trips to Belgium.[1122]

527. Subsequently, the Federal Administrative Court analysed the *Ruiz Zambrano* and *McCarthy* cases of the ECJ extensively.[1123] The Federal Administrative Court pointed out that the ECJ did not follow AG Sharpston's proposal to recognise a right of residence on the territory of the Member States based on citizenship of the Union and independent from the right to move between the Member States. In these cases, the ECJ ruled that 'Article 21 TFEU is not applicable to a Union citizen who has never exercised his right of free movement, who has always resided in a Member State of which he is a national and who is also a national of another Member State, provided that the situation of that citizen does not include the application of measures by a Member State that would have the effect of depriving him of the genuine enjoyment of the substance of the rights conferred by virtue of his status as a Union citizen or of impeding the exercise of his right of free movement and residence within the territory of the Member States'.[1124]

528. The Federal Administrative Court considered that the facts at issue were similar to those of the *McCarthy* case. According to the Federal Administrative Court, in these cases – unlike in the *Ruiz Zambrano* case, which concerned minor Union citizens and the refusal of a right of residence of the third country national parents – the refusal of a right of residence of the third country national spouse does not have the effect that the Union citizen is obliged to leave the territory of the Union. In particular, the Union citizen has an unconditional right of residence in his State of origin. The Federal Administrative Court ruled that the present situation fell outside the scope of application of Union law.

529. Immediately afterwards, the Federal Administrative Court referred to the ECJ's case law that 'any discrimination which nationals of a Member State may suffer under the law of that State falls within the scope of that law and must therefore be dealt with within the framework of the internal legal system of that State'.[1125] In this context, the Federal Administrative Court assessed whether the application of the '*Aufenthaltsgesetz*', concerning family members

---

[1121] See inter alia ECJ case C-370/90 *Singh* [1992] ECR I-4265 and ECJ case C-291/05 *Eind* [2007] ECR I-10719.

[1122] German Federal Administrative Court 22 June 2011, 1 C 11.10, para 9.

[1123] Ibid para 10.

[1124] ECJ case C-434/09 *McCarthy* [2011] ECR I-3375, para 56. The Federal Administrative Court paraphrased this partially.

[1125] ECJ joined cases C-64/96 and C-65/96 *Uecker and Jacquet* [1997] ECR I-3171, para 23.

of German citizens who cannot claim a residence right on the basis of Union law, is compatible with Article 3(1) German Constitution, entailing the principle of equality.[1126] The Court considered that it is unclear whether, in view of the obligation of the implementation of Union law and the resulting concern of different legal systems, equal or comparable cases in the sense of Article 3(1) Basic Law are at stake at all.[1127] The Court ruled that the difference is objectively justified at least since the different treatment results from the coexistence of Union law and national law.[1128] Accordingly, the Federal Administrative Court held that the application of the '*Aufenthalsgesetz*' on family members of immobile Union citizens, who cannot benefit from a residence right on the basis of Union law, does not violate national law, in particular Article 3(1) Basic Law.

530. Several Administrative Appeal Courts of the Länder have confirmed the Federal Administrative Court's position.[1129] Accordingly, the more stringent conditions of the '*Aufenthaltsgesetz*' continue to apply to German citizens in a purely German situation.

2.3.2.3. Division of Competences Precedes Assessment in the Light of the Principle of Equality

531. In sum, the German administrative courts see reverse discrimination primarily from the perspective of division of competences. Since a Member State has the competence to treat purely internal situations as it pleases, there is no need to compare situations under Union law to purely internal situations. In particular, the Administrative Appeal Court of Hesse argued that unequal treatment, in the

---

1126 German Federal Administrative Court 22 June 2011, 1 C 11.10, para 11.

1127 Ibid: '*dabei kann dahinstehen, ob angesichts der Verpflichtung zur Umsetzung unionsrechtlicher Vorgaben und der dadurch bedingten Betroffenheit unterschiedlicher Rechtsreise überhaupt gleiche oder vergleichbare Sachverhalte im Sinne des Art. 3 Abs. 1 GG vorliegen*'.

1128 Ibid: '*Denn die aus dem Nebeneinander von Unionsrecht und nationalem Recht entstehende Ungleichbehandlung ist jedenfalls sachlich gerechtfertigt*'.

1129 See eg Administrative Appeal Court of Berlin-Brandenburg 19 March 2012, OVG 3 B 21.11 in which the Administrative Appeal Court of Berlin-Brandenburg had to rule upon a case regarding a Gambian citizen who claimed a right of residence on the basis of family reunification with his parents who lived in Bremen and who had two other children with German nationality. After summarising the ECJ's judgments in *Ruiz Zambrano*, *McCarthy* and *Dereci* (paras 23–25), the Administrative Appeal Court considered that the German brothers of the claimant had not exercised their right to free movement (para 26). Next, the Administrative Appeal Court considered that refusal to grant a visa to the claimant did not lead to the German brothers being deprived of the genuine enjoyment of the substance of the rights conferred upon them by virtue of their status as Union citizen, since they could stay with their parents on the German territory (para 26). See also inter alia Administrative Appeal Court of Lüneberg 4 October 2011, 4 ME 184/11, paras 8–10. See also HAILBRONNER and THYM, *Report on the Free Movement of Workers in Germany in 2011–2012*, p 14 <http://www.ru.nl/law/cmr/research/projects/fmow-2/national-reports-fmw/> accessed 15.06.2016.

sense of Article 3(1) Basic Law, is at stake where it can be attributed to one single authority. The Federal Administrative Court considered that even if you were to compare the situations, the difference in treatment is objectively justified in general; that is, it results directly from the division of competences between the EU and the Member States. Hence, reverse discrimination is seen as a side effect of the division of competences.

532. In other words, the German administrative courts' assessment of reverse discrimination in the light of the principle of equality stops immediately at the beginning of the assessment because it is preceded by an assessment in the light of the division of competences. In the light of our working hypothesis, this should only apply to cases of compensation by Union law.

However, as has been argued in the introduction to this section, in certain cases Union law overcompensates in the area of family reunification. Accordingly, the national authority should follow the hypothesis of overcompensation by Union law when making the assessment of the reverse discrimination. This would allow an assessment of the merits, which is currently prevented by the German Administrative Courts' reasoning.

2.4. A CHANGE OF APPROACH IN AUSTRIA AND BELGIUM

2.4.1. Developments in Austrian Legislation on Family Reunification

2.4.1.1. Austrian Constitutional Court in 1997: Difference in Treatment is Discriminatory

533. In *Dereci*, the ECJ ruled that when a right of residence cannot be obtained on the basis of Directive 2004/38 or on the basis of the Treaty provisions on Union citizenship, because the present situation falls outside their scope of application, it might be that 'on the basis of other criteria, *inter alia*, by virtue of the right to the protection of family life, a right of residence cannot be refused'.[1130]

534. The Austrian Constitutional Court took this approach in its judgment of 17 June 1997 – hence 14 years before the ECJ's *Dereci* judgment. The case concerned a Romanian[1131] citizen who was married to an Austrian citizen. When his request for a residence permit on the basis of the '*Aufenthaltsgesetz*'[1132] was rejected, he subsequently claimed a visa on the basis of the Articles 28 and 29

[1130] ECJ case C-256/11 *Dereci*, para 69 and above nn 318–24.

[1131] Romania became a Member State of the EU in 2007.

[1132] Austrian Residence Act, *Austrian Federal Law Gazette* 466/1992.

'*Fremdengesetz*',[1133] that is, via his spouse's status of Union citizen.[1134] Again his request was rejected, this time because Austrian citizens were not considered to be included in the term Union citizens of Article 28 '*Fremdengesetz*' and, hence, the complainant could not be seen as a favoured third country national in the sense of Article 29 '*Fremdengesetz*'.[1135]

535. The Austrian Constitutional Court first considered that the reasoning of the respondent authority clearly leads to the inferior treatment of Austrian citizens compared with citizens of other EU Member States.[1136] According to the Court, this difference in treatment is discriminatory in the sense of the Articles 14 and 8 ECHR since no objective and reasonable justification is apparent and since no clear and legitimate aim is being pursued.[1137] The Austrian Constitutional Court ruled that Article 29 '*Fremdengesetz*' should, in any case, be interpreted in the sense that the residence permit of third country national with EU citizens is subjected to the same rules as the residence permit of Austrian citizens.[1138] The Court explicitly considered that this is the only interpretation that is compatible with the demands of Article 8 *juncto* Article 14 ECHR.[1139]

536. Correspondingly, the Austrian legislation was amended.[1140] From then onwards Austrian citizens and EU citizens were treated equally in the area of family reunification.

However, this did not remain the case for very long because the Austrian legislator reintroduced reverse discrimination in this area when Directive 2004/38 was transposed.[1141] The new federal Act, concerning settlement and residence in Austria, applies to 'aliens', who are defined as persons not possessing Austrian nationality, and to Austrian citizens who have made use of their right to free movement.[1142]

2.4.1.2. Austrian Constitutional Court in 2009: Autonomy of National Legislator to Treat Purely Internal Situations Differently

537. This new legislation was the subject of a case before the Austrian Constitutional Court in a procedure concerning partial annulment. In particular,

[1133] Austrian Aliens Act, *Austrian Federal Law Gazette* 838/1992.
[1134] Austrian Constitutional Court 17 June 1997, no 14 863.
[1135] By decision of 28 December 1995 of the District Commission of Bregenz. See Austrian Constitutional Court 17 June 1997, no 14 863, II, 2.1.
[1136] Austrian Constitutional Court 17 June 1997, no 14 863, II, 2.3.
[1137] Ibid. [1138] Ibid. [1139] Ibid.
[1140] Austrian Aliens Act, *Austrian Federal Law Gazette* 75/1997.
[1141] By the federal Act concerning settlement and residence in Austria, *Austrian Federal Law Gazette* 100/2005, which entered into force 1 January 2006.
[1142] Articles 1, 2 and 57 of the Federal Act concerning settlement and residence in Austria.

the provisions regarding the family members of Austrian citizens 'who have used their right of free movement' were challenged.[1143]

538. Agreeing with the Austrian government, the Austrian Federal Constitutional Court ruled that, according to Union law, the (national) legislator is free to regulate situations that have no link with Union law differently than situations that do have a link with Union law.[1144] The Austrian Federal Constitutional Court held that the distinction made by the new Residence and Settlement Act is objectively justified.[1145]

539. In particular, the Court highlighted that the decisive criterion for this distinction is the realisation of free movement; it does not depend on nationality. The Court pointed out that this connecting factor of the realisation of free movement serves as an assurance and promotion of the exercise of free movement and other rights enshrined in the Union Treaties by Austrian nationals. The Court ruled that, from the perspective of transposition of Union law, it is necessary to grant a residence permit under the simplified provisions to third country nationals who are family members of those Austrian citizens who have used their right to free movement.

540. On the other hand, the Court ruled that in cases which do not have a connection with Union law, the individual Member State has a broader discretion as to the definition of those to whom a residence permit ought to be granted. The Court ruled that the legislator is entitled to regulate purely internal situations according to its own understanding of what is needed for a well-organised immigration policy. In the Court's view, this is precisely what the legislator had done in the new Settlement and Residence Act.[1146] Accordingly, the Federal Constitutional Court rejected the action for annulment.

1143 Austrian Constitutional Court 16 December 2009, no 18 968.

1144 Ibid para II 2.9.

1145 Ibid: [*Dennoch erachtet der Verfassungsgerichtshof die im NAG getroffene Unterscheidung weiterhin für sachlich gerechtfertigt. Dem Gesetzgeber steht es nach dem Recht der europäischen Union nämlich insoweit frei, an das Gemeinschaftsrecht anknüpfende Sachverhalte anders zu regeln als solche ohne Bezug zum Gemeinschaftsrecht, weshalb diesbezüglich – wie die Bundesregierung zutreffend ausführt – ein die aufenthaltsrechtliche Ungleichbehandlung rechtfertigender Unterschied im Tatsächlichen vorliegt*].

1146 Ibid: [*In Fällen, die keinen Bezug zum Gemeinschaftsrecht aufweisen, kommt aber den einzelnen Mitgliedstaaten ein weiterer Gestaltungsspielraum in der Frage zu, wem ein Aufenthaltsrecht eingeräumt wird. Der Gesetzgeber ist daher berechtigt, rein innerstaatliche Sachverhalte nach seinen eigenen Vorstellungen von den Erfordernissen eines geordneten Fremdenwesens zu regeln. Dies geschieht durch jene Bestimmungen des NAG, die die allgemeinen Voraussetzungen für die Erteilung von Aufenthaltstiteln normieren*]. Emphasis added.

541. The Austrian Constitutional Court resigned itself to the choice of the legislator to treat family reunifications with Austrian citizens in a purely internal situations more strictly following the reintroduction of reverse discrimination in this area by the legislator in 2006, even though it had ruled in 1997 that the reverse discrimination regarding family reunification was discriminatory in the sense of the Articles 14 and 8 ECHR. The Austrian Constitutional Court based its judgment of 16 December 2009 on the residual competence of the Member States to regulate purely internal situations. When doing so, the Member States have the discretion to treat these situations differently than situations falling within the scope of Union law, on the condition that the difference in treatment be objectively justified. The Constitutional Court did not really elaborate on why this difference in treatment is objectively justified. In this respect, it referred to the legislator's freedom to pursue its own immigration policy; however, it did so without examining whether the stricter treatment of one's own nationals in a purely internal situation is an appropriate and proportional measure.

2.4.2. Developments in Belgian Legislation on Family Reunification

542. The position of the legislator on family reunification has changed over time not only in Austria, but also in Belgium. While Belgian legislation on family reunification autonomously aligned with Union law initially – by extending the Union provisions to purely internal situations – reverse discrimination was created by subjecting family members of Belgian citizens to stricter conditions in 2011. The Belgian Constitutional Court reviewed the Act of 2011 in the light of the principle of equality, as enshrined in Articles 10 and 11 of the Constitution.

2.4.2.1. Autonomous Legislative Alignment in the Area of Family Reunification

543. Initially, a clear example of autonomous legislative alignment could be found in the Belgian Aliens Act concerning family reunification. Then Article 40(6) determined that 'with the EEC-foreigner are … equated, the spouse of a Belgian citizen who accompanies or joins him or her, as well as their direct descendants who are under the age of 21 or are dependent, their dependent direct relatives in the ascending line and the spouse of those direct relatives in the descending and ascending line who accompany or join them'. In other words, the listed family members of a Belgian citizen were equated with EEC-foreigners. As can be seen from the *travaux préparatoires*, it was the will of the legislator that family members of a Belgian citizen 'would not be treated less favourably' than the family members of citizens from other EU Member States.[1147] Although

[1147] *Parliamentary Documents* Chamber of Representatives, 1977–78, no 144/7, 9.

it was not explicitly formulated like this during parliamentary debates, this provision was interpreted in the sense that the Belgian legislator wanted to avoid reverse discrimination by granting family members of a Belgian citizen in a purely internal situation the same rights as the rights that Union law grants to 'mobile' Union citizens.[1148]

544. The Belgian legislator transposed Directive 2004/38 through an amendment of the Belgian Aliens Act, by Act of 25 April 2007.[1149] At that time, ex Article 40(6) was repealed and Article 40*ter*[1150] was inserted which determined that 'the provisions of this chapter that are applicable to the family members of a Union citizen who accompany or join him, are [also] applicable to family members of a Belgian citizen who accompany or join him. Concerning the ascendants referred to in Article 40*bis*(2)(1)4°, the Belgian citizen has to demonstrate that he has stable, regular and sufficient resources in order to prevent that they become a burden of the public authorities during their residence in the country, and that he has a sickness insurance that covers the risk of the family members concerned in Belgium.' Accordingly, the complete equation of family members of a Belgian citizen to Union citizens was terminated since the family members involved were no longer equated to Union citizens themselves, but to family members of Union citizens.[1151] Moreover, a reverse discrimination was inserted in relation to those Belgian citizens who wanted to be accompanied by their ascendants, since they were subjected to the additional condition of demonstrating sufficient resources and the requirement for healthcare insurance.[1152] This modification has been prompted by the desire 'to avoid [the situation whereby] ascendants of Belgian citizens at their arrival in Belgium end up in precarious circumstances and become a burden for the public authorities'.[1153]

1148 See amongst others Belgian Council of State 15 May 2009 no 193.348, 5/9 and Vanheule, 'Recente ontwikkelingen in de verblijfswetgeving' in Foblets and Vanheule (eds), *Vreemdelingenrecht, Themis*, die Keure 2011–12, pp 88–89.

1149 Act of 25 April 2007, *BS* 10 May 2007.

1150 In the meantime repealed by Act of 8 July 2011 (see above nn 550–553).

1151 Verschueren, 'Het verblijfsrecht van EU-burgers en hun familieleden' in Foblets and others (eds), *De Nieuwe Vreemdelingenwet België in lijn met de Europese regelgeving, Migratie- en migrantenrecht recente ontwikkelingen, Deel 12*, die Keure 2007, pp 172–73.

1152 As opposed to Union citizens in a cross-border situation who are not subjected to that condition.

1153 *Parliamentary Documents* Chamber of Representatives 2006–07, no 2845/001, 44. According to Sabrine Dawoud this reverse discrimination of Belgian citizens for family reunification with ascendants did not have much impact in practice (Dawoud, 'Gezinshereniging en omgekeerde discriminatie: de Belgische context', Studiedag Centrum voor Gelijkheid van Kansen en voor Racismebestrijding, 6 December 2011).

2.4.2.2. *Intermezzo*: Problems Concerning the Scope and Interpretation of Autonomously Aligned Legislation

545. Although at first glance, autonomous legislative alignment seems to be a clear and straightforward way of remedying reverse discrimination, on closer examination, problems concerning its scope and interpretation arise. This is demonstrated by the disagreement that exists within the Belgian Council of State on how to interpret autonomously aligned legislation: the Dutch-speaking and the francophone sections seem to hold opposing views when ruling on decisions made by the first-instance court or regarding decisions related to the application of the Aliens Law by the Council for Alien Law Litigation.

546. The Dutch-speaking section of the Council of State considered that Article 40(6) Belgian Aliens Act provides an equivalent for persons who do not fall within the scope of application of Directive 2004/38.[1154] It deemed that the equation in the national Belgian legislation does not, by definition, constitute a transposition of the Directive precisely because it relates to cases not falling within the scope of application of the Directive.[1155] It concluded that Article 40(6) Belgian Aliens Act cannot be assessed on the basis of Directive 2004/38.[1156] The Dutch-speaking section of the Council of State seems to be of the opinion that the Belgian judge, regarding purely Belgian situations at least, can diverge from the authoritative interpretation given to Directive 2004/38 by the Court of Justice, such as in the *Chen* case.[1157]

547. The French-speaking section of the Council of State had to examine a case decided upon by the Council for Alien Law Litigation.[1158] The latter had considered that the ascendant of a Belgian citizen could only obtain the right to reside on Belgian territory if he or she depends upon the Belgian citizen, and this condition was not fulfilled in the case at issue.[1159] The Council for Alien Law Litigation recognised that in the *Chen* case a right of residence was granted to a third country national who was a non-dependent ascendant from a Union citizen.[1160] The Council for Alien Law Litigation considered that only the *effet utile* of the child's right of residence justified the parent, who is that minor's primary caretaker, being allowed to reside with the child in the host Member State.[1161] However, the Council for Alien Law Litigation judged that in the instance of a third country national, the parent of a Belgian minor

---

1154 Belgian Council of State, 18 September 2009 no 196 182, 9/10.
1155 Ibid. 1156 Ibid.
1157 ECJ case C-200/02 *Zhu and Chen* [2004] ECR I-9925.
1158 Belgian Council of State 15 May 2009 no 193 348.
1159 Ibid 5/9. 1160 Ibid. 1161 Ibid.

who has always resided in Belgium and who has never made use of his rights of free movement, it is not possible to find a derogation from the condition of dependency on the Belgian national in name of the equality of treatment sought by the legislator in the legal framework traced by Article 40.[1162] Hence, the Council for Alien Law Litigation seemed to share the vision of the Dutch-speaking section of the Council of State; Article 40 Belgian Aliens Act should not be analogously interpreted with Directive 2004/38.

548. The French-speaking section of the Council of State, however, judged that the judgment contested before it violated Article 40 Belgian Aliens Act in the light of the assimilation sought by the legislator between family members of a Belgian citizen and family members of a Union citizen.[1163] Consequently, the French-speaking section of the Council of State disagreed with the Dutch-speaking section and the Council for Alien Law Litigation. It decided that the equation, by the Belgian legislator, implies that Article 40(6) should be interpreted completely in line with the interpretation given to Directive 2004/38, including in the *Chen* case law.

549. The advantage of interpreting the national legislation – which has autonomously been aligned with the Union legislation – in the same way as the Court of Justice interprets the Union legislation is obvious: situations are treated alike independently of whether a purely internal situation or a situation falling under Union law is at stake. If the national legislator has opted for legislative alignment, in order to ensure equal treatment independent from a cross-border element, an analogous interpretation is the most logical option. However, a counter-argument may be found in the fact that the ECJ's interpretation may be unexpected and far-reaching. Then it could be argued that the national legislator never had the intention to provide national legislation in the same way.[1164]

2.4.2.3. Introduction of Reverse Discrimination in the Field of Family Reunification in 2011

550. In 2011, the Belgian legislator ended the equating of family members of Belgian citizens with family members of Union citizens.[1165] In particular, three

---

[1162] Ibid 6/9. [1163] Ibid.

[1164] See also above n 146 regarding references for preliminary rulings where the main proceedings concern a purely internal situation.

[1165] Act of 8 July 2011 [*Wet van 8 juli 2011 tot wijziging van de wet van 15 december 1980 betreffende de toegang tot het grondgebied, het verblijf, de vestiging en de verwijdering van vreemdelingen wat betreft de voorwaarden tot gezinshereniging*]. The underlying reasons were discussed earlier (see above n 6).

more stringent conditions for family reunification with Belgian citizens in a purely internal situation were inserted.

551. First, the right to family reunification with relatives in the ascending line for an adult Belgian citizen in a purely internal situation henceforth ceases to exist.[1166] By contrast, other adult Union citizens benefit under Directive 2004/38 from the right to unite with their direct relatives in the ascending line.[1167]

552. Secondly, alongside the proof of decent housing and health insurance coverage, the present Article 40*ter* Belgian Aliens Act determines that when a Belgian citizen in a purely internal situation wants his family members to be allowed to join him, he has to demonstrate that he has 'stable, adequate and regular resources'. This condition is deemed to be met when he shows proof of income of at least 120 per cent of the minimum level of income support.[1168] Conversely, this income condition does not exist for economically active Union citizens who have made use of their right of free movement and their family members. When a Union citizen is a worker or a self-employed person on the territory of another Member State, there are no additional conditions to meet to be entitled to a right of residence for more than three months.[1169] Non-economically active citizens must demonstrate 'sufficient resources'; this condition is assessed by taking 'the nature and frequency of personal incomes' into account.[1170]

553. Thirdly, the difference in treatment concerned the age requirements for spouses and partners. Article 40*ter* Belgian Aliens Act determines that for the family reunification of a Belgian citizen with his spouse or partner, it is required that both be older than 21 years old. Conversely, if a Union citizen wants to reunite with his spouse who is a third country national, no age requirement applies.[1171]

1166 They are no longer listed in Article 40*ter* Belgian Aliens Act.

1167 Article 2(2)d *juncto* Article 3(1) Directive 2004/38. It should be noted however that the Belgian legislator has formalised in Article 40*ter* Belgian Aliens Act the existing practice of granting a residence permit to the ascendants of a minor who is a Belgian citizen. In Union law, on the contrary, the right of the minor who is a Union citizen to be accompanied or joined by his or her ascendants has so far only been recognised in the case law of the Court of Justice (the so-called *Chen* case law) and not by legislative instruments at Union level.

1168 Article 40*ter* Belgian Aliens Act.

1169 Article 7(1)(a) Directive 2004/38 and Article 40(4), 1° and 40*bis*(4), first para Belgian Aliens Act.

1170 Article 7(1)(b) Directive 2004/38. Article 8(4) Directive 2004/38 determines that 'Member States may not lay down a fixed amount which they regard as "sufficient resources", but they must take into account the personal situation of the person concerned.' Article 40*bis*(4), second para Belgian Aliens Act.

1171 For 'mobile' Union citizens there is no age requirement for spouses (Article 40*bis*(2)1 Belgian Aliens Act). Conversely, Article 40*bis*(2)c provided that an age requirement of 21 was

554. Simultaneously, the Belgian legislator has inserted stricter conditions on family reunification with both Belgian citizens and Union citizens. The legislator has determined criteria to demonstrate the durable and stable character of the relationship.[1172] In cases of family reunification with children, the Belgian citizen or Union citizen and his or her spouse or partner should have the right to custody over the child.[1173] Finally, the reference period in which the conditions have to be maintained has been extended to three years.[1174]

2.4.2.4. The Judgments of the Belgian Constitutional Court of 26 September 2013

555. With the judgments of 26 September 2013, the Belgian Constitutional Court took a position on the compatibility of reverse discrimination with Articles 10 and 11 of the Constitution for the first time. Prior to that time, the Constitutional Court had always avoided taking a position on reverse discrimination.[1175] In its judgments of 26 September 2013, the Constitutional Court ruled, on the one hand, on the questions referred by the Belgian Council of State for a preliminary ruling on Article 9 of the Act of 8 July 2011, amending Article 40*ter* Belgian Aliens Act[1176] and on the action for annulment brought against the conditions for family reunification set out in the Act of 8 July 2011 on the other.[1177] Here, the focus will be on the part of the judgment concerning reverse discrimination.[1178] The Belgian Constitutional Court assessed the three aforementioned stricter requirements for 'immobile' Belgian citizens in the light of the principle of non-discrimination and equality, as enshrined in Articles 10 and 11 of the Constitution.

applicable to registered partnerships. However, in its judgment of 26 September 2013, the Constitutional Court abolished this age condition for registered partnership with a 'mobile' Union citizen to the extent that the same exception as for third country nationals (in Article 10(1)5°) was not foreseen – that is, the required age has been brought back to 18 years if it is demonstrated that the partners previously lived together for at least one year.

1172 Article 40*bis*(2)2°a) Belgian Aliens Act.

1173 Ibid Article 40*bis*(2)3°.

1174 Ibid Article 40*quater*(1).

1175 See more in Verbist, 'Omgekeerde discriminatie en de Belgische rechtsorde: op zoek naar een standpunt' in Alen and Theunis (eds), *Leuvense Staatsrechteijke Standpunten, Deel III*, die Keure 2012, pp 407–10; Verbist, 'Reverse Discrimination – A Belgian Perspective' in Guild, Rotaeche and Kostakopoulou (eds), *The Reconceptualization of European Union Citizenship*, Brill Nijhoff 2014, pp 276–82 and Bombois, 'La "discrimination à rebours" et son appréhension par la cour constitutionelle belge' in Cariat and Nowak (eds), *Le droit de l'Union européenne et le juge belge – Het recht van de Europese Unie en de Belgische rechter*, Bruylant 2015, pp 369–74.

1176 Belgian Constitutional Court 26 September 2013, no 123/2013.

1177 Ibid no 121/2013.

1178 See more extensively Verbist, 'De arresten van 26 september 2013 van het Grondwettelijk Hof: "omgekeerde discriminatie" inzake gezinshereniging is geen schending van het grondwettelijk gelijkheidsbeginsel' [2014] *T Vreemd* 93–106.

556. Before the Constitutional Court, the federal government had argued that the situation of Belgian citizens who have never used their right to free movement cannot be compared with the situation of mobile Union citizens to the extent that the latter benefit from specific legislation – Article 40*bis* and Articles 41 to 47 Belgian Aliens Act – which is the implementation of obligations flowing from Directive 2004/38.[1179] The Belgian Constitutional Court held that although according to the case law of the Court of Justice, a situation of reverse discrimination cannot violate the general Union principle of equality and non-discrimination, the same may not apply with regard to Articles 10 and 11 of the Belgian Constitution.[1180] The Court pointed out that Articles 10 and 11 of the Belgian Constitution aim to ensure that the norms that apply in the Belgian legal order comply with the principles of equality and non-discrimination. The Court added that Articles 10 and 11 of the Constitution have a general scope, prohibiting all discrimination regardless of its origin. The rights and freedoms that flow from international treaty provisions, which bind Belgium, are included in the rights and freedoms which should be guaranteed without discrimination. Accordingly, the Belgian Constitutional Court ruled that accepting the argument of the federal government would render the scrutiny on equality and non-discrimination 'meaningless'.[1181]

557. The Constitutional Court ruled that the three aforementioned differences in treatment can be justified by the legislation's aim of controlling migration flows.[1182] According to the Court, the national legislator has a broad discretion in the context of immigration policy given the complex considerations that should be made regarding the requirements of European law.[1183] Consequently, the Court considered the stricter conditions for Belgian citizens in a purely Belgian situation a relevant measure.[1184] Since the Court found neither a disproportionate impairment of the principle of equality nor of the right to the protection of family life,[1185] it concluded that Article 40*ter* Belgian Aliens Act – in

1179 Belgian Constitutional Court 26 September 2013, no 121/2013, para B.47 and Belgian Constitutional Court 26 September 2013, no 123/2013, para B.5.1.

1180 Belgian Constitutional Court 26 September 2013, no 121/2013, para B.48 and Belgian Constitutional Court 26 September 2013, no 123/2013, para B.5.2.

1181 Belgian Constitutional Court 26 September 2013, no 121/2013, para B.49 and Belgian Constitutional Court 26 September 2013, no 123/2013, para. B.5.3 where the Court used the word [*zinledig*].

1182 Belgian Constitutional Court 26 September 2013, no 121/2013, para B.52.2 and Belgian Constitutional Court 26 September 2013, no 123/2013, para B.6.2.

1183 Belgian Constitutional Court 26 September 2013, no 121/2013, para B.52.2 and Belgian Constitutional Court 26 September 2013, no 123/2013, para B.6.2.

1184 Belgian Constitutional Court 26 September 2013, no 121/2013, para B.52.2 and Belgian Constitutional Court 26 September 2013, no 123/2013, para B.6.2.

1185 Belgian Constitutional Court 26 September 2013, no 121/2013, paras B.53–B.56.2 and Belgian Constitutional Court 26 September 2013, no 123/2013, para B.6.7.3.

particular, for not treating Belgian citizens who have never used their right on free movement and their family members in the same way as Union citizens and their family members as meant in Article 40*bis* of the same Act – does not violate Articles 10, 11 and 22 of the Constitution, whether or not in combination with Article 8 ECHR.[1186]

558. Then, the Constitutional Court examined the claim that Article 40*bis* Belgian Aliens Act violates Articles 10 and 11 of the Constitution, in combination with Articles 2 and 3 of Directive 2004/38 to the extent that the conditions for family reunification which apply to family members of a citizen of another Member State of the European Union, do not apply to the family members of a Belgian citizen who has used his right of free movement. The Court ruled that this difference in treatment constituted a violation of Articles 10 and 11 of the Constitution.[1187] However, according to the Court, this discrimination does not originate in Article 40*bis* Belgian Aliens Act, but in the absence of a legal provision which allows Belgian citizens who have effectively and genuinely made use of their right to free movement to reside in Belgium with their family members upon compliance with conditions which are not stricter than those which were imposed by the host Member State on the basis of Union law.[1188]

2.4.2.5. The Constitutional Court's Judgments of 26 September 2013: Analysis

i. The Comparability of Purely Internal Situations and Cross-Border Situations

559. The first question which the Court had to answer in its judgments of 26 September 2013, was whether the situations were comparable or not. This is the first step in the application of the principles of equality and non-discrimination as applied by the Belgian judiciary; the position taken at this point determines whether or not the legal measure is further assessed in the light of the principle of equality and non-discrimination.[1189]

560. If the Constitutional Court had accepted the Council of Ministers' argument of non-comparability, this would have implied that the stricter conditions for family reunification with Belgian citizens would escape from further assessment in the light of the principle of equality, as enshrined in the Articles 10 and 11 of the Constitution. That is, using the words of Rimanque,

---

1186 Belgian Constitutional Court 26 September 2013, no 121/2013, para B.57 and Belgian Constitutional Court 26 September 2013, no 123/2013, para B.8.

1187 Belgian Constitutional Court 26 September 2013, no 121/2013, para B.58.8.

1188 Ibid.

1189 However, the step of comparability often fails to appear in the Court's legal reasoning. De Prins, Vrielink and Sottiaux, *Handboek discriminatierecht*, Kluwer 2005, pp 250–52.

'in the absence of comparability the problem of equality does not arise'.[1190] The author added that in that case 'the difficult questions concerning the justification and the seriousness of the inequality are avoided'.[1191] However, the Constitutional Court did not follow this logic.

561. In particular, the Constitutional Court rejected the Council of Ministers' argument of non-comparability precisely because this would make the judgment as to whether or not the principle of equality is respected 'meaningless'.[1192] The likely underlying reason is that the Constitutional Court did not want every purely internal situation to be considered incomparable with situations falling under Union law, since in that case situations of reverse discrimination would always escape from judicial review – not just at the European level, but also at the national level.[1193]

562. Subsequently, the Court considered that Articles 10 and 11 of the Constitution aim to ensure that the rules that apply in the Belgian legal order respect the principle of equality. Two norms which are applicable in the Belgian legal order are certainly at stake.[1194] More specifically, it has been argued that it lies in the logic of a global control of equality itself that a difference in treatment does not escape from assessment by the Court for the simple reason that one of the situations under comparison is indirectly governed by a provision which is elaborated by an authority other than the national legislator, but which is reproduced by the latter and which takes effect in the same legal order.[1195]

1190 Rimanque, 'De paradoxale werking van het gelijkheidsbeginsel' [1992–93] *RW* 9. Author's translation of: [*bij afwezigheid van vergelijkbaarheid [rijst] het gelijkheidsprobleem niet*].

1191 Ibid. Author's translation of: [*de lastige vragen omtrent de verantwoording en de ernst van de ongelijkheid worden vermeden*].

1192 The Belgian Constitutional Court confirmed the comparability of a purely internal situation and a cross-border situation falling under 90/436/EEC 'Convention on the elimination of double taxation in connection with the adjustment of profits of associated enterprises' in the context of reverse discrimination in Belgian Constitutional Court 7 November 2013, 149/2013. In particular, it explicitly held that it was relevant to compare the situations although one of the situations contains a cross-border element and the other situation does not (para B.5.2).The Belgian Constitutional Court held that the stricter treatment of purely internal situations regarding taxation of enterprises was compatible with the principle of equality as enshrined in Articles 10 and 11 of the Belgian Constitution.

1193 This interpretation seems to be confirmed by consideration B.48 of the Court: [*hoewel, gelet op de rechtspraak van het Hof van Justitie ter zake, een verschil in behandeling … dat ongunstig is voor de burgers van de Unie die nooit hun recht van vrij verkeer hebben uitgeoefend, het algemeen beginsel van het recht van de Europese Unie van gelijkheid en niet-discriminatie wegens de specifieke kenmerken van die rechtsorde en het beperkte toepassingsgebied ervan, niet kan schenden, zou hetzelfde niet kunnen gelden ten aanzien van de artikelen 10 en 11 van de Grondwet*].

1194 The situation of Belgian citizens who have not made use of their right to free movement is determined by Article 40*ter* Belgian Aliens Act. The situation of Union citizens who have used their right on free movement is determined by Articles 40*bis* and 41–47 Belgian Aliens Act, which constitutes Belgium's implementation of Directive 2004/38.

1195 Bombois, 'La "discrimination à rebours" et son appréhension par la cour constitutionelle belge' in Cariat and Nowak (eds), *Le droit de l'Union européenne et le juge belge – Het recht van de Europese Unie en de Belgische rechter*, Bruylant 2015, p 380.

563. Thereafter, the Court added that those Articles have a general scope, they prohibit reverse discrimination, irrespective of their origin. However, until now, the Constitutional Court seemed to be of the opinion that only a difference in treatment that originates in the action of one legislator can be reviewed in the light of the principles of equality and non-discrimination. This can at least be inferred from the Constitutional Court's settled case law that a different treatment in areas in which the Belgian communities and regions have own competences, the consequence is of a different policy which is permitted by the autonomy which is granted to them by the Constitution.[1196] The autonomy would be devoid of purpose if such a difference in treatment would be considered to violate Articles 10 and 11 of the Constitution.[1197] Accordingly, the analysis of competences should precede the analysis of equality.[1198]

This so-called doctrine of the single source, or of the autonomous source,[1199] also applies to a difference in treatment in which the federal State, on the one hand, and the communities of the regions on the other hand, have their own competences.[1200] In those cases, the Constitutional Court is even more explicit, since it uses a slightly different formulation: a difference in treatment 'which originates in the application of norms of different legislators exercising their own competences'[1201] or 'in the division of competences between the State and the regions'[1202] cannot in itself be considered to violate the principle of equality and non-discrimination.[1203]

564. Reverse discrimination is precisely a difference in treatment that results from the application of norms of different legislators: a more favourable Union provision against a stricter national provision. Accordingly, the question arises

---

1196 See inter alia Belgian Constitutional Court 10 June 1993, no 44/93, para B.3 and Belgian Constitutional Court 14 December 2005, no 190/2005, para B.4.7. See Vande Lanotte and Goedertier, *Handboek Belgisch Publiekrecht*, die Keure 2013, p 340.

1197 Vande Lanotte and Goedertier, *Handboek Belgisch Publiekrecht*, die Keure 2013, p 340.

1198 Vanpraet, 'België in Europa: de bevoegdheidsverdelende regels en het (con)federalisme in het kwadraat' in Vandenbossche and Drogenhenbroeck (eds), *Europese voorschriften en Staatshervorming*, die Keure 2013, pp 361–62.

1199 Ibid 363.

1200 See inter alia Belgian Constitutional Court 24 September 2003, no 119/2003, paras B.3.1–B.3.4 and Belgian Constitutional Court 5 May 2011, no 63/2011, para B.3.4.

1201 Belgian Constitutional Court 5 May 2013, no 63/2011, para B.3.4. Author's translation of: [*Het betreft immers een verschil in behandeling dat zijn oorsprong vindt in de toepassing van normen van verschillende wetgevers bij de uitoefening van hun eigen bevoegdheden. Een zodanig verschil kan op zich niet worden geacht strijdig te zijn met het beginsel van gelijkheid en niet-discriminatie*].

1202 Belgian Constitutional Court 24 September 2003, no 119/2003, para B.3.4. Author's translation of: [*Het verschil in behandeling vindt derhalve zijn oorsprong in de bevoegdheidsverdeling tussen de Staat en de gewesten en is verantwoord door de autonomie die krachtens de Grondwet aan de onderscheiden wetgevers toekomt*].

1203 It is unclear whether the different wordings are a deliberate choice of the Constitutional Court. See Feyen, *Beyond Federal Dogmatics*, Lund University Publications 2013, pp 171–72.

as to whether, in principle, the doctrine of the autonomous or single source could, by analogy, be applied to reverse discrimination assessed from a national perspective.[1204] The answer is negative according to the Belgian Constitutional Court since it decided in September 2013 to apply the principle of equality, as enshrined in the Belgian Constitution, to situations of reverse discrimination in order to ensure that national rules implementing Union law do not create a difference in treatment that is detrimental to own nationals and which would not be reasonably justified.

565. The question remains as to what exactly distinguishes the different treatment that results from different policies pursued by the communities, the regions and the federal government when they have autonomous competences, on the one hand, and a different treatment which results from different policies pursued by the European Union and by Belgian authorities in their respective spheres of competence on the other. What about 'the autonomy' of Belgium in relation to the European Union? The Constitutional Court did not refer to its case law on the autonomy of the communities and the regions; hence, the explanation for this distinction cannot be inferred from the judgment.[1205]

566. It is possible to explain the distinction in a rather formalistic way. That is to say, the two provisions creating the situation of reverse discrimination are issued by the Belgian legislator. In particular, Article 40*ter* Belgian Aliens Act regulates the situation of Belgian citizens who have not made use of their right of free movement. Articles 40*bis* and 41 to 47 Belgian Aliens Act regulate the situation of Union citizens who have exercised their right to free movement. Obviously, the content of the latter is exclusively commanded by Union law, that is to say, it is the implementation in Belgian law of Directive 2004/38.

1204 It has been argued that a consideration regarding a difference in treatment which cannot be attributed to one single source could not only have been expressed by the Constitutional Court in the *Flemish Care Insurance* case, but also by the Court of Justice. See in this respect Velaers and Vanpraet, 'De materiële en territoriale bevoegdheidsverdeling inzake sociale zekerheid en sociale bijstand (II)' [2009] *TBP* 195, 213.

1205 The same question can be posed in the context of the Austrian Constitutional Court's case law assessing a situation of reverse discrimination in the light of the Austrian principle of equality (above nn 449–53 and 533–41). In particular, the Austrian Constitutional Court also has settled case law according to which the principle of equality does not apply to a different treatment which results from divergent rules of the *Länder* amongst each other, nor of the difference in treatment which results from the different rules between a *Land* and the *Bund*. Nevertheless, the Austrian Constitutional Court ruled in 1999 and 2004 that a situation of reverse discrimination violated the Austrian principle of equality. However, in contrast to the Belgian Constitutional Court's judgment, the Austrian Constitutional Court did not discuss the issue of comparability in the judgments referred to above at all, but immediately considered whether the difference in treatment could be justified.

However, the distinction can also be explained in a more substantive way. According to Bombois, it is the territorial and normative connection between the European and national legal orders that distinguishes the situation of reverse discrimination from the exercise of each federated entity's legislative autonomy.[1206] That is to say, the Member States share responsibility in the establishment of EU law. By contrast, federated entities are only responsible for those measures that they establish for their own territory and they do not contribute to the establishment of legislation of another federated entity. Moreover, while EU law and the legislation of the Member States apply to the same territory, the legislation of different federated entities does not apply to the same territory in principle.[1207]

567. The Constitutional Court justified the application of Articles 10 and 11 of the Constitution via Article 14 ECHR and the case law of the European Court of Human Rights. The Court considered that 'to the rights and freedoms which must be ensured without discrimination, belong the rights and freedoms which result from international treaty provisions which bind Belgium. In particular, article 14 of the ECHR prohibits every discrimination in the enjoyment of rights protected under the Convention, including the right to family life.'[1208] Subsequently, the Court referred to the the European Court of Human Rights' *Hode and Abdi* judgment in which the latter ruled that 'where a measure results in the different treatment of persons in analogous positions, the fact that it fulfilled the State's international obligation will not it itself justify the difference in treatment'.[1209] It seems that the Belgian Constitutional Court put this forward as a reason to review the different treatment of purely internal and cross-border situations in light of the principle of equality.

568. It has been argued that if this interpretation by the Belgian Constitutional Court is correct, then the *Hode and Abdi* judgment would prohibit other European constitutional courts from also assuming that two situations which are opposed

1206 Bombois, 'La "discrimination à rebours" et son appréhension par la cour constitutionelle belge' in Cariat and Nowak (eds), *Le droit de l'Union européenne et le juge belge – Het recht van de Europese Unie en de Belgische rechter*, Bruylant 2015, p 381.

1207 Except from the juxtaposition of a federal law and a regional decree, see ibid fn 144.

1208 Author's translation of Belgian Constitutional Court 26 September 2013, no 121/2013, para B.48.

1209 Ibid para B.49, referring to ECHR 6 November 2012, *Hode and Abdi v United Kingdom*, para 55. See also Belgian Constitutional Court 26 September 2013, no 122/2013, para B.9. In the latter case, the Belgian Constitutional Court held that the stricter treatment of family members of Belgian citizens in a purely internal situation regarding integration incomes was compatible with the principle of equality as enshrined in Articles 10 and 11 of the Constitution.

in the framework of a reverse discrimination are incomparable.[1210] However, as has been argued repeatedly above, in the light of our working hypothesis, the comparability of purely internal situations and cross-border situations in the context of a reverse discrimination depends upon whether Union law overcompensates or compensates, respectively. This does not seem incompatible with the European Court of Human Rights' consideration that 'where a measure results in the different treatment of persons in analogous positions, the fact that it fulfilled the State's international obligation will not it itself justify the difference in treatment'.[1211] That is to say, this consideration can be read in the light of our working hypothesis in which the concept of (over)compensation can be seen as an addition to or refinement of this consideration.

ii. The Autonomy of the Belgian Legislator to Treat Purely Internal Situations Differently

569. In its judgments of 26 September 2013, the Constitutional Court tried to balance its concern of ensuring judicial review of situations of reverse discrimination with its concern to guarantee the autonomy of the Belgian legislator in principle to treat purely internal situations differently than situations falling under Union law. At different stages of the assessment, and in the light of Articles 10 and 11 of the Constitution, the Court underlined that the Belgian legislator can treat purely Belgian situations more strictly and that this does not necessarily constitute a violation of Articles 10 and 11 of the Constitution.

570. First, before reviewing the Act in the light of the principle of equal treatment, the Constitutional Court considered that since the provisions of Union law on free movement and citizenship do not apply to purely internal situations, then the Member States can determine the conditions for family reunification with their own nationals whose situation does not fall under Union law. In this respect, the Court pointed out that different goals underpin the legislation in the Union and in Belgium.[1212]

1210 Bombois, 'La "discrimination à rebours" et son appréhension par la cour constitutionelle belge' in Cariat and Nowak (eds), *Le droit de l'Union européenne et le juge belge – Het recht van de Europese Unie en de Belgische rechter*, Bruylant 2015, p 380.

1211 ECHR 6 November 2012, *Hode and Abdi v United Kingdom*, para 55.

1212 Belgian Constitutional Court 26 September 2013, no 121/2013, para B.45: [... *De bestreden bepaling past derhalve in het streven van de wetgever naar een ordentelijk immigratiebeleid en streeft een doelstelling na die verschillend is van die welke aan de basis ligt van het Unierecht inzake vrij verkeer. ... Aldus zijn de lidstaten bevoegd om te bepalen onder welke voorwaarden de familieleden van een eigen onderdaan wiens situatie geen aanknopingspunt heeft met het Unierecht, een verblijfstitel kunnen verkrijgen*].

571. Secondly, upon considering that the purely internal situations and the situations falling under Union law are comparable, the Court immediately added that the sole fact that the Belgian legislator only implements Union law for persons falling within the scope of Union law, but not for Belgian citizens who have not exercised their right of free movement, does not violate the principles of equality and non-discrimination.[1213]

572. Thirdly, the goal of controlling migration flows was accepted as being the most important justification for the three differences in treatment that are detrimental for family reunification with a Belgian citizen in a purely internal situation. In this respect, the Court stressed that the legislator has a broad discretion in the context of immigration policy which requires a complex balancing act and has to take into account the obligations flowing from Union law.[1214]

573. Even though the argument regarding the Belgian legislator's autonomy to treat purely internal situations differently, and in particular more strictly, could justify almost any situation of reverse discrimination in principle, this is not the automatic result of the Belgian Constitutional Court's assessment of reverse discrimination. In a period of less than one year, the Belgian Constitutional Court had to rule upon three other cases of reverse discrimination. In two of them, the Court held that the situation of reverse discrimination was compatible with Articles 10 and 11 of the Belgian Constitution.[1215]

However, in the third case, regarding State responsibility for an infringement attributable to a national court, the Belgian Constitutional Court itself made a detour via Union law.[1216] Although the case in the main proceedings did not have a link with Union law, the Court took into account the Court of Justice's relevant case law considering the necessity of harmonising the guarantees granted by Union law on the one hand and domestic law on the other.[1217] The Constitutional Court rejected one interpretation of Article 1382 of the Belgian Civil Law as incompatible with Articles 10 and 11 of the Belgian Constitution;[1218] however, it suggested an alternative reasoning based on the Court of Justice's case law, which is compatible with Articles 10 and 11 of the Belgian Constitution.[1219]

1213 Belgian Constitutional Court 26 September 2013, no 121/2013, para B.50.2.

1214 Ibid para B.52.2.

1215 Belgian Constitutional Court 26 September 2013, no 122/2013 and Belgian Constitutional Court 7 November 2013, no 149/2013.

1216 Belgian Constitutional Court 30 June 2014, no 99/2014.

1217 Ibid para B.21, author's translation of: [*Rekening houdend met de noodzaak om de waarborgen die zijn toegekend door het recht van de Europese Unie, enerzijds, en door het interne recht, anderzijds, te harmoniseren, houdt het Hof rekening met de rechtspraak van het Hof van Justitie*].

1218 Ibid para B.23.

1219 Ibid paras B.24–25.

iii. Different Impact of the Stricter Conditions for Purely Internal Situations

574. In its assessment of the relevance and proportionality of the differences in treatment between a Belgian citizen and his family members on the one hand and a Union citizen and his family members on the other, the Belgian Constitutional Court took into account the right to respect of family life, as enshrined in Article 22 of the Constitution and Article 8 ECHR.[1220]

575. The Court considered that the three differences in treatment can be justified by the legislator's aim of controlling migration flows.[1221] The Court pointed out that the Belgian legislator took into account that, by various legislative amendments, access to Belgian nationality had been facilitated in recent years.[1222] Although this is the result of a legislative choice, this circumstance justifies the relevance of the different treatment according to the Court.[1223]

576. Next, the Belgian Constitutional Court assessed the proportionality of the three specific differences in treatment between a Belgian citizen and his family members on the one hand and a Union citizen and his family members on the other individually. Regarding the right to family reunification with ascendants, the Court held that by admitting family reunification of minor Belgian citizens with both of their parents, the legislator took into account the special connection between young children and their parents.[1224] By contrast, if an adult Belgian citizen lives separately from his parents, this is, according to the Belgian Constitutional Court, the result of a personal choice in most cases. Moreover, the Court considered that the ascendants of adult Belgian citizens can apply for a residence permit on the basis of Title I of the Belgian Aliens Act.[1225]

577. Regarding the requirement of resources, the Court considered that the legislator established a reference amount, which results in no further examination if it is reached. By contrast, if the income is less than the reference amount, then the competent authority should examine and decide on the basis of the specific facts at issue.[1226] Therefore, the Court held that the legislator struck a fair balance between the aim of ensuring the continuation of the system of social assistance and the aim of exercising the right to family life in circumstances which respect human dignity.[1227]

[1220] The Court had announced to take the right to respect for family life in particular into account in the examination whether the difference in treatment is based on a pertinent criterion and whether or not it causes disproportionate results.

[1221] Belgian Constitutional Court 26 September 2013, no 121/2013, para B.52.2.

[1222] Ibid para B.52.1.

[1223] Ibid para B.52.2.

[1224] Ibid para B.54.2.

[1225] Ibid para B.54.2.

[1226] Ibid para B.55.2.

[1227] Ibid para B.55.5.

578. Regarding the age requirement for spouses and partners, the Court considered that this requirement does not prevent a residence permit, but only defers it temporarily. Moreover, young adults are protected against the risks of marriages of convenience and forced marriages.[1228]

579. In sum, according to the Court, the fact that an adult Belgian citizen has no right to family reunification with his parents, the stricter conditions regarding the stable, adequate and regular resources for the Belgian citizen who requests family reunification, and the stricter condition of age are a not disproportionate infringement of the right to family life. Accordingly, the Constitutional Court ruled that the contested situation of reverse discrimination is not discrimination in the sense of Articles 10 and 11 of the Belgian Constitution.

580. Although the Belgian Constitutional Court assessed whether or not a disproportional condition was at stake for each of the three conditions separately, it is submitted that there is a conceptual difference between the three conditions. In the first instance, you have conditions that involve changing parameters, such as the age and resources requirements. The age requirement is a temporal delay which changes automatically over time. The resources requirement can be changed by the Union citizen itself, by searching for a job and proving financial independence – without claiming that this is a simple change, but it is a possibility. It is submitted therefore that the compatibility of these two requirements with Articles 10 and 11 of the Belgian Constitution is acceptable.

581. In the second instance, you have unalterable conditions, such as the absence of the right for major Belgian citizens to family reunification with ascendants. The third country national (grand)parents are not entitled to join, whether or not they are taken care of and whether or not they are a burden on the Belgian social security. That the Belgian Constitutional Court considered that ascendants of major Belgian citizens can apply for a residence permit on the basis of Title I of the Belgian Aliens Act should be taken into account – the Court was probably referring here mainly to Articles 9 and 9*bis* Belgian Aliens Act. However, in practice it seems very hard to get a residence permit by taking this path.[1229] Accordingly, de facto adult Belgian citizens have no right to

1228 Ibid para B.56.2.

1229 Statisch jaarverslag 2014, Dienst vreemdelingenzaken, 29 <https://dofi.ibz.be/sites/dvzoe/NL/Documents/Statistisch%20jaarverslag%202014%20NL_v2.pdf>.

family reunification with their ascendants. It is difficult to see how this is not a disproportional infringement of the right to family life. If the Belgian legislator wanted to limit the number of ascendants who obtain a residence permit, why not subject this right to strict and objective conditions instead of withholding it altogether?

iv. Belgian Citizens who have Exercised their Right of Free Movement

582. A final remark on the Constitutional Court's judgments of 26 September 2013 concerns the reasoning regarding the situation of a Belgian citizen who has exercised his right of free movement. The Court ruled that the absence of a legal provision on this particular situation constitutes a violation of Articles 10 and 11 of the Constitution. However, in the light of European law, the Constitutional Court had the choice between two more straightforward alternatives by which to assess a Belgian citizen's situation who had exercised his right of free movement.[1230]

583. First, the Constitutional Court could have interpreted Article 40*bis* Belgian Aliens Act as being consistent with Union law.[1231] Article 40*bis*(1) determines that 'without prejudice to the more favourable provisions in legislation or in European regulations [sic] which the family members of Union citizens could claim, the provisions hereafter apply to them'.[1232] Obviously, a Belgian citizen is also a Union citizen, but in order to benefit from Union law, he first has to come within the scope of Union law. If a Belgian citizen has exercised his right of free movement, then Article 40*bis* can be applied, where this Article is interpreted in a manner consistent with the wording and goal of Directive 2004/38.

584. Secondly, the Constitutional Court could have ruled that Article 40*ter* Belgian Aliens Act needs to be set aside for a Belgian citizen who has exercised his right of free movement.[1233] The Court did use this technique – and rightly – when it assessed the arguments regarding the rights conferred upon by the status of Union citizenship.[1234] In particular, the Court ruled that Article 40*ter*

1230 Verbist, 'De arresten van 26 september 2013 van het Grondwettelijk Hof: "omgekeerde discriminatie" inzake gezinshereniging is geen schending van het grondwettelijk gelijkheidsbeginsel' [2014] *T Vreemd* 93–106.

1231 See inter alia ECJ case C-106/89 *Marleasing* [1990] ECR I-4135, para 8.

1232 Author's translation of: [*onverminderd de meer voordelige bepalingen vervat in wetten of Europese verordeningen waarop de familieleden van de burger van de Unie zouden kunnen aanspraak maken zijn de hierna volgende bepalingen op hen van toepassing*].

1233 See inter alia ECJ case 106/77 *Simmenthal* [1978] ECR 629, paras 17 and 21.

1234 This part of the judgment is not described here. See Verbist, 'De arresten van 26 september 2013 van het Grondwettelijk Hof: "omgekeerde discriminatie" inzake gezinshereniging is geen schending van het grondwettelijk gelijkheidsbeginsel' [2014] *T Vreemd* 93–106, 100.

is consistent with Articles 10 and 11 of the Constitution in combination with the provisions of Union law on the condition that Article 40*ter* is set aside, if in a specific case the refusal of a right of residence of a family member would have the effect of obliging a Belgian citizen to leave the territory of the European Union.[1235]

2.5. THE UNIQUE ITALIAN POSITION: FROM A PROHIBITION ON REVERSE DISCRIMINATION IN THE AREA OF FAMILY REUNIFICATION TO A GENERAL PROHIBITION ON REVERSE DISCRIMINATION

2.5.1. The Italian Council of State Regarding Family Reunification

585. The Italian Council of State took a clear position on reverse discrimination in the field of family reunification in its Opinion of 8 November 1995.[1236] In this case, the Italian government considered the requests of numerous Italian citizens, including ex third country nationals, who had acquired Italian nationality, for family reunification with family members who were third country nationals.[1237] Since these requests could not be granted in the sense of Article 4 Law 943/1986, which exclusively refers to third country nationals, the government considered that the norms provided for Union citizens in the legislative Decree 470/1992 should be extended to Italian citizens as Union citizens.[1238] The Council of State shared this view.[1239]

586. The Council of State considered that the question arises, by default, of an explicit provision that grants to Italian citizens the right to ask for family reunion with family members that are third country nationals.[1240] It continued that Article 4 Law 943/1986 only contains such a right in favour of third country nationals who ask to reunite with their family in Italy and that Article 5 DPR

1235 Belgian Constitutional Court 26 September 2013, no 121/2013, paras B. 59.7–8.

1236 Council of State, First Section, Opinion of 8 November 1995, 679/95, not published, consult the author.

1237 Ibid para 1.

1238 Law of 30 December 1986, no 943 [*Norme in materia di collocamento e di trattamento dei lavoratori extracomunitari immigrati e contro le immigrazioni clandestine*] *GU* no 8, 12 January 1987. Legislative Decree of 26 November 1992, no 470 [*Attuazione delle direttive 90/364/ CEE, 90/365/CEE e 90/366/CEE in materia di diritto di soggiorno dei cittadini comunitari, dei lavoratori salariati e non salariati che hanno cessato la propria attivita' professionale e degli student*] *GU* no 286, 4 December 1992. Council of State, First Section, Opinion of 8 November 1995, 679/95, para 1.

1239 Council of State, First Section, Opinion of 8 November 1995, 679/95, para 2.

1240 Ibid pp 2–3.

1656/1965 – inserted by Article 1 legislative Decree 470/1992 – provides the right of family reunification with third country nationals who are family members in favour of citizens of EU Member States who reside in Italy.[1241] The Council observed that this last provision, implementing Union Directives 90/64, 90/365 and 90/366 concerning the right of economically non-active Union citizens or students, could be interpreted such that it only refers to citizens of other EU Member States who reside on the Italian territory.[1242]

According to the Council of State, however, such an interpretation would imply an objective discrimination that exists to the detriment of Italian citizens, residing in Italy, who have family members who are third country nationals. Italian citizens would then be in an inferior situation compared to both citizens of other EU Member States and third country nationals regarding the possibility of benefitting from family reunification.[1243] The Council of State ruled that such an unreasonable solution, which infringes the principles of equality and rationality, as enshrined in Article 3 of the Constitution, requires that the normative lacuna be filled by way of 'explanatory interpretation'[1244] by recourse to the above-cited provision of the legislative Decree 470/1992 which cannot be read otherwise than referring also to Italian citizens, given that they are also citizens of the Union.[1245]

587. Hence, the Italian Council of State concluded that the situation of reverse discrimination was incompatible with the Italian principle of equality. It remedied the situation of reverse discrimination by way of a 'lacuna-filling' interpretation of the Italian legislation.

2.5.2. *The Italian Legislator: Autonomous Alignment*

2.5.2.1. Legislative Autonomous Alignment in Family Reunification

588. The legislative Decree 30/2007 transposes Directive 2004/38 on the right of citizens of the Union and their family members to move and reside freely within the territory of the Member States.[1246] It employs a very similar structure and language to Directive 2004/38. Article 3 of the legislative Decree 30/2007 determines that the provisions of the present legislative Decree, if they are more

1241 Ibid p 3. Decree of the President of the Republic of 30 December 1965, no 1656 [*Norme sulla circolazione e il soggiorno dei cittadini degli stati membri della c.e.e.*] *GU* no 55, 3 March 1966.

1242 Council of State, First Section, Opinion of 8 November 1995, 679/95, para 2, p 3.

1243 Ibid.

1244 Ibid: '*interpretazione integrativa*'.

1245 Council of State, First Section, Opinion of 8 November 1995, 679/95, para 2, pp 3–4.

1246 Legislative Decree of 6 February 2007, no 30, *GU* no 72, 27 March 2007.

favourable, apply to non-Italian family members of Italian citizens.[1247] Hence, the Italian legislator has autonomously aligned its legislation in the domain of family reunification.[1248]

2.5.2.2. General Legislative Autonomous Alignment

589. Moreover, the Italian legislator imposed a general obligation to prevent situations of reverse discrimination against their own citizens in purely internal situations. It was argued that the Italian Constitutional Court 1997 judgment, discussed above, was the legislator's inspiration to establish a general prohibition on reverse discrimination.[1249]

590. Article 2(h) of Law 62/2005 determines that the legislative Decree has to ensure that equal treatment of Italian citizens compared to citizens of other EU Member States is effectively guaranteed, in a way which ensures a maximum level of harmonisation between the internal legislation of the different Member States and which avoids discrimination to the detriment of Italian citizens, where they are subjected to legislation which is more restrictive than that which is applied to the citizens of other Member States.[1250]

1247 [Article 23. *Applicabilita' ai soggetti non aventi la cittadinanza italiana che siano familiari di cittadini italiani*
Le disposizioni del presente decreto legislativo, se piu' favorevoli, si applicano ai familiari di cittadini italiani non aventi la cittadinanza italiana.].

1248 Luxembourg too has autonomously aligned its legislation in the field of family reunification. Article 12 of the Law of 29 August 2008 determines that family members of a Luxembourg citizen, Union citizen or third country national, are treated in the same way as family members of a Union citizen. Conversely, see Belgium above nn 550 ff.

1249 Above nn 437–42. According to Hanf, the Constitutional Court's judgment 443/1997 can 'be read as codification or execution of a constitutional duty derived by the Italian Constitutional Court from the principle of equality' (Hanf, '"Reverse Discrimination" in EU Law: Constitutional Aberration, Constitutional Necessity, or Judicial Choice?' (2011) 18 *MJ* 29, fn 102). See also Zoppi, 'Le discriminazioni a rovescio' (2006) 4 *Diritto comunitario e degli scambi internazionali* 795, 812: [*L'intervento normative, reso opportune dall'onerosità dell'intervento della Corte costituzionale, ...*].

1250 Law of 18 April 2005, no 62 concerning provisions implementing the obligations arising from the membership of Italy to the European [Community, now Union] *GU* no 96, 27 April 2005. The legislative decree concerning family reunification hence seems to be an example of this general obligation. Author's translation of: [*i decreti legislativi assicurano che sia garantita una effettiva parità di trattamento dei cittadini italiani rispetto a quelli degli altri Stati membri dell'Unione europea, facendo in modo di assicurare il massimo livello di armonizzazione possibile tra le legislazioni interne dei vari Stati membri ed evitando l'insorgere di situazioni discriminatorie a danno dei cittadini italiani nel momento in cui gli stessi sono tenuti a rispettare, con particolare riferimento ai requisiti richiesti per l'esercizio di attività commerciali e professionali, una disciplina più restrittiva di quella applicata ai cittadini degli altri Stati membri*].

591. This position was confirmed in 2009 when by Law 88/2009[1251] Article 14*bis* was inserted into Law 11/2005.[1252] Article 14(2) determines that national legislative provisions or internal practices do not apply to Italian citizens when they produce discriminatory effects compared to the conditions and treatment of Union citizens residing or established on the Italian territory.[1253]

2.5.2.3. Extensive Implications of General Legislative Autonomous Alignment

592. An illustration of the extensive implications of this kind of legislation can be found in the Regional Administrative Court of Veneto's judgment in the area of the classic freedom of movement for persons, regarding Italian civil engineers in particular.[1254] The case concerned Article 52 of the regional Decree 2537/1925 which denied civil engineers who obtained their degree in Italy access to certain professional activities – regarding immovable property listed in legislative Decree 490/99 – whereas civil engineers who obtained their degree in other Member States could not be denied access to those activities.

593. The Regional Administrative Court of Veneto ruled in favour of the complainants on the basis of two convergent lines of reasoning. The first one was based on the Italian Constitutional Court's case law, the second on the Italian legislator's position.

In particular, the Regional Administrative Court of Veneto first assessed the provision in the light of Article 3 of the Constitution, which enshrines the principle of equality.[1255] In this respect, the Court of Veneto recalled the

1251 Law of 7 July 2009, no 88 concerning the provisions implementing the obligations arising from the membership of Italy to the European [Union] *GU* no 161, 14 July 2009.

1252 Law of 4 February 2005, no 11 concerning general norms on the belonging of Italy to the normative process of the European Union and of the procedures implementing [Union] obligations, *GU* no 37 15 February 2005.

1253 [*Article 14bis (Parità di trattamento) – 1. Le norme italiane di recepimento e di attuazione di norme e princı`pi della Comunita` europea e dell'Unione europea assicurano la parità di trattamento dei cittadini italiani rispetto ai cittadini degli altri Stati membri dell'Unione europea residenti o stabiliti nel territorio nazionale e non possono in ogni caso comportare un trattamento sfavorevole dei cittadini italiani. 2. Nei confronti dei cittadini italiani non trovano applicazione norme dell'ordinamento giuridico italiano o prassi interne che producano effetti discriminatori rispetto alla condizione e al trattamento dei cittadini comunitari residenti o stabiliti nel territorio nazionale.*].

1254 Regional Administrative Court of Veneto 15 November 2007, no 3630. (The Court previously referred a question on the constitutional legitimacy of the contested provision to the Italian Constitutional Court. The latter, however, considered the question manifestly inadmissible since the contested provision was of a regulatory nature. See Ordinance of the Regional Administrative Court of Veneto 28 September 2005, no 3600 and Ordinance of the Constitutional Court of 16 April 2007, no 130.)

1255 Regional Administrative Court of Veneto 15 November 2007, no 3630, pp 4–5.

Constitutional Court's case law according to which homogeneous situations cannot be treated differently, unless differentiation has been objectively justified. In particular, in its judgment 443/1997, discussed above,[1256] the Constitutional Court held that in the assessment of compliance with the constitutional principle of equality under Article 3 of the Constitution, the possible discriminatory effects resulting from the application of Union law cannot be ignored. The Court of Veneto held that the discrimination at issue was 'certainly unjust and irrational' regarding the case of Italian civil engineers. Therefore, the Court ruled that the contested provision, Article 52 of regional Decree 2537/1925 violated the principle of equality as enshrined in Article 3 of the Constitution.

Secondly, the Court of Veneto pointed out that Article 52 of regional Decree 2537/25 also violated 'the principle of equality introduced by Article 2, I, h) of Law 62/2005'.[1257] The Court ruled that, although this principle is established for legislative decrees which implement specific Union Directives, it should be considered to have a general application.[1258] Otherwise, it would create unequal treatment contradictory with the same ratio of the principle. The Regional Administrative Court of Veneto annulled the contested decision on the basis of the preceding considerations.

1256 Above nn 437–42.

1257 Regional Administrative Court of Veneto 15 November 2007, no 3630, p 5.

1258 See also Zoppi, 'Le discriminazioni a rovescio' (2006) 4 *Diritto comunitario e degli scambi internazionali* 795, 812: '*L'intervento normativo … sembra risolvere una volta per tutte il problema della discriminazion a rovescio*'.

CONCLUSION PART II

1. CONCLUSION BY AREA?

594. Apart from Italy, the Member States under analysis remedy reverse discrimination in some cases and allow it in others. Part II has discussed the assessments by national authorities of situations of reverse discrimination on the basis of the area in which these cases could be situated. The question arises as to whether a conclusion can be drawn on the basis of the area in which the reverse discrimination arises. In particular, it might be that reverse discrimination in the area of the free movement of goods is considered to be less problematic than in the area of freedom of movement for persons. That is to say, the free movement of goods is generally considered to be a less sensitive area than the freedom of movement for persons.

595. It was found that there were three out of five cases in the area of the free movement of goods in which the national authority allowed reverse discrimination,[1259] while there were only three out of ten cases in the area of the freedom of movement for persons in which reverse discrimination was allowed.[1260, 1261] Admittedly, only a limited number of assessments of reverse discrimination by national authorities were examined. Hence, this finding should not be given too much weight.

1259 That is, reverse discrimination was prohibited by the Italian Constitutional Court regarding industrially dried pasta and by the German Federal Administrative Court regarding the purity requirement of beer. By contrast, reverse discrimination was allowed by the French Council of State regarding ethyl alcohol, by the French Court of Cassation regarding emmenthal and so far by the Belgian legislator regarding mayonnaise.

1260 That is, reverse discrimination was prohibited by the Austrian Constitutional Court regarding professional qualifications and regarding the acquisition of immovable property, by the French Constitutional Court regarding the restoration of classified historic monuments by a certain type of architects, by the German Federal Constitutional Court in two cases regarding the Skilled Trades Order, by the French Court of Cassation regarding employment conditions and by the Italian Constitutional Court regarding the duration of contracts. By contrast, reverse discrimination was allowed by the French Council of State regarding both proof of good behaviour and declaration for tourist guides and by the French Court of Cassation regarding expatriation allowance.

1261 In the area of family reunification, the Member States under analysis, except from Italy, allow reverse discrimination.

596. Moreover, there appear to be no persuasive arguments for the proposition that situations of reverse discrimination of goods should never be considered to be problematic or that situations of reverse discrimination in the area of freedom of movement for persons should always be considered to be problematic. It is submitted that the key to distinguishing problematic from unproblematic situations of reverse discrimination lies less in the area of goods versus persons, and more in the concept of compensation versus overcompensation by Union law.

2. APPLICATION OF THE WORKING HYPOTHESIS TO THE NATIONAL LEVEL

2.1. INTERPRETATION OF COMPENSATION AND OVERCOMPENSATION AT NATIONAL LEVEL

597. In Part II, the working hypothesis based on the concept of compensation and overcompensation to the national level was applied. That is to say, for each situation of reverse discrimination assessed at national level, we examined whether a mere compensation or an overcompensation by Union law was at stake. Analysis was given of the national authority's assessment in the light of the working hypothesis which suggests a different approach to be followed on the basis of the assessment of compensation or overcompensation by Union law.

2.2. NATIONAL ASSESSMENT IN CASES OF COMPENSATION BY UNION LAW

598. According to our working hypothesis, in cases of compensation by Union law, a mere difference in treatment is at stake. In other words, the purely internal situations and the cross-border situations are considered to be different situations that are treated differently. However, this does not imply a predefined result in the case of compensation; it is not the case that a compensation issue means that reverse discrimination has to be allowed by the national authority in any event, according to the working hypothesis. In particular, the national authority can either stop its assessment of reverse discrimination immediately after considering that a mere difference in treatment is at stake, or it can assess the purely internal situation in the light of national law.

599. If the national authority decides to assess the purely internal situation as such in the light of national law, there is, it is submitted, no need to make a comparison with situations falling under the scope of Union law. Accordingly, it has been argued that substantial rights as enshrined in national law, such as the right to choose an occupation and the right to family life for instance, are appropriate for the assessment of reverse discrimination in which Union law merely compensates a disadvantage resulting from the exercise of free movement.

By contrast, the national principle of equality is conceptually not – or at least less – appropriate since the situations are not comparable, but different in the case of compensation of Union law. This implies that the analysis under the national principle of equality should stop right there. For instance, it was argued above that the Austrian Constitutional Court ought to assess the prior authorisation of acquiring immovable property in purely internal situations in the light of the freedom of movement or the right to own property, as enshrined in Articles 4 and 5 Basic Law of 21 December 1867, and not in the light of the principle of equality as enshrined in Austrian law.

600. Although it is this author's preference that an assessment be made on the basis of substantial rights, as enshrined in national law, in cases of compensation by Union law, this does not prevent the national authority from drawing inspiration from the way in which the issue has been regulated at the Union level. For instance, this is what the German Federal Constitutional Court did in its judgment of 2005 regarding registration in the Skilled Trades Register. In particular, the Court took the distinct treatment of craftsmen from other EU Member States providing services in Germany into consideration. However, it was on the basis of the open wording of Article 8 Skilled Trades Order and in the light of Article 12(1) Basic Law enshrining the right to choose an occupation that the Court decided that a generous interpretation of Article 8 Skilled Trades Order was required.

2.3. NATIONAL ASSESSMENT IN CASES OF OVERCOMPENSATION BY UNION LAW

601. In cases of overcompensation by Union law, in light of our working hypothesis, the national authority has to assess the situation of reverse discrimination in the light of national law, explicitly comparing or taking into account the situation falling under Union law. This does not imply that all situations in which reverse discrimination is a result of overcompensation by Union law should be prohibited at the national level. However, it is submitted that the national authority should not accept justifications for reverse discrimination which is the result of overcompensation by Union law too easily. That is to say, cases of compensation by Union law, and hence mere differences in treatment, are already filtered out.

602. Taking the impact of the stricter conditions for purely internal situations explicitly into account is, in the author's opinion, crucial. For instance, the Belgian Constitutional Court ruled on more restrictive conditions for their own nationals in purely internal situations in the field of family reunification. The Court assessed the reverse discrimination – the result of overcompensation by Union law – in light of the principle of equality as enshrined in Belgian constitutional law. In particular, the Belgian Constitutional Court considered the three stricter conditions to be justified.

Whereas this author is in agreement with the compatibility of the requirements regarding resources and age with the constitutional principle of equality and the right to family life, there are serious doubts as to whether the denial of a right to family reunification with ascendants from an adult Belgian citizen is proportional in the light of the principle of equality and the right to family life. That is, the first two conditions involve changing parameters. The age requirement is a temporal delay which changes automatically over time. The resources requirement can, at least in theory, be changed by the Union citizen itself, by searching for a job and by proving financial independence. By contrast, the third condition cannot be altered. The third country national (grand)parents are not entitled to join whether or not they are taken care of and whether or not they are a burden upon the Belgian social security.

603. The principle of equality as enshrined in national law is, it is argued, the most appropriate instrument for the assessment of cases of reverse discrimination resulting from a overcompensation by Union law, for the national authority to employ. This is because it allows comparison between purely internal and cross-border situations and also for the balancing of justifications and the impact of the stricter conditions for purely internal situations.

3. EVALUATION OF THE APPLICATION OF THE WORKING HYPOTHESIS TO THE NATIONAL LEVEL

3.1. PUTTING OF COMPENSATION AND OVERCOMPENSATION IN PRACTICE AT NATIONAL LEVEL

604. When evaluating the working hypothesis, it is important first of all to remember that a narrower or broader interpretation of overcompensation has the effect of potentially defining the scope of Union law in a broader or narrower sense respectively. Secondly, the assessment of whether a compensation or an overcompensation is at stake, is a more difficult exercise at national level than at Union level. That is, whereas the ECJ has to decide in a specific case, the national court has to make an assessment *in abstracto* as to whether or not the compensation by Union law is a proportional remedy to the disadvantage suffered by the Union citizen or good.

605. Accordingly, caution has been exercised so that a situation is not labelled too quickly as comprising an overcompensation by Union law when assessing an example of reverse discrimination at the national level. In particular, in the area of family reunification, it has been argued that the national authority should assess the situation of reverse discrimination as a case of overcompensation by Union law. Although a mere compensation by Union law is at stake in some cases, the national authority cannot make the assessment of compensation or overcompensation *in abstracto*. Since there is a real risk of overcompensation, it has been argued that the national authority should begin from the premise that an overcompensation is at stake in the area of family reunification.

606. The interpretation of whether a compensation or an overcompensation is at stake seems to depend largely upon what exactly should be considered to be a restriction to free movement. In the event that one defends a more restrictive interpretation of restrictions to free movement within the EU, then this will obviously lead to more cases of overcompensation of Union law. Although the interpretation of restrictions is highly relevant, it has only been examined briefly in Part I. In particular, a more restrictive interpretation was defended and two proposals were discussed in this regard.[1262] However, an application of the working hypothesis starting from different understandings on restrictions to free movement within the EU would be a very interesting avenue for further research.

607. The appraisal that the interpretation of (over)compensation relates to the interpretation of restrictions to free movement, probably points out the main drawback of the application of the working hypothesis to the national level. That is to say, if the national authority has to assess whether the EU grants more rights than necessary in order not to restrict the freedom of movement within the EU, this might be considered as questioning the ECJ and re-interpreting the ECJ's interpretation of Union law. However, on the basis of Article 267 TFEU the Court of Justice has jurisdiction to give preliminary rulings concerning the interpretation of the Treaties. Consequently, this might question the putting into practice at national level of the concept of compensation and overcompensation. Accordingly, the question will be addressed as to whether an alternative for the working hypothesis should be provided for the assessment of reverse discrimination at national level.

1262 Above nn 206–19.

3.2. ALTERNATIVES TO THE APPLICATION OF THE WORKING HYPOTHESIS AT NATIONAL LEVEL

608. Two alternatives for the application of the working hypothesis at national level are discussed. First under consideration is the argument of the division of competences between the EU and the Member States as being conclusive in each case of reverse discrimination. Secondly, it is considered whether the national authority should apply the principle of equality in each case of reverse discrimination – not only in cases of overcompensation by Union law.

609. Assessing reverse discrimination in the light of the vertical division of competences between the EU and the Member States is what the German administrative courts do in the area of family reunification. They argue that the difference in treatment between purely internal situations and situations falling within the scope of application of Union law is objectively justified in general because it results directly from the division of competences between the EU and the Member States. This approach implies that no situation of reverse discrimination is problematic.

610. However, it is submitted that the division of competences is not a conclusive argument because of the territorial and normative connection between the European and national legal orders. That is to say, the Member States have a shared responsibility in the establishment and execution of EU law. Especially in the area of family reunification, it is submitted that the vertical division of competences between the EU and its Member States should not be considered as a decisive argument from the start of the assessment. Admittedly, the rules on the vertical division of competences may play a role at a different level. That is, the argument of autonomy of the national legislator can still be relevant in cases of overcompensation in which the national authority applies the principle of equality as enshrined in national law, in particular in the assessment of proportionality.[1263]

611. Another alternative to the working hypothesis for the assessment of reverse discrimination at national level, is the application of the principle of equality as enshrined in national law to each case of reverse discrimination – not only in cases of overcompensation as suggested by the working hypothesis. Hence, this alternative can be understood as a criticism of the assessment of reverse discrimination in the light of a substantial right – which is suggested in

---

[1263] Above nn 569–73.

cases of compensation by Union law. However, as the German purity requirement of beer case demonstrates, the assessment on the basis of a substantial right also allows for the balancing of the different interests at stake.[1264] Accordingly, the assessment in the light of a substantial right is not *per se* less appropriate than an assessment in the light of the principle of equality. In both cases, the application in a specific case largely depends upon the responsibility the national authorities take.[1265]

612. Nevertheless, the assessment in the light of a substantial right in case of compensation by Union law versus the assessment in the light of the principle of equality in case of overcompensation by Union law has a double advantage. First, it indicates whether the purely internal situation and the cross-border situation should be compared. There is no need to compare them in case of compensation by Union law, while there is in case of overcompensation by Union law. Secondly, it indicates whether the case of reverse discrimination is unproblematic or problematic.

613. Although the working hypothesis might need refinement as regards its operationalisation at national level, it can be concluded overall that it is a conceptually valid hypothesis also at national level. The idea behind it is certainly not to criticise the ECJ but to encourage the national authority to reflect on the situation in the EU context. If there are aspects specific to the cross-border situation which justify the grant of rights by Union law, then the national authority does not have to take these into account when ruling upon the purely national situation. In that case, the purely internal situation and the cross-border situation are not comparable, a mere compensation by Union law is at stake. By contrast, if there are no elements specific to the cross-border situation, the latter can be compared with a purely internal situation. In that case, the national authority should follow the approach suggested for an overcompensation by Union law, that is to say, the principle of equality as enshrined in national law. This allows comparing of purely internal and cross-border situations and it allows balancing justifications and the impact of the stricter conditions for purely internal situations.

Hence, the concept of compensation and overcompensation applied at national level can be seen as a way in order to make implicit assumptions explicit. However, caution must be exercised when the national authority makes the assessment whether Union law merely compensates or overcompensates.

1264 Above nn 430–36.

1265 Above n 435, comparing the German Federal Administrative Court's judgment on the purity requirement of beer with the French Court of Cassation's judgment on emmenthal.

4. SOME FINAL THOUGHTS ON ADDRESSING REVERSE DISCRIMINATION AT THE NATIONAL LEVEL

614. It is admitted that it might seem strange that Union law creates a problem, by giving more rights than it ought to, and that the national legal systems have to 'solve' it. However, as has been argued in Part I, it is up to the EU in the first place to straighten out these situations of overcompensation. If this does not happen, the national legal systems have to deal with it as well as possible. It is submitted that the national authorities should fill the gaps that remain in the protection from reverse discrimination in cases of overcompensation by Union law.[1266]

615. However, there are limits to addressing reverse discrimination at the national level. In particular, Poiares Maduro has argued that 'national political processes may be dominated by some national interests which would gain by the maintenance of reverse discrimination, at the expense of other national interests'.[1267] Moreover, he has pointed out that the strong risks of majoritarian bias may lead to an under-representation of minority interests.[1268] However, it should be emphasised that the national judicial instances may still review the national measure at issue.

616. Finally, it should be noted that the Member States are, at least in theory, able to prevent reverse discrimination arising from secondary Union law. That is to say, when negotiating secondary Union law, the national representatives in the Council should reflect on whether they would be prepared to extend the rules to their own nationals in purely internal situations or whether they would accept that their own citizens are treated less favourably. They should discuss the national position at issue at the national level ahead of time and defend this at the Union level. A real dialogue between the Union legislative level and the individual Member State legislative level seems important here. Moreover, advance awareness of reverse discrimination and an explicit debate about it at the national level seem an important step towards an open and reasoned assessment of reverse discrimination by the national authorities.

[1266] See also Spitaleri who considers national rules as '*sede ulteriore*' in which situations of reverse discrimination can be remedied. However in contrast to the opinion offered here, Spitaleri sees national rules as a last resort with a view to achieving equality between internal and cross-border situations. Spitaleri, *Le discriminiazioni alla rovescia nel diritto comunitario*, Università di Trieste 2005, p 160: [*gli ordinamenti nazionali ... una sede ulteriore, dove queste possone essere ulteriormente 'filtrate' in vista di una complete parificazione tra fattispecie interne e comunitarie*].

[1267] Poiares Maduro, 'The Scope of European Remedies: The Case of Purely Internal Situations and Reverse Discrimination' in Kilpatrick, Novitz and Skidmore (eds), *The Future of European Remedies*, Hart Publishing 2000, pp 135–36.

[1268] Ibid p 137.

PART III

REVERSE DISCRIMINATION IN A FEDERAL STATE CONTEXT

617. This work has distinguished between 'classic cases' of reverse discrimination and cases of reverse discrimination in a federal state context.[1269] Parts I and II discussed 'classic cases' of reverse discrimination in which a Member State treats its own nationals in a purely internal situation more strictly than Union citizens falling within the ambit of Union law. Part III will focus on 'specific cases' of reverse discrimination. These concern situations of reverse discrimination in a federally structured Member State. That is to say, it may happen that the reverse discrimination only affects some of the Member State's own nationals, in particular those who do not fall under the jurisdiction of the regional authority granting certain rights to the nationals falling under its jurisdiction.

618. Regional authorities often reserve benefits to persons residing in the territory falling under their jurisdiction. For instance, residents can benefit from free or discounted access to public services, such as swimming pools, museums, theatres, sports events, etc, or residents may have the right to use their own language vis-à-vis public authorities.[1270] In order to comply with the Treaty provisions on free movement and the principle of non-discrimination on grounds of nationality, the regional authority treats nationals of other EU Member States like their own residents and grants them the same benefits. Accordingly, specific cases of reverse discrimination may arise.

619. A notorious example of a specific case of reverse discrimination in a federal state context is the *Flemish Care Insurance* case, which will be discussed

---

1269 See also DAUTRICOURT and THOMAS, 'Reverse Discrimination and Free Movement of Persons Under Community Law: All for Ulysses, Nothing for Penelope?' (2009) 34 *ELRev* 443: 'an important distinction has to be drawn between, on the one hand, the specific category of reverse discrimination resulting from the existence of internal repartition of competences within a Member State and, on the other, reverse discrimination which does not result from the federal organisation of the state but exclusively from the fact that some nationals have not made use of their [Union] free movement rights'.

1270 VAN DER STEEN, 'Zuiver interne situaties: geen omwenteling, wel inperking' (2008) *NTER* 301, 305.

in detail as a common thread throughout this part. For now, it suffices to point out that the system of Flemish care insurance as determined by the Decree excluded from its benefits Belgian citizens who worked in the Dutch-speaking region or in the bilingual region of Brussels Capital, but who lived in the French- or German-speaking region and who never exercised their right to free movement. This complex case of reverse discrimination is the result of both the ECJ's and the Belgian Constitutional Court's judgment on the case. That is, on the basis of Union law, Union citizens who had exercised their right to free movement had to be included. By contrast, the Belgian Constitutional Court ruled that Belgian citizens living in the French- or German-speaking region who had never exercised their right on free movement could not be included because the Flemish legislator is not competent for this category of persons. The extraterritorial application of the Flemish Decree would be a violation of the Belgian constitutional rules on internal division of competences.

620. Chapter 6 will discuss cases of reverse discrimination in a federal state context from the perspective of Union law. After describing the Union's approach towards the federal structure of its Member States generally, it will go on to discuss the ECJ's case law on specific cases of reverse discrimination. Next, the ECJ's case law on State aid will be analysed, in which the autonomy of regional authorities is recognised under certain conditions. Finally, the possibility of preventing specific situations of reverse discrimination at the Union level by recognising regional authorities when assessing restrictions to free movement, will be examined.

Chapter 7 will discuss cases of reverse discrimination in a federal state context from the perspective of Belgium and Germany.[1271] The chapter will analyse the examples through the legal ground which was decisive for the national authority, that is to say, those national rules concerning the division of competences, the rules on internal free movement and the principle of equality as enshrined in national law.

621. The question arises as to whether the working hypothesis, as set out in Parts I and II, in the context of 'classic' cases of reverse discrimination can also be applied to 'specific' cases of reverse discrimination. In particular, can the distinction between problematic and unproblematic cases of reverse discrimination on the basis of (over)compensation by Union law also be made if the stricter treatment only applies to some of the Member States' own nationals? This will be assessed both at the Union level (in Chapter 6) and at the national, in particular the regional, level (in Chapter 7).

1271 Although Austria is one of the five Member States under analysis, and it has a federal State structure, no relevant illustrations in Austria of specific cases of reverse discrimination were found.

CHAPTER 6

UNION PERSPECTIVE ON REVERSE DISCRIMINATION IN A FEDERAL STATE CONTEXT

1. THE STATUS OF REGIONS FROM A UNION PERSPECTIVE

622. This chapter will first describe the attitude of the EU vis-à-vis regions in general. This will be done by drawing both upon the Treaties and the Court's case law on these matters.

623. It should be pointed out that different denominations are used regarding the terminology in the context of federally structured Member States. The Treaties refer to 'regions' and 'regional and local authorities'. The ECJ also uses the term 'infra-State bodies', in particular in the context of cases on State aid. Finally, Advocates General have used the terms 'decentralised authority' and 'devolved administrations'. In general, this book uses the denominations employed in the Treaties, but when discussing ECJ cases or the opinion of an Advocate General, the denominations put forward by them will be used.

1.1. THE ECJ'S CASE LAW ON THE INTERNAL DIVISION OF COMPETENCES WITHIN A MEMBER STATE

1.1.1. The Autonomy of the Member States in the Allocation of Internal Powers

624. It is the ECJ's well-established case law that a Member State may freely allocate internal legislative powers as it sees fit and implement Union law by measures from regional or local authorities.[1272] In other words, the question as to which entity of a Member State ought to implement or transpose Union law is not a matter of Union law, but one which is governed by the national rules concerning

[1272] See inter alia ECJ case 96/81 *Commission v Netherlands* [1982] ECR I-1791, para 12 and, more recently, ECJ case C-87/02 *Commission v Italy* [2004] ECR I-5975, para 38.

the internal division of competences within that Member State.[1273] However, the Union measures at issue have to be implemented correctly.[1274]

1.1.2. The ECJ Does Not Accept Hiding behind Domestic Rules on State Structure

625. Although each Member State is free to organise its internal structure, the fact remains that it alone is responsible towards the Union, under Article 258 TFEU, for compliance with its obligations under Union law.[1275] If EU law is not implemented correctly by the regional or local authority, then the Member State is held liable and the latter may not take shelter behind the national constitutional rules on the internal division of competences in order to avoid the ECJ finding that the Member State has failed to fulfil its obligations under Union law.[1276] In this context, the Court has consistently ruled that 'a Member State cannot plead provisions, practices or situations prevailing in its domestic legal order, including those resulting from the constitutional organisation of that State, to justify the failure to observe obligations arising under [Union] law'.[1277]

626. In order to ensure compliance with obligations arising under international and supranational law, the central authority of the state may substitute the regional authority in some Member States.[1278] In Belgium, for instance, the federal Parliament or the federal executive can temporarily act instead of one of its communities or regions, the two types of regional authorities in Belgium,[1279] when the Belgian State is condemned by an international or supranational court following a failure to act on behalf of this community or region to comply with

---

1273 Opinion AG Trstenjak 3 February 2009 in C-428/07 *Horvath*, para 95.

1274 Ibid. In particular, the ECJ held that 'it is not for the Commission to rule on the division of competences by the institutional rules proper to each Member State, or on the obligations which may be imposed on federal and Laender authorities respectively. It may only verify whether the supervisory and inspection procedures established according to the arrangements within the national legal system are in their entirety sufficiently effective to enable the Community requirements to be correctly applied' (ECJ case C-8/88 *Germany v Commission* [1990] ECR I-2321, para 13).

1275 See inter alia ECJ case C-33/90 *Commission v Italy* [1991] ECR I-5987, para 24; ECJ case C-388/01 *Commission v Italy*, cited in fn 55, para 27; ECJ case C-87/02 *Commission v Italy* [2004] ECR I-5975, para 38. See in connection with Article 260 TFEU ECJ case C-610/10 *Commission v Spain*, para 132.

1276 See inter alia ECJ case C-323/96, *Commission v Belgium* [1998] ECR I-5063, paras 40–42; ECJ case C-87/02 *Commission v Italy* [2004] ECR I-5975, para 38; ECJ case C-102/06 *Commission v Austria* [2006], not published in the European Court Reports, para 9; and ECJ case C-212/06 *Flemish Care Insurance* [2008] ECR I-1683, para 58.

1277 See inter alia ECJ case C-212/06 *Flemish Care Insurance* [2008] ECR I-1683, para 58.

1278 The possibility of substitution exists in Belgium, Austria, Germany, Spain and the UK. See references for each country in Lenaerts and Van Nuffel, *European Union Law*, Sweet & Maxwell 2011, p 630.

1279 See below n 636 on the Belgian State structure.

an international or supranational obligation.[1280] The Belgian State can recover all costs from the regional authority concerned incurred by its failure to act.[1281]

627. Moreover, in *Internationale Handelsgesellschaft*, the Court held that the alleged infringement of national constitutional rules on state structures does not affect the validity of a Union measure or its effect within a Member State.[1282] Here, the ECJ clearly explained the underlying reasons for its case law. It considered that 'recourse to the legal rules or concepts of national law in order to judge the validity of measures adopted by the institutions of the [Union] would have an adverse effect on the uniformity and efficacy of [Union] law. The validity of such measures can only be judged in the light of [Union] law. In fact, the law stemming from the Treaty, an independent source of law, cannot because of its very nature be overridden by rules of national law, however framed, without being deprived of its character as [Union] law and without the legal basis of the [Union] itself being called in question.'[1283] It seems that the same kind of logic underpins the Court's case law regarding the obligation to fulfil obligations under Union law.

628. Rather than being a *sui generis* position in Union law, the case law of the Court of Justice corresponds to a well-established rule of international law to that effect, as enshrined in Article 27 of the Vienna Convention on the Law of Treaties (VCLT). This Article, regarding 'internal law and observance of treaties', determines that 'a party may not invoke the provisions of its internal law as justification for its failure to perform a treaty'.[1284] This is traditionally known as 'federal blindness' from the perspective of international law. It is submitted that the way in which AG Trstenjak has put it is to be preferred: '[T]he reverse side of this neutrality of the [Union] legal order vis-à-vis the organisational

---

1280 Article 169 Belgian Constitution *juncto* Article 16(3) Special Law of 8 August 1980.

1281 Article 16(3) Special Law of 8 August 1980. Including any costs for reparations that have to be made. In this respect, Lenaerts and Van Nuffel argued that 'each Member State must ensure that individuals obtain reparation for damage caused to them by non-compliance with Union law, whichever public authority is responsible for the breach and whichever public authority is in principle, under the law of the Member State concerned, responsible for making reparation' (LENAERTS and VAN NUFFEL, *European Union Law*, Sweet & Maxwell 2011, pp 629–30).

1282 ECJ case 11/70 *Internationale Handelsgesellschaft* [1970] ECR 1125, para 3.

1283 Ibid.

1284 Article 27 VCLT: 'Internal law and observance of treaties. A party may not invoke the provisions of its internal law as justification for its failure to perform a treaty. This rule is without prejudice to article 46.'

Article 46 VCLT: 'Provisions of internal law regarding competence to conclude treaties (1) A State may not invoke the fact that its consent to be bound by a treaty has been expressed in violation of a provision of its internal law regarding competence to conclude treaties as invalidating its consent unless that violation was manifest and concerned a rule of its internal law of fundamental importance. (2) A violation is manifest if it would be objectively evident to any State conducting itself in the matter in accordance with normal practice and in good faith.'

structure of the Member States is that to the same extent as a Member State is entitled to allocate its powers internally as it sees fit and as prescribed by its constitutional order, it is prevented from relying on domestic circumstances in order to circumvent its obligations under [Union] law.'[1285] This formulation shows better the origins of this principle of international law: international law only regulates the relationships between the different States; it shows respect for the sovereignty of the States and does not interfere in their internal affairs.[1286]

629. The European Court of Human Rights (ECtHR) in Strasbourg applies this principle as well. It determined explicitly that 'the European Convention does not contain a "federal clause" limiting the obligations of the federal State for events occurring on the territory of the states forming part of the federation'.[1287] The ECtHR repeatedly ruled that, in view of the Convention, the only issue of relevance is the State's international responsibility, 'irrespective of the national authority to which the breach of the Convention in the domestic system is imputable'.[1288] The Convention not only obliges the federal level of the contracting States to respect the rights and freedoms enshrined in the Convention, but also requires that the federal authority of the contracting State prevents and remedies any breach of the Convention at federated levels.[1289] The contracting State 'cannot take shelter behind' its federal structure when the Convention is not respected at a subordinated level of that same State.[1290]

1.2. THE STATUS OF REGIONS IN THE TREATIES

630. Whereas the Treaties initially only referred to the Member States and not to their regions, they now take the status of the Member States' regions into account. Various Treaty provisions explicitly refer to regions in some Member States, especially in the wake of the Lisbon Treaty.[1291]

631. First of all, Article 4(2) TEU provides that 'the Union shall respect the equality of Member States before the Treaties as well as their national identities,

---

1285 Opinion AG Trstenjak in 3 February 2009 in C-428/07, *Horvath*, para 96.

1286 Ibid fn 47.

1287 ECtHR case *Assanidze v Georgia*, 8 April 2004, para 141.

1288 Ibid para 146; *Foti and Others v Italy*, judgment of 10 December 1982, Series A no 56, p 21, para 63; *Zimmermann and Steiner v Switzerland*, judgment of 13 July 1983, Series A no 66, p 13, para 32; and *Lingens v Austria*, judgment of 8 July 1986, Series A no 103, p 28, §46.

1289 ECtHR case *Assanidze v Georgia*, 8 April 2004, para 146 and *Ireland v the United Kingdom*, judgment of 18 January 1978, Series A no 25, pp 90–91, para 239.

1290 ECtHR case *Assanidze v Georgia*, 8 April 2004, para 146 and *Ireland v the United Kingdom*, judgment of 18 January 1978, Series A no 25, p 64, para 159.

1291 The following analysis is based on Van Nuffel, 'Does EU Decision-Making Take into Account Regional Interests?' in Cloots, De Baere and Sottiaux (eds), *Federalism in the EU*, Hart Publishing 2012, pp 193–94.

inherent in their fundamental structures, political and constitutional, inclusive of regional and local self-government'.[1292] This general obligation for the EU to respect regional autonomy was introduced by the Lisbon Treaty. This provision clearly indicates that regional and local self-government is protected as a part of a Member State's national identity, and not as a self-standing 'regional identity'.[1293] In this respect, Van Nuffel has emphasised that the Treaties do not protect a right for regions to claim autonomy towards the national or European legislator; they only protect the freedom of a Member State to organise its internal State structure in a decentralised or federal manner.[1294] Hence, this interpretation of Article 4(2) still corresponds to the original idea behind the principle of international law which is codified in Article 27 VCLT.

632. Secondly, the principles of subsidiarity and proportionality entail the general obligation for the EU 'to ensure that decisions are taken as closely as possible to the citizens of the Union'.[1295] Article 5 TEU and Protocol No 2 on the application of the principles of subsidiarity and proportionality explicitly refer to the regional and local level. Article 5(3) TEU states that pursuant to the principle of subsidiarity, the Union shall act only if and insofar as the objectives of the action can be better achieved at Union level. Otherwise, it is left to the Member States to take decisions 'either at central level or at regional and local level'.[1296] In accordance with the principle of proportionality, Union action cannot go beyond what is necessary to achieving the Treaties' objectives.[1297] Article 5 of Protocol No 2 provides that proposals of directives should assess 'its implications for the rules to be put in place by Member States, including, where necessary, the regional legislation'. Moreover, any burden falling upon 'the Union, national governments, regional or local authorities, economic operators and citizens' must be considered when drafting legislative acts.[1298]

Van Nuffel has drawn attention to the fact that 'regional authorities are mentioned at the same level as any other authority of the Member State'; hence, their interest should also only be taken into account to the same extent as the interests of other actors.[1299] Furthermore, he emphasised that the proportionality

1292 See more in Cloots, 'National Identity and the European Court of Justice', Dissertation, KU Leuven 2013.

1293 Van Nuffel, 'Does EU Decision-Making Take into Account Regional Interests?' in Cloots, De Baere and Sottiaux (eds), *Federalism in the EU*, Hart Publishing 2012, p 193.

1294 Ibid 193 and 195.

1295 Preamble Protocol No 2 on the application of the principles of subsidiarity and proportionality.

1296 Article 5(3) TEU.

1297 Article 5(4) TEU.

1298 Article 5 Protocol No 2.

1299 Van Nuffel, 'Does EU Decision-Making Take into Account Regional Interests?' in Cloots, De Baere and Sottiaux (eds), *Federalism in the EU*, Hart Publishing 2012, p 194.

principle does not require that EU legislation takes into account each possible difference that would exist between Member States or between regions.[1300] By contrast, the proportionality principle is only violated where ignoring certain particularities of regions or Member States would render the EU legislation at issue inappropriate to achieving its objective, or when its objective could be also achieved by means of measures that better accommodate these particularities or that are less onerous.[1301]

633. Finally, the Treaties also require that the Union takes regional differences into account in different domains.[1302] Van Nuffel has identified the different concerns underlying these provisions.[1303] He pointed out that the need to respect regional differences in economic policies may be inspired by the need to ensure the efficiency of actions at Union level.[1304] Taking regional differences into account may also aim to respect the region's cultural diversity as well as to leave regional politically sensitive issues untouched.[1305] Van Nuffel has emphasised that, in all of those areas, the 'Treaty provisions require the EU institutions to account for regional differences as a matter of fact' rather than requiring the respect of regional autonomy in the sense of taking the interest of a particular region as defined by that region itself into account.[1306]

2. ECJ'S CASE LAW ON REVERSE DISCRIMINATION IN A FEDERAL STATE CONTEXT

634. This section discusses the Court's case law on reverse discrimination in a context in which self-governing powers are allocated to regional or local entities. In particular, in the *Flemish Care Insurance* case, the ECJ had the opportunity to take a position on reverse discrimination in a federal State context since the Flemish Decree at issue excluded only those Belgian nationals falling under the jurisdiction of another regional authority of Belgium. Since the *Flemish Care Insurance* case is the only case in which the ECJ had to rule on a legislative measure of a regional authority which established itself a specific situation of reverse discrimination to date, it will be analysed extensively.

1300 Ibid. 1301 Ibid.

1302 See for instance the disparities in employment in the various regions (Articles 46(d) and 91(2) TFEU) and the diversity in various agricultural regions (Article 39(2)(a) TFEU). Article 167(1) TFEU determines that 'The Union shall contribute to the flowering of the cultures of the Member States, while respecting their national and regional diversity and at the same time bringing the common cultural heritage to the fore'.

1303 Van Nuffel, 'Does EU Decision-Making Take into Account Regional Interests?' in Cloots, De Baere and Sottiaux (eds), *Federalism in the EU*, Hart Publishing 2012, pp 193–94.

1304 Ibid p 193. 1305 Ibid pp 193–94. 1306 Ibid p 194.

635. Next, the section will examine two cases in which the specific situation of reverse discrimination (may) result from the ECJ's judgment of finding an infringement of Union law regarding cross-border situations, rather than from the regional authority's legislative measure. The *Las* and *Libert* judgments will be discussed to this end.

636. The three ECJ judgments discussed in this section concern Belgium's complex State structure, which consist of both communities and regions.[1307] In particular, Belgium consists of three communities: the Flemish, the French and the German (-speaking) communities.[1308] These communities are competent in cultural, educational, personal and linguistic matters.[1309] Moreover, Belgium is composed of three regions: the Flemish region, the Walloon Region and Brussels-Capital Region and which partially territorially overlap with the communities.[1310] The regions have a wide range of competences, mainly economic ones.[1311] Finally, four linguistic regions exist within Belgium: the Dutch-speaking region, the French-speaking region, the bilingual Brussels-Capital region and the German-speaking region.[1312]

2.1. *FLEMISH CARE INSURANCE* CASE: SPECIFIC SITUATION OF REVERSE DISCRIMINATION AS A DIRECT CONSEQUENCE OF THE FLEMISH DECREE

637. By the Decree of 30 March 1999, the Flemish community organised a system of care insurance covering non-medical assistance and services for people suffering from serious and prolonged disability.[1313] The initial Decree imposed obligations and conferred entitlements on the basis of a residence criterion. People residing in the Dutch-speaking region were obliged to participate in the insurance scheme; persons residing in the bilingual Brussels-Capital region were allowed to participate if they so choose.

1307 For an overview, in English, of the Belgian federal state structure see Feyen, *Beyond Federal Dogmatics*, Lund University Publications 2013, pp 60–66 and Peeters, 'The Federal Structure: Kingdom, Regions and Communities' in Craenen (ed), *The Institutions of Federal Belgium: An Introduction to Belgian Public Law*, Acco 1996, pp 55–69.

1308 Article 2 Belgian Constitution. The Dutch, French and German texts of the Belgian Constitution refer to '*gemeenschappen*', '*communautés*' and '*Gemeinschaften*' respectively.

1309 Articles 127–30 Belgian Constitution.

1310 Article 3 Belgian Constitution. The Dutch, French and German texts of the Belgian Constitution refer to '*gewesten*', '*régions*' and '*Regionen*' respectively.

1311 Article 134 Belgian Constitution and Article 6 Special Law governing institutional reform of 8 August 1980.

1312 Article 4 Belgian Constitution. The Dutch, French and German texts of the Belgian Constitution refer to '*taalgebieden*', '*régions linguistiques*' and '*Sprachgebiete*' respectively.

1313 Decreet van 30 maart 1999 houdende de organisatie van de zorgverzekering, *BS* 28 mei 1999 ('Care Insurance Decree').

638. In response to the objections by the European Commission, on the basis of a violation of Regulation 1408/71[1314] and the principles of free movement within the European Union, the scope of application of the Flemish Care Insurance Decree has been extended to residents of an EU Member State who do not live in Belgium, but who work in the Dutch-speaking region or in the bilingual Brussels-Capital region.[1315] The consequence of this amendment was that residents from another EU Member State who work in the Dutch-speaking region or in the bilingual region of Brussels-Capital respectively, had to or could participate in the care insurance system, while people living in the French- or German-speaking regions, but who worked in the Dutch-speaking region or in the bilingual region of Brussels-Capital did not have the opportunity to do so. The governments of the French community and the Walloon region challenged the Care Insurance Decree before the Belgian Constitutional Court.[1316] The latter decided to refer questions to the Court of Justice for a preliminary ruling.

1314 Regulation (EEC) No 1408/71 of the Council of 14 June 1971 on the application of social security schemes to employed persons and their families moving within the Community. The regulation uses the criterion of *lex loci laboris* for the determination of its scope of application.

1315 [Decreet van 30 april 2004 houdende de wijziging van het decreet van 30 maart 1999, *BS* 9 juni 2004]. Article 4 of the Decree of 30 March 1999, as amended by the Decree of 30 April 2004, defines as follows the classes of persons who must or may be affiliated to the care insurance scheme: '§1. Any person residing within the Dutch-speaking region must join a care insurance scheme approved by this Decree. …

§2. Any person residing within the bilingual region of Brussels-Capital may on a voluntary basis join a care insurance scheme approved by this Decree.

§2bis Any person referred to in paragraphs 1 and 2 to whom, on the basis of the rules governing the law applicable under Regulation (EEC) No 1408/71, the social security scheme of another Member State of the European Union or of another State party to the European Economic Area applies as of right shall not fall within the scope of this Decree.

§2ter Any person not residing in Belgium to whom, on the basis of the rules governing the applicable law under Regulation (EEC) No 1408/71, the social security scheme in Belgium applies as of right because of his employment in the Dutch-speaking region must join a care insurance scheme approved by this Decree. The provisions of this Decree concerning persons referred to in paragraph 1 shall apply by analogy.

Any person not residing in Belgium to whom, on the basis of the rules governing the applicable law under Regulation (EEC) No 1408/71, the social security scheme in Belgium applies as of right because of his employment in the bilingual region of Brussels-Capital may elect to join a care insurance scheme approved by this Decree. The provisions of this Decree concerning persons referred to in paragraph 2 shall apply by analogy.'

Hence, the residence criterion remained the main criterion, but was complemented with the criterion of *lex loci laboris* for persons not living in Belgium. See also *Arbitragehof* 19 April 2006, no 51/2006.

1316 Then called the Court of Arbitration. On 7 May 2007, the name of the Court was changed, by amendment of the Belgian Constitution, to the *Cour constitutionnelle/Grondwettelijk Hof/Verfassungsgerichtshof* (Constitutional Court) *BS* 8 May 2007, 25101 and 25102.

2.1.1. *The ECJ's* Flemish Care Insurance *Judgment*

639. In its judgment of 1 April 2008, the Court of Justice distinguished between persons who work in the Dutch-speaking region or the bilingual Brussels-Capital region and who do not qualify for the advantages of the care insurance since they are living in another part of the national territory depending on whether or not they have used their right to free movement.[1317]

640. On the one hand, the Court ruled explicitly that Union law does not apply to Belgian citizens who work in the Dutch-speaking region or in the bilingual region of Brussels-Capital, but who live in the French- or German-speaking region and have never exercised their freedom to move within the European Union, since this constitutes a purely internal situation.[1318] The Court, however, remarked that the 'interpretation of provisions of [Union] law might possibly be of use to the national court, having regard too to situations classed as purely internal, in particular if the law of the Member State concerned were to require every national of that State to be allowed to enjoy the same rights as those which a national of another Member State would derive from [Union] law in a situation considered to be comparable by that court.'[1319]

641. On the other hand, it may be that employed or self-employed workers who fall within the ambit of Union law are excluded from the care insurance scheme, that is, as well as citizens of other EU Member States who work in the Dutch-speaking region or the bilingual Brussels-Capital region but who live in the French- or German-speaking region, as Belgian citizens in the same situation who have made use of their right to freedom of movement.[1320] The Court of Justice considered that the Articles 45 and 49 TFEU 'militate against any national measure which, even though applicable without discrimination on grounds of nationality, is capable of hindering or rendering less attractive the exercise by [Union] nationals of the fundamental freedoms guaranteed by the Treaty'.[1321] The Court ruled that *in casu* the national legislation constitutes a restriction of the fundamental freedoms, since the migrant workers, who pursue or contemplate the pursuit of employment or self-employment in the Dutch-speaking region or Brussels-Capital region either suffer the loss of eligibility for the benefits of the care insurance or are limited in their choice of the place to which they transfer their residence.[1322]

642. According to well-established case law, national measures that hinder the exercise of fundamental freedoms guaranteed by the Treaty may be allowed if

1317 ECJ case C-212/06 *Flemish Care Insurance* [2008] ECR I-1683, paras 35–36.
1318 Ibid paras 37–38.
1319 Ibid para 40.
1320 Ibid para 41.
1321 Ibid para 45.
1322 Ibid para 48.

three cumulative conditions are met: they pursue a legitimate objective in the public interest, are appropriate to ensuring the attainment of that objective and do not go beyond what is necessary to attain the objective pursued.[1323] As justification, the Flemish government submitted that the residence requirement is inherent to the division of competences within the Belgian federal State and, more particularly, that the Flemish community has no competence with respect to persons residing in one of Belgium's other linguistic regions.[1324] The Court of Justice, however, rejected this argument by referring to its established case law that 'a Member State cannot plead provisions, practices or situations prevailing in its domestic legal order, including those resulting from the constitutional organisation of that State, to justify the failure to observe obligations arising under [Union] law'.[1325] The Court decided that the exclusion of persons who work in the Dutch-speaking region or in the bilingual Brussels-Capital region and who live in the French- or German-speaking community from a social security scheme and entitlement to the benefits provided by that scheme was contrary to the free movement of workers (Article 45 TFEU) and establishment (Article 49 TFEU), insofar as these people have made use of their right to freedom of movement within the European Union.[1326]

2.1.2. *Analysis of the ECJ's* Flemish Care Insurance *Judgment*

643. Legal scholars have discussed the ECJ's judgment on the Flemish care insurance scheme extensively.[1327] The analysis here will focus on two important criticisms: the insufficient respect for the constitutional traditions of the Member States and the excessive interpretation of the scope of application of EU free movement rights.

644. First, the ECJ's judgment has been criticised for the lack of respect paid to the Belgian internal division of competences.[1328] Regarding those situations falling within the ambit of Union law, the ECJ considered that

---

1323 Ibid para 55 and references there.

1324 Ibid para 57.

1325 Ibid para 58. See above nn 625–29.

1326 Ibid para 60.

1327 See inter alia Am Ende, 'But Not the Walloons! Internal Quarrel – or a Case for the Court?' [2008] *ELR* 114, 114–17; Feyen, 'Zorgen voor morgen: implicaties van het arrest van het Grondwettelijk Hof over discriminaties in de Vlaamse zorgverzekering: Een juridische veldslag' [2009] *TBPK* 169, 169–174; Storme, 'Vlaamse Zorgverzekering. Een lange weg naar een geschikte aanknopingsfactor' [2008] *NjW* 614–23; Van Elsuwege and Adam, 'The Limits of Constitutional Dialogue for the Prevention of Reverse Discrimination' (2009) 5 *EuConst* 327–95 and Velaers and Vanpraet, 'De materiële en territoriale bevoegdheidsverdeling inzake sociale zekerheid en sociale bijstand (II)' [2009] *TBP* 195, 195–218.

1328 Cloots, 'Germs of Pluralist Judicial Adjudication: Advocaten Voor de Wereld and Other References from the Belgian Constitutional Court' (2010) 47 *CMLRev* 645, 663.

the residence requirement in the Flemish Decree constituted an unjustified obstacle to freedom of movement for workers and of establishment. The Court simply rejected the argument given by the Flemish government concerning the requirements inherent in the division of competences within the Belgian federal structure by referring to its settled case law that 'a Member State cannot plead provisions, practices or situations prevailing in its domestic legal order, including those resulting from the constitutional organisation of that State, to justify the failure to observe obligations arising under [Union] law'.[1329] However, Cloots has argued that the ECJ in this way 'disregarded constitutional provisions reflecting a compromise that was achieved after a period of deep national crisis and difficult negotiations, a compromise vital to the continued existence of the Belgian State'.[1330] She considered that this rejection, in only one paragraph, is striking since the ECJ had attached greater weight to national constitutional rules when balancing whether national measures capable of hindering the exercise of fundamental freedoms guaranteed by the Treaty can be justified in previous judgments.[1331] Cloots has admitted that in those earlier judgments, the ECJ relied less on the constitutional status of these provisions, and more on the values which they enshrine, in particular the protection of fundamental rights and an official language.[1332] Nevertheless, and especially in the light of Article 4(2) TEU regarding the EU's respect for regional and local levels of self-government, she argued that the ECJ should clarify the reasons for not attaching the same weight to national constitutional provisions concerning State structure than to fundamental rights or language requirements.[1333]

645. Secondly, the scope of application of the Union provisions on free movement as interpreted by the Court in its judgment of 1 April 2008 is analysed. In that respect, the ECJ started its reasoning by referring to its settled case law that the Union provisions on fundamental freedoms do not only militate against national measures which discriminate on grounds of nationality, but which are also capable of hindering or rendering the exercise by Union nationals of the fundamental freedoms guaranteed by the Treaties less attractive.[1334] The Court

---

1329 ECJ case C-212/06 *Flemish Care Insurance* [2008] ECR I-1683, para 58.

1330 Cloots, 'Germs of Pluralist Judicial Adjudication: Advocaten Voor de Wereld and Other References from the Belgian Constitutional Court' (2010) 47 *CMLRev* 645, 663.

1331 Ibid 663–64, referring to the cases ECJ case C-112/00 *Schmidberger* [2003] ECR I-5659 and ECJ case C-36/02 *Omega* [2004] ECR I-9609 (concerning fundamental rights) and ECJ case C-379/87 *Groener* [1989] ECR 3967 (concerning language requirements).

1332 Cloots, 'Germs of Pluralist Judicial Adjudication: Advocaten Voor de Wereld and Other References from the Belgian Constitutional Court' (2010) 47 *CMLRev* 645, 664. See ECJ case C-112/00 *Schmidberger* [2003] ECR I-5659, para 74; ECJ case C-36/02 *Omega* [2004] ECR I-9609, paras 34–35 and ECJ case C-379/87 *Groener* [1989] ECR 3967, para 19.

1333 Cloots, 'Germs of Pluralist Judicial Adjudication: Advocaten Voor de Wereld and Other References from the Belgian Constitutional Court' (2010) 47 *CMLRev* 645, 664.

1334 ECJ case C-212/06 *Flemish Care Insurance* [2008] ECR I-1683, para 45 and references there.

ruled that the Flemish Care Insurance Decree constituted these restrictive effects, since Union citizens might be discouraged from making use of their freedom of movement and from leaving their Member State of origin to stay in or to move to Belgium, 'by reason of the fact that moving *to certain parts of Belgium* would cause them to lose the opportunity of eligibility for the benefits which they might otherwise have claimed'.[1335] The ECJ added that the restrictive effects of the Flemish Care Insurance Decree's residence requirement were not too indirect and uncertain to be considered as obstacles contrary to Articles 45 and 49 TFEU.[1336] Furthermore, the Court recalled that according to its case law, the Treaty articles on free movement prohibit 'any restriction, even minor'.[1337]

646. It can be seen from the above that the ECJ interprets the concept of restriction on fundamental freedoms in a very extensive manner. Part I of this text noted the risks of an overly broad interpretation of the concept of restriction.[1338] What is remarkable about the *Flemish Care Insurance* case is the fact that the ECJ also considers a limitation of the choice of the place of residence *within* a Member State to be a limitation of the EU free movement provisions.[1339] In the light of our working hypothesis, this can be seen as being an indication that an overcompensation by Union law was at stake. In particular, it is questionable whether the limitation of the choice of the place of residence *within* a Member State is considered to be a disadvantage resulting from the exercise of free movement that should be remedied.

647. Moreover, it has been argued that the ECJ took the criterion of the exercise of free movement out of the context in which it was originally developed.[1340] In the cases to which the ECJ referred, Ms Scholz, Mr Terhoeve and Mr Hartmann were deprived of a benefit in their Member State of origin either because they had previously worked in another Member State[1341] or because they had moved to another Member State.[1342] The ECJ ruled that the national legislation in question constituted either an unjustified indirect discrimination[1343] or an obstacle to

---

1335 Ibid paras 47–48 (emphasis added).

1336 Ibid para 51.

1337 Ibid para 52 and references there.

1338 Above nn 206–19.

1339 Velaers and Vanpraet, 'De materiële en territoriale bevoegdheidsverdeling inzake sociale zekerheid en sociale bijstand (II)' [2009] *TBP* 195, 205. See also Verschueren, 'De regionalisering van de sociale zekerheid in België in het licht van het arrest van het Europees Hof van Justitie inzake de Vlaamse Zorgverzekering' [2008] *BTSZ* 177, 206–07.

1340 Cloots, 'Germs of Pluralist Judicial Adjudication: Advocaten Voor de Wereld and Other References from the Belgian Constitutional Court' (2010) 47 *CMLRev* 645, 663.

1341 ECJ case C-419/92 *Scholz* [1994] ECR I-505, paras 3–4 and ECJ case C-18/95 *Terhoeve* [1999] ECR I-345, para 28.

1342 ECJ case C-212/05 *Hartmann* [2007] ECR I-6303, para 18.

1343 ECJ case C-419/92 *Scholz* [1994] ECR I-505, paras 11–12 and ECJ case C-212/05 *Hartmann* [2007] ECR I-6303, paras 30–37.

the freedom of movement for workers[1344] in these cases. In *Scholz*, *Terhoeve* and *Hartmann*, the previous exercise of EU free movement rights constituted a relevant cross-border element precisely because of the fact that Ms Sholz, Mr Terhoeve and Mr Hartmann had worked or had moved to another Member State which resulted in their being denied a certain advantage under national law. The idea behind this, from the perspective of Union law, is that a Member State cannot treat its own nationals less favourably in the event that they have used their right of free movement within the EU since this less favourable treatment could dissuade Union citizens from effectively making use of their freedom of movement.

Cloots has argued that in the *Flemish Care Insurance* case, by contrast, the ECJ used the criterion of previous exercise of free movement as 'a trigger for' the application of Union free movement rights.[1345] She concluded that the ECJ used an 'arbitrary criterion for distinguishing situations which are not purely internal and where, hence, a residence condition for affiliation to the Flemish Care Insurance Scheme is illegitimate' in this case.[1346] In other words, Cloots appears to question the lack of a causal link between the cross-border element and the right invoked under Union law, as discussed in Part I.[1347]

648. Finally, it has been argued that the Court could have chosen an alternative reasoning. In particular, it has been considered that the ECJ could have followed its case law that migration between Member States can lead to better as well as to less favourable social protection depending on the Member State's social security system in which the person is going to work.[1348] In the absence of harmonisation, a difference in treatment in social protection between Member States cannot, as such, be considered as an impediment of the free movement within the EU.[1349] Hence, in the light of the working hypothesis, this alternative reasoning could have avoided an overcompensation by Union law.

1344 ECJ case C-18/95 *Terhoeve* [1999] ECR I-345, paras 39–41.

1345 Cloots, 'Germs of Pluralist Judicial Adjudication: Advocaten Voor de Wereld and Other References from the Belgian Constitutional Court' (2010) 47 *CMLRev* 645, 663: 'Consequently, the fact a person exercised his right to free movement in the past was converted from a reason for which that person may not be deprived of a certain advantage into a trigger for the application of EU law and for the entitlement to a benefit that would otherwise have been refused to him.'

1346 Ibid 662–63.

1347 Above nn 186–91.

1348 Verschueren, 'De regionalisering van de sociale zekerheid in België in het licht van het arrest van het Europees Hof van Justitie inzake de Vlaamse Zorgverzekering' [2008] *BTSZ* 177, 207, referring to ECJ joined cases C-393/99 and C-394/99 *Inasti e.a.* [2002] ECR I-2829, paras 50–51. See also Velaers and Vanpraet, 'De materiële en territoriale bevoegdheidsverdeling inzake sociale zekerheid en sociale bijstand (II)' [2009] *TBP* 195, 205.

1349 ECJ joined cases C-393/99 and C-394/99 *Inasti e.a.* [2002] ECR I-2829, paras 50–51; Preamble Regulation 883/2004, para 4 and Opinion AG Maduro in C-3/08, para 17.

649. The Belgian Constitutional Court's subsequent judgment on the Flemish Care Insurance Decree will be examined in further detail in Chapter 7. At this point, however, it suffices to say that the exact combination of the reasoning of the ECJ and the Belgian Constitutional Court resulted in a complex and specific case of reverse discrimination. In particular, the final result was that the only category of persons who could not benefit from the advantages of the Flemish Care Insurance were Belgian citizens working in Flanders or Brussels, but living in the French- or German-speaking region and who never exercised their right to free movement.

2.2. SPECIFIC SITUATION OF REVERSE DISCRIMINATION AS A POSSIBLE CONSEQUENCE OF THE ECJ'S *LAS* AND *LIBERT* JUDGMENTS

2.2.1. Las *Case Regarding the Flemish Decree on Use of Languages*

2.2.1.1. ECJ's *Las* Judgment

650. Mr Las, a Dutch citizen resident in the Netherlands, was employed as a Chief Financial Officer for an unlimited period by PSA Antwerp, a company established in Antwerp (Belgium) but which belongs to a multinational group operating port terminals whose registered office is in Singapore. His contract of employment, which was drafted in English, stipulated that Mr Las was to carry out his work principally in Belgium although some work would be carried out from the Netherlands.

Four years later, by way of a letter in English, Mr Las was dismissed with immediate effect. Pursuant to Article 8 of his employment contract, PSA Antwerp made a 'payment in lieu of notice' equal to three months' salary and an additional payment equal to six months' salary to Mr Las. However, Mr Las claimed a considerably higher amount in compensation. As the parties failed to reach an agreement, Mr Las brought an action before the Labour Court of Antwerp.

651. Mr Las argued that the Flemish Decree on Use of Languages provides for the use of Dutch in undertakings whose place of business is established in the Dutch-speaking part of Belgium. In particular, he asserted that Article 8 of his employment contract, which was drafted in English, was vitiated by absolute nullity because it infringed upon the provisions of the Flemish Decree on Use of Languages.

Conversely, PSA Antwerp contended that the Decree cannot be applied to situations in which a person exercises his right of freedom of movement as a worker. According to PSA Antwerp, the Decree constitutes an obstacle to that fundamental freedom which cannot be justified by overriding reasons of general interest. PSA Antwerp added that in the present case the employment contract had to be respected because it reflected the will of the parties expressed in a language intelligible to each party, namely English, especially since the CEO of PSA Antwerp was unfamiliar with Dutch. The Labour Court of Antwerp decided to stay proceedings and refer the question to the ECJ of whether the freedom of movement for workers within the EU (Article 45 TFEU) precludes legislation such as the Flemish Decree on Use of Languages.

652. The ECJ made two preliminary remarks. First of all, the ECJ pointed out that the circumstances in the main proceedings fell within the scope of Article 45 TFEU, since the case concerned an employment contract concluded between a Dutch citizen residing in the Netherlands and a company established in Belgium.[1350] In other words, it considered that the situation at stake was not purely internal. Secondly, the Court stated that workers as well as employers may rely on Article 45 TFEU.[1351] Referring to earlier judgments, the ECJ considered that in order to be genuinely effective, the right of workers to engagement and employment without discrimination necessarily involves the employer's right to engage and to employ them in accordance with the rules on the freedom of movement for workers.[1352]

653. Regarding the existence of a restriction, the ECJ considered that by imposing the use of Dutch in all acts and documents on employment relations, in respect both of Belgian nationals and of foreign nationals employed by undertakings established in the Dutch language region, the Decree in question is prone to have a dissuasive effect on those employees and employers who are unfamiliar with Dutch.[1353] Therefore, the Court found that the Decree on Use of Languages constituted a restriction on the freedom of movement for workers.[1354]

654. The Belgian government named three reasons why the Flemish Decree was required: first, to promote the use of one of its official languages; second, to protect employees by enabling them to examine employment documents in their own language; and third, to ensure the efficacy of administrative and judicial supervision.[1355] Although the ECJ acknowledged that these three objectives were

1350 ECJ case C-202/11 *Las*, para. 17. See also ECJ case C-202/11 *Las*, Opinion AG Jääskinen, paras 22–23.

1351 ECJ case C-202/11 *Las*, para 18.

1352 Ibid and references there to earlier judgments. See also ECJ case C-202/11 *Las*, Opinion AG Jääskinen, para 24.

1353 ECJ case C-202/11 *Las*, paras 21–22.

1354 Ibid para 22.

1355 Ibid para 24.

legitimate interests which can, in principle, justify a restriction on the exercise of fundamental freedoms recognised in the Treaty, it ruled that the legislation at issue is not proportionate to those objectives.[1356] The Court considered that the penalty in the present case, the absolute nullity of that contract, went beyond what was strictly necessary to obtaining the aforementioned objectives.[1357] The permission to draft a second version of this contract in a language known to all parties concerned would be appropriate and less prejudicial to the freedom of movement for workers.[1358] The Court decided that Article 45 TFEU precludes 'legislation of a federated entity of a Member State … which requires all employers whose established place of business is located in that entity's territory to draft cross-border employment contracts exclusively in the official language of that federated entity, failing which the contracts are to be declared null and void by the national courts of their own motion.'[1359]

2.2.1.2. Analysis of the ECJ's *Las* Judgment

655. In the light of our working hypothesis, it can be argued that a clear case of compensation by Union law was at stake here. In particular, imposing the use of Dutch upon all employment relations for undertakings whose place of business is established in the Dutch-speaking region was undoubtedly a restriction to the use of the rights of free movement to those Union citizens who are unfamiliar with Dutch. Moreover, a heavy penalty was provided in cases of non-compliance; that is to say, the absolute nullity of the contract. Accordingly, ruling that Article 45 TFEU precludes such a legislation as that at issue in the main proceedings was a proportional compensation for the disadvantage resulting from the exercise of free movement.

656. The ECJ's *Las* judgment may result in a specific situation of reverse discrimination, depending on the reaction at the Belgian or Flemish levels, since the Court of Justice explicitly ruled on cross-border employment contracts alone. The subsequent judgment by the referring court in the main proceedings is less important regarding the emergence of a specific situation of reverse discrimination, since it can settle the dispute in the main proceedings on the basis of the ECJ's *Las* judgment – the referring court itself limited its question, as to whether the legislation at issue was contrary to the freedom of movement within the EU, regarding only those 'employment relations with an international character'.[1360] Consequently, immediately after the ECJ's *Las* judgment, the

---

[1356] Ibid paras 25–33.
[1357] Ibid para 33.
[1358] Ibid para 32.
[1359] Ibid para 34.
[1360] Ibid para 15.

Flemish Decree on Use of Languages only applies to employment relations with a purely Belgian character.

Next, it was possible, in theory, that this difference in treatment was challenged before the Belgian Constitutional Court or that the Flemish Parliament decided – in the light of the ECJ's *Las* judgment and possibly also in the light of the Belgian Constitution – to modify the Decree both for cross-border and purely Belgian employment relations. As will be discussed in Chapter 7, the Flemish Parliament decided to adapt the Decree only for cross-border situations and, accordingly, created a specific situation of reverse discrimination.

2.2.2. Libert *Case Regarding the Flemish Decree on 'Living in Your Own Region'*

2.2.2.1. ECJ's *Libert* Judgment

657. The *Libert* case concerned the Decree of the Flemish Region of 27 March 2009 on land and real estate policy and, in particular, Book 5 thereof which is entitled 'Living in Your Own Region'.[1361] In particular, Article 5(2)(1) provides that a specific condition applies to the transfer of land and buildings constructed thereupon when they are located both within a 'residential extension area'[1362] and in a target commune which appears on the most recent list published in the *Belgian Official Journal*.[1363] The land and the buildings may be transferred only to persons who have, in the opinion of a provincial assessment committee, a sufficient connection with the commune. The special transfer requirement expires 20 years after the initial transfer.

According to the second paragraph of Article 5(2)(1), a person has a sufficient connection with the commune if he or she can demonstrate one or more of the following three conditions. The first condition is that the person interested in purchasing or leasing the immovable property has been continuously resident in the target commune or in a neighbouring commune for at least six years prior to the transfer. The second alternative condition requires that the prospective buyer or tenant must, on the date of the transfer, carry out activities in the commune in question which occupy on average at least half a working week. According to the third alternative condition, the prospective buyer or tenant must have a professional, family, social or economic connection with the commune as a result of a significant circumstance of long duration. Article 5(2)(3) Flemish Decree provides that the provincial assessment committee and third parties who

1361 *BS* 15 May 2009, 37 408. Case C-203/11 also concerns Book 4 of this Decree, but those questions will not be discussed here.

1362 Laid down by the Royal Decree of 28 December 1972.

1363 In particular the Order of the Flemish Government of 19 June 2009.

are adversely affected may apply for the annulment of a transfer which has taken place in disregard of the special condition.

658. Book 5 of the Flemish Decree on Land and Real Estate Policy was challenged before the Belgian Constitutional Court in a procedure for annulment. The Belgian Constitutional Court decided to stay proceedings and refer the question to the ECJ as to whether 'Articles 21 TFEU, 45 TFEU, 49 TFEU, 56 TFEU and 63 TFEU and Articles 22 and 24 of Directive 2004/38 preclude legislation, such as Book 5 Flemish Decree, which makes the transfer of immovable property in the target communes subject to verification, by a provincial assessment committee, that there exists a "sufficient connection" between the prospective buyer or tenant and those communes'.[1364]

659. As a preliminary remark, the Flemish government asserted that the EU provisions relied upon by the applicants were not applicable since the actions in the main proceedings concerned purely internal situations. That is to say, the Belgian nationals were resident in Belgium and the undertakings were established under Belgian law. Hence, all the relevant elements were confined within the borders of one Member State.

The ECJ recognised, in principle, this claim referring to its settled case law that 'the Treaty rules governing freedom of movement for persons and the measures adopted to implement them cannot be applied to activities which have no factor linking them with any of the situations governed by EU law and which are confined in all relevant respects within a single Member State'.[1365] However, the Court emphasised that nationals or undertakings of another EU Member State could be affected by the provisions of the Flemish Decree because they may also be interested in purchasing or in long-term leasing immovable property in the areas mentioned above.[1366] Moreover, the Court drew attention to the fact that the questions referred were raised in specific proceedings before the Belgian Constitutional Court, that is, in proceedings for the annulment of a legislative measure of national law.[1367] Since the Flemish Decree applies both to Belgian nationals and to citizens of other Member States, the decision of the Belgian Constitutional Court would also clearly have an effect on nationals from other EU Member States.[1368]

660. Subsequently, the ECJ considered that the specific transfer requirement of a 'sufficient connection' with the target commune not only prevented people

1364 ECJ joined cases C-197/11 and C-203/11 *Libert e.a.*, para 31. The other 11 questions in case C-203/11 will not be discussed here.

1365 ECJ joined cases C-197/11 and C-203/11 *Libert e.a.*, para 33.

1366 Ibid para 34.

1367 Ibid para 35. See also Opinion AG Mazák, para 23.

1368 Ibid.

without this connection with the commune to purchase or rent immovable property, but also deterred Union citizens who own or rent a property in any given commune from leaving them to reside in another Member State or to pursue a professional activity there.[1369] The Court ruled that the provisions of Book 5 of the Flemish Decree obviously constituted restrictions on the fundamental freedoms, as enshrined in Articles 21, 45 and 49 TFEU and Articles 22 and 24 of Directive 2004/38.[1370] The Court also made a finding of restrictions on the free movement of services (Article 56 TFEU) and of capital (Article 63 TFEU).[1371]

661. Next, the Court considered whether the provisions of the Flemish Decree that hindered the exercise of EU fundamental freedom may nevertheless be allowed on the condition that these provisions pursue an overriding reason of general interest, that they are appropriate to the attainment of the objective and that they are proportionate.[1372] In this regard, the Flemish government stated that the rules are intended to guarantee housing in residential extension areas for less affluent local members of the population.[1373] After recognising that social housing policy in a Member State can constitute a legitimate objective in the public interest,[1374] the ECJ considered whether the Flemish Decree was a necessary and appropriate measure thereto.[1375]

662. The Court considered that the 'sufficient connection' with the target commune which the prospective buyer or tenant had to demonstrate before the provincial assessment committee went beyond what is necessary for the attainment of the objective pursued, since the three conditions mentioned in Article 5(2)(1)(2) may also be met by persons with sufficient resources who need no social protection on the property market.[1376] Moreover, the Court pointed out that less restrictive measures could meet the objective pursued.[1377] Finally, and still according to the ECJ, the third condition concerning a significant professional, social or economic connection of long duration was too vague and could not adequately circumscribe discretion of the provincial assessment committee.[1378] The Court concluded that 'Articles 21 TFEU, 45 TFEU, 49 TFEU, 56 TFEU and 63 TFEU and Articles 22 and 24 of Directive 2004/38 preclude legislation, such as Book 5 of the Flemish Decree, which makes the transfer

1369 ECJ joined cases C-197/11 and C-203/11 *Libert e.a.*, paras 39–40.

1370 Ibid para 41.

1371 Ibid paras 42–47.

1372 Ibid para 49.

1373 Ibid paras 50–51. See also the *Travaux préparatoires* mentioned in the referring judgment of the Belgian Constitutional Court, 6 April 2011, no 50/2011, B.65.2.

1374 ECJ joined cases C-197/11 and C-203/11 *Libert e.a.*, para 52.

1375 Ibid paras 53–59.

1376 Ibid paras 54–55.

1377 Ibid para 56.

1378 Ibid paras 57–59.

of immovable property in the target communes subject to verification, by a provincial assessment committee, that there exists a "sufficient connection" between the prospective buyer or tenant and those communes'.[1379]

2.2.2.2. Analysis of the ECJ's *Libert* Judgment

663. In contrast to the *Flemish Care Insurance* case – which concerned a similar situation – the ECJ did not make a distinction in the *Libert* judgment between people who have made use of their right to free movement, and hence fall within the scope of application of Union law, and people who have not made use of their right to free movement, and hence fall under their Member State of origin's national legislation. The most obvious explanation for this is that neither the parties nor the Advocate General invoked this argument.

664. In the *Libert* case, the Court seemed to emphasise the specific nature of the procedure in which the national judge referred: a procedure of annulment of the Flemish Decree. The decision by the Belgian Constitutional Court of whether or not to annul the contested provisions affects not only Belgian citizens and undertakings but also the citizens and undertakings of other EU Member States. In this sense, the *Libert* judgment can be linked to the *Guimont* line of cases, discussed above,[1380] which establish an indirect exception to the purely internal situation doctrine via Article 267 TFEU.

665. In the light of our working hypothesis, it can be argued that the ECJ's *Libert* judgment constitutes a mere compensation by Union law. In particular, requiring a 'sufficient connection' with the target commune not only prevents people without such a connection to purchase or rent immovable property, but also deters Union citizens from owning or renting such a property from residing and working in another Member State. This clearly constitutes a restriction to free movement within the EU. Disapplying the requirement of a 'sufficient connection' in cross-border situations can be considered to be a compensation by Union law since the requirement may have a strong deterring effect from exercising the rights of free movement.

666. As far as cross-border situations are concerned, the Belgian Constitutional Court is bound by the preliminary ruling of the Court and had to annul the Flemish Decree to that extent. However, it depends on the way in which the

---

[1379] Ibid para 60.

[1380] Above nn 137 ff.

Belgian Constitutional Court ruled on purely internal situations whether or not a specific situation of reverse discrimination emerges.

In its judgment of 7 November 2013, the Belgian Court took the ECJ's reasoning in the *Libert* case into consideration. It ruled that Book 5 of the Flemish Decree on Land and Real Estate Policy violated Articles 10 and 11 of the Constitution in combination with Articles 21, 45, 49, 56 and 63 TFEU and Articles 22 and 24 of Directive 2004/38. Since the Constitutional Court did not make a distinction between purely internal situations and those situations falling under Union law, it appears that the contested provisions have been annulled for both types of situation. This judgment of the Belgian Constitutional Court will be discussed in greater detail in Chapter 7, but for now it can be concluded that the combination of the ECJ and the Belgian Constitutional Court's judgments did not result in a specific situation of reverse discrimination.

2.3. ECJ'S CASE LAW ON SPECIFIC SITUATIONS OF REVERSE DISCRIMINATION: TWO CONCLUDING OBSERVATIONS

667. First, is should be pointed out that the application of the working hypothesis, based on compensation or overcompensation, seems perfectly possible in the context of reverse discrimination within a federal state. On the one hand, regarding the *Flemish Care Insurance* case specifically, it has been argued that an overcompensation by Union law was at stake, that is, that the limitation of the choice of place of residence within a Member State should not be considered to be a disadvantage resulting from the exercise of free movement which should be remedied. Nevertheless, the ECJ held that a restriction on the freedom of movement was at stake and that a specific situation of reverse discrimination resulted therefrom. On the basis of our working hypothesis, situations of reverse discrimination resulting from an overcompensation by Union law are problematic and should be solved in the first place at the Union level. The solution here seems to lie in a stricter interpretation of the concept of restriction to freedom of movement within the EU. In particular, the ECJ should not have considered the Flemish Care Insurance scheme to be a restriction to the freedom of movement within the EU.

On the other hand, regarding the *Las* and *Libert* judgments, it has been argued that a compensation by Union law was at stake. Accordingly, the specific situations of reverse discrimination possibly resulting therefrom – depending on the subsequent action taken at the national/regional level – can be considered to be a mere difference in treatment.

668. Secondly, it should be emphasised that in each of the judgments discussed, the ECJ took the Belgian State and not the Dutch-speaking region as the relevant reference frame through which to assess the case. However, if the ECJ had taken the Dutch-speaking region to be the reference framework by which to rule on an alleged restriction on free movement within the EU, then these specific forms of reverse discrimination in a federal State context could not have arisen at Union level. This is an interesting line of thought which will be developed further in the following section.

3. RECOGNITION OF THE AUTONOMY OF REGIONAL AUTHORITIES BY THE ECJ IN THE CONTEXT OF STATE AID

669. In her Opinion in the *Flemish Care Insurance* case, AG Sharpston has emphasised that a paradox exists between the goal of the Union to abolish barriers to freedom of movement between the Member States and the fact that decentralised authorities of Member States may nevertheless establish barriers within that Member State.[1381] Therefore, AG Sharpston proposed, in her Opinion in the *Flemish Care Insurance* case, that we consider the relevant regulatory authority, either the Member States or the decentralised authorities within a Member State, to be the relevant reference framework when ruling on potential barriers to freedom of movement within the EU. She thereby referred to cases of State aid, in which the Court has certainly taken the status of the autonomous infra-State body at issue into account.[1382]

670. The following sections will consider, first, the cases on State aid in which the Court recognised the autonomy which Member States confer on their infra-State bodies. Then, they will proceed to analyse whether the Court limits these kind of considerations to the area of State aid.

3.1. ECJ'S JUDGMENTS ON STATE AID RECOGNISE THE AUTONOMY OF INFRA-STATE BODIES

3.1.1. ECJ's Azores *Judgment*

671. In the case of *Portugal v Commission*, the so-called *Azores* case,[1383] the ECJ considered an autonomous region of a Member State as the relevant

[1381] Opinion AG Sharpston 28 June 2007 in C-212/06, *Flemish Care Insurance*, para 116.
[1382] Ibid fn 67.
[1383] ECJ case C-88/03 *Azores* [2006] ECR I-7115.

reference framework for the first time. The Azores constitutes an autonomous region of Portugal with their own political and administrative bodies.[1384] The autonomous region receives its own tax revenues as well as a part of the State tax revenue.[1385] Moreover, the autonomous region has the right to exercise its own fiscal competence and to adapt national fiscal provisions to regional particularities.[1386] Accordingly, the regional legislative assembly of the Azores has adopted a decree in order to exercise its power of adaptation of State taxes to the region's specificities.[1387] In particular, the Decree provides for reductions in the rates of income and corporation tax that are applicable to all economic agents, natural and legal persons, insofar as they are subject to income or corporation tax in the Azores region.

672. After classifying the measures as State aid according to the procedure of Article 108(2) TFEU, the Commission concluded that the tax reductions applicable to firms that operate outside the financial sector were compatible with the internal market.[1388] In contrast, the reductions regarding undertakings operating in the financial sector were declared incompatible with the internal market and Portugal was ordered to take all necessary measures to recover the aid made available for this sector. Portugal lodged an action for annulment against the Commission's Decision before the ECJ.[1389]

673. Since Article 107(1) TFEU prohibits State aid 'favouring certain undertakings or the production of certain goods', the ECJ considered that it was appropriate to examine, first, whether the Azores tax reductions were selective in nature. This was also precisely the bone of contention between the Commission and Portugal.

According to the Commission, it clearly follows from the Treaties that the selectivity of a measure must be determined with reference to the national

---

1384 Article 6(2) Portuguese Constitution of 2 April 1976, as amended.

1385 Article 227(1)j Portuguese Constitution.

1386 Article 227(1)i Portuguese Constitution and Law no 13/98 of 24 February 1998 on the finances of the autonomous regions [Lei No 13/98 de 24 de Fevereiro. Lei de Finanças das Regiões Autónomas, Diário da República I, series A, No 46, of 24 February 1998, 746]. The Portuguese State defined the conditions for this regional financial autonomy by Law 13/98 of 24 February 1998 on the finances of the autonomous regions [Lei No 13/98 de 24 de Fevereiro. Lei de Finanças das Regiões Autónomas, Diário da República I, series A, No 46, of 24 February 1998, 746].

1387 Regional Legislative Decree No 2/99/A of 20 January 1999, as amended by Regional Legislative Decree No 33/99/A of 30 December 1999.

1388 According to the Commission, it falls under the derogation in Article 107(3)(a) TFEU.

1389 The focus here is on the first plea of the Portuguese government in support of its action, ECJ case C-88/03 *Azores* [2006] ECR I-7115, paras 38–85.

framework, in this case the Portuguese territory.[1390] Hence, the Commission argued that the advantages reserved for undertakings operating in the Azores region were selective in nature. In contrast, the Portuguese government submitted that the reference framework had to involve the region concerned where the scope of tax concessions is limited to the area of jurisdiction of the competent regional authority.[1391] Portugal argued that the reduction of income and corporation tax was not a selective measure, but a general one, since the reduction was applicable to all undertakings subject to tax in that region.[1392]

674. The ECJ agreed with Portugal's position. The Court ruled that 'the reference framework need not necessarily be defined within the limits of the Member State concerned, so that a measure conferring an advantage in only one part of the national territory is not selective on that ground alone for the purposes of Article [107(1) TFEU]'.[1393] The Court pointed out that it may be that by its autonomous status, in relation to the central government, an infra-State body plays a fundamental role in defining the political and economic conditions in which the undertakings operate.[1394] In those areas it is the infra-State body that constitutes the relevant context.[1395] The Court explicitly rejected the Commission's argument that taking the region to be the relevant reference framework would be inadmissible, according to the wording of the Treaty and to the well-established case law in this field.[1396]

675. The court defined three requirements that must be satisfied in order for a decision taken by a regional or local authority to be regarded as an exercise of sufficiently autonomous powers.[1397] First, the infra-State body must have an independent political and administrative status. Secondly, the decision must have been adopted without the central government being able to intervene in the content of the decision directly. Thirdly, the financial consequences of a tax concession for undertakings in the region may not be offset by aid or subsidies from other regions or by the central government. Hence, the infra-State body should assume the political and financial consequences of its measures.

Regarding the tax concessions adopted by the Azores region, the Court held that they did not fulfil all the requirements set out above since the tax reductions were offset by a financing mechanism which was managed at the level of the central government.[1398] Thus the Court concluded that the tax concessions at issue were selective measures.[1399]

[1390] Ibid para 42.
[1391] Ibid para 39.
[1392] Ibid.
[1393] Ibid para 57.
[1394] Ibid para 58.
[1395] Ibid.
[1396] Ibid para 59.
[1397] Ibid paras 67–68.
[1398] Ibid paras 69–78.
[1399] Ibid para 79.

3.1.2. *ECJ's* Trabajadores de la Rioja *Judgment*

676. In the *Trabajadores de la Rioja* case, which concerned a similar issue, the three requirements set out in *Azores* were developed further. The ECJ replied to a question referred by the Supreme Court of Justice of the Autonomous Community of the Basque Country regarding tax measures of the three 'historical territories' of Vizcaya, Alava and Guipuzcoa ('the foral authorities') which belong to the Basque Country's autonomous community. The measures at issue provided for a tax rate lower than the basic rate in Spanish national legislation and for tax concessions which did not exist in Spanish national legislation.[1400] The referring court asked whether those measures which affected the jurisdiction of the respective infra-State body had to be considered in the light of Article 107(1) TFEU on State aid as selective and, accordingly, had to be notified to the Commission on the basis of Article 108(3) TFEU.[1401]

677. Referring to the *Azores* judgment, the ECJ confirmed that in order to determine whether the measure at issue is selective, the reference framework does not necessarily need to be defined within the limits of the Member State concerned.[1402] If a measure confers an advantage upon only one part of the national territory, then it cannot on that ground alone be considered as a selective measure in the context of Article 107 TFEU.[1403] Subsequently, the Court clarified the three criteria set out in the *Azores* judgment and emphasised that it is up to the national judge to examine and to decide whether they are satisfied in the main proceedings.[1404]

678. First, the Court made clear that when the three criteria set out in the *Azores* judgment are fulfilled, the infra-State body plays a fundamental role in the definition of the political and economic environment of the undertakings which operate on the territory within its competence.[1405] The Court explicitly rejected the Commission's contention that a precondition exists for the operation of the three conditions set out in the *Azores* judgment.[1406] The Court emphasised that

---

1400 ECJ joined cases C-428/06 to C-434/06 *Trabajadores de la Rioja* [2008] ECR I-6747, paras 21–25 contain the references to the tax legislation at issue.

1401 Ibid para 32.

1402 Ibid paras 46–47.

1403 Ibid para 47.

1404 Ibid paras 110 and 139–40. The Court repeatedly stated that the referring judge is responsible for assessing whether the tax measures at issue are selective measures in the context of State aid, since in the preliminary ruling proceeding the Court's task is limited to interpreting the Treaty provisions, in particular Article 107(1) TFEU. By contrast, the *Azores* judgment was given in an action for annulment lodged by Portugal against a Commission decision. Therefore, the Court itself had to give a final assessment as to whether the Commission had justly judged that the tax measures constituted State aid. (See also Opinion AG Kokott in ibid paras 59–60.)

1405 Ibid paras 54–56.

1406 Ibid para 53.

the conditions of institutional autonomy, procedural autonomy and economic and financial autonomy are the only conditions that must be satisfied in order to take the territory falling within the competence of an infra-State body to be the relevant reference framework when assessing the selectivity of this infra-State body's decision.[1407]

679. Next, the Court provided guidelines for the national court in order to determine whether the second requirement of 'procedural autonomy' was fulfilled in the case at issue.[1408] The essential criterion here is whether the infra-State body can adopt a decision independently, without the central government being able to interfere directly regarding its content.[1409] Generally, the procedural autonomy of the infra-State body is not called into question where that body has 'the obligation to take into consideration the State interest in order to respect the limits of the areas of competence which are accorded to it'.[1410]

680. Finally, the Court further clarified the third criterion, 'economic and financial autonomy', according to which the region must assume the financial consequences of the tax measures which it adopts.[1411] The Court added that mere financial transfers between the infra-state body and the central State alone cannot suffice to prove the contrary.[1412] These transfers may take place for reasons unconnected to the tax measures.[1413] Hence, a causal relationship between the financial transfers and the tax measures is needed in order to challenge the infra-State body's financial autonomy.

3.1.3. *General Court's* Gibraltar v Commission *judgment*

681. The General Court also does not automatically consider regional tax measures to be selective measures in the context of State aid. In the *Gibraltar v Commission* case, the General Court[1414] ruled that the Commission had erroneously taken the UK to be the relevant reference framework.[1415] The Court concluded that the reference framework corresponds exclusively to the

1407 Ibid para 60.
1408 Ibid para 110.
1409 Ibid para 107, referring to ECJ case C-88/03 *Azores* [2006] ECR I-7115, para 67.
1410 ECJ joined cases C-428/06–C-434/06 *Trabajadores de la Rioja* [2008] ECR I-6747, para 108.
1411 Ibid para 123, referring to ECJ case C-88/03 *Azores* [2006] ECR I-7115, para 67.
1412 ECJ joined cases C-428/06–C-434/06 *Trabajadores de la Rioja* [2008] ECR I-6747, para 135.
1413 Ibid.
1414 Then called the Court of First Instance.
1415 EGC joined cases T-211/04 and T-215/04 *Gibraltar v Commission* [2008] ECR II-3745, paras 76–116.

geographical limits of the territory of Gibraltar, since Gibraltar satisfied the three conditions set out in the *Azores* judgment on the tax regime.[1416]

682. An appeal was lodged before the Court of Justice against this judgment by which the General Court annulled the Commission decision concerned. The Court of Justice ruled that even where a tax measure is not regionally selective, it can still be materially selective – in only conferring advantages to certain companies on the regional territory – and hence would qualify as State aid.[1417]

3.1.4. A Balancing Act in Cases on State Aid Involving Regional Authorities

683. As an interim conclusion, we can refer to AG Kokott's analysis of this case law in her Opinion in the *Trabajadores de la Rioja* case. In particular, the Advocate General observed that the Court managed to successfully balance two principles.[1418] On the one hand, respect is shown for the autonomy that is granted by the Member State's Constitution to its decentralised authorities. This corresponds to the EU's obligation under Article 4(2) TEU to respect its Member States' national identities, including their constitutional structures.[1419] This implies that encroachment upon the constitutional division of competences within a Member State must be avoided. On the other hand, by setting out three requirements relating to the autonomy in order to consider the decentralised authority to be sufficiently autonomous in the matter at issue, the Court ensures that the Member State cannot take shelter behind its constitutional order through a purely formal transfer of legislative powers. This is in keeping with the Court's settled case law that 'a Member State cannot plead provisions, practices or situations prevailing in its domestic legal order, including those resulting from the constitutional organisation of that State, to justify the failure to observe obligations arising under [Union] law'.[1420] In sum, the ECJ guarantees, in this way, the 'effective enforcement of EU law while respecting each Member State's constitutional choices as to the conferral of regional autonomy'.[1421]

1416 Ibid paras 85–115.

1417 ECJ joined cases C-106/09 P and C-107/09 P *Commission v Gibraltar*, paras 184–86. See also eg ECJ case C-169/08 *Presidente del Consiglio dei Ministri v Regione Sardegna* [2009] ECR I-10821, paras 59–63.

1418 Opinion AG Kokott in C-428/06 to C-434/06, paras 54–57 about the *Azores* judgment. The same remark applies to the Court's judgment in the *Trabajadores de la Rioja* case.

1419 Lenaerts and Cambien considered that 'in a sense, the ECJ's reasoning is a reference avant la letter to the first sentence of current art. 4 (2) TEU, as modified by the Treaty of Lisbon', Lenaerts and Cambien, 'Regions and the European Court: Giving Shape to the Regional Dimension of the Member States' (2010) 35 *ELRev* 609, 634.

1420 See inter alia ECJ case C-212/06 *Flemish Care Insurance* [2008] ECR I-1683, para 58 and references there.

1421 Lenaerts and Cambien, 'Regions and the European Court: Giving Shape to the Regional Dimension of the Member States' (2010) 35 *ELRev* 609, 634.

3.2. DOES THE ECJ RECOGNISE THE AUTONOMY OF REGIONAL AUTHORITIES IN OTHER AREAS AS WELL?

3.2.1. Recognition of Regional Authorities for Implementation of Union Law: Horvath

684. In the *Horvath* case, AG Trstenjak suggested applying the criteria for determining selectivity in the law on State aid *mutatis mutandis* to the question of the relevant reference framework for assessing a difference in treatment in the light of the Union principle of non-discrimination.[1422] The case concerned the implementation of Regulation 1782/2003 establishing common rules for direct support schemes under the common agricultural policy and establishing certain support schemes for farmers in the UK.[1423] The common agricultural policy, and in particular the implementation of the aforementioned regulation, is a matter which has been transferrd – or 'devolved' – to Scotland, Wales and Northern Ireland. The UK government generally remains competent only with respect to England. With a view to complying with the requirements of Regulation 1782/2003, the UK government, with respect to England alone and each of its devolved administrations, adopted separate rules defining minimum requirements which vary slighty. Mr Horvath, a farmer in England who was entitled to income support under the Union rules, challenged the English implementation rules on the basis that the implementation rules in Scotland, Wales and Northern Ireland were more favourable which amounted to an unlawful discrimination under Union law.

685. In her Opinion, AG Trstenjak argued that the criteria used by the Court in the *Azores* judgment could be helpful in the present situation since it concerned an assessment of whether there is a difference in treatment between economic operators or not in both cases.[1424] In other words, the reference framework is needed to assess the selectivity of a measure in the area of State aid, while the reference framework includes the categories of persons or things

---

[1422] Opinion AG Trstenjak 3 February 2009 in C-428/07, *Horvath*, paras 102–08.

[1423] Regulation 1782/2003 establishing common rules for direct support schemes under the common agricultural policy and establishing certain support schemes for farmers and amending Regulations 2019/93, 1452/2001, 1453/2001, 1454/2001, 1868/94, 1251/1999, 1254/1999, 1673/2000, 2358/71 and 2529/2001 [2003] *OJ* L 270/1.

[1424] Opinion AG Trstenjak 3 February 2009 in C-428/07, *Horvath*, paras 102–06, especially para 106: 'I believe that it is reasonable to apply such an approach to the present situation, because the criteria employed by the Court are an aid in assessing the existence of a situation which, irrespective of the sector-specific terminology – "selectivity" in the case of the law on aid – ultimately constitutes no more than a difference in treatment between economic operators'.

in the comparison in the light of the principle of discrimination. Although the terminology is different, the analysis is similar. Hence, the Advocate General suggested that in order to assess the discriminatory character of the provisions concerned, it should be possible to limit the relevant reference framework to the autonomous regional authority which has its own rule-making powers by virtue of the national Constitution.[1425] In the present case, the reference framework would be England, as a constituent part of the UK, with the powers of a regional authority in the sphere of agriculture.[1426]

686. Subsequently, AG Trstenjak referred to the Court's case law in which it focuses on the source of the alleged discrimination in order to determine the relevant reference framework.[1427] The Advocate General immediately pointed out that this approach is, in essence, based upon the same considerations as the *Azores* case law.[1428] She referred to the ECJ's case law in specific cases of discrimination in which it ruled that no discrimination exists if the differences in treatment cannot be attributed to one single source, since in that case no body is responsible for the inequality.[1429] It is also settled case law, in the context of the implementation of Union law, that any disparities in treatment which result from differences existing between the laws of the various Member States cannot alone give rise to discrimination.[1430] Otherwise, the legislative freedom of the Member States would be impaired.[1431]

1425 Ibid para 107.

1426 Ibid para 108.

1427 Ibid paras 109 ff.

1428 Ibid para 109.

1429 Ibid. According to AG Trstenjak this approach has been applied primarily in the context of Article 157 TFEU (para 110).

It should be noted, however, that this is not only settled case law in specific cases of discrimination, but also in the context of the general Union principle of non-discrimination of Article 18 TFEU, see inter alia ECJ case C-403/03 *Schempp* [2005] ECR I-6421, para 34 and references there: 'it is settled case-law that Article [18 TFEU] is not concerned with any disparities in treatment, for persons and undertakings subject to the jurisdiction of the [Union], which may result from divergences existing between the various Member States, so long as they affect all persons subject to them in accordance with objective criteria and without regard to their nationality'.

1430 Opinion AG Trstenjak 3 February 2009 in C-428/07, *Horvath*, para 113 with references to inter alia ECJ joined cases 185/78 to 204/78 *Van Dam en Zonen* [1979] ECR 2345, para 10 and ECJ case C-177/94 *Perfili* [1996] ECR I-161, para 17. See also ECJ case C-137/00 *The Queen* [2003] ECR I-7975, para 124: 'Whilst it is true that Article [18 TFEU] prohibits every Member State from applying its competition law differently on grounds of the nationality of the parties concerned, the fact remains that Article [18 TFEU] is not concerned with any disparities in treatment which may result, for persons and undertakings subject to the jurisdiction of the [Union], from divergences existing between the laws of the various Member States, so long as the latter affect all persons subject to them, in accordance with objective criteria and without regard to their nationality'.

1431 Ibid para 114.

AG Trstenjak suggested applying the same reasoning when the Constitution of the Member State provides that devolved administrations have legislative competence in different constituent parts of that Member State.[1432] She found an additional reason in the fact that Union law does not preclude the implementation of Union law at the regional or local levels.[1433] In this respect, the Advocate General referred to Judge Matscher's dissenting Opinion in the case of *Dudgeon v UK* before the ECtHR.[1434] He argued that 'the diversity of domestic laws, which is characteristic of a federal State, can in itself never constitute a discrimination, and there is no necessity to justify diversity of this kind. To claim the contrary would be to disregard totally the very essence of federalism.'[1435]

687. In sum, AG Trstenjak argued that in the present case, England, as a constituent part of the UK, was the relevant reference framework according to the ECJ's case law on both the requirement of the selectivity of State aid and the need for one single source of discrimination.[1436] This implied that unequal situations in the constituent parts of the UK could arise because a crucial criterion for the application of the non-discrimination principle had not been met; the unequal treatment could not be attributed to one single public authority.[1437]

688. The Court of Justice came to the same conclusion as the Advocate General; however, it did so without mentioning its case law on the selectivity of State aid. It based its decision solely on its previous case law concerning the need to identify one single source of discrimination. The Court began its reasoning by referring to its settled case law according to which 'the prohibition on discrimination is not concerned with any disparities in treatment which may result, between the Member States, from divergences existing between the legislation of the various Member States so long as that legislation affects equally all persons subject to it'.[1438] Subsequently, the Court applied this case law to the relationship between regional authorities within a single Member State. The Court held that divergences between the measures of the competent, devolved authorities cannot, on that ground alone, constitute discrimination.[1439]

1432 Ibid para 115.

1433 Ibid paras 115 and 98. In particular, Regulation No 1782/2003 even calls for this implementation in order to ensure a differentiated implementation of the Common Agricultural Policy. See ibid para 115, referring to paras 90 and 93.

1434 See ibid fn 69.

1435 Dissenting opinion of Judge Matscher in the judgment of the European Court of Human Rights of 22 October 1981, *Dudgeon v United Kingdom* (Application No 7525/76).

1436 Opinion AG Trstenjak 3 February 2009 in C-428/07, *Horvath*, para 116.

1437 Ibid paras 116–17.

1438 Ibid para para 55.

1439 Ibid paras 57–58.

3.2.2. *Recognition of Regional Authorities in the Assessment of Restrictions to Free Movement?*

3.2.2.1. AG Sharpston's Proposal in the *Flemish Care Insurance* Case

689. In her Opinion in the *Flemish Care Insurance* case, AG Sharpston questioned the paradox that exists between the Union's goal to abolish barriers to the freedom of movement between the Member States and the fact that decentralised authorities of Member States may nevertheless establish barriers within that Member State.[1440] The Advocate General asked the following rhetorical question: 'what sort of a European Union is it if freedom of movement is guaranteed between Dunkirk (France) and De Panne (Belgium), but not between Jodoigne and Hoegaarden?'[1441] Sharpston considered that were the decentralised authorities of Member States to have the relevant competences to introduce barriers to free movement between themselves, then this could undermine the internal market without internal borders between the EU Member States.[1442] This issue cannot be understated, especially in the light of an evolution towards regional devolution in several Member States.[1443] Therefore, AG Sharpston has suggested that the ECJ should, in examining the dismantling of restrictions to the freedom of movement within the EU, regard 'the entities that have the relevant regulatory authority (be these Member States or decentralised authorities within a single Member State)'.[1444]

690. AG Sharpston hereby referred to the criteria that the Court set out in the *Azores* judgment. She argued that the Belgian communities and regions' position is equivalent to that of a Member State, since they act as autonomous legislators within their spheres of competence.[1445] She concluded that 'were Flanders an independent Member State of the Union, the impossibility for those living in Wallonia but working in Flanders to affiliate to the Flemish care insurance scheme would clearly fall foul of the Treaty'.[1446]

691. Moreover, AG Sharpston pointed out that the ECJ has already extended the prohibition on tariff barriers to a similar prohibition on regional borders within a Member State.[1447] This case law is based on the idea that internal frontiers are incompatible with the internal market and, according to AG Sharpston, the same reasoning could be applied to the freedom of movement for persons since, just as with the provision on internal tariff barriers, 'the Treaty draftsmen may well have taken it for granted when envisaging freedom

1440 Opinion AG Sharpston 28 June 2007 in C-212/06, *Flemish Care Insurance*, para 116.
1441 Ibid.
1442 Ibid para 118.
1443 Ibid.
1444 Ibid para 117.
1445 Ibid para 120.
1446 Ibid.
1447 Ibid para 122.

of movement for persons within the [Union] that internal obstacles within a single Member State such as the one at issue in the present case would have been abolished'.[1448] She found an additional stimulus for doing so in the provisions on Union citizenship.[1449] In particular, she pointed out that Article 21 TFEU could be interpreted as providing the freedom both to move and to reside without prior movement between Member States.[1450]

3.2.2.2. Possibility of Preventing Specific Situations of Reverse Discrimination at Union Level

692. AG Sharpston's proposal is very interesting in the context of reverse discrimination. If the ECJ in the *Flemish Care Insurance*, *Las* and *Libert* judgments had taken the regional authority – the Dutch-speaking region or Flemish community – to be the relevant reference framework, then specific situations of reverse discrimination would have been prevented at the Union level. Instead, a 'traditional' violation of the Treaty provisions on free movement would be at stake. In particular, regarding the Flemish Care Insurance Decree, people living in the French- or German-speaking regions, but working in the Dutch-speaking region, would either suffer the loss of eligibility for the benefits of the care insurance or are limited in their choices of the place to which they transfer their residence. If the Dutch-speaking region were an independent Member State, this would clearly be a traditional restriction of free movement within the European Union.

693. As explained above, the ECJ did not follow AG Sharpston's suggestion in this respect. The Court did not take the decentralised authority to be the relevant reference framework when ruling upon potential barriers to the freedom of movement within the Union.[1451] The Court probably did not want to interfere in the Member States' internal affairs. However, from the perspective of the promotion of free movement, these complex specific cases of reverse discrimination are hard to accept since Member States can reintroduce barriers to freedom of movement within the country's borders while the EU strives to abolish barriers to freedom of movement beyond national borders. This is probably the reason why the Court explicitly considered that the referring court, namely the Belgian Constitutional Court, could apply the same interpretation of

---

[1448] Ibid paras 123–32, in particular paras 128–30.
[1449] Ibid para 133.
[1450] Ibid para 144.
[1451] See also Dautricourt and Thomas, 'Reverse Discrimination and Free Movement of Persons Under Community Law: All for Ulysses, Nothing for Penelope?' (2009) 34 *ELRev* 454, 443 and 453–54 who argued, referring to *Angonese*, that the cross-border element should be assessed at the regional level where regional entities are competent to introduce barriers to the freedom of movement.

Union law that the ECJ gave for Union citizens who have exercised their right of free movement to situations in which Belgian citizens have not exercised their right of free movement.[1452] Hence, in cases of reverse discrimination, in contexts in which self-governing powers are allocated to regions, the principle of respect for the internal allocation of competences of a Member State has to be balanced against the principle of effective enforcement of the Treaty provisions on free movement.

694. The fact is that the ECJ thought through the full consequences of the autonomy of a region, by regarding them to be the relevant reference framework in the area of both State aid and in the implementation of Union law, but it has not extended this approach to the area of possible impediments to free movement in the EU. This difference between State aid cases and the *Horvath* case, on the one hand, and the *Flemish Care Insurance* case, on the other, can be explained by drawing a distinction between the 'passive' and 'active' aspect of the constitutional autonomy of decentralised authorities.[1453] The ECJ has thus far only recognised the passive aspect, ruling that the existence of territorial selectivity or a violation of the principle of equality is not demonstrated by the mere fact that an autonomous region has adopted rules applicable to the territory under its jurisdiction. However, the ECJ has not (yet?) recognised the active aspect of decentralised authorities' constitutional autonomy; that is, the possibility that their normative acts impede free movement within a Member State.

The question arises as to whether the EU could intervene in the latter case. It could be argued that this falls outside the scope of application of the Treaty provisions on free movement and, hence, outside EU competences as well.[1454] Or, it could be argued that the ECJ might recognise, in specific circumstances, this active aspect of a Member State's federal State structure as well. In particular, if the barriers created by autonomous regions within Member States take considerable proportions and actually impede free movement within the European Union as a whole, it is not unlikely that the ECJ will intervene.

695. Although AG Sharpston's proposal makes perfect sense from the perspective of the promotion of freedom of movement within the EU, it would probably be very hard to accept from the perspective of the Member States.

1452 ECJ case C-212/06 *Flemish Care Insurance* [2008] ECR I-1683, para 40.

1453 Bombois, 'La "discrimination à rebours" et son appréhension par la cour constitutionelle belge' in Cariat and Nowak (eds), *Le droit de l'Union européenne et le juge belge – Het recht van de Europese Unie en de Belgische rechter*, Bruylant 2015, p 390.

1454 See inter alia van der Steen who argued that the fact that the ECJ did not follow AG Sharpston's proposal is based on Article 5 TEU enshrining the principle of conferral. In particular, van der Steen argued that Belgian citizens who have not exercised their rights of free movement fall outside the competences and aims which are granted to the EU (van der Steen, 'Zuiver interne situaties: geen omwenteling, wel inperking' (2008) *NTER* 301, 304).

That is to say, extending the view on regions developed in the area of State aid to restrictions on free movement could be considered to be a violation of the Member State's sovereignty. Whereas the concept of State aid is a self-contained aspect of European Union law, restrictions on free movement are much broader in scope conceptually. Therefore, such an extension of the case law would have a huge impact upon the regional authorities' competences.

696. By contrast, Van der Mei approached the issue from the perspective of EU citizenship, leaving more room for the Member States and their regional authorities.[1455] In particular, he has observed that EU citizenship does not force the ECJ to find a solution to specific situations of reverse discrimination, since EU citizenship primarily requires equal treatment between own citizens and citizens from other Member States.[1456] He argued that this can, in principle, also be realised by reconsidering the conclusion that citizens of other EU Member States can claim an equal treatment on the basis of Union law in a federated entity in which he or she does not reside or work. Van der Mei admitted that this approach might not seem desirable from the perspective of the promotion of free movement; however, he argued that this approach remains worthy of consideration nevertheless.

In particular, in the light of Article 18 TFEU, Van der Mei argued that it makes more sense to compare citizens of other Member States to the whole group of home Member State's citizens and that the former only have to be treated equally, if and to the extent that, the own citizens residing in another federated entity are entitled to that same right. He explained that the question of whether or not a resident of Friesland should have equal access to public services in Groningen is, in the first instance a question regarding national citizenship which should be treated on the basis of national law. He posed the question thus: if Dutch law allows Groningen to treat its own residents more favourably than residents of Friesland, why would EU law preclude this? That is to say, if national citizenship leaves room for such a difference in treatment, why would EU citizenship not do likewise? Van der Mei has argued that EU citizenship should leave the differences between citizens of the same nationality undisturbed. After all, 'citizenship of the Union shall be additional to and not replace national citizenship'.[1457]

697. So far, the ECJ has followed neither Sharpston's proposal nor Van der Mei's view. However, it may be that a solution by the ECJ, which risks being considered as incompatible with the principle of conferral, is not appropriate,

---

1455 Van der Mei, 'EU-burgerschap en de reikwijdte van het verbod van discriminatie op grond van nationaliteit' (2009) *NTER* 275, 285–86.

1456 Referring to ECJ joined cases C-22/08 and C-23/08, *Vatsouras and Koupatantze* [2009] ECR I-4585.

1457 Article 9 TEU.

and rather what is required is intervention by the Union legislator. That is to say, fully in line with the principle of conferral, the Member States, as *Herren der Verträge*, are able to amend the Treaties in order that the relevant regulatory authorities are taken into account when ruling upon potential barriers to the freedom of movement within the EU, which are not necessarily the Member States but also decentralised authorities.

This amendment could be accompanied by the recognition of relevant regulatory decentralised authorities as privileged parties for an action of annulment of acts of Union institutions on the basis of Article 263 TFEU and by the provision of representatives of these relevant regulatory decentralised authorities to the Council of Ministers and the Committee of Permanent Representatives of the Governments of the Member States.

698. However, so far, specific situations of reverse discrimination are not being prevented at the Union level. Where such situations arise, it is up to the Member States to deal with them. Whether and how the Member States, and their autonomous regions, can remedy these situations will be discussed in Chapter 7.

CHAPTER 7

NATIONAL PERSPECTIVES ON REVERSE DISCRIMINATION IN A FEDERAL STATE CONTEXT

699. This chapter examines specific forms of reverse discrimination from two national perspectives, specifically from the Belgian and German perspectives. In particular, it examines the grounds on which national authorities decide whether to remedy the specific form of reverse discrimination at stake or not. First of all, these forms of reverse discrimination may be assessed in the light of the national rules on the division of competences. Secondly, specific situations of reverse discrimination may be assessed in the light of internal free movement within a federally structured Member State. Thirdly, as in 'classic' cases of reverse discrimination, the principle of equality, as enshrined in national law, comes into play. Finally, it should be added that national authorities do not always assess a situation of reverse discrimination on the basis of national law, but sometimes – incorrectly – on the basis of Union law.[1458]

[1458] An example of reverse discrimination in a federally structured Member State, in which the argument of primacy of Union law was decisive for the Flemish government, concerns the Flemish Decree on Land and Real Estate Policy. On the basis of the Special Finance Law, regions can only establish increases or reductions on personal income tax on inhabitants of the region concerned (Article 6(2) 3° and 4° *juncto* Article 7(1), 1° Special Finance Law, *BS* 17 January 1989). However, the Flemish government argued that given the primacy of European law over Belgian (constitutional) provisions, it was possible to invoke Article 63 TFEU in order that creditors established outside the territory of the Flemish region were also included, to the extent that they were liable to the personal income tax. The Flemish government said that judging them differently would imply that the tax competences of the regional legislator are de facto diluted, because the regional legislator could only adopt tax measures in violation of European law. These considerations were not made explicit in the final text of Articles 3(1)(3)–3(1)(9) of the Flemish Decree concerned (Explanatory Memo, Parl. Doc. Flemish Parl. 2008–09, No 2012/1, 107–08).

Although the use of the primacy argument in order to apply Union law in purely internal situations is, it is submitted, an incorrect application of Union law, the case illustrates that the Flemish regional legislator is well aware of the tension that exists between the national constitutional rules on internal division of powers and the freedom of movement within the EU.

700. In Belgium, the debate around reverse discrimination in a federal State context started with the case of the *Flemish Care Insurance*. Chapter 6 discussed the ECJ's *Flemish Care Insurance* judgment. This chapter will discuss the Belgian sequel, in particular the judgment of the Belgian Constitutional Court of 21 January 2009.[1459] The Flemish Decree was questioned in the light of the principle of equality, the principle of internal free movement and the rules on the internal division of powers. Actually, this case touches upon all the problematic aspects of a specific form of reverse discrimination in a federal State context. The Belgian Constitutional Court's judgment will be discussed in detail in Section 1 below because this argument was decisive for the Belgian Constitutional Court and further reference to the judgment will be made in Sections 2 and 3.

1. NATIONAL RULES ON THE INTERNAL DIVISION OF COMPETENCES

1.1. THE BELGIAN CONSTITUTIONAL COURT'S JUDGMENT ON THE FLEMISH CARE INSURANCE

701. In its judgment of 21 January 2009, the Belgian Constitutional Court reproduced the distinction that the ECJ drew between people who work in the Dutch-speaking region[1460] or in the bilingual Brussels-Capital region, but who live in the French- or German-speaking regions, depending on whether or not they have made use of the right to free movement within the EU.[1461] The Belgian Constitutional Court concluded, entirely in line with the reasoning of the ECJ, that the exclusion of Union citizens who have exercised their right to free movement within the EU from the Flemish Care Insurance Decree constituted a violation of Articles 10 and 11 of the Belgian Constitution read together with the Articles 45 and 49 TFEU.[1462] Following the Court of Justice's reasoning, the Belgian Constitutional Court decided that the rules on the internal allocation of powers, and the territorial incompetence of the Flemish

1459 Numerous contributions were written about this judgment, see inter alia Feyen, 'Zorgen voor morgen: implicaties van het arrest van het Grondwettelijk Hof over discriminaties in de Vlaamse zorgverzekering: Een juridische veldslag' [2009] *TBPK* 169, 169–74; Van Elsuwege and Adam, 'The Limits of Constitutional Dialogue for the Prevention of Reverse Discrimination' (2009) 5 *EuConst* 327–99; Velaers and Vanpraet, 'De materiële en territoriale bevoegdheidsverdeling inzake sociale zekerheid en sociale bijstand (II)' [2009] *TBP* 195–218; and Verschueren, 'Europese krijtlijnen voor een sociaal federalisme' in Cantillon, Popelier and Ninke (eds), *De gelaagde welvaartsstaat. Naar een Vlaamse sociale bescherming in België en in Europa?*, Intersentia 2010, pp 227–58.

1460 [*Nederlandse taalgebied*].

1461 Belgian Constitutional Court 21 April 2009, no 11/2009, para B.6-B.7.

1462 Ibid paras B.8.1–B.10.3. The Belgian Court repeatedly quoted the ECJ's C-2012/06 judgment.

community towards persons living on the territory of other language-speaking regions in Belgium in particular, could not be a justification for the contested difference in treatment.[1463]

702. The Constitutional Court confirmed the principle of a territorial allocation of powers, as enshrined in Articles 128(2) and 130(2) of the Constitution,[1464] but pragmatically reduced its impact by the extension of the Flemish community's competence towards people living on the French- or German-speaking territory, to the extent that they had exercised their right to free movement within the EU.[1465] In particular, the Court took the following factors into account: 'the necessity flowing from Union law, the fact that only a limited group of persons is concerned and the fact that reimbursements will be refused or reduced if the user has a claim to coverage of the same costs on the basis of other legal provisions'.[1466] The Court concluded that the extension of the Flemish community's competence did not affect the competences of the French- and German-speaking communities disproportionally.[1467]

703. Next, the Court ruled on the situation of Belgian citizens who had not exercised their right to free movement within the EU.[1468] Since this concerned a purely internal situation, the Court examined the arguments only in the light of internal, namely Belgian, law.[1469] The Court considered that Articles 128(2) and 130(2) Belgian Constitution established a system of allocation of powers based exclusively on territoriality. According to the Court, making an exception for persons who had not used their right to free movement was incompatible with these constitutional rules.[1470] Hence, the Belgian Constitutional Court did not follow the ECJ's 'suggestion' of applying the same interpretation of free movement within the European Union to purely internal situations; it did not allow an extraterritorial application of the Flemish Care Insurance Decree for persons in purely internal situations, because that would be incompatible with the constitutional rules on the internal division of powers.[1471]

1463 Ibid para B.10.2.

1464 Ibid: [*Ofschoon de Vlaamse Gemeenschap in beginsel geen bevoegdheden heeft ten aanzien van de categorie van personen die in het Franse of het Duitse taalgebied wonen*].

1465 See also VELAERS and VANPRAET, 'De materiële en territoriale bevoegdheidsverdeling inzake sociale zekerheid en sociale bijstand (II)' [2009] *TBP* 195, 206.

1466 Belgian Constitutional Court 21 January 2009, no 11/2009, para B.10.2. Author's translation of: [*rekening houdend met de uit het Europees [Unie]recht voorvloeiende noodzakelijkheid, met het feit dat het om een relatief beperkte groep van personen gaat en met ... [het feit dat] tenlastenemingen zullen worden geweigerd of verminderd indien de gebruiker aanspraak heeft op dekking van dezelfde kosten krachtens andere wettelijke of decretale bepalingen*].

1467 Ibid. 1468 Ibid paras B.11.1 ff. 1469 Ibid paras B.11.1–B.11.2.

1470 Ibid paras B.12.2, B.12.3 and B.14.

1471 ECJ case C-212/06 *Flemish Care Insurance* [2008] ECR I-1683, para 40 and VELAERS and VANPRAET, 'De materiële en territoriale bevoegdheidsverdeling inzake sociale zekerheid en sociale bijstand (II)' [2009] *TBP* 195, 210 and 212.

704. The Constitutional Court recognised that whether these persons are discriminated against in the exercise of their right to free movement within Belgium is questionable.[1472] However, the Court entertained the view that the difference in treatment, or the 'possible discrimination', originates in the Flemish Care Insurance Decree on no account, but in the lack of analogous measures adopted by the French- or German-speaking communities or even by the federal legislator.[1473] Moreover, the Court concluded that it should not investigate whether these persons are discriminated in the exercise of free movement, as enshrined in Article 6(1), VI, 3 Special Law of 8 August 1980. Finally, the Constitutional Court ruled that since the arguments regarding Articles 23 and 191 of the Constitution could not lead to another conclusion, it was not necessary to examine the matter any further.[1474]

1.2. ANALYSIS OF THE BELGIAN CONSTITUTIONAL COURT'S JUDGMENT ON THE BASIS OF THE INTERNAL RULES ON DIVISION OF COMPETENCES

705. The Court of Justice and the Belgian Constitutional Court entertain different views regarding the significance of the rules on internal division of powers.[1475] It is the Court of Justice's settled case law that the constitutional organisation of a Member State cannot justify the failure to observe obligations arising under Union law regarding those situations that fall within the scope of Union law.[1476] However, the Belgian Constitutional Court concluded precisely on the basis of the principle of exclusive territorial division of competences, as enshrined in the Constitution, that the scope of application of the Flemish Decree on Care Insurance could not be extended to purely internal situations involving residents of the French- and German-speaking region. Hence the Constitutional Court did not follow the ECJ's 'suggestion', as noted above.[1477] On the other hand, the Constitutional Court, in order to respond to the Court of Justice's judgment, allowed an extraterritorial exception for the extension of competence of the Flemish community towards residents of the French- or German-speaking regions, to the extent that they made use of their right of free movement.

706. Although the Court of Justice and the Constitutional Court's judgments regarding the Flemish care insurance were fitted by both courts in their settled

1472 Belgian Constitutional Court 21 January 2009, no 11/2009, para B.13.2.
1473 Ibid paras B.15.1–B.16 in which the Court spoke about the [*eventuele discriminatie*].
1474 Ibid para B.17.
1475 Van Elsuwege and Adam, 'The Limits of Constitutional Dialogue for the Prevention of Reverse Discrimination' (2009) 5 *EuConst* 334, 336–37.
1476 ECJ case C-212/06 *Flemish Care Insurance* [2008] ECR I-1683, paras 57–58.
1477 Above n 640.

case law,[1478] the result is remarkable to say at least. That is to say, the only category of persons who cannot benefit from the advantages of the Flemish care insurance are those Belgian citizens who work in Flanders or Brussels, but who live in the French- or German-speaking regions and who have never exercised their right to free movement.

Not surprisingly, the paradoxical effects, stemming from the combination of the ECJ's and Belgian Constitutional Court's judgments have been criticised.[1479] That is to say, both a French citizen living in Dunkirk and working in De Panne and a Belgian citizen living in Jodoigne and working in Leuven who has exercised his right to free movement can benefit from the Flemish Care Insurance. However, a Belgian citizen living in Jodoigne and working in Leuven who has not exercised his right to free movement cannot join the Flemish Care Insurance scheme. In this context, it is helpful to refer back to AG Sharpston's proposal in this case, taking the relevant regulatory authority as the relevant reference framework into account, the Flemish community in this case.[1480] Moreover, Belgian scholars pointed out that this perplexing result is caused by different connecting factors: the criterion of the place of work applies to situations falling under Union law while the place of residence applies to purely internal situations.[1481]

707. In this respect, the question was raised as to whether it would have been better for the Belgian Constitutional Court to recognise the criterion of the place of work as the connecting factor, instead of the criterion of residence.[1482] That is to say, the paradoxical effects are not the result of the Belgian principle of the division of powers as such, based on exclusivity and territoriality, but instead is the result of its interpretation by opting for the criterion of residence as being the most important connecting factor.[1483] In particular, in order to indicate the exclusively competent legislator the connecting factor should be determined

---

1478 Van Elsuwege and Adam, 'The Limits of Constitutional Dialogue for the Prevention of Reverse Discrimination' (2009) 5 *EuConst* 334, 337.

1479 Storme, 'Vlaamse Zorgverzekering. Een lange weg naar een geschikte aanknopingsfactor' [2008] *NjW* 614, 621–23 and Velaers and Vanpraet, 'De materiële en territoriale bevoegdheidsverdeling inzake sociale zekerheid en sociale bijstand (II)' [2009] *TBP* 195, 217.

1480 Above nn 689–91.

1481 Feyen, *Beyond Federal Dogmatics*, Lund University Publications 2013, pp 268–75; Storme, 'Vlaamse Zorgverzekering. Een lange weg naar een geschikte aanknopingsfactor' [2008] *NjW* 614, 622–23; and Velaers and Vanpraet, 'De materiële en territoriale bevoegdheidsverdeling inzake sociale zekerheid en sociale bijstand (II)' [2009] *TBP* 195, 217.

1482 Velaers and Vanpraet, 'De materiële en territoriale bevoegdheidsverdeling inzake sociale zekerheid en sociale bijstand (II)' [2009] *TBP* 195, 217. See Storme, 'Vlaamse Zorgverzekering. Een lange weg naar een geschikte aanknopingsfactor' [2008] *NjW* 614, 623 who formulates it more resolutely.

1483 Storme, 'Vlaamse Zorgverzekering. Een lange weg naar een geschikte aanknopingsfactor' [2008] *NjW* 614, 621 and 623 and Velaers and Vanpraet, 'De materiële en territoriale bevoegdheidsverdeling inzake sociale zekerheid en sociale bijstand (II)' [2009] *TBP* 195, 217.

in the light of 'the subject, the nature and possibly the goal of the attributed substantive competence'.[1484]

708. Recognising the place of work as the connecting factor within Belgium would have had several other advantages.[1485] First of all, no specific situation of reverse discrimination would exist in which Belgian citizens are treated differently depending on whether or not they have exercised their right to free movement.[1486] Moreover, this would definitely comply with the principle of exclusive territorial competence, given that the extraterritorial exception in favour of the Flemish legislator's competences would no longer be necessary.[1487] According to Storme, the Belgian economic and monetary Union should play a more important role in the Constitutional Court's case law and the decision to opt for the criterion of place of work would also fit within this view.[1488] Last, but not least, the use of the criterion of place of work within Belgium would also imply a better integration of the Belgian constitutional order within the European legal order.[1489] Storme has even argued that the case of the Flemish care insurance should act as an incentive to the regional legislators in determining future criteria for the scope of application of a legal measure, 'to take into account a careful balance of conflicting rules with a broad perspective, taking into account all constitutional principles as well as the embedding in European and international context'.[1490]

1484 Storme, 'Vlaamse Zorgverzekering. Een lange weg naar een geschikte aanknopingsfactor' [2008] *NjW* 614, 621–23 and Velaers and Vanpraet, 'De materiële en territoriale bevoegdheidsverdeling inzake sociale zekerheid en sociale bijstand (II)' [2009] *TBP* 195, 217–18. Author's translation of: [*het onderwerp, de aard en eventueel het doel van de toegewezen materiële bevoegdheid*].

1485 Velaers and Vanpraet, 'De materiële en territoriale bevoegdheidsverdeling inzake sociale zekerheid en sociale bijstand (II)' [2009] *TBP* 195, 217.

1486 Storme, 'Vlaamse Zorgverzekering. Een lange weg naar een geschikte aanknopingsfactor' [2008] *NjW* 614, 621–23 and Velaers and Vanpraet, 'De materiële en territoriale bevoegdheidsverdeling inzake sociale zekerheid en sociale bijstand (II)' [2009] *TBP* 195, 217.

1487 Velaers and Vanpraet, 'De materiële en territoriale bevoegdheidsverdeling inzake sociale zekerheid en sociale bijstand (II)' [2009] *TBP* 195, 217.

1488 Storme, 'Vlaamse Zorgverzekering. Een lange weg naar een geschikte aanknopingsfactor' [2008] *NjW* 614, 622–23.

1489 Storme, 'Vlaamse Zorgverzekering. Een lange weg naar een geschikte aanknopingsfactor' [2008] *NjW* 614, 621–23 and Velaers and Vanpraet, 'De materiële en territoriale bevoegdheidsverdeling inzake sociale zekerheid en sociale bijstand (II)' [2009] *TBP* 195, 217.

1490 Storme, 'Vlaamse Zorgverzekering. Een lange weg naar een geschikte aanknopingsfactor' [2008] *NjW* 614, 623. Author's translation of: [*De perikelen in verband met het Zorgverzekeringsdecreet moet de aanleiding zijn voor de regelgevers van de deelgebieden om bij het vastleggen van toepassingscriteria in de toekomst steeds een zorgvuldige conflictenrechtelijke afweging te maken met een breed perspectief en rekening houdend met alle constitutionele principes evenals met de inbedding in de Europese en inernationale context*]. This position does correspond with AG Sharpston's view (Opinion AG Sharpston 28 June 2007 in C-212/06, *Flemish Care Insurance*, paras 84–97).

On the other hand, the fact that totally different logics underpin the choice of the criteria should not be forgotten, in particular, that they assume different groups of solidarity.[1491] In particular, the Flemish care insurance is a type of 'aid to persons' that is traditionally connected to the place of residence.[1492]

709. In the previous chapter, it was argued that the specific situation of reverse discrimination in the *Flemish Care Insurance* case resulted from an overcompensation by Union law.[1493] In cases of overcompensation by Union law and in the light of the working hypothesis, the national authority has to assess the situation of reverse discrimination in the light of national law by explicitly comparing or taking the situation falling under Union law into account. Although this does not imply that all situations in which reverse discrimination is a result of overcompensation by Union law should be prohibited at national level, the national authority should not too easily accept justifications in order to allow such cases of reverse discrimination. In particular, in case of the Flemish care insurance, recognising the place of work as a connecting factor seems to be an excellent solution to the problematic situation of reverse discrimination. That is, it would not only solve the reverse discrimination, it would also be compatible with the Belgian constitutional rules on the division of competences and, moreover, it would lead to a better integration of the Belgian system within the European system.

2. INTERNAL FREE MOVEMENT

710. The right to internal free movement is not enshrined in the Belgian Constitution. The Belgian Constitutional Court derived from the constitutional reforms of 1970 and 1980 that 'the new Belgian State system is founded on an economic and monetary union' in its *Water Export* landmark judgment.[1494] Subsequently, with the constitutional reform of 1988–89, the term 'economic and monetary union' was introduced in the Special Law governing Institutional Reform of 8 August 1980[1495] as a limitation on the region's competences in

---

1491 Velaers and Vanpraet, 'De materiële en territoriale bevoegdheidsverdeling inzake sociale zekerheid en sociale bijstand (II)' [2009] *TBP* 195, 217–18.

1492 Cloots, 'Germs of Pluralist Judicial Adjudication: Advocaten Voor de Wereld and Other References from the Belgian Constitutional Court' (2010) 47 *CMLRev* 645, 667 and Velaers and Vanpraet, 'De materiële en territoriale bevoegdheidsverdeling inzake sociale zekerheid en sociale bijstand (II)' [2009] *TBP* 195, 218. See also Opinion Belgian Council of State 16 March 2004, Parl. St. Vl. Parl. 2003-04, no 1970/2, para 10.

1493 Above n 667.

1494 Belgian Constitutional Court 25 February 1988, no 47/1988, para 6.B.4.

1495 Hereafter SLIR.

economic matters. Article 6(1) VI SLIR determines that the regions exercise their powers with due consideration of the principles of the freedom of movement for persons, goods, services and capital, and of the freedom of trade and commerce, as well as with due consideration of the economic and monetary union, as determined by the law and by international treaties. At present, the economic and monetary union is considered to be a general principle that limits all competences, as well those of the regions as of other authorities.

711. The right to internal free movement is enshrined in the German Basic Law. In particular, Article 11 Basic Law provides that 'all Germans shall have the right to move freely throughout the federal territory'.[1496] The right to internal free movement seems to play only a minor role in German constitutional law.[1497] So far, Article 11 Basic Law has only been invoked once in the context of reverse discrimination in a case regarding university tuition fees, which will be discussed in the following section.[1498]

712. The main question in this section is whether the interpretation of the principle of internal free movement runs parallel to the Court of Justice's interpretation of the principle of free movement within the EU.[1499] Feyen has concisely summarised the dilemma for Belgium in this respect. On the one hand, if Belgian fundamental freedoms are thought of as being in line with the European ones, then the Belgian constitutional division of powers risks becoming fundamentally eroded.[1500] On the other hand, if the principle is differently conceptualised in the Belgian and European legal orders, then situations of reverse discrimination will inevitably emerge.[1501]

1496 The second paragraph of Article 11 Basic Law provides 'This right may be restricted only by or pursuant to a law, and only in cases in which the absence of adequate means of support would result in a particular burden for the community, or in which such restriction is necessary to avert an imminent danger to the existence or the free democratic basic order of the Federation or of a Land, to combat the danger of an epidemic, to respond to a grave accident or natural disaster, to protect young persons from serious neglect, or to prevent crime'.

1497 It is hard to find the legal doctrine discussing Article 11 Basic Law. For instance in Heun, *Constitutional Systems of the World. The Constitution of Germany*, Hart Publishing 2011, Article 11 is not discussed at all (see Table of Legislation, xxvii). The same remark applies to Kommers and Miller, *The Constitutional Jurisprudence of the Federal Republic of Germany*, Duke University Press 2012. Moreover, only very few cases before the German Federal Constitutional Court mention Article 11 Basic Law.

1498 Below nn 749–53.

1499 See also Feyen, 'Economic and Monetary Union: Caught between Brussels and Luxembourg?' in De Baere, Sottiaux and Cloots (eds), *Federalism in the European Union*, Hart Publishing 2012, pp 392–404.

1500 Ibid p 404.

1501 Ibid.

2.1. BELGIAN CONSTITUTIONAL COURT ON THE BELGIAN ECONOMIC AND MONETARY UNION

2.1.1. Belgian Constitutional Court's Flemish Care Insurance *Judgment*

713. Although the Belgian Constitutional Court did not answer the question, as to the compatibility of the Decree on Flemish Care Insurance in the light of the Belgian economic and monetary union, it follows from the fact that the Belgian Constitutional Court did not follow the ECJ's 'suggestion' regarding purely internal situations that the Belgian principle of internal free movement is not necessarily interpreted in the same way as its European counterpart.[1502] Moreover, in two previous judgments regarding the Flemish care insurance, the Court explicitly ruled that 'by its limited behaviour and the effects thereof' the Flemish care insurance does not endanger the economic and monetary union.[1503] Although the question arises of why the Court avoided confirming this in its judgment of 2009, it can be derived from the two previous judgments that according to the Belgian Constitutional Court that not every restriction to internal free movement is forbidden by Article 6(1) VI SLIR.[1504]

714. Although this reading of the Belgian Constitutional Court's judgment on internal free movement is uncontroversial, Belgian legal scholars are divided on how the Belgian Constitutional Court should interpret the principle of the Belgian economic and monetary union in the context of reverse discrimination.

715. On the one hand, it is argued that forbidding restrictions on free movement in a European context should be avoided, while they are admitted in a national context. Accordingly, specific forms of reverse discrimination would be avoided in a federal State context. This can be achieved either by applying the EU free movement provisions to those entities that have the relevant regulatory authority – *in casu* the decentralised authority within a single Member State – or by interpreting the Belgian economic and monetary union as being completely identical to its European counterpart.

1502 See also ibid p 401 (in which Feyen wrote that 'the very fact that the BCC reproduced the distinction between purely internal situations and situations falling within the ambit of EU law in its 2009 judgment implies that, at least potentially, the BCC remains willing to construe the Belgian EMU requirements differently from the Court of Justice's reading of the fundamental freedoms') and Velaers and Vanpraet, 'De materiële en territoriale bevoegdheidsverdeling inzake sociale zekerheid en sociale bijstand (II)' [2009] *TBP* 195, 210 (who argued that otherwise, the Belgian Court would have declared the argument of the government of the French community to be well-founded).

1503 Belgian Court of Arbitration 13 March 2001 no 33/2001, para B.3.9.2 and Belgian Court of Arbitration 19 April 2006 no 51/2006, para B.10.3.

1504 Velaers and Vanpraet, 'De materiële en territoriale bevoegdheidsverdeling inzake sociale zekerheid en sociale bijstand (II)' [2009] *TBP* 195, 210–11.

Van Elsuweghe and Adams support the first view, building on AG Sharpston's Opinion in the *Flemish Care Insurance* case.[1505] They defend a flexible reasoning of the concept of Member State, by recognising the federated entity to be the relevant legal framework to which the Union provisions of free movement apply in the context of reverse discrimination.

The second view has been defended by Storme who has argued in the context of the *Flemish Care Insurance* case that the inhabitants of the French- or German-speaking regions clearly find themselves in a situation similar to that of a Dutch citizen who lives in the Netherlands, but who works in the Dutch-speaking region.[1506] Therefore, on the basis of the Belgian economic and monetary union, they should benefit from free movement within Belgium.[1507] Storme has explicitly added that this would seriously affect the federated entities' actions: they should carefully consider legislation taking all constitutional rules as well as the embedding in the European and international context into account.[1508]

716. On the other hand, there is some defence in Belgian legal doctrine of the interpretation in some cases of the Belgian economic and monetary union differently from – hence more narrowly than – the ECJ's broad interpretation of the EU fundamental freedoms. Velaers and Vanpraet argue that the Belgian constitutional rules on division of powers, which are based on the principle of territoriality and exclusivity, set limits on the principle of internal free movement.[1509] In other words, the authors who defend this position want to avoid the Belgian State structure from being undermined.

In the light of the ECJ's current extensive reading of the Treaty provisions on freedom of movement, and the presence of restrictions thereto in particular, it is submitted that a stricter interpretation of the Belgian economic and monetary union can be supported in some cases. However, if the ECJ did tighten up its concept of restrictions to the freedom of movement,[1510] a parallel reading of the Belgian economic and monetary union with its European counterpart would definitely be defensible.

1505 Stanislas and Van Elsuwege, 'Situations purment internes, discriminations à rebours et collectivités autonomes après l'arrêt sur l'assurance soins flamande' (2008) *CDE* 655, 705–10.

1506 Storme, 'Vlaamse Zorgverzekering. Een lange weg naar een geschikte aanknopingsfactor' [2008] *NjW* 614, 622.

1507 Ibid 622.

1508 Ibid 622–23.

1509 See inter alia Vanpraet, *De latente staatshervorming*, die Keure 2011, pp 192 and 199; Velaers and Vanpraet, 'De materiële en territoriale bevoegdheidsverdeling inzake sociale zekerheid en sociale bijstand (II)' [2009] *TBP* 195, 211 (furthermore, in the context of the Flemish care insurance, the authors highlighted the significant role of the residence criterion in the Belgian federal State: ibid).

1510 Above nn 206–19.

2.1.2. *Belgian Constitutional Court on Inheritance Tax*

717. Another Belgian example concerns inheritance tax, which constitutes a regional competence in Belgium.[1511] The Flemish decree regarding this matter provided an exemption from inheritance tax that is applied to family companies; in particular it applies to those companies in which at least 50 per cent of the share capital was held by the deceased and/or his spouse, in the three years preceding the death of the deceased, but only on the condition that the undertaking or company has employed at least five full-time workers in the Flemish region in the three years preceding the death of the deceased.[1512]

718. The Court of First Instance of Hasselt referred a question for a preliminary ruling to the Court of Justice regarding this provision. The Court of Justice held that 'in the absence of valid justification, Article [49 TFEU] precludes inheritance tax legislation of a Member State which excludes from the exemption from that tax available for family undertakings those undertakings which employ in the three years preceding the date of death of the deceased at least five workers in another Member State, whereas it grants such an exemption where the workers are employed in a region of the first Member State'.[1513]

719. This contested provision has, consequently, been amended by Article 20 of the Flemish Decree of 21 December 2007.[1514] Pursuant to this amendment, the exemption from inheritance tax is only allowed 'on condition that the undertaking or company in the twelve quarters preceding the death, at least 500,000 euro salary costs were paid for workers employed in the European Economic Area'.

It is clear from the parliamentary records that the Flemish Decree has been amended following the judgment of the Court of Justice in the *Geurts and Vogten* case. Although the Court of Justice only ruled on the incompatibility of the condition of employees in the Flemish region with the freedom of establishment for cross-border situations, the regional legislator decided to repeal the criterion of employment in the Flemish region altogether nevertheless. Accordingly, the regional legislator has chosen to apply the same criteria to both cross-border situations involving workers from other Member States and purely internal

---

1511 Article 3(1)4 Special Law of 16 January 1989 concerning the financing of the Communities and the Regions *BS* 3 August 2001. The example discussed here concerns the Flemish region; for an example concerning the bilingual region of Brussels-Capital see Belgian Council of State, Opinion 49.458/2 of 11 April 2011 and Article 2 Ordinance of the bilingual region of Brussels-Capital 16 December 2011, *BS* 2 February 2012.

1512 Article 60a (subsequently 60*bis*) Inheritance Tax Code laid down by Royal Decree no 308 of 31 March 1936 [*Wetboek der successierechten*] *BS* 7 April 1936.

1513 ECJ case 464/05 *Geurts and Vogten* [2007] ECR I-9325, para 29.

1514 *BS* 31 December 2007.

situations involving workers from the Flemish region, the Walloon region and the Brussels-Capital region. Without explicitly referring to the concern of avoiding reverse discrimination, the regional legislator's choice comes down to autonomous alignment with the rules that are applicable to mobile Union citizens.

720. In 2010, the Belgian Constitutional Court was asked to rule on the old version of the Decree, prior to its amendment in 2007, in the light of the Belgian economic and monetary union as enshrined in Article 6(1) VI SLIR.[1515] First, the Belgian Constitutional Court considered that since the regions are made competent explicitly, by special law, to change the amount of inheritance tax due, it would be possible that the amount of that tax would differ from region to region. This difference in itself cannot be a violation of the economic and monetary union.[1516] The fact that this can influence the taxpayer's behaviour is a possible side effect of each taxation.

However, the Belgian Constitutional Court ruled that the specific reduction at issue impeded investment in companies which do not employ five workers in the Flemish region and, thus, hinders their freedom of establishment and capital. The Belgian Constitutional Court referred here explicitly to the ECJ's judgment in *Geurts and Vogten*.[1517] Although the Court recognised that the continuation of family undertakings and the guarantee of employment may, under certain circumstances and conditions, be acceptable justifications for a regional tax reduction, it ruled that in the present case the condition of employment in the Flemish Region was not necessary to attaining that goal.[1518] The Belgian Constitutional Court concluded that the contested provision of the Flemish

---

1515 See also Alen and Muylle, *Handboek van het Belgisch Staatsrecht*, Kluwer 2011, p 405.

1516 Belgian Constitutional Court, Case 83/2010, 8 July 2010, para B.8: [*Aangezien de bijzondere wetgever de gewesten uitdrukkelijk heeft toegestaan de vrijstellingen van het successierecht te wijzigen, kan daaruit voortvloeien dat het bedrag van dat recht van gewest tot gewest verschilt. Zulk een verschil houdt op zichzelf geen schending van de economische en monetaire unie in. Het feit dat de vrijstelling het gedragspatroon van een belastingplichtige kan beïnvloeden, is bovendien een mogelijk neveneffect van elke belasting of van de modaliteiten ervan*].

1517 Ibid para B.9: [*De invoering van de specifieke vrijstelling voor erfgenamen van activa in familiale ondernemingen of van aandelen in familiale vennootschappen is van dien aard dat de investering in bedrijven die niet minstens vijf werknemers tewerkstellen in het Vlaamse Gewest, wordt bemoeilijkt of verhinderd. De maatregel belemmert derhalve de vrijheid van vestiging en beperkt bijgevolg het vrije verkeer van kapitaal (zie ook HvJ, 25 oktober 2007, C-464/05, punten 16 en 17)*].

1518 Ibid: [*Ofschoon het voortbestaan van familiale ondernemingen en het waarborgen van tewerkstelling in die ondernemingen, in bepaalde gevallen en onder bepaalde omstandigheden, een aanvaardbare rechtvaardiging kunnen vormen voor een gewestelijke regeling die een belastingvoordeel toekent, is niet aangetoond dat die rechtvaardiging te dezen voorhanden is (ibid., punt 26)*]. Hence, here too the Belgian Court referred to the ECJ's judgment.

Decree on inheritance tax constituted a violation of the Belgian economic and monetary union.[1519]

721. The ECJ and the Belgian Constitutional Court reached a similar conclusion by pursuing a similar line of reasoning.[1520] Although the justifications for the continuation of family undertakings and the guarantee of employment were accepted as reasons of general public interest, the condition of employment in the Flemish region was considered to be inappropriate to attaining that goal. Therefore, both courts ruled that the condition violated the freedom of movement.

722. Feyen has pointed out that the Belgian Constitutional Court 'failed, however, to give reasons for why it aligned itself so easily with the Court of Justice in the inheritance tax case'.[1521] The author wondered why, in this case, the Belgian Constitutional Court thought it was appropriate 'to apply the European EMU conception to a purely internal situation'.[1522] It is probable that the fact that the Decree had already been amended – the condition had been substituted by employment in the EEA – played an important role.[1523] This certainly appears to be the most likely explanation. Given that employment in the Walloon region and in Brussels-Capital region was already included in the provision on the tax exemption, it was clear that political consensus existed on the issue and, hence, it was 'easier' for the Belgian Constitutional Court to rule that the old exclusion of employment in those two regions violated the Belgian economic and monetary union.

2.2. BELGIAN COUNCIL OF STATE ON THE BELGIAN ECONOMIC AND MONETARY UNION

723. Three Opinions will be discussed – in diverse matters – of the Belgian Council of State from which it appears that the Belgian Council of State's interpretation of the Belgian principle of internal free movement starts from an analogous application to that of the ECJ's interpretation of the principle of free movement within the EU. An evolution in the direction of an increasingly transparent and nuanced formulation of the Council of State's position can be noticed in the consecutive cases.

1519 Ibid para B.10.

1520 Feyen, 'Economic and Monetary Union: Caught between Brussels and Luxembourg?' in De Baere, Sottiaux and Cloots (eds), *Federalism in the European Union*, Hart Publishing 2012, p 403.

1521 Ibid p 404.

1522 Ibid.

1523 See also ibid fn 67.

2.2.1. *Inheritance Tax for Legacies in Favour of the Bilingual Brussels-Capital Region*

724. The first Opinion regards the exemption of inheritance tax for legacies in favour of the bilingual Brussels-Capital region solely.[1524] The European Commission initiated an infringement procedure against Belgium regarding this rule. In particular, in its reasoned opinion of 30 September 2010, the European Commission argued that this provision of inheritance tax was incompatible with the Treaty provisions on free movement of capital, since foreign public legal entities and public institutions are taxed according to the normal rate.[1525]

Accordingly, the draft ordinance, laid down by the bilingual Brussels-Capital region, added legacies in favour of foreign public legal entities to the exemption. However, the draft ordinance still excluded legacies in the federal State's favour and in favour of the other regions in Belgium.

725. The Belgian Council of State argued that the draft ordinance deterred the testator from donating a legacy in favour of the federal State and in favour of the other regions in Belgium, which are similar entities to the ones for which an exemption is foreseen.[1526] Referring to the reasoned opinion of the European Commission for situations which fall under Union law,[1527] the Belgian Council of State held that the exclusion of legacies in favour of the federal State and the other regions in Belgium constituted a violation of Article 6(1) VI, 3 SLIR, enshrining the Belgian economic and monetary union.[1528] Here, the Belgian Council of State clearly drew its inspiration from the European Commission's interpretation of the principle of free movement within the EU, when it assessed the exact same provision of the Codex on inheritance tax.[1529]

1524 Belgian Council of State, Opinion of 11 April 2011, no 49.458/2 on [*voorontwerp van ordonnantie tot wijziging van het Wetboek der Successierechten*].

1525 Ibid 2/7.

1526 Ibid 4/7.

1527 Ibid: [*naar het voorbeeld van hetgeen in het met redenen omkleed advies van de Europese Commissie wordt gesteld voor de rechtstoestanden die onder de toepassing vallen van het Europese recht*].

1528 Ibid. The European Commission ruled in its reasoned opinion that the provision at issue violated Article 63 TFEU, the free movement of capital within the EU, since similar foreign legal entities could not benefit from the tax exemption (see 4–2/7).

1529 See also Belgian Council of State, Opinion of 4 September 2012, no 51.737/1/V. The Opinion concerned a draft decision of the Flemish government of 19 November 2010 amending its decision on Energy which implements Directive 2009/28/EC on the promotion of the use of energy from renewable sources. In its Opinion, the Belgian Council of State argued that the prohibition on taking into account projects which are outside the Flemish region is incompatible with the Belgian economic and monetary union (as regards investments localised in another Belgian region) and with the free movement of services and capital (as regards investments in another EU Member State). Here, the Belgian Council of State drew the parallel between the principle at Belgian and at Union level, without referring to an action of a Union institution in the specific context at issue.

2.2.2. *Flemish Integration Policy*

726. The second (series of Opinions) significant in the context of the interpretation of the Belgian economic and monetary union compared to its European counterpart concerns the Flemish integration policy.[1530] The Flemish Decree on Integration Policy of 7 June 2013 replaces two older decrees and their various amendments.[1531] In its Opinion on the legislative proposal that led to this Flemish Decree on Integration Policy, the Council of State considered that the proposal took into consideration its comment, in a previous Opinion, that the European principles on free movement apply *mutatis mutandis* to purely internal situations on the basis of Article 6(1) VI, 3 SLIR.[1532]

727. In particular, this legislative proposal exempted those foreigners and Belgian nationals seeking to be registered in Flanders after having been registered in a town in a language region other than the Dutch-speaking region from the requirement to follow an integration programme.[1533] The Council of State observed that if internal free movement has the same meaning as free movement within the EU, then a person who is registered in a town of another language region and who returns to the Dutch-speaking region must be exempted from the duty of integration on the sole ground that he has exercised his right to free movement, just like any person who was first registered in another language region and just like any person who, after an initial registration in a town in the Dutch-speaking region, exercises the right of free movement in the European sense.[1534]

728. The Belgian Council of State not only assessed the legislative proposal in the light of internal free movement, but also in the light of the principle of equality. According to the Council of State, the exemptions foreseen for persons who have exercised the right to free movement begs the question as to whether it is still justified to impose an integration duty upon people with Belgian nationality who are being registered in Belgium for the very first time. The Council of State argued that it was not the issue of competence that was

1530 Here, the two most recent Opinions are discussed.

1531 The Flemish Decree of 7 June 2013 abolishes the Decree of 28 April 1998 on the Flemish integration policy as amended by the Decrees of 30 April 2009, 23 December 2010 and 6 July 2012 and the Decree of 28 February 2003 as amended by the Decrees of 14 July 2006, 1 February 2008 and 17 February 2012.

1532 Opinion Council of State 52 163/3 of 6 November 2012, Parl. St. Vl. Parl. 2012–13, 1867/1, 169 referring to Opinion Belgian council of State No 39 856/3 of 21 March 2006 on a legislative proposal which has led to the Decree of 14 July 2006, Parl. St. Vl. Parl. 2005–06, 850/1.

1533 Article 27(1), 1° and 3° draft of Decree, Parl. Doc. 2012–13, No 1867/1, 108 and 198.

1534 Opinion Council of State 52 163/3 of 6 November 2012, Parl. St. Vl. Parl. 2012–13, 1867/1, 8/20.

at stake, but rather the issue of equal treatment. The Council argued that, in principle, a difference in treatment as a consequence of the EU right to free movement could not be considered to be 'an unjustified discrimination'. However, it is possible to treat people who have a certain connection with Belgian citizens in the same way as Union citizens (and people equated with them) although they can neither invoke the right to free movement within the EU nor do they make use of the internal free movement.[1535]

729. Subsequently, an amendment was proposed to extend the requirement of integration classes to any person who is first registered in the bilingual Brussels-Capital region or the French-speaking region and moves to the Dutch-speaking region within the period of a year. It was argued that the intention was not to affect people who were already integrated in the bilingual Brussels-Capital or the French-speaking regions and who subsequently move to the Dutch-speaking region.[1536] Only those people who were first established in Brussels or Wallonia and who move to Flanders within the period of one year are obliged to follow an integration programme.

In its Opinion on the amendment at issue, the Council of State considered that these people's right to internal free movement is limited in this way, but that it is has not been made clear in the explanation of the amendment by which goal this is justified and whether the measure is proportionate.[1537] The Council of State argued that this should be expressed in the parliamentary proceedings. This amendment was accepted in the text adopted by the Plenary session, however, without explaining precisely why this measure was justified and proportionate.[1538]

730. It is hard to derive with certainty from these Opinions on the Flemish integration policy whether the *mutatis mutandis* application of the European principles of free movement on purely internal situations is an obligation in every event or only an observation in the case at issue. On the one hand, the Council of State considered that its previous comment that the European principles on

[1535] Ibid.
[1536] Parl. Doc. 2012–13, 1867/4, 4.
[1537] Ibid 1867/6, 7.
[1538] Ibid 1867/8, 42 where it was argued, without further explanation, that in this way an inequality had been remedied. Moreover, it was observed that although this amendment closed loopholes by submitting newcomers, who went via Brussels and Wallonia to Flanders, to an integration programme, the 12-month period during which this was possible was no guarantee of a sufficient integration in Flanders; in particular, concerning the language element (Handelingen 29 May 2013, plenary session 38 (2013–13) 75). By contrast, others were of the opinion that after 12 months people can no longer be considered to be newcomers, since they probably have an employment contract or income support and will have received social assistance to find a job and to be integrated (ibid 90).

free movement apply by analogy to purely internal situations on the basis of Article 6(1) VI, 3 SLIR, was taken into account. On the other hand though, the Council considered that '*if* internal free movement has the same meaning as free movement within the EU',[1539] then an extra exemption to the duty of integration should be added. Clarification can be found in the Opinion on the draft Decree amending the Decree on Use of Languages discussed in the following subsection.

2.2.3. *Amendment of Decree on Use of Languages After the ECJ's* Las *Judgment*

2.2.3.1. Council of State's Opinion on Amendment of Decree on Use of Languages

731. In its Opinion on the draft Decree amending the Decree on Use of Languages, the Council of State assessed the specific situation of reverse discrimination in the light of the constitutional principle of equality and the Belgian economic and monetary union. In order to answer the objections of the ECJ's *Las* judgment, discussed above,[1540] the Flemish Decree on Use of Languages had to be changed. The draft Decree still provides, in principle, that the language to be used for relations between employers and employees, as well as for company acts and documents required by law, shall be Dutch.[1541] However, a second paragraph has been added that establishes the possibility of making an exception to this principle: it is possible to draft in addition an authentic version of such contracts in an official language of the European Union known to all the parties concerned for individual employment contracts.[1542] This exception is possible where the employee finds themselves in one of the following situations: (1) he has his place of residence on the territory of another EU Member State or of one of the members of the EEA; or (2) he has his place of residence on the Belgian territory and he has exercised his right to free movement of workers or his free movement of establishment as guaranteed by Articles 45 and 49 TFEU.

In other words, the draft Decree introduces a specific form of reverse discrimination that is detrimental to the persons falling within another federated entity's jurisdiction. That is to say, for Belgian nationals residing in the bilingual Brussels-Capital and the French-speaking regions and who have never exercised their rights of freedom of movement for workers and establishment, it is not possible to draft, in addition to the contract in Dutch, a contract in another language, for instance French.

1539 Emphasis added.
1540 Above nn 650–54.
1541 Draft Article 5 of the Decree on Use of Languages.
1542 Ibid second paragraph.

732. In its Opinion regarding this draft Decree, the Council of State considered that it has the effect that for those employees who do not find themselves in one of the two above mentioned situations, the language used in the employment contract is Dutch exclusively.[1543] Documents or acts that are contrary to the provisions of the Language Decree are to be considered null and void; the nullity is to be determined by the court of its own motion.[1544] The Council of State considered that these situations, in which Union law is not applicable, should be assessed in the light of the constitutional principles of equality and non-discrimination and in the light of the general framework of the Belgian economic and monetary union.[1545]

733. As regards the principle of equality, the Council of State considered that the draft Decree has the effect of establishing a difference in treatment between citizens – Belgian citizens as well as those citizens who do not have the nationality of a Member State of the European Union – who have not exercised their right to free movement of workers and citizens who did use this right on free movement as specified in draft Article 5(2) the Decree on the Use of Languages. In particular, the first category of persons does not have the possibility to also draft an authentic version of their individual employment contract in an official language of the EU other than Dutch.[1546]

The Council of State considered that although, according to the case law of the Court of Justice, a difference in treatment between persons which is detrimental for Union citizens who have never exercised their right to free movement, cannot violate the general principles of Union law of equality and non-discrimination – on the basis of the limited scope of application thereof, it is possible that the same does not count for Articles 10 and 11 Belgian Constitution.[1547] Assuming that the two categories would be insufficiently comparable, because the legislator wanted to implement the obligations flowing from Union law for only one of them, would make the assessment in the light of the principle of equality 'meaningless'.[1548]

The Council of State considered that the mere circumstance that the draft Decree is intended to adapt the internal legislation to Union law is insufficient to justify the difference in treatment which is disadvantageous for persons who

---

1543 Opinion Council of State 3 December 2013 no 54.334/AV, para 8.

1544 Article 10 of the Decree on Use of Languages.

1545 Opinion Council of State 3 December 2013 no 54.334/AV, para 9.

1546 Ibid para 10.1.

1547 Ibid para 10.2, referring to Belgian Constitutional Court 26 September 2013, no 121/2013, para B.48 and Belgian Constitutional Court 26 September 2013, no 123/2013, para B.5.2.

1548 Opinion Council of State 3 December 2013 no 54.334/AV, para 10.2, referring to Belgian Constitutional Court 26 September 2013, n 121/2013, para B.49 and Belgian Constitutional Court 26 September 2013, no 123/2013, para B.5.3.

never exercised their right to free movement.[1549] The legislator is not obliged to provide identical rules for citizens falling under Union law and those citizens who do not fall under Union law, given the different goals of Union law and internal law. However, the difference in treatment has to be justified in order to comply with Articles 10 and 11 Belgian Constitution.[1550] According to the Council of State, the supervision of this justification coincides, to a large extent, with the supervision of the compliance with the economic and monetary union.[1551]

734. As regards the Belgian economic and monetary union, the Council of State considered that it follows from Article 6, VI, 3 SLIR that the Flemish Community needs to take the principles of freedom of movement for persons within the Belgian legal order into account when exercising its competence regarding the use of languages.[1552] The Council considered that the European principles on free movement apply *mutatis mutandis* to internal situations on the basis of this provision.[1553] The Council added here that this does not necessarily imply that the application of these principles, in particular regarding the proportionality review of the goals pursued, leads to the same result as in the European legal order.[1554] The Council of State has pointed out that the restrictions on internal free movement can be underpinned by goals other than the goals that are the basis for the restriction on free movement, as determined by the Court of Justice in the *Las* judgment, and it is possible to take into account other considerations when assessing the proportionality and pertinence of these restrictions.[1555] The Council of State ruled that the compliance with the principles of free movement in the internal Belgian legal order should be assessed, inter alia, in light of the constitutional principles on which the Belgian State structure is based, such as the division in language regions (Article 4 Constitution), the freedom of the use of the languages spoken in Belgium (Article 30 Constitution) and the Flemish and French communities' competence to regulate the use of languages in social relations between employers and their employees in their region.[1556]

735. Subsequently, the Council of State assessed whether there was a sufficient justification for this difference in treatment and the restriction on internal free

---

1549 Opinion Council of State 3 December 2013 no 54.334/AV, para 10.3, referring to Belgian Constitutional Court 26 September 2013, no 121/2013, para B.49 and Belgian Constitutional Court 26 September 2013, no 123/2013, para B.5.3.

1550 Opinion Council of State 3 December 2013 no 54.334/AV, para 10.3, referring to Belgian Constitutional Court 26 September 2013, no 121/2013, para B.50.2 and Belgian Constitutional Court 26 September 2013, no 123/2013, para B.5.5.

1551 Opinion Council of State 3 December 2013 no 54.334/AV, para 10.5.

1552 Ibid para 11.1.

1553 Ibid, referring to the Opinion discussed above.

1554 Ibid.

1555 Ibid.

1556 Ibid. On the principle of territoriality and language legislation in Belgium see Velaers, 'Territorialiteit versus personaliteit: een never ending story?' in Cantillon, Popelier, Sinardet and Velaers (eds), *België, quo vadis?*, Intersentia 2012, pp 75–106.

movement in the light of the two aforementioned constitutional principles. In this respect, the Flemish government argued that the Decree on Use of Languages addresses a three-fold need: (1) the promotion and encouragement of the use of Dutch, (2) the social protection of employees and (3) the facilitation of the related administrative controls.[1557] It pointed out that the draft Decree only amends the rules for those Union citizens who fall under the scope of application of Union law in order to comply with the obligations under Union law,[1558] while at the same time in order to respect the aforementioned objectives to the utmost. Moreover, the Flemish government referred to the judgments of the Belgian Constitutional Court of 26 September 2013 'in a similar case' in which the latter ruled that it is possible to treat Union citizens differently depending on whether they have used their right to free movement within the EU, if a sufficient justification exists.[1559] In this respect it referred back to the three objectives mentioned above and which were acknowledged by the Court of Justice in the *Las* case as overriding reasons of general interest. According to the Flemish government, the draft Decree intends to create a respectful and qualitative work environment and, hence, pursues an objective which is different from the one which underpins the Union provisions on free movement. Finally, the Flemish government considered that the mandatory use of Dutch be limited to individual employment relations; it is not applicable to corporate communications.

However, the Council of State ruled that the Flemish government's arguments insufficiently justifed the compatibility of the draft Decree with the principle of equality and the principles of internal free movement, given the fact that the Constitutional Court's reasoning in its judgment of 121/2013, regarding the rules on family reunification, could not simply be copied to the case at issue.[1560] The Council of State pointed out that the legislation must sufficiently demonstrate which specific internal objectives and arguments justify the relevance of the distinction between employees who have used their right to free movement and those employees who did not, as well as the proportionality of the different treatment.[1561]

2.2.3.2. Comparison with the Belgian Constitutional Court's Judgment on Family Reunification

736. Comparing this Opinion of the Council of State regarding the Flemish Decree on Use of Languages to the judgments of the Belgian Constitutional

1557 Opinion Council of State 3 December 2013 no 54.334/AV, para 12. This paragraph contains the arguments put forward by the representative of the Flemish government in order to justify the draft Decree.

1558 In particular with the *Las* judgment (ECJ case C-202/11, *Las*).

1559 Belgian Constitutional Court 26 September 2013, no 121/2013, above nn 701–04.

1560 Opinion Council of State 3 December 2013 no 54.334/AV, para 13.

1561 Ibid.

Court on family reunification discussed above[1562] reveals both similarities and differences in their respective reasoning. In particular, both judicial instances were of the opinion that purely internal situations and situations falling under the scope of Union law are comparable to one another. Both added that treating these situations differently should be reasonably justified.

737. However, the appreciation differs of whether a sufficient justification is present. The Belgian Constitutional Court accepted the goal of pursuing a Belgian migration policy as a justification quite easily. It did not find a disproportionate infringement of the right of respect for family life nor of the principle of equality.

By contrast, the Council of State considered the justification put forward by the Flemish government to be insufficient. The Flemish government had pointed out that the draft Decree only amends the rules for Union citizens falling under the scope of application of Union law in order to both comply with the *Las* judgment and, at the same time, to respect the objectives of promoting the use of Dutch, socially protecting employees and facilitating administrative controls to the utmost. In this respect, the Flemish government referred to the judgments of the Belgian Constitutional Court in cases of family reunification. However, according to the Council of State, the Constitutional Court's reasoning in those judgments could not simply be transposed from the context of family reunification to the context of the Decree on Use of Languages. The Council of State ruled that an acceptable justification should sufficiently clarify which specific internal objectives and arguments justify the relevance of the distinction between employees who have exercised their right to free movement and the employees who have not, as well the proportionality of the different treatment. Hence, the Belgian Council of State seems more stringent in accepting a sufficient justification for a situation of reverse discrimination than the Belgian Constitutional Court.

738. The Flemish Decree of 14 March 2014 has changed the Decree on Use of Languages of 1973 in the sense of the draft Decree.[1563] In order to meet the objections of the Council of State, the Flemish legislator tried to argue why the difference in treatment between purely Flemish situations and situations falling under Union law is justified in greater detail.[1564] After referring to the principle of conferral, it was argued that the stricter treatment aimed to create a respectful and high-quality working environment, which was a goal distinct from the

1562 Above nn 701–04.

1563 Flemish Decree of 14 March 2014 amending Articles 1, 2, 4, 5, 12 and 16 of the Decree on Use of Languages of 19 July 1973.

1564 Flemish Parliament 2340/1 (2013–14) submitted 6 January 2014 <http://docs.vlaamsparlement.be/docs/stukken/2013-2014/g2340-1.pdf>, 10–12.

one underlying Union free movement law. Moreover, it was pointed out that the obligatory use of Dutch was limited to employment relations and did not apply to collective communication in which it was already required to provide translations in specific cases.

2.2.4. Freedom of Movement within the EU and Internal Free Movement Not Necessarily Convergent According to Belgian Case Law

739. The main question examined in this section was whether Belgian case law interprets the principle of internal free movement in a parallel manner with that of the Court of Justice's interpretation of the principle of free movement within the EU. The answer, for both the Belgian Constitutional Court and the Belgian Council of State, seems to be 'not necessarily'. No specific situations of reverse discrimination arise where the concepts are interpreted in a convergent manner. However, if the concepts are interpreted differently, specific situations of reverse discrimination emerge.

740. On the one hand, the Belgian Constitutional Court and the Belgian Council of State applied the 'European principle of free movement' *mutatis mutandis* to internal free movement, in the case of inheritance tax, and in the case of inheritance tax and the Flemish integration policy respectively.

On the other hand, the Belgian Constitutional Court and the Belgian Council of State have interpreted the Belgian economic and monetary union differently from the ECJ's interpretation of the freedom of movement, regarding the Flemish Care Insurance Decree and the Decree on Use of Languages, respectively. Whereas this follows from the Belgian Constitutional Court's *Flemish Care Insurance* judgment only implicitly, the Council of State has developed a more elaborate reasoning of the Belgian economic and monetary union vis-à-vis the ECJ's interpretation of freedom of movement within the EU. That is to say, the Council of State considered that the 'European principles on free movement' apply *mutatis mutandis* to internal situations on the basis of Article 6, VI, 3 SLIR; however, this does not necessarily imply that this leads to the same result as in the European legal order. In particular, other considerations and other goals can be taken into account regarding the proportionality review; the compliance with the principles of free movement in the internal Belgian legal order should be assessed, inter alia, in light of the constitutional principles on which the Belgian State structure is based.[1565]

[1565] In the context of the Decree on Use of Languages, the Council of State referred to Article 4 Belgian Constitution, enshrining the division in language regions, Article 30 Belgian Constitution, enshrining the freedom of the use of the languages spoken in Belgium and to

3. THE PRINCIPLE OF EQUALITY AS ENSHRINED IN NATIONAL LAW

3.1. BELGIAN CONSTITUTIONAL COURT

3.1.1. Flemish Care Insurance *Judgment: No Assessment in the Light of Articles 10 and 11 Belgian Constitution*

741. Although the Constitutional Court recognised in its *Flemish Care Insurance* judgment that whether Belgian citizens who have never exercised their right of free movement are discriminated against in the exercise of their right on free movement within Belgium is something that can be questioned,[1566] it did not actually answer this question. The Court entertained the view that the difference in treatment or the possible discrimination cannot originate from the Flemish Care Insurance Decree, but from the lack of comparable measures adopted by the French- or German-speaking communities or even by the federal legislator.[1567]

742. However, the Council of State explicitly answered this question, in its Opinion of 16 March 2004 on the draft Decree amending the Decree of 30 March 1999 regarding the organisation of the care insurance scheme. That is to say, the Council of State concluded that there would not be an inconsistency with Articles 10 and 11 of the Constitution.[1568] The Council of State also ruled that there arises from Union law an obligation for the regional legislator which 'justifies that for the category of persons who benefit from European legislation, an exemption is provided from the general applicable scheme'.[1569] The Council of State decided that '[given the system of exclusive competences within the Belgian legal order], the residence criterion also [seems to be] an adequate criterion to situate the care insurance within the language region for which the Flemish Community is competent'.[1570]

---

the competence of the Flemish and French communities to regulate the use of languages in social relations between employers and their employees in their region.

1566 Belgian Constitutional Court 21 January 2009, no 11/2009, para B.13.2.

1567 Ibid paras B.15.1–B.16.

1568 Opinion Belgian Council of State 16 March 2004, *Parliamentary documents* Flemish Parliament 2003–04, no 1970/2, para 10. See VELAERS and VANPRAET, 'De materiële en territoriale bevoegdheidsverdeling inzake sociale zekerheid en sociale bijstand (II)' [2009] *TBP* 195, 212.

1569 Opinion Belgian Council of State 16 March 2004, *Parliamentary documents* Flemish Parliament 2003–04, no 1970/2, para 10. Author's translation of: [*Een dergelijke verplichting verantwoordt dat, voor de categorie van personen die het voordeel van de Europese regelgeving genieten, wordt voorzien in een afwijking van de algemeen geldende regeling*].

1570 Ibid. Author's translation of: [*Voorts blijkt het woonplaatscriterium, gelet op het stelsel van exclusieve bevoegdheden binnen de Belgische rechtsorde, ook een adequaat criterium te zijn*

743. The question arises as to why the Belgian Constitutional Court did not apply its single source doctrine. That is to say, the Court did not consider that the unequal treatment that flows from the Flemish Care Insurance Decree was a direct consequence of the territorial division of competences within Belgium. Accordingly, an unequal treatment of different situations would have been at issue here, which does not constitute discrimination in the sense of Articles 10 and 11 of the Constitution. As explained above,[1571] it is the Constitutional Court's settled case law that a different treatment in areas in which the communities and the regions have their own competences, is the consequence of a different policy which results from the autonomy which is granted to them by the Constitution; this difference in treatment cannot in itself be considered to be incompatible with Articles 10 and 11 of the Constitution.[1572] Otherwise, the autonomy of the decentralised authorities would be meaningless.[1573]

The doctrine of the single source or of the autonomous source also applies to a difference in treatment in which the federal State on the one hand, and the communities or the regions on the other, have their own competences.[1574] In those cases, the Constitutional Court is even more straightforward, since it uses a slightly different formulation: a difference in treatment 'which originates in the application of norms of different legislators exercising their own competences'[1575] or 'in the division of competences between the State and the regions'[1576] cannot in itself be considered to violate the principles of equality and non-discrimination.[1577]

om de zorgverzekering te situeren in het taalgebied waarvoor de Vlaamse Gemeenschap bevoegd is].

1571 Above n 563.

1572 See inter alia Belgian Court of Arbitration 14 November 1991, no 33/91, para B.4.1; Belgian Court of Arbitration 10 June 1993, no 44/93, para B.3 and Belgian Court of Arbitration 30 June 2004, no 119/2004, para B.4.2.

1573 See inter alia Belgian Court of Arbitration 10 June 1993, no 44/93, para B.3 and Belgian Court of Arbitration 30 June 2004, no 119/2004, para B.4.2. See Ande Lanotte and Goedertier, *Handboek Belgisch Publiekrecht*, die Keure 2013, p 340.

1574 See inter alia Belgian Constitutional Court 24 September 2003, no 119/2003, paras B.3.1–B.3.4 and Belgian Constitutional Court 5 May 2011, no 63/2011, para B.3.4.

1575 Belgian Constitutional Court 5 May 2013, no 63/2011, para B.3.4. Author's translation of: [*Het betreft immers een verschil in behandeling dat zijn oorsprong vindt in de toepassing van normen van verschillende wetgevers bij de uitoefening van hun eigen bevoegdheden. Een zodanig verschil kan op zich niet worden geacht strijdig te zijn met het beginsel van gelijkheid en niet-discriminatie*].

1576 Belgian Constitutional Court 24 September 2003, no 119/2003, para B.3.4. Author's translation of: [*Het verschil in behandeling vindt derhalve zijn oorsprong in de bevoegdheidsverdeling tussen de Staat en de gewesten en is verantwoord door de autonomie die krachtens de Grondwet aan de onderscheiden wetgevers toekomt*].

1577 It is unclear whether the different wordings is a deliberate choice of the Constitutional Court. See Feyen, *Beyond Federal Dogmatics*, Lund University Publications 2013, pp 171–72.

744. According to Vanpraet, the single source doctrine does not apply to 'transversal competences'.[1578] The question arises as to whether this was the case for the Flemish care insurance. However, it is not entirely clear what precisely Vanpraet understands transversal competences to entail. A better understanding of what Vanpraet might intend requires a more detailed discussion of the division of competences within Belgium.

745. The basic principle in the Belgian federal State structure is the exclusive territorial division of competences.[1579] In this regard, it is important that the single source doctrine applies, because otherwise the autonomy of the federated entities and the federal government would be devoid of purpose.

746. Although exclusive competence is the starting point, other types of competence exist within Belgium; that is to say, shared exclusive competences, actual concurring competences, limited concurring competences and parallel competences also exist in the division of competences within Belgium.[1580] What about these deviating techniques of division of competences and of the application of the single source doctrine? Regarding shared exclusive competences no problem of comparison exists because different authorities regulate other aspects of one area. Hence, different situations are at stake. A problem also does not exist for actual concurring competences because federated entities are only competent to regulate where the federal government has not regulated in the area at stake. Moreover, no problem arises for limited concurring competences because the federal government establishes the general rules and the federated entities can complement it by making stricter rules, but not by making more lenient rules.

However, in the context of parallel competences, the question of whether or not the single source doctrine applies is relevant. That is to say, parallel competences imply a cumulative exercise of one area of competences by and at different levels of government. As can be seen in the Belgian Constitutional Court's *Flemish Care Insurance* judgment, the federal legislator can also establish care insurance on the basis of its competences in social security. Accordingly, a parallel competence arises in the *Flemish Care Insurance* case.[1581] A possible conclusion is that the single source doctrine does not apply to parallel competences.

1578 Vanpraet, 'België in Europa: de bevoegdheidsverdelende regels en het (con)federalisme in het kwadraat' in Vandenbossche and Drogenhenbroeck (eds), *Europese voorschriften en Staatshervorming*, die Keure 2013, pp 366–67.

1579 Articles 128(2) and 130(2) Belgian Constitution and Alen and Muylle, *Handboek van het Belgisch Staatsrecht*, Kluwer 2011, p 397.

1580 Alen and Muylle, *Handboek van het Belgisch Staatsrecht*, Kluwer 2011, pp 397–402.

1581 Velaers and Vanpraet, 'De materiële en territoriale bevoegdheidsverdeling inzake sociale zekerheid en sociale bijstand (II)' [2009] *TBP* 195, 214–16.

3.1.2. *Belgian Constitutional Court Prevents Specific Reverse Discrimination in Land and Real Estate Policy*

747. The Belgian sequel to the ECJ's *Libert* judgment, discussed above,[1582] could have created a specific situation of reverse discrimination. In practice, however, that did not happen. In its judgment of 7 November 2013, the Belgian Constitutional Court completely followed the ECJ's reasoning in the *Libert* case regarding Book 5 of the Decree of the Flemish region, which is entitled 'Living in Your Own Region'.[1583] The Belgian Constitutional Court considered that it appeared from the ECJ's judgment that the specific transfer requirement of a 'sufficient connection' to the target commune, which the prospective buyer or tenant must demonstrate before the provincial assessment committee, constituted a restriction to the fundamental freedoms. That restriction, and in particular the three alternative conditions, were not directly related to the objective of protecting local people without sufficient resources on the property market exclusively. Moreover, the conditions caused disproportional consequences while less restrictive measures could meet the objective pursued. Accordingly, the Constitutional Court ruled that Book 5 of the Decree of the Flemish region on land and real estate policy violated Articles 10 and 11 of the Constitution in combination with Articles 21, 45, 49, 56 and 63 TFEU and Articles 22 and 24 Directive 2004/38; therefore, it was annulled entirely.[1584]

748. It was argued above[1585] that the ECJ's *Libert* judgment constitutes a mere compensation by Union law. The Belgian Constitutional Court could have made a distinction between purely internal situations and situations falling under Union law. The Belgian Constitutional Court could have annulled the contested provisions only to the extent that they concerned situations falling under Union law. This would have led to a specific situation of reverse discrimination that could have been considered as a mere difference in treatment. Or, after having drawn a distinction between cross-border and purely internal situations, the Belgian Constitutional Court could have applied an analogous interpretation of the Belgian economic and monetary union to the ECJ's interpretation of freedom of movement in the *Libert* judgment; this would have led to an equal treatment of cross-border and purely internal situations.

However, unlike in the *Flemish Care Insurance* case, no distinction was made between purely internal situations and situations falling under Union law in the *Libert* case, neither by the ECJ, nor by the Belgian Constitutional Court. Moreover, the case was not assessed in the light of the Belgian economic and

---

1582 Above nn 657–66.

1583 Belgian Constitutional Court 7 November 2013, no 144/2013, paras B.5.1–5.4.

1584 Ibid para B.5.4.

1585 Above n 665.

monetary union since neither of the parties had invoked this argument. On the basis of the ECJ's judgment, the Constitutional Court annulled the contested provisions in their entirety and, hence, no form whatsoever of (reverse) discrimination exists.

3.2. GERMAN FEDERAL CONSTITUTIONAL COURT ON UNIVERSITY TUITION FEES

749. In May 2013, the German Federal Constitutional Court ruled on a provision of the Land Bremen which charged only out-of-state students university tuition fees from the third to the fourteenth semester. Conversely, in-state residents of Bremen were credited with a study account of 14 semesters so they did not have to pay the tuition themselves.[1586] The Administrative Court of Bremen referred to the Federal Constitutional Court the question of whether this legislation was compatible with Article 11 Basic Law, enshrining the right to internal free movement, and with Article 12(1) in combination with Article 3(1) Basic Law, enshrining the right to choose an occupation and the principle of equality, respectively.

750. The German Federal Constitutional Court considered that since 'education is generally the preliminary stage for taking up a profession', Article 12(1) Basic Law 'guarantees the right to freely choose an educational facility'.[1587] The Court ruled that charging general tuition fees was compatible with the Basic Law insofar as they were socially responsibly and not prohibitive.[1588]

751. However, the Court held that charging only those students who did not reside in Bremen these fees was incompatible with Article 12(1) in combination with Article 3(1) Basic Law.[1589] In this respect, the Court considered that students residing within or outside of Bremen are in a comparable situation, since both make use of the educational opportunities offered by Bremen.[1590] If only out-of-state students were charged tuition fees, then this constituted an unequal

1586 Article 6, 1st sentence *juncto* Articles 3(1) and 2(1) Bremen Act on Study Accounts of 18 October 2005. The Land Bremen revoked this legislation in 2010 (see German Federal Constitutional Court 8 May 2013, 1 BvL 1/08, para 7).
A similar situation exists in the UK and in particular in Scotland. Whereas Scottish students and students from other EU Member States get free university tuition, students from England, Wales and Northern Ireland have to pay to study at Scottish universities (Barnard, *The Substantive Law of the EU: The Four Freedoms*, Oxford University Press 2013, p 238).

1587 German Federal Constitutional Court 8 May 2013, 1 BvL 1/08, para 21 (official translation in English).

1588 Ibid paras 19–37.

1589 Ibid paras 38 ff.

1590 Ibid para 42.

treatment which needed justification in the light of Article 3(1) Basic Law.[1591] The Court found no sound factual reasons that would justify Bremen's differentiating tuition provisions.[1592] In particular, the German Federal Constitutional Court held that the residence of a student and the resultant affiliation with the Land of Bremen could not, in itself, constitute a justification.[1593]

752. In this respect, the Court ruled that the principle of equality is 'not applicable where different legislatures treat issues differently'.[1594] The Court specified that, in principle, a State legislature can, within its own sphere of jurisdiction, enact provisions which differ from the legislation of other States, even if this entails a more favourable treatment of in-state residents in practice.[1595] The Court held that the sole fact that some Länder charge university tuition fees, while other Länder do not, is not a violation of the right to equal treatment in itself.[1596]

However, the Court added that the principle of equal treatment does apply if the legislation of a specific Land treats in-state residents and out-of-state residents differently.[1597] According to the Court, the unequal treatment at issue could not be justified 'because of the specific nature of the situation being regulated'.[1598] The Court ruled that 'if a matter falls within the jurisdiction of the state legislature, but the issue concerned extends by its nature beyond the state's borders and, as in the case at hand, affects the participatory right to free and equal access to higher education that is recognised in all … states equally, then one-sided benefits for residents of one state are permissible only according to heightened requirements for their justification'.[1599] Therefore, the Court held that the contested provision violated the right, under Article 12(1) in combination with Article 3(1) Basic Law, to equal access to higher education across State borders, since the university is a nationwide educational system.[1600]

753. Although Bremen's Administrative Court clearly doubted the compatibility of the Bremen Act on Study Accounts with Article 11 Basic Law, the Federal Constitutional Court did not consider the right on internal free movement at all. The Federal Constitutional Court based its reasoning entirely on the right to occupational freedom, as enshrined in Article 12, in combination with the principle of equality, as enshrined in Article 3 Basic Law. The Federal Constitutional Court referred to its settled case law according to which the principle of equality is not applicable when different legislators treat issues within their own sphere of jurisdiction differently.[1601] The Court clarified that

---

1591 Ibid paras 41–42.
1592 Ibid paras 43 ff.
1593 Ibid para 44.
1594 Ibid para 45.
1595 Ibid.
1596 Ibid.
1597 Ibid.
1598 Ibid para 46.
1599 Ibid.
1600 German Federal Constitutional Court 8 May 2013, 1 BvL 1/08, paras 38 and 46.
1601 Compare with the settled case law of the Belgian Constitutional Court, above n 563.

the fact that some federal States charge tuition fees, while others do not, cannot be subjected to review in the light of the principle of equality. Conversely, the principle of equal treatment is applicable 'if, as in this case, there is a different treatment of in-state residents and others under the law of a single federal state'. According to the Constitutional Court, this unequal treatment based on residence could not be justified since higher education is an interrelated nationwide system, making free and equal access thereto necessary across State borders. Hence, the German Federal Constitutional Court, in contrast to the Belgian Constitutional Court in the *Flemish Care Insurance* case, explicitly explained why it applied the principle of equality as enshrined in Article 3 Basic Law.

CONCLUSION PART III

754. The question arises as to whether there is a substantial difference between classic cases of reverse discrimination, on the one hand, and specific cases of reverse discrimination in a federal state context, on the other. This author does not think so. Specific cases of reverse discrimination are also a possible side effect of the limited scope of application of regulations of different levels of government. However, the situation is more complex since an extra level of government is added in the case of specific cases of reverse discrimination, namely, the regional level within a Member State. Since no substantial difference exists between classic and specific cases of reverse discrimination, it was possible to apply the working hypothesis based on (over)compensation to the latter cases too.

1. SPECIFIC SITUATIONS OF REVERSE DISCRIMINATION FROM THE UNION PERSPECTIVE

755. Specific situations of reverse discrimination could be prevented at the Union level, by the ECJ or by the Union legislator. The ECJ could do so on the basis of two divergent positions. First, when assessing restrictions to the freedom of movement within the EU, the ECJ could regard the relevant regulatory authority – be it the Member States or decentralised authorities within a single Member State – as the relevant frame of reference. If the regional authority is taken to be the relevant reference framework, the Flemish community in the *Flemish Care Insurance* case for instance, we would no longer be confronted with a specific situation of reverse discrimination, not even with a 'traditional' case of reverse discrimination. Instead, a 'traditional' violation of the Treaty provisions on free movement would be at stake. This position is mainly defensible from the perspective of the promotion of freedom of movement within the EU, but it seems too undermining for the Member States' federal State structure.

756. Secondly, in the light of Article 18 TFEU, the ECJ could compare citizens of other Member States to the whole group of citizens of the home Member State, instead of comparing citizens of other Member States with the small group of citizens who benefit from more favourable treatment by their regional authority. From this perspective, citizens from other Member States only have to be treated equally, and to the extent that their own citizens residing in another federated entity are entitled to that same right. This position obviously gives more regulatory autonomy to the Member States, but it seems hard to accept from the perspective of the promotion of the freedom of movement within the EU.

757. Finally, the Union legislator could prevent specific situations of reverse discrimination. In particular, the Member States as *Herren der Verträge* are able to amend the Treaties in order that the relevant regulatory authority is taken into account regarding the assessment of potential barriers to the freedom of movement within the EU, which is not necessarily a Member State but could also be a decentralised authority.

758. Since these proposals are, as yet, merely theoretical, specific situations of reverse discrimination are not prevented at the Union level. Accordingly, it is possible to apply the working hypothesis, based on the concept of compensation and overcompensation, to the three ECJ judgments which might have led to a specific situation of reverse discrimination – depending on the national authorities' subsequent choices.

759. In particular, it has been argued that the *Flemish Care Insurance* judgment is an example of overcompensation by Union law, since the ECJ should not have considered the limitation of a choice of residence within a Member State to be a restriction to free movement within the EU. By contrast, it was argued that in its *Las* and *Libert* judgments, the ECJ did not overcompensate. That is, by imposing the use of Dutch in all employment-related documents, employees and employers unfamiliar with Dutch were directly affected in their access to employment in the Dutch language region in Belgium. Moreover, demonstrating a sufficient connection with the target commune prevented people without this connection from purchasing or renting immovable property in that same commune, while also deterring people who own or rent a property in this commune from leaving and going to another Member State to work and reside.

2. SPECIFIC SITUATIONS OF REVERSE DISCRIMINATION FROM NATIONAL PERSPECTIVES

760. Since specific situations of reverse discrimination are not prevented at the Union level, the Member States have to deal with them. National and regional authorities base their assessment of specific situations of reverse discrimination on the national rules regarding the division of competences, rules on internal free movement and the principle of equality as enshrined in national law. Specific situations of reverse discrimination seem mainly to be an issue in Belgium, in particular in the wake of the *Flemish Care Insurance* case.

761. The working hypothesis was also applied to the assessment of specific situations of reverse discrimination at national level. Since it was argued that the ECJ's *Flemish Care Insurance* judgment was a case of overcompensation by Union law, it follows that the national authority should assess the situation of reverse discrimination explicitly taking those situations that fall under Union law into account. However, the Belgian Constitutional Court did not explicitly compare purely Belgian situations and cross-border situations and decided not to allow an extraterritorial application of the Flemish care insurance on the basis of the national rules on division of competences. It has been argued here that the recognition of the place of work as a connecting factor would have been a good solution to the Flemish care insurance issue, since it would solved the the issue of reverse discrimination, it would be compatible with the Belgian constitutional state structure and it would take the situations falling within the scope of application of Union law into account.

Since the ECJ's *Las* and *Libert* judgments were considered to be cases of compensation by Union law, the possible resulting situations of reverse discrimination can be considered in terms of mere differences in treatment. Hence, the national authority can simply consider purely internal situations and cross-border situations to be different and can treat them differently; in other words, allowing reverse discrimination. This is what the Flemish legislator did in the aftermath of the *Las* judgment. In particular, the Flemish legislator changed the Decree on Use of Languages regarding cross-border situations, but maintained that the language to be used for employment relations is Dutch for purely internal situations. By contrast, in the aftermath of the *Libert* judgment, the Belgian Constitutional Court annulled the condition of 'living in one's own region', implying a sufficient connection with the target commune without making a distinction between cross-border and purely internal situations. Hence, no specific situation of reverse discrimination occurs in the latter area.

CHAPTER 8
CONCLUSION

762. In this work, three main research questions were examined, on the basis of which the general conclusion is structured. First, we analysed to what extent reverse discrimination continues to fall within the scope of law of the Member States or within the ambit of Union law. Secondly, we examined the grounds on which the Member States decide whether or not to remedy reverse discrimination. Thirdly, there was analysis of whether reverse discrimination should be considered as a problem that requires a solution in each case. Moreover, if a solution is required, who should provide this solution: the EU, the Member States, regions or several levels of government acting together?

1. REVERSE DISCRIMINATION AS A SIDE EFFECT OF THE SCOPE OF APPLICATION OF UNION LAW

1.1. SITUATIONS OF REVERSE DISCRIMINATION FALL WITHIN THE SCOPE OF APPLICATION OF NATIONAL LAW

763. According to the settled case law of the ECJ, the Treaty provisions on free movement and citizenship do not apply to purely internal situations of which all the relevant aspects are confined to one single Member State. Therefore, a Member State may treat its own nationals in purely internal situations less favourably than persons falling within the scope of application of these Treaty provisions. Hence, the limited scope of application of the Treaty provisions on free movement and citizenship may lead to a situation of reverse discrimination. In particular, reverse discrimination can be considered as a side effect of the fact that national law and Union law are applicable to the same territory, however, each of them with its own limited scope of application.

764. It is settled case law of the Court of Justice that situations of reverse discrimination are not prohibited by Union law. Accordingly, situations of reverse discrimination fall within the scope of law of the Member States and they have to deal with it. It has been argued in this book that the ECJ's traditional approach remains valid since reverse discrimination has to be considered a possible side effect of the limited scope of application of Union law which is based on the division of competences between the EU and the Member States as governed by the principle of conferral of powers.

765. It has been argued that a general prohibition of reverse discrimination at Union level would only be possible by changing primary law, that is to say, by a Treaty amendment of the Treaty provisions on freedom of movement and Article 18 TFEU. However, this seems not only politically unfeasible in the near future, it also seems unnecessary and undesirable.

First, the supposition that a general prohibition of reverse discrimination at Union level would lead to a better protection of Union citizens in all cases was challenged. The more favourable conditions for those who fall within the scope of Union law often impose fewer requirements in order to benefit from a certain right. However, the stricter conditions for purely internal situations can not only be seen as a less favourable treatment for purely internal situations, but also as a way of achieving higher standards of protection.

Secondly, a general prohibition of reverse discrimination at Union level would imply that policy decisions actually pass from national level to the EU. However, national institutions seem to be better suited to assess situations of reverse discrimination than EU institutions because they are familiar with the national rules, principles and interests which are at stake.

Finally, it was emphasised that currently remedies for reverse discrimination are available at both Union and national level. Correcting reverse discrimination at Union level is possible by way of maximum harmonisation of legislation in a specific area. In the absence of such harmonsiation, the Member States can correct the situation of reverse discrimination.

1.2. THE ECJ'S INTERPRETATION OF A PURELY INTERNAL SITUATION

766. The extent to which reverse discrimination falls within the scope of law of the Member States depends on the interpretation of a purely internal situation. It is the Court of Justice which ultimately interprets whether a situation is purely internal or whether it falls under the scope of application of Union law.

767. The ECJ accepts very generously a sufficient connection with Union law, bringing a situation as much as possible within the scope of Union law. Two techniques used by the ECJ to consider more and more situations as falling within the scope of Union law were distinguished. First, the Court stretches the notion of movement to its outer limits – a cross-border element as actual movement between Member States is far from a necessary condition. Secondly, the Court reduces the importance of movement in the light of Union citizenship by accepting more abstract elements which are inherent to the situation as a sufficient link with Union law.

768. Although the precise degree of connection with Union law which is required in order to fall within its scope remains opaque, some indications can be inferred from recent case law. It is remarkable that the most significant aspect of recent developments in the Court's case law on a sufficient link with Union law concern derived rights of residence for third country nationals who are family members of Union citizens in the home Member State of the Union citizen. Accordingly, reverse discrimination in the area of family reunification is the main illustration used in this book.[1602]

769. In the *O and B* case, the Court of Justice gave some further guidance on how much movement is required in order to derive a right of residence for a third country national family member on the basis of Article 21 TFEU. In particular, the Court held that only genuine residence, understood as periods of residence by the Union citizen of more than three months in another Member State, during which family life has been created or strengthened can result in a derived right of residence in the Union citizen's home Member State for third country nationals, family members. Moreover, the Court of Justice held that weekends or holidays' spent in another Member State do not generate such a derived right of residence from Article 21 TFEU, not even when all the short periods are considered together.

770. As regards the reduction of the importance of movement, the *Ruiz Zambrano* judgment is of particular importance. Since the children of Ruiz Zambrano, Belgian citizens and hence Union citizens, had never left Belgium, it was argued that Union law did not apply in the case at issue because the main proceedings concerned a purely internal situation. The Court of Justice gave no response to this remark and held that national measures 'which have the effect of depriving citizens of the Union of the genuine enjoyment of the substance of the rights conferred by virtue of their status as citizens of the Union' are incompatible with Article 20 TFEU.

Two main questions arose after this judgment: had the Court of Justice abandoned its purely internal situation doctrine and what does 'deprival of the genuine enjoyment of the substance of the rights conferred by virtue of their status as citizens of the Union' actually mean? The Court of Justice answered these questions in subsequent cases, providing a narrow reading of the *Ruiz Zambrano* judgment.

[1602] Also in each of the five Member States under analysis, the issue of reverse discrimination has been very much at the centre of recent debates.

771. The first question was answered two months later in the *McCarthy* judgment in which the Court of Justice confirmed its purely internal situation doctrine. In *Dereci*, the Court of Justice clarified that the *Ruiz Zambrano* criterion is specific in character and applies only exceptionally. The Court held that it refers to a de facto obligation for a Union citizen to leave the territory of the Union as a whole. By contrast, mere economic reasons or keeping the family together on the territory of the Union are not sufficient in order to meet the aforementioned criterion. In *O and S*, the Court emphasised that the relationship of dependency – legal, financial or economic – between the Union citizen and the third country national is decisive since that dependency would lead to the Union citizen being obliged, in fact, to leave the territory of the European Union as a whole.

772. The demarcation line between the scope of application of the Treaty provisions on free movement (and citizenship) and the scope of application of national law coincided at first with cross-border situations and purely internal situations respectively. However, this no longer applies currently. Either a cross-border element or an intrinsic connection with Union law can constitute a sufficient connection with Union law in order to fall within the scope of application of the Treaty provisions on freedom of movement and citizenship. Accordingly, the boundaries between the scope of application of EU law and national law have been shifted in favour of the former.

2. DIVERGING NATIONAL PERSPECTIVES ON REVERSE DISCRIMINATION

773. If purely internal situations are treated more strictly in an area which is not harmonised, it is up to the Member States individually to decide whether or not they remedy the situation of reverse discrimination. That is to say, reverse discrimination often arises because Union law requires a Member State to treat Union citizens falling within its scope of application in another way than the Member States originally planned for their own citizens. In such a situation, the national authorities may tackle the reverse discrimination by extending the more favourable treatment provided by Union law to their own nationals in purely internal situations. In particular, they can use different legal concepts in order to assess a situation of reverse discrimination: the principle of equality as enshrined in national law, substantial rights such as the right to respect for family life or the freedom to choose an occupation, and rules on the division of competences, both between the EU and the Member States and on the internal division of competences within one Member State.

774. Only one of the five Member States under analysis, namely Italy, consistently prohibits reverse discrimination. In particular, in Italy reverse discrimination is considered to be incompatible with the principle of equality as enshrined in Italian law. By contrast, Austria, Belgium, France and Germany remedy reverse discrimination in some cases and allow it in other cases. As regards these four Member States no general conclusion can be drawn by Member State by legal concept, or by area.

However, in the area of family reunification, a general tendency – with the exception of Italy – is visible. That is to say, the national legislators in Belgium, France, Austria and Germany treat family reunification with their own nationals in a purely internal situation less favourably than Union citizens and their family members falling under Union law. Although the less favourable treatment of own citizens concerns different aspects in these four Member States – going from a prior evaluation procedure to the absence of the right for adult citizens to family reunification with ascendants – the courts in each of the four Member States followed the choice of the national legislator to pursue a more restrictive immigration policy.

3. DISTINGUISHING PROBLEMATIC AND UNPROBLEMATIC CASES OF REVERSE DISCRIMINATION

775. Finally, the book turned to the third research question of whether we should consider reverse discrimination as a problem that requires a solution in each case? Moreover, if a solution is required, who should provide this solution: the EU, the Member States, regions or several levels of government acting together?

3.1. REDEFINING THE SCOPE OF APPLICATION OF THE TREATY PROVISIONS ON FREE MOVEMENT AND CITIZENSHIP

776. It was argued that reverse discrimination has to be considered as a side effect of the limited scope of application of the Treaty provisions on free movement and citizenship which is based on the division of competences between the EU and the Member States. Moreover, it was argued that the lack of clarity in the dividing line between the scope of application of Union law and that of national law causes the perception that reverse discrimination is unfair and has to be remedied. Accordingly, redefining the scope of application of the Treaty provisions on free movement and citizenship in a clear and acceptable manner, in particular respecting the vertical division of competences between the EU and Member States as governed by the principle of conferral, could alter this perception.

777. In particular, it was suggested that the scope of application of the Treaty provisions on free movement and citizenship be redefined in a more narrow way. Accordingly, fewer situations would benefit from the more favourable treatment of Union law, but it would be clear and justifiable as to why they fell within the scope of Union law and why other situations were purely internal and fell within the scope of application of national law. After a more limited redefinition of the scope of application of the Treaty provisions on free movement and citizenship, the remaining situations of reverse discrimination would have to be accepted as disparities which are a by-product of the multi-levelled structure of the European Union.

778. Implementing this suggestion in practice is clearly challenging. Accordingly, three ways in which the scope of application of the Treaty provisions on free movement and citizenship could be defined in a more limited way were distinguished.

779. First, a narrower interpretation of 'restrictions' to the freedom of movement fits with this aim. In this regard, the book considered AG Tizzano's proposal in his Opinion in *Caixa Bank* to adopt a non-discrimination approach together with a direct market access approach and Barnard's proposal that non-discriminatory national rules should benefit from a presumption of legality. Although the section on tightening up the concept of restrictions to freedom of movement was only a brief digression in this work, it certainly deserves more research. In particular, more proposals could be analysed and it would be interesting to apply them to the cases discussed in this book.

780. Secondly, it was emphasised that the ECJ should provide more guidance on what constitutes a sufficient connection with Union law. Moreover, it was argued that the ECJ should systematically and openly assess whether a causal link is present between this connection with Union law and the right invoked under Union law. Only if both a sufficient connection with Union law and a causal link are present would the situation fall within the scope of application of the Treaty provisions on free movement and citizenship. In this way, legal certainty would be enhanced. Moreover, it would also prevent an important form of abuse of Union law in which an artificial connection with Union law is created. That is to say, situations with artificial connections with Union law would be revealed and would not be allowed to benefit from Union law.

781. Thirdly, a working hypothesis was developed, based on the distinction between compensation and overcompensation by Union law in order to distinguish unproblematic cases of reverse discrimination from problematic ones. It was applied to situations of reverse discrimination both at Union level and at national level. Since specific cases of reverse discrimination in a federal

State context are also a possible side effect of the limited scope of application of regulations of different levels of government, it was possible to apply the working hypothesis in this context as well. Although the situation is more complex since an extra level of government is added in specific cases of reverse discrimination, namely, the regional level within a Member State, no substantial difference exists between classic and specific cases of reverse discrimination for the application of the working hypothesis.

3.2. WORKING HYPOTHESIS BASED ON THE CONCEPT OF (OVER)COMPENSATION BY UNION LAW

3.2.1. The Distinction Between Compensation and Overcompensation by Union Law

782. The idea of compensation is that if Union law only compensates for a disadvantage resulting from the use of free movement, a mere difference in treatment and no discrimination is at stake. In this case, the purely internal situations and the situation with a sufficient connection with Union law are considered as different situations which can be treated differently. Union law creates substantive equality. The situation of reverse discrimination is not considered to be problematic.

783. By contrast, if it appears that Union law grants more rights than needed in order to compensate for a disadvantage suffered as a result from the exercise of free movement or when rights are granted where no disadvantage would have resulted from the use of the fundamental freedoms, an overcompensation by Union law is at stake. In that case, the reverse discrimination is problematic because similar situations are treated differently without a sufficient justification.

784. Hence, the distinction between overcompensation or mere compensation is a way in order to assess whether the situations are similar or different respectively. If they are similar, they should be treated alike. If they are different, they can be treated differently.

The application of the principle of equality requires a balancing act. First of all, comparing two persons or things, requires 'a common standard of measurement' in each particular case. It is important to explicitly identify this 'common standard of measurement' or '*tertium comparationis*' or 'relevant reference framework' in order to apply the principle of equality in a transparent way. As regards reverse discrimination and the principle of equality, the question arises whether purely internal situations and cross-border situations are comparable. It was argued that this depends on whether a compensation or an overcompensation by Union law is at stake. Accordingly, the concept of (over)compensation can be considered as providing this common standard of measurement in order to assess whether the two components of the reverse discrimination are similar or different, as the first step in the application of the principle of equality. The concept can help to make the assessment of cases of reverse discrimination more transparent, to make implicit assumptions explicit.

785. If a situation of reverse discrimination is a result of an overcompensation by Union law, the question arises at which level of governance a solution for the reverse discrimination should be provided. This author has argued that, in case of overcompensation by Union law, the reverse discrimination should be remedied in the first place at Union level. Both the Union legislator – by way of harmonisation – and the Court of Justice can take steps to prevent reverse discrimination resulting from overcompensation. Where there is no Union action in case of overcompensation, the national authorities can remedy the situation of reverse discrimination.

3.2.2. Interpretation of '(Over)Compensation' and 'Disadvantage Resulting from Exercise of Free Movement'

786. The working hypothesis is based on the distinction between compensation and overcompensation by Union law for a disadvantage resulting from the exercise of rights of free movement within the EU. A first question that raises is what precisely may be a disadvantage resulting from the exercise of free movement? It seems that often obstacles of administrative and financial nature are at stake. It is important to emphasise that the disadvantage resulting from the exercise of free movement should be assessed in each particular case. In line with this book's preference for a narrower interpretation of restrictions to the freedom of movement, the presence of a disadvantage should not be accepted too easily. This assessment is closely related to the next question whether the compensation meets the disadvantage in a proportional manner: if only a small disadvantage occurs for which only a small benefit is granted, a mere compensation is at stake which does not pose a problem.

787. By contrast, if Union law goes too far in compensating a disadvantage, overcompensation arises. The proportionality of compensating is easier to observe at European level than at national level. This applies in particular to the Court of Justice because it has to decide in a specific case. For instance in the *Carpenter* case, the Court of Justice arguably overcompensated the disadvantage for Mr Carpenter and his family.

788. It is admitted that the concepts of (over)compensation, disadvantage suffered from the exercise of free movement and proportionality are open to discussion. In order to indicate guiding principles in order to interpret these concepts, we can refer back to the starting point that reverse discrimination has to be considered as a side effect of the limited scope of application of Union law which is based on the division of competences between the EU and the Member States. Accordingly, the first principle which comes into play is the principle of conferral as enshrined in Article 5(2) TEU. That is to say, the EU can only take action if this forms part of the competences conferred upon it by the Treaties. Two complementing principles of the principle of conferral are the principle of proportionality and the principle of subsidiarity as enshrined in Article 5(3)(4) TEU and Protocol No 2 on the application of the principles of subsidiarity and proportionality. According to the principle of subsidiarity, in areas of shared competences, the EU should only act if the tasks cannot be performed effectively at a lower level, that is to say, by the Member States at central, regional or local level. According to the principle of proportionality, the Union action cannot exceed what is necessary to achieve the aims of the Treaties.

789. Finally, it should be pointed out that the open character of the concept of (over)compensation need not only be seen as a weakness, but also a strength, in particular because of its flexibility. Thus, whilst overcompensation by Union law is now seen mainly in the area of family reunification, it is hard to predict whether or not there will be another area in the future in which the EU will do the same thing and overcompensate. Nevertheless, this formula will remain applicable because it allows evolutions over time.

3.2.3. Reverse Discrimination in Case of Mere Compensation by Union Law

790. In the light of the working hypothesis, in case of compensation by Union law, a mere difference in treatment is at stake. In other words, the purely internal situations and the situations with a sufficient connection with Union law are considered to be different situations which are treated differently. At Union level, no action whatsoever is required since the reverse discrimination is a side effect of the limited scope of application of the Treaty provisions on free movement and citizenship. The differentiation of rights has to be accepted as a by-product of the organisation of the EU in which authority is divided between different levels of government.

791. The national authority too can stop its assessment of reverse discrimination right there and accept it as a mere difference in treatment. However, it is also able to assess the purely internal situation in the light of national law. Hence, the working hypothesis does not imply a predefined result in case of compensation by Union law; it is not because a compensation is at stake that reverse discrimination has to be allowed in any event by the national authority on the basis of the working hypothesis.

792. If the national authority decides to assess the purely internal situation as such in the light of national law, it is submitted that there is no need to make a comparison with situations falling within the scope of Union law. Accordingly, it was argued that substantial rights as enshrined in national law, as for instance the right to choose an occupation and the right to family life, are appropriate for the assessment of reverse discrimination in which Union law merely compensates a disadvantage resulting from the exercise of free movement.

By contrast, it is submitted that the national principle of equality is conceptually not – or at least less – appropriate since in case of compensation by Union law the situations are not comparable, but different. This implies that the analysis under the national principle of equality should stop right there.

3.2.4. Reverse Discrimination in Case of Overcompensation by Union Law

3.2.4.1. A Solution at Union Level

793. It was argued that in case of overcompensation by Union law, the reverse discrimination is problematic. Moreover, it was argued that an overcompensation by Union law should be remedied in the first place at Union level. Both the Union legislator and the Court of Justice can take steps in order to prevent reverse discrimination resulting from overcompensation. In particular, reverse discrimination can be prevented at Union level by way of maximum harmonisation. Moreover, the ECJ can take responsibility for preventing cases of overcompensation by Union law by confining its interpretation of the concept of restriction to the freedom of movement and by assessing the presence of a causal link between the connection with Union law and the right invoked under Union law.

794. It was argued that the right to family reunification on the basis of Union law has evolved from a compensation to an overcompensation. The perception has been created that an artificial cross-border element suffices in order to rely on Union law for a right of residence for a third country national family member. The idea that rights to non-EU family members are arbitrarily granted on the basis of Union law is difficult to accept.

795. The most coherent and acceptable solution in the delicate area of family reunification – touching upon the emotionally highly important right to live together with one's family – is to harmonise the law in this area. That is to say, to determine the conditions under which a Union citizen has a right to family reunification whether or not he can demonstrate a connection with Union law. In particular, Article 79 TFEU provides an explicit legal basis to determine the conditions of entry and residence of third country nationals, unequivocally including them for the purpose of family reunification. It is remarkable that the inclusion of static Union citizens was already suggested by the European Commission in its first proposal for the Family Reunification Directive 2003/86. However, broad political support was lacking then and, it would appear, it is currently still lacking.

796. Admittedly, there are recent indications that the awareness of overcompensation in the matter of family reunification is growing. First, in *O and B*, the ECJ tried to give some more specific guidance on the required cross-border element. In particular, it required genuine residence – of more than three months – in a host Member State during which family life has been created or strengthened.

Moreover, in the deal on the renegotiation of the UK's EU membership, the Commission made the political commitment to make a proposal to amend the Citizenship Directive if the main draft decision had entered into force. Although this did not happen, since on 23 June 2016 the majority of the population of the UK voted in favour of leaving the EU, the Commission's Declaration is still relevant in light of the growing awareness of overcompensation in the area of family unification. In particular, the Commission Declaration stated that it would propose 'to exclude, from the scope of free movement rights, third country nationals who had no prior lawful residence in a Member State before marrying a Union citizen or who marry a Union citizen only after the Union citizen has established residence in the host Member State. Accordingly, in such cases, the host Member State's immigration law will apply to the third country national.'[1603] This would have led to fewer instances of abuse of Union law. Thus, it would have addressed marriages 'with third country nationals for the purpose of making use of free movement as a route for regularising unlawful stay in a Member State or for bypassing national immigration rules applying to third country nationals'.[1604]

797. Objections may be raised against the proposal that cases of overcompensation by Union law should in the first place be remedied at Union level. One could argue that it is very unlikely that a step back will be taken in the EU project. It would be contrary to the argument of 'path dependency'.[1605] However, it is submitted that this proposal is a legally valid and politically sustainable approach for the issue of reverse discrimination. For instance, the deal on the renegotiation of the UK's EU membership and in particular the close

1603 European Council meeting (18 and 19 February 2016) conclusions, annex 7, p 35.
1604 Ibid annex 1, section D, p 21.
1605 On path dependency see inter alia Stone Sweet, 'Path Dependence, Precedent and Judicial Power' in Shapiro and Stone Sweet (eds), *On Law, Politics and Judicialization*, Oxford University Press 2002, pp 112–35.

cooperation between the European Council and the European Commission in this case demonstrated that taking a small step back at Union level is not utopian. In particular, it shows that political will exists to reconsider some fundamental aspects of the current reading of EU free movement law and Union citizenship.[1606] Moreover, as can be seen from the planned amendment of the Citizenship Directive, an explicit recognition of re-transferring competences to the Member States for specific aspects of, for instance immigration law, is a political acceptable option.

3.2.4.2. A Solution at National Level

798. If the situation of overcompensation by Union law is not remedied at Union level, it is up to the Member States to deal with the problematic situation of reverse discrimination resulting from it. In particular, the national authority has to assess the situation of reverse discrimination in the light of national law, explicitly comparing or taking into account the situation falling under Union law. This does not imply that all situations in which reverse discrimination is a result of overcompensation by Union law should be prohibited at national level. However, the national authority should not accept too easily justifications for reverse discrimination which is the result of overcompensation by Union law. That is to say, cases of compensation by Union law and hence mere differences in treatment are already filtered out.

799. It is submitted that the principle of equality as enshrined in national law is the most appropriate instrument for the national authority to asses a case of reverse discrimination resulting from an overcompensation by Union law. This is because it allows for a comparison of purely internal and cross-border situations and it allows for the balancing of justifications and the impact of stricter conditions for purely internal situations.

800. Criticisms may be formulated against the application of the concepts of compensation and overcompensation at national level. One could argue that if the national authority has to assess whether the EU grants more rights than actually necessary in order not to restrict the freedom of movement within the EU, it is questioning the ECJ when the latter is the competent authority to interpret the Treaties on the basis of Article 267 TFEU. However, the idea behind the application of the working hypothesis at national level is certainly not to criticise the ECJ but to encourage the national authority to reflect on

1606 The focus here is on the attitude of the European institutions, in contrast to the way in which the UK conducted the political debate (critical comments on the attitude of the latter can certainly be made).

the situation in the EU context. It should contribute to an open and reasoned assessment of reverse discrimination by the national authorities. Admittedly, caution must be exercised when the national authority makes the assessment whether Union law merely compensates or overcompensates.

801. Although the working hypothesis might need refinement as regards putting it into practice at national level, it can be concluded that it is a conceptually valid hypothesis also at national level. In particular, the assessment in the light of a substantial right in case of compensation by Union law versus the assessment in the light of the principle of equality in case of overcompensation by Union law has a double advantage. First, it indicates whether the purely internal situation and the cross-border situation should be compared. Secondly, it indicates whether the case of reverse discrimination is unproblematic or problematic.

802. Overall, it can be concluded that the distinction between compensation and overcompensation is a sound concept in order to distinguish unproblematic from problematic cases of reverse discrimination respectively. The majority of situations of reverse discrimination should not be considered a problem, but rather a mere consequence of the limited scope of application of the Treaty provisions on free movement and citizenship. These cases should be accepted as disparities which are the result of the European Union's multi-levelled structure of government.

BIBLIOGRAPHY

Acierno S, 'The Carpenter Judgment: Fundamental Rights and the Limits of the Community Legal Order' (2003) 28 *ELRev* 398.

Ackermann T, 'Case Note on C-148/02, Garcia Avello' (2007) 44 *CMLRev* 141.

Adam S and Van Elsuwege P, 'Situations purement internes, discriminations à rebours et collectivités autonomes après l'arrêt sur l'assurance soins flamande' (2008) *CDE* 655.

—— and ——, 'Citizenship Rights and the Federal Balance Between the European Union and its Member States: Comment on Dereci' (2012) 37 *ELRev* 176.

Adinolfi A, 'The Judicial Application of Community Law in Italy' (1998) 35 *CMLRev* 1313.

Alen A and Muylle K, *Handboek van het Belgisch Staatsrecht*, Kluwer 2011.

Alter K J, 'Law, Political Science and Legal Studies. A Political Science Perspective' (2002) 3 *EUP* 113.

Am Ende M, 'But Not the Walloons! Internal Quarrel - Or a Case for the Court?' (2008) *ELR* 114.

Aristotle, *Nicomachean Ethics*.

——, *Politics*.

Bamforth N and O'Cinneide C, *Discrimination Law: Theory and Context*, Thomson Sweet & Maxwell 2008.

Barnard C, *EC Employment Law*, 3rd ed, Oxford University Press 2006.

——, 'Restricting Restrictions: Lessons for the EU from the US?' (2009) 68 *CLJ* 575.

——, *The Substantive Law of the EU: The Four Freedoms*, Oxford University Press 2013.

Bombois T, 'La "discrimination à rebours" et son appréhension par la cour constitutionelle belge' in Cariat N and Nowak J (eds), *Le droit de l'Union européenne et le juge belge - Het recht van de Europese Unie en de Belgische rechter*, Bruylant 2015.

Bossuyt M, *L'interdiction de la discrimination dans le droit international des droits de l'homme*, Bruylant 1976.

Cals S, *La discrimination à rebours et le droit communautaire*, Université de Toulouse 2001.

Cambien N, 'Citizenship of the Union as a Cornerstone of European Integration', Dissertation, KU Leuven 2011.

——, 'Mogen statische Unieburgers worden gediscrimineerd op het vlak van gezinshereniging? Enkele beschouwingen bij de arresten Ruiz Zambrano en McCarthy van het Hof van Justitie' (2011) 3 *T Vreemd* 241.

——, 'Recente ontwikkelingen op het vlak van gezinshereniging van Belgen en Unieburgers: a long and winding road?' in *Migratie en migrantenrecht deel 16*, die Keure 2015.

Cannizzaro E, 'Esercizio di competenze comunitarie e discriminazioni "a rovescio"' (1996) 2 *Il diritto dell'Unione Europea* 351.

——, 'Producing 'Reverse Discrimination' through the Exercise of EC Competences' (1997) 17 *YEL* 29.

Caporaso J, 'The European Union and Forms of State: Westphalian, Regulatory or Post-modern' (1996) 34 *JCMS* 29.

Carlier J Y, 'Case Note on C-200/02, Zhu Chen' (2005) 42 *CMLRev* 1121.
Chang R S, 'Reverse Racism! : Affirmative Action, the Family and the Dream that is America' (1995–96) *Hastings Const LQ* 1115.
Cloots E, 'Germs of Pluralist Judicial Adjudication: Advocaten voor de Wereld and Other References from the Belgian Constitutional Court' (2010) 47 *CMLRev* 645.
——, 'National Identity and the European Court of Justice', Dissertation, KU Leuven 2013.
Cluzel-Métayer L, 'Le principe d'égalité et de non-discrimination dans la jurisprudence du Conseil d'Etat et de la Cour de cassation: analyse comparée dans le domaine de l'emploi' (2010) *RFDA* 309.
Cornu G, *Vocabulaire juridique*, Presses Universitaires de France 2011.
Costello C, 'Metock: Free Movement and "Normal Family Life" in the Union' (2009) 46 *CMLRev* 587.
Craig P, 'Integration, Democracy and Legitimacy' in Craig P and de Burca G (eds), *The Evolution of EU Law*, 2nd ed, Oxford University Press 2011.
—— and de Burca G, *EU Law. Text, Cases, and Materials*, 6th ed, Oxford University Press 2015.
Currie S, 'Accelerated Justice or a Step Too Far? Residence Rights of Non-EU Family Members and the Court's Ruling in Metock' (2009) 34 *ELRev* 310.
Dashwood A, 'The Limits of European Community Powers' (1996) *ELRev* 113.
——, 'The Relationship Between the Member State and the European Union/European Community' (2004) 41 *CMLRev* 355.
D'Oliveira H U J, 'Is Reverse Discrimination Still Possible Under the Single European Act?' in *Forty Years On: The Evolution of Postwar Private International Law in Europe: Symposium in Celebration of the 40th Anniversary of the Centre of Foreign Law and Private International Law, University of Amsterdam, on 27 october 1989*, Kluwer 1990.
De Prins D, Vrielink J and Sottiaux S, *Handboek discriminatierecht*, Kluwer 2005.
Daniele G, 'La Corte di Giustizia rompe il vaso di pandora della cittadinanza europea' (2012) *Giornale Dir Amm* 39.
Daniele L, 'Non-discriminatory Restrictions to the Free Movement of Persons' (1997) 22 *ELRev* 191.
Dautricourt C and Thomas S, 'Reverse Discrimination and Free Movement of Persons Under Community Law: All for Ulysses, Nothing for Penelope?' (2009) 34 *ELRev* 454.
Davies G, *Nationality Discrimination in the European Internal Market*, Kluwer Law International 2003.
de Burca G, 'The Role of Equality in European Community Law' in Dashwood A and O'Leary S (eds), *The Principle of Equal Treatment in EC Law*, Sweet & Maxwell 1997.
Della Chà A, 'Challenge of Internal Rules on Grounds of Reverse Discrimination: An Open Issue' (2002) 16 *Diritto del commercio internazionale* 145.
Drago R, 'Note de jurisprudence, Conseil d'Etat 27 juillet 1797' (1980) *RDP* 214.
Editorial Comments, 'Freedoms Unlimited? Reflections on Mary Carpenter v. Secretary of State' (2003) 40 *CMLRev* 537.
——, 'Two-speed European Citizenship? Can the Lisbon Treaty Help Close the Gap?' (2008) 45 *CMLRev* 1.
Epiney A, *Umgekehrte Diskriminierungen*, Carl Heymans Verlag KC 1995.
Feyen S, 'Zorgen voor morgen: implicaties van het arrest van het Grondwettelijk Hof over discriminaties in de Vlaamse zorgverzekering: Een juridische veldslag' (2009) *TBPK* 169.

——, 'Economic and Monetary Union: Caught Between Brussels and Luxembourg?' in Cloots E, De Baere G and Sottiaux S (eds), *Federalism in the European Union*, Hart Publishing 2012.
——, *Beyond Federal Dogmatics*, Leuven University Press 2013.
Follesdal A and Hix S, 'Why There is a Democratic Deficit in the EU: A Response to Majone and Moravcsik' (2006) 44 *JCMS* 533.
Goossens E, 'Pleidooi voor de veralgemeende invoering van de Europese erfrechtverklaring in het Belgisch recht' (2013) *Not.Fisc.M.* 204.
Hailbronner K and Thym D, 'Case Note on Case C-34/09, Ruiz Zambrano' (2011) 48 *CMLRev* 1253.
Hanf D, "Reverse Discrimination' in EU Law: Constitutional Aberration, Constitutional Necessity, or Judicial Choice?' (2011) 18 *MJ* 29.
Hart H L A, *The Concept of Law*, 2nd ed, Oxford University Press 1994.
Heirbaut D and Storme M, 'The Belgian Legal Tradition: From a Long Quest for Legal Independence to a Longing for Dependence?' (2006) 14 *ERPL* 645.
Heun W, *Constitutional Systems of the World. The Constitution of Germany*, Hart Publishing 2011.
Hix S, *The Political System of the European Union*, 2nd ed, Palgrave Macmillan 2005.
Iliopoulou A and Jauréguiberry A, 'La première condamnation d'une discrimination à rebours. A propos de l'arrêt du Conseil d'Etat du 6 octobre 2008' (2009) *RFDA* 132.
Jadoul L and Vanneste F, 'Casenote on Case C-60/00 Carpenter' (2003) 9 *ColJourEurLaw* 447.
Joppke C, *Challenge to the Nation-State: Immigration in Western Europe and the United States*, Oxford University Press 1998.
Kelemen R D, *Eurolegalism. The Transformation of Law and Regulation in the EU*, Harvard University Press 2011.
Kestemont L, 'Methods for Traditional Legal Research' in *Reader 'Methods of Legal Research'*, KULeuven–University of Tilburg 2014–15.
Kochenov D, 'Case Note on C-135/08, Rottmann' (2010) 47 *CMLRev* 1831.
Kommers D P and Miller R A, *The Constitutional Jurisprudence of the Federal Republic of Germany*, Duke University Press 2012.
Kostakopoulou D, 'Co-creating European Union Citizenship: Institutional Process and Crescive Norms' (2012–13) 15 *Cambridge Yearbook of European Legal Studies* 271.
Lane R and Nic Shuibhne N, 'Case Note on Case C-281/98, Angonese' (2000) 37 *CMLRev* 1237.
Lansbergen A, 'Metock, Implementation of the Citizens' Rights Directive and Lessons for EU Citizenship' (2009) *Journal of Social Welfare and Family Law* 285.
Lefevre S, 'The Interpretation of Community Law by the Court of Justice in Areas of National Competence' (2004) 29 *ELRev* 501.
Lenaerts K, 'L'égalité de traitement en droit communautaire. Un principe unique aux apparences multiples' (1991) *CDE* 41.
——, '"Civis europaeus sum": From the Cross-border Link to the Status of Citizen of the Union' (2011) *Online journal on Free Movement of Workers Within the European Union* 6.
——, Arts D and Maselis I, *Procedural Law of the European Union*, Sweet & Maxwell 2006.
—— and Cambien N, 'Regions and the European Court: Giving Shape to the Regional Dimension of the Member States' (2010) 35 *ELRev* 609.

——, Maselis I and Gutman K, *EU Procedural Law*, Nowak J (ed), Oxford University Press 2014.
—— and Van Nuffel P, *European Union Law*, Sweet & Maxwell 2011.
Maas W, *Creating European Citizens*, Rowman & Littlefield 2007.
MacCormick N, *Questioning Sovereignty*, Oxford University Press 1999.
Menon A and Weatherill S, 'Democratic Politics in a Globalising World: Supranationalism and Legitimacy in the European Union', LSE working papers 13/2007.
Moravcsik A, 'In Defence of the "Democratic Deficit": Reassessing Legitimacy in the European Union' (2002) 40 *JCMS* 603.
Nic Shuibhne N, 'Free Movement of Persons and the Wholly Internal Rule: Time to Move On?' (2002) 39 *CMLRev* 771.
——, 'The Resilience of Market Citizenship' (2010) 47 *CMLRev* 1597.
——, 'Seven Questions for Seven Paragraphs' (2011) 36 *ELRev* 161.
——, '(Some of) the Kids are All Right: Comment on McCarthy and Dereci' (2012) 49 *CMLRev* 349.
——, 'The "Constitutional Weight" of Adjectives' (2014) 39 *ELRev* 153.
——, 'Limits Rising, Duties Ascending: The Changing Legal Shape of Union Citizenship' (2015) 52 *CMLRev* 889.
Nowak J and Rotunda R D, *Constitutional Law*, 8th ed, West 2010.
Nowak J, 'Case Note, Case C-34/09, Gerardo Ruiz Zambrano v. Office national de l'emploi (ONEM) & Case C-434/09, Shirley McCarthy v. Secretary of State for the Home Department' (2011) 17 *ColJourEurLaw* 673.
——, 'Case Note C-93/12 ET Agrokonsulting' (2014) 3 *SEW* 144.
O'Leary S, *The Evolving Concept of Community Citizenship. From the Free Movement of Persons to Union Citizenship*, Kluwer Law International 1996.
Papadopoulou R E, 'Situations purement internes et droit communautaire: un instrument jurisprudentiel à double fonction ou une arme à double tranchant?' (2002) *CDE* 95.
Peers S, 'Free Movement, Immigration Control and Constitutional Conflict' (2009) 5 *EU Const* 173.
——, 'EU Law Analysis: EU Citizens' Access to Benefits: The CJEU Clarifies the Position of Former Workers', http://eulawanalysis.blogspot.be/2015/09/eu-citizens-access-to-benefits-cjeu.html (last visited 4 April 2016).
——, 'EU Law Analysis: Free Movement and Social Benefits for Economically Inactive EU Citizens: The Dano Judgment in Historical Context', http://eulawanalysis.blogspot.be/2014/11/free-movement-and-social-benefits-for.html (last visited 4 April 2016).
Pickup D M W, 'Reverse Discrimination and Freedom of Movement for Workers' (1986) 23 *CMLRev* 156.
Poiares Maduro M, 'The Scope of European Remedies: The Case of Purely Internal Situations and Reverse Discrimination' in Kilpatrick C, Novitz T and Skidmore P (eds), *The Future of European Remedies*, Hart Publishing 2000.
Prechal S, de Vries S and van Eijken H, 'The Principle of Attributed Powers and the Scope of EU Law' in Besselink L, Pennings F and Prechal S (eds), *The Eclipse of the Legality Principle in the European Union*, Kluwer 2011.
Prechal S, 'Interne situatie en prejudiciële vragen' (2015) 11 *SEW* 494.
Rimanque K, 'De paradoxale werking van het gelijkheidsbeginsel' [1992–93] *RW* 6.

Ritter C, 'Purely Internal Situations, Reverse Discrimination, Guimont, Dzodzi and Article 234' (2006) 31 *ELRev* 710.

Scharpf F, 'Economic Integration, Democracy and the Welfare State' (1997) 4 *JEPP* 18.

Schmidt S K, 'Judicial Europeanisation: The Case of Zambrano in Ireland' (2014) 37 *West European Politics* 769.

Sevinga K, 'Bevoegdheid van het Hof van Justitie: de ene interne situatie is de andere niet' (2014) *NTER* 196.

Shaw J, 'Between Law and Political Truth? Member State Preferences, EU Free Movement Rules and National Immigration Law' (2015) 17 *Cambridge Yearbook of European Legal Studies* 247.

Snell J, 'The Notion of Market Access: A Concept or a Slogan?' (2010) 47 *CMLRev* 437.

Sørensen K E, 'Abuse of Rights in Community Law: A Principle of Substance or Merely Rhetoric?' (2006) 43 *CMLRev* 423.

Spaventa E, 'From Gebhard to Carpenter: Towards a (Non-)economic European Constitution' (2004) 41 *CMLRev* 743.

——, 'Seeing the Wood Despite the Trees? On the Scope of Union Citizenship and its Constitutional Effects' (2008) 45 *CMLRev* 13.

——, 'Family Rights for Circular Migrants and Frontier Workers: O and B, and S and G' (2015) 52 *CMLRev* 753.

Spitaleri F, *Le discriminiazioni alla rovescia nel diritto comunitario*, Università di Trieste 2005.

Stone Sweet A, 'Path Dependence, Precedent and Judicial Power' in Shapiro S and Stone Sweet A (eds), *On Law, Politics and Judicialization*, Oxford University Press 2002.

Storme H, 'Vlaamse Zorgverzekering. Een lange weg naar een geschikte aanknopingsfactor' (2008) *NjW* 614.

Strik T, *Besluitvorming over asiel- en migratierechten*, Boom Juridische Uitgevers 2011.

Tribe L, *American Constitutional Law*, 3rd edn, Foundation Press 2000.

Tryfonidou A, 'Reverse Discrimination in Purely Internal Situations: An Incongruity in a Citizens' Europe' (2008) 35 *LIEI* 67.

——, *Reverse Discrimination*, Kluwer Law International 2009.

——, 'In Search of the Aim of the EC Free Movement of Persons Provisions: Has the Court of Justice Missed the Point?' (2009) 46 *CMLRev* 1591.

——, '(Further) Signs of a Turn of the Tide in the CJEU's Citizenship Jurisprudence, Case C-40/11 Iida, Judgment of 8 November 2012, Not Yet Reported' (2013) 20 *MJ* 302.

van der Mei A P, 'EU-burgerschap en de reikwijdte van het verbod van discriminatie op grond van nationaliteit' (2009) *NTER* 275.

van der Steen I, 'Zuiver interne situaties: geen omwenteling, wel inperking' (2008) *NTER* 301.

Van Eijken H, 'Ruiz Zambrano the aftermath: de impact van artikel 20 VWEU op de Nederlandse rechtspraak' (2012) 18 *NTER* 41.

—— and de Vries S A, 'A New Route into the Promised Land? Being a European Citizen after Ruiz Zambrano' (2011) 36 *ELRev* 704.

Van Elsuwege P and Adam S, 'The Limits of Constitutional Dialogue for the Prevention of Reverse Discrimination' (2009) 5 *EuConst* 327.

——, 'Shifting the Boundaries? European Union Citizenship and the Scope of Application of EU Law' (2011) 38 *LIEI* 263.
—— and Kochenov D, 'On the Limits of Judicial Intervention: EU Citizenship and Family Reunification Rights' (2011) 13 *EJML* 443.
——, 'The Phenomenon of Reverse Discrimination: An Anomaly in the European Constitutional Order?' in Rossi L S and Casolari F (eds), *The EU After Lisbon, Amending or Coping with the Existing Treaties*, Springer 2014.
Van Gerven W, *The European Union. A Polity of States and Peoples*, Stanford University Press 2005.
Van Gestel R and Micklitz H-W, 'Revitalizing Doctrinal Legal Research in Europe: What About Methodology', EUI Working Papers Law 2011/05.
Van Hoecke M, 'Preface' in Van Hoecke M (ed), *Methodologies of Legal Research*, Hart 2011.
Van Nuffel P, 'Does EU Decision-Making Take into Account Regional Interests?' in Cloots E, De Baere G and Sottiaux S (eds), *Federalism in the EU*, Hart Publishing 2012.
Vande Lanotte J and Goedertier G, *Handboek Belgisch Publiekrecht*, die Keure 2013.
Vanheule D, 'Recente ontwikkelingen in de verblijfswetgeving' in Foblets M-C and Vanheule D (eds), *Vreemdelingenrecht, Themis*, die Keure 2011–12.
Vanpraet J, 'België in Europa: de bevoegdheidsverdelende regels en het (con)federalisme in het kwadraat' in Vandenbossche E and Drogenhenbroeck S V (eds), *Europese voorschriften en Staatshervorming*, die Keure 2013.
——, *De latente staatshervorming*, die Keure 2011.
Vanvoorden K, 'Stelt het arrest Jia een einde aan de België route?' (2007) 2 *T Vreemd* 72.
——, 'Case Note on C-200/02, Zhu Chen' (2005–06) 12 *ColJEurL* 305.
Velaers J and Vanpraet J, 'De materiële en territoriale bevoegdheidsverdeling inzake sociale zekerheid en sociale bijstand (II)' [2009] *TBP* 195.
——, 'Territorialiteit versus personaliteit: een never ending story?' in Cantillon B, Popelier P, Sinardet D and Velaers J (eds), *België, quo vadis?*, Intersentia 2012.
Verbist V, 'De invloed van het Unieburgerschap op zuiver interne situaties' [2011] *RW* 510.
——, 'Omgekeerde discriminatie en de Belgische rechtsorde: op zoek naar een standpunt' in Alen A and Theunis J (eds), *Leuvense Staatsrechteijke Standpunten, Deel III* , die Keure 2012.
——, 'De arresten van 26 september 2013 van het Grondwettelijk Hof: "omgekeerde discriminatie" inzake gezinshereniging is geen schending van het grondwettelijk gelijkheidsbeginsel' (2014) *T Vreemd* 93.
——, 'Reverse Discrimination – A Belgian Perspective' in Guild E, Rotaeche C J G and Kostakopoulou D (eds), *The Reconceptualization of European Union Citizenship*, Brill Nijhoff 2014.
——, 'De toegang tot sociale bijstand voor voormalig economisch actieve onderdanen van een gastlidstaat: Case Note on C-67/14, Alimanovic' (2016) 5 *SEW* 233–236.
Verhoeven A, *The European Union in Search of a Democratic and Constitutional Theory*, Kluwer Law International 2002.
Verschueren H, 'Het verblijfsrecht van EU-burgers en hun familieleden' in Foblets M-C and others (eds), *De Nieuwe Vreemdelingenwet België in lijn met de Europese regelgeving, Migratie-en migrantenrecht recente ontwikkelingen, Deel 12*, die Keure 2007.
——, 'De regionalisering van de sociale zekerheid in België in het licht van het arrest van het Europees Hof van Justitie inzake de Vlaamse Zorgverzekering' [2008] *BTSZ* 177.

—, 'Reverse Discrimination: An Unsolvable Problem?' in Minderhoud P and Trimikliniotis N (eds), *Rethinking the Free Movement of Workers: The European Challenges Ahead*, Wolf Legal Publishers 2009.
Vick D W, 'Interdisciplinarity and the Discipline of Law' (2004) 31 *J Law & Soc* 163.
Walker N, 'Subsidiarity and the Deracination of Political Community: The EU and Beyond', Edinburgh School of Law Research Paper Series 2015/31.
Walter A, *Reverse Discrimination and Family Reunification*, Wolf Legal Publishers 2008.
Weatherill S, 'Competence Creep and Competence Control' (2004) 23 *YEL* 1.
Westen P, 'The Empty Idea of Equality' (1982) 95 *Harvard Law Review* 537.
—, *Speaking of Equality*, Princeton University Press 1990.
White R C A, 'A Fresh Look at Reverse Discrimination?' (1993) 18 *ELRev* 527.
Woods L and Watson P, *Steiner & Woods EU Law*, 12th ed, Oxford University Press 2014.
Zoppi I, 'Le discriminazioni a rovescio' (2006) 4 *Diritto comunitario e degli scambi internazionali*.

www.ingramcontent.com/pod-product-compliance
Ingram Content Group UK Ltd.
Pitfield, Milton Keynes, MK11 3LW, UK
UKHW051920100926
8556IPUK00021B/1272

9 781780 684581